Light from the East

TITLES IN THE SERIES

Nature, Reality, and the Sacred:
The Nexus of Science and Religion
Langdon Gilkey

The Human Factor:
Evolution, Culture, and Religion
Philip Hefner

On the Moral Nature of the Universe
Nancey Murphy and George F. R. Ellis

Theology for a Scientific Age:
Being and Becoming—Natural and Divine
Arthur Peacocke

The Faith of a Physicist
John Polkinghorne

The Travail of Nature:
The Ambiguous Ecological Promise
of Christian Theology
H. Paul Santmire

God, Creation,
and Contemporary Physics
Mark William Worthing

Unprecedented Choices: Religious Ethics
at the Frontiers of Genetic Science
Audrey R. Chapman

Whatever Happened to the Soul?
Warren S. Brown, Nancey Murphy,
and H. Newton Malony, editors

The Mystical Mind: Probing the Biology
of Religious Experience
Eugene d'Aquili and
Andrew B. Newberg

Nature Reborn:
The Ecological and Cosmic Promise
of Christian Theology
H. Paul Santmire

Wrestling with the Divine:
Religion, Science, and Revelation
Christopher C. Knight

Doing without Adam and Eve:
Sociobiology and Original Sin
Patricia A. Williams

Nature, Human Nature, and God
Ian G. Barbour

In Our Image:
Artificial Intelligence
and the Human Spirit
Noreen L. Herzfeld

Minding God:
Theology and the Cognitive Sciences
Gregory R. Peterson

Participating in God:
Creation and Trinity
Samuel M. Powell

Light from the East

Theology, Science, and the
Eastern Orthodox Tradition

Alexei V. Nesteruk

FORTRESS PRESS

MINNEAPOLIS

LIGHT FROM THE EAST
Theology, Science, and the Eastern Orthodox Tradition

Library of Congress Cataloging-in-Publication Data
Nesteruk, Alexei V.
  Light from the East : theology, science, and the Eastern Orthodox tradition / Alexei V. Nesteruk.
    p. cm.
Includes bibliographical references and index.
  ISBN 0-8006-3499-3 (pbk. : alk. paper)
  1. Orthodox Eastern Church. I. Title.
  BX320.3.N47 2003
  261.5'5'088219—dc21   2003007217

Manufactured in the U.S.A.
07   06   05   04   03   1   2   3   4   5   6   7   8   9   10

To my mother and to the memory of my father

Contents

Preface

Nowadays, when postmodernity has penetrated to modern educational systems as well as to research in social sciences, arts, philosophy, and theology, a project that attempts to treat the problem of theology and science from a particular perspective—one based on the living tradition of the Orthodox Church enduring through centuries with no considerable innovations—can seem a risky enterprise. Not only is the concept of truth, which is the central point in Orthodox theology, an unpopular topic in scientific and cultural circles, but Orthodox Christian tradition and Greek Patristic ideas (from which this tradition originates) are now known only to the community of Orthodox believers and a few professionals in academic theology. This implies that Christian Orthodoxy could not enter the dialogue with science on the same scale as happened with the Western Christian theology. This is why the theology of Eastern Christianity needs to be articulated for the Western reader in the modern context of the ongoing dialogue between science and religion.

In what sense, then, can the monolithic Orthodox theology, contraposed to the varieties of religious thought in the West, make valuable insights in the dialogue with science, which, if viewed historically, represents pluralism of ideas about nature and its methods and theories? Christian Orthodoxy never developed its own "natural theology" and never tried to incorporate scientific achievements in its own conceptual frame. Rather, it avoided pluralism and fragmentation by never being contrasted or related to the sciences, for theology itself represented by its essence not an academic discipline but the way of living with God and in God—that is, as the way to truth less through knowledge (which has always been considered a danger of the old Gnosticism) and more through an immediate experience of God as both personal spiritual life and participation in ecclesial community.

This is why theology of the Orthodox faith should be seen as cumulative experience of faith in God, evolving within the boundaries of faith that are expressed in dogmatic definitions. Since the Orthodox Church is considered the ongoing building of the body of Christ—and the affirmation of the presence of the Holy Spirit in it—theology, as a manifestation of this in verbal, written, musical, and other forms, allows one to employ any expression of faith as long as its boundaries are not crossed.

This means that the pluralism of Orthodox theology exists as many ways of expressing faith, all united in the silent mystery of the Divine, which is beyond any discursive shape and image. Orthodoxy has no pluralism in the Western sense, as a variety of theologies of particular individuals and specific historical periods. Orthodoxy has no variety of religious ideologies. All Orthodox theologians, whether Greek, Romanian, or Russian, use Patristic thought as an ultimate standard of theologizing. This does not mean that no development of theology is possible. Modern Greek theologians, for example, develop their subject by incorporating some modern philosophical ideas of Heidegger and Levinas, whereas Russian theologizing is more cautious. This demonstrates that pluralism of thought exists in modern Orthodox theology but does not lead to fragmentation of the whole experience of the church as the whole and its perception of the unity in the living tradition. The reference to Patristic synthesis, which is the ground and pillar of Orthodox theologizing, thus becomes an inevitable point of departure in any engagement of Orthodox theology with science.

The fundamental question in both theology and science is the question of truth. The achievement of the Greek Patristic synthesis was to link the problem of truth with the idea of liturgical experience in order to proclaim that truth, as ontological truth, is accessible only through and within communion with God in ecclesial community. This can have implications for the science-religion dialogue. Indeed, the traditional split in religion and science into truth in theology and truth in science is rooted in most cases in the disconnection of each one's truth from the idea that both science and theology have the common ground of truth, the common source of their ontological otherness: God, whose being—as well as ours in God—is revealed through communion.

The split between theology and science can be overcome if both are reinstated to their proper relationship to the eucharist, understood in cosmic terms as the offering of creation back to God through art, science, and technology. Scientific activity can be treated as a *cosmic eucharistic work* (a "cosmic liturgy"). Science thus can be seen as a mode of religious experience, a view obvious to those scientists who participate in ecclesial communities but as yet undemonstrated to those outside such communities. This idea is an inspiration behind this book.

I am very happy to point out that apart from my Orthodox background and scholarship, I have been deeply influenced by the ideas of Thomas Torrance. By referring to Patristic ideas, Torrance strongly advocated that the mediation between theology and science be established based on the unity of their ontological grounds, which should be anticipated if one believes in the incarnation of the Logos of God. The cosmic liturgy of human creativity thus coincides with the contemplation of the Logos of God made intelligible, by whom this world was made and in whom the universe is hypostatically inherent.

Many events and circumstances, as well as many colleagues, teachers, and friends, contributed directly and indirectly to the writing of this book. I would like to acknowledge those who were crucial to its completion.

My son, Dmitri, was not only a witness of my work on this book for the past four years but also my spiritual companion and the invisible keeper of my hypostatic balance between heavenly thoughts and the practicalities of life. I am enormously grateful to him as well for computer support, particularly with the figures. I am cordially grateful to George Horton, a first reader of this book, for many suggestions and, in particular, for checking my English. I would like to thank my colleagues the Institute of Orthodox Studies in Cambridge for help with the theological side of this book, in particular Bishop Basil (Osborne) of Sergievo, Bishop Kallistos (Ware) of Dioklea, Mother Joanna (Moore), George Bebawi, Markus Plested, and Andrew Louth.

The work for this book was carried out during three years of my involvement in the Oxford Templeton Seminars, where many of the book's ideas were tested. I am grateful to all participants and lecturers at these seminars for their help and encouragement, in particular to John Roche, Alister McGrath, Donald Yerxa, Karl Giberson, Randy Maddox, Samuel Powell, Alan Padget, Dennis Temple, Ernan McMullin, Thomas Lindell, Wayne Norman, Stephen Pope, Peter Hill, John Brooke, and David Lindberg.

The book was prepared while I was lecturing at the University of Portsmouth, and I would like to thank my colleagues and friends Christopher Dewdney and David Matravers for giving me an arena to test some of the ideas through teaching courses. The participation of David Matravers in my life in general, as well as indirectly in this book's writing, by helping me with the basic living and working conditions in Great Britain was crucial. I thank him from the very depths of my heart.

The concluding phase of this project was generously supported by the John Templeton Foundation through sabbatical grant #1573 (Eastern Orthodox Perspective in Science and Theology). I am grateful to the Foundation for this support.

1

Introduction

Orthodoxy and Science: Special Experience

It is widely accepted in historical terms that Western Christianity had the first, deep impact on natural sciences, which led later to the problem of the relationship between science and religion as a cultural, academic, and ecclesial issue. Arthur Peacocke, a leading scholar in the science and theology dialogue within the Anglican tradition, admits in his book *Theology for a Scientific Age* that the experience of Eastern Christianity in engagement with science is different.[1] The Orthodox theologian S. Harakas also argues, in one of the rare papers on the Orthodox perspective in science, that "Orthodox Christianity has a special approach to science."[2] Despite the recognition of the "difference" of this experience, the meaning of this difference has not yet been fully articulated and investigated anywhere in the literature.

This book formulates in stages some aspects of the Orthodox approach to the problem of science and religion. In some ways, this attempt will be orientated toward a specific historical form of Orthodox religious experience as compared with Western Christianity. The "specialness" of the Orthodox experience in relationship with science and its difference from the Western forms of the dialogue between science and religion are ultimately determined by such essential theological underpinnings as the nature of theology, the nature of the human ability to know God, and the understanding of humankind's place in the universe and role in the mediation between the world and God.

The evolving differences between the Western and the Eastern Christian approaches to the natural sciences themselves constitute a serious historical problem: why the impact of Greek Classical culture with Christianity in Western Europe, which had been articulated by St. Augustine of Hippo and eight centuries later by Roger Bacon, has an absolutely different long-term effect on scientific development and the progress of technology when compared to eastern parts of Europe, where people's ways of living and theologizing were for many centuries closer to the Greek Patristic tradition, and different from the Latin tradition, to which St. Augustine belonged.[3] One mystery involves why, by the twelfth century, Greek Patristic thought and Byzantine theology, with their deeply cosmic dimensions, were nearly forgotten in Western Europe.[4] This book does not pretend to be a complete historical research; it argues, nevertheless, that what was forgotten—that is, the so-called Greek Patristic synthesis, which forms the basis for all Orthodox theologizing—contains in itself the secret of that special attitude to science that Orthodox theology followed throughout the centuries.

One might argue that the specificity of the Orthodox attitude to science is shaped by historical and geographical factors, such as the detachment of the Greek-speaking Byzantine Empire and Eastern European countries (which adopted Orthodoxy from Byzantium) from the West. With the fall of the Byzantine Empire in the fifteenth century, followed by the eclipse of Orthodoxy and its relationship with Western Christianity, the era of Enlightenment and technological revolutions was slow to influence Orthodox peoples, whereas discussions on science and religion in the West had by that time already become historical facts and subjects of textbooks.[5] One can argue that this historical delay in part caused the gap between science and religion in the Orthodox world and that, as a result, the Orthodox experience of interaction with science is "belated" and "undeveloped."

The liberation of the Balkans from Ottoman domination in the nineteenth century spurred the Orthodox revival in Greece and Eastern Europe. It coincided with a spiritual revival in Russia, where the first serious discussions on science and religion started in the late 1800s and early 1900s. Interestingly, however, the Russian prerevolutionary interest in science and religion never seriously dealt with questions of the natural sciences as such. Rather, science and religion were discussed in the context of the problem of faith and knowledge, which, as we understand it today, is a more general theological and philosophical problem than the dialogue between science and theology.[6]

Without saying too much about the seventy years following the revolution of 1917, it is clear that the problem of faith and knowledge was never discussed seriously, in any respect, in Soviet Russia. The atheistic formula and the idol of scientific progress substituted for religion on pages of journals and books excluded any constructive and meaningful mediation between science and any theology (not only Orthodox theology). A serious attitude to the problem of science and religion in Russia has begun to develop only in the past decade, as shown by conferences in St. Petersburg and Moscow, some publications and translations of the modern Western monographs, and educational courses in Russian universities, which are taught by a few enthusiasts.

Such a historical and geographical "explanation" of the specificity of the Orthodox experience with respect to science suffers from a lack of recognition that Orthodoxy, despite being "natural" in its historical motherland of Eastern Europe, is now a worldwide phenomenon. One can observe the growth of diasporic Orthodox churches in Western Europe, in the United States, and beyond. Orthodoxy becomes a part of the spiritual experience of people from historically non-Orthodox countries. Regardless, there is still no deep engagement between science and Orthodox

faith in the pan-Orthodox world today; there are no discussions of science and theology within the Orthodox context even in the countries where these discussions are
widespread in the Western theological tradition. In fact, Orthodox theology lacks any
attempt to qualify and evaluate modern science and technology even in theological
terms, to say nothing of the development of such topics as nature and its scientific
knowledge in theological discourse. Members of the Orthodox clergy recognize this
gap. For example, Metropolitan Paulos Mar Gregorios openly expresses his regret
that an understanding of the place of humans in the cosmos remains undeveloped:
"It is striking how little attention is given by Orthodox theologians to issues relating
to the human role within the cosmos. Only a few articles have been devoted to topics
such as creation, nature, and time."[7]

Publications on science and theology in the Orthodox context amount to only
three dozens book and papers (a showing hardly to be compared with the hundreds
of titles on science and religion written within Western Christianity).[8] These include
two books by P. Sherrard that have a strongly negative evaluation of modern science's
misuse in technological implications, two books on Orthodox bioethics, and some
short researches on science and religion in general.[9]

Some contemporary Orthodox theologians briefly mention the issue of science
and religion and indirectly indicate ways of approaching this problem. Examples
from these theologians' work will make it possible to examine the methodology of
mediation between theology and science more thoroughly later in this book.

We start by recalling that Greek Patristic theology, which underlies all Orthodox
thinking, contains a cosmic dimension; it is cosmic theology, for it is preoccupied not
only with the reality of heavenly things and future events but also with the fate of the
visible cosmos and of humans, as part of it, in the perspective of its ultimate transfiguration through the union with God, its creator. It is exactly this cosmic dimension in Orthodox theology that is often forgotten or ignored while evaluating its
impact on the grandeur of modern scientific enterprise. Some contemporary
Orthodox theologians have articulated this problem; the Romanian theologian
Father Dumitru Staniloae, for example, appealed for the reconciliation of the views
of Patristic theology in its cosmic dimension with modern science:

> A theology which is concerned to emphasize the destiny of mankind and the mean-
> ing of history cannot avoid facing the world in which men actually live out their
> lives. Orthodox theology has therefore become—together with Western theology—
> a theology of the world, returning through this aspect to the tradition of the Eastern
> Fathers themselves who had a vision of the cosmos recapitulated in God. From this
> point of view the most important problem for the Orthodox theology of tomorrow
> will be to reconcile the cosmic vision of the Fathers with a vision which grows out of
> the results of the natural sciences. . . . Theology today must remain open to embrace
> both humanity and the cosmos; it must take into account both the aspirations of all
> mankind and the results of modern science and technology.[10]

From this perspective, we can assert that the problem of mediation between Orthodox theology and modern science constitutes a challenge of creating a "new Patristic synthesis" of theology and science. In other words, there is no way for Orthodox theology to deal with the problems that science poses to modern civilization by disregarding the views about the cosmos, and the position of human beings in it, that have been developed by the Greek church fathers. To avoid "reinventing the bicycle" in theology, the Fathers' views should not be neglected when creating an innovative philosophical understanding of theology and science. Without the experience of the Fathers, the resulting synthesis would be outside the Orthodox tradition and thus would inevitably be incomplete and inadequate.

In addition, theology in the Orthodox context has never been considered solely an academic discipline, detached from the living experience of God in both personal worship and the liturgical life of ecclesial communities. If science is to be involved in relationship with theology, it inevitably must become an existential mode of humanity, whose existence in theological terms can be expressed as communion with God. Science, then, should be seen as a mode of communion with God. This would mean that theology and science are similar in that both are existential activities of human beings in their communion with God. The mediation between theology and science thus becomes their reinstatement to a similar status with respect to human existence as communion with God. This thought was expressed by Metropolitan J. Zizioulas of Pergamon in his book *Being as Communion:*

> Science and theology for a long time seemed to be in search of different sorts of truth, as if there were not one truth in existence as a whole. This resulted from making truth subject to the dichotomy between the transcendent and the immanent, and in the final analysis from the fact that the "theological" truth and the "scientific" truth were both disconnected from the idea of communion, and were considered in terms of a subject-object framework which was simply the methodology of analytical research. . . . If theology creatively uses the Greek patristic synthesis concerning truth and communion and applies it courageously to the sphere of the Church, the split between the Church and science can be overcome. The scientist who is a Church member will be able to recognize that he is carrying out a *para-eucharistic work,* and this may lead to the freeing of nature from its subjection beneath the hands of modern technological man.[11]

Scientific research and activity, then, can be treated as religious experience. Any tension between theology and science disappears, for they both flourish from the same human experience of existence-communion. Science thus cannot be detached from theology; it is in the complex with theology that it can be properly understood and treated. Therefore, the *communal* (liturgical) dimension of Greek Patristic synthesis provides another methodological rule of mediation between theology and science, namely, that this mediation can never be detached from the experience of the living God in ecclesial communities. The mediation between theology and science itself acquires the features of ecclesial activity.

It is important to realize, however, that if science, by virtue of its genuine nature, is involved in theological discourse, then science can receive its qualification from a theological perspective in discursive terms. Namely, it is theology that can provide insights on the value and the meaning of science for human society. The fundamental claim of modern theology, which is reminiscent of the ancient writings of Gregory the Theologian (Naziansus), is that science as such is incomplete and cannot provide knowledge of the essence of its objects. Sherrard is eager to articulate this point:

> Modern science, based as it is on a rationality subordinated to non-spiritual categories, likewise can never attain a knowledge of anything in itself, no matter how much it concerns itself with experiment and observation or how far it carries its function of dissection and analysis. This is the situation to which modern science has been condemned and in which it continues to be trapped. It is compelled by its very premises to ignore in things those qualities that transcend their finite appearance and the reason's capacity for logical analysis and deduction.[12]

Here we approach another important issue from Orthodox theological experience: its fundamental *apophaticism* in questions concerned with the ultimate origin of created things and their meaning, which is rooted in a limited human capacity to reason about things that are sometimes beyond reasoning and are accessible only to the highest human faculty of faith and the direct cognition of things. Apophaticism in this context means freedom granted to church members to explore experientially their personal way of life in God. This implies that science as such needs to be complemented by a wider human vision of things, one generally expressed in metaphysical concerns as well as in religion. To deny this dimension and its importance for human life leads to atheism and an illusion of reaching truth through scientific "closures" of observations and measurements. The Greek Orthodox theologian C. Yannaras argues about this forcefully:

> For the man who denies or rejects metaphysical question, who does not trust the experience of the personal revelation of God, the world—material reality—often becomes a refuge or an alibi for his flight from the problem of God. He invokes the certainties of physics in order to prove the propositions of metaphysics to be uncertain and untrustworthy. He takes refuge in the clarity of quantitative measurements in order to escape the difficulty of the qualitative challenges which verify life. . . . Mythologized "science" is today the opium for the metaphysical enervation of the masses.[13]

It now becomes clear that for the proper understanding of its meaning and usage, science should be involved in metaphysical inquiry and theological discourse, thus being placed in the context of the general spiritual progress of humankind, which is not exhausted at all by scientific progress. It is here that Orthodox theology takes a different turn from the Western trend with respect to science, judging it from a religious perspective but not simply employing science in order to illustrate established religious views. D. Staniloae argues this point:

> While Western theology, which has only now abandoned the rationalist formulae of scholasticism under the pressure of the present intellectual revolution, seeks to explain the doctrines of the faith just as exhaustively by means of rationalist formulae of another kind, especially those based on the results of the natural sciences, Orthodox theology considers that these same scientific results have thrown even greater light upon the infinite mystery of the divine interpersonal life and upon the ineffable mystery of the human subject, as well as upon the personal relations which obtain among these human subjects and between them the God who transcends reason.[14]

Staniloae continues:

> In its estimation of the role of scientific progress in the understanding of dogma Orthodox theology is in agreement with Western theology. What distinguishes it from the latter is the fact that it takes scientific progress into account only in so far as science makes a contribution to the progress of the human spirit, and only in so far as it deepens in man the experience of his own spiritual reality and of the supreme spiritual reality, neither of which can be reduced to the physical and chemical level.[15]

Orthodox theology asserts that reality, understood in a wide theological sense, is much wider than that which is known to human beings through their reason and scientific research. If human reason is subjected to this lure of all-embracing knowledge and disregards the human spiritual experience of contemplating realities that are above and beyond the visible and intellectual, it inevitably arrives at the idol of scientific progress, which can only know this reality "objectively" (that is, not from within its inward existence) and manipulate it technologically, so that humility in grasping the sense of existence is lost: "We have become so accustomed to the scientific-technological stance that we have lost the faculty of addressing reality as a whole, of seeing in it the source and sustainer of life, of responding to it with reverence and receptivity, and of surrendering ourselves to it in all-fulfilling love. We have lost the capacity to respond with our whole being to the being of the Wholly Other who presents himself to us through the created universe."[16]

Apophaticism becomes a synonym of humility if one risks arguing about nature and life in ultimate terms. It is here that such words as *wisdom* and *spirit* reflect the true nature of knowledge, which leads inevitably to the maker and sustainer of all that exists. In no way, however, is science excluded from the human search for truth: it is simply concerned with the created order of things, which in some mysterious way contains the pointers to the Divine, the ground and truth of all creation. As

Bishop Kallistos (Ware) of Diokleia expressed this: "As creator God is always at the heart of each thing, maintaining it in being. On the level of scientific inquiry, we discern certain processes or sequences of cause and effect. On the level of spiritual vision, which does not contradict science, but looks beyond it, we discern everywhere the creative energies of God, upholding all that is, forming the innermost essence of all things. But while present everywhere in the world, God is not to be identified with the world."[17]

If science, seen in a theological perspective, is destined to deepen the spiritual experience of humankind and to extend its immediate perception of reality beyond human senses and the visible, then the challenge becomes to develop a balanced language, accessible to both science and theology, that could cope with the difficulties of the ill-articulated entities that constitute religious experience of reality as a whole. This is a serious problem, and it is exactly that which this books attempts to review and develop. The task is enormously difficult, for it has to transcend any simple logic of either the naive reconciliation of science and theology or, alternatively, a brutal demarcation of each field with no hope of establishing any mediation. The danger of oversimplifying the relationship between science and theology is clearly seen from some comments by Philip Sherrard with which it is difficult to agree. Let us look carefully at another quotation from him:

> Indeed, nearly all attempts to reconcile religion and science have been made by theologians, not by scientists (who appear to be more perceptive in this respect). What such a reconciliation generally involves is an attempt to adapt the principles of religion—transcendent and immutable—to the latest findings of science, and so to make religion "reasonable" or in keeping with the "spirit of the age" by appearing "scientific." Naturally, the particular scientific hypotheses in the name of which this adaptation is carried out are often discarded by scientists themselves by the time the theologians completed their task. . . . There can be no greater disservice done to the Christian religion than to tie it up with scientific views which in their very nature are merely temporary. Far from religion and science mutually supporting each other it may be said that the more one is involved with science and its methods the more likely is one to become impervious to the experience of those realities which give religion its meaning.[18]

Certainly it is reasonable to argue that scientific development is in a state of infinite advance and that all its discoveries and theories have limited validity if seen from the "point of view of eternity." This implies that all cataphatic claims of modern science for knowing ultimate truth and possessing the ultimate theory must be declined on the grounds of their a priori limited validity originating from sensory and mental boundaries implied in human scientific advance.[19] However, it does not have to reject science from the equation in search for truth, for it supplies us with the human projection of truth in the created and contingent world, which is created by God. This observation suggests, rather, that religious truth has a different ontology, one that far transcends the expanding horizon of scientific knowledge. The Russian theologian V. Lossky has expressed this thought by saying that any properly scientific synthesis can easily be incorporated by theology.[20] It is true, however, that neither science nor religion should assimilate the other and adapt the other's methods in its own approach to truth; at present, scientific enterprise, which is built on the ideal of rational knowledge, is deprived of taking into account such not easily articulated aspects of existence as human consciousness, the world of culture, and the sphere of human spiritual experience. This problem must not threaten the dialogue between science and theology; on the contrary, it must encourage modern thinkers to develop an intellectual context and its corresponding language that could operate with both physical realities and the realities of the spiritual life in God.[21] This is a real challenge for scientists and theologians to be professionals in both fields, that is, to be rational with what concerns the realities of this age and, at the same time, to be mystical with what lies in the foundation of the visible world, which carries in itself the signs of the invisible and uncreated.

Bishop Basil (Osborne) of Sergievo refers to the figure of Dionysius Areopagite to illustrate the challenge of modern thinkers in talking on equal footing about nature and what lies beyond it in God:

> Dionysius [the Areopagite] was able to speak, in his day, using a language about the real world that was common currency among educated people in his time. Theologians, today, find this very hard to do. We very much need to find a contemporary language with which to speak about the world as we know it through science and then relate this to our spiritual concerns and to God. Our discourse . . . must revolve around three poles: God, man and nature. And if we cannot speak convincingly about nature, how are we going to speak convincingly about man who is part of nature? Indeed, how are we to speak convincingly about God? . . . We humans . . . need to commune with the world, to live with it at the level of the explicate, perceptual world. But for the integration of our whole being, we will also need to be able to do this at the level of the mind. Dionysius was able to do this, and has enabled many others to do so as well. A modern Dionysius, to produce the same effect, will have to possess a language about the material world . . . that opens out easily onto the world of the mind and of the spirit. Theologians themselves are unlikely to produce this necessary mode of speech, though they should certainly be invited to join others in assessing it.[22]

It seems to be true that theologians need both to transcend their own "specialty" in order to acquire the language of science and that scientists should become theologians in a nontrivial sense, that is, to not only generalize their theories to the level of philosophical limits but also acquire the mode of *contemplation* of the world, which leads them to the personal God, as well as makes it possible to express what is contemplated through new language. Can this synthesis be achieved? This book tries to provide some answers.

It is clear from the discussion here that the problem of the relationship between theology and science as seen in the perspective of the living Orthodox tradition escapes the simplistic models of interaction and classification schemes (such as whether science and theology are compatible, should assimilate each other, or are in a state of consonance) that are so popular in contemporary discussions in the West. The dialogue between theology and science demands the development of a theo-logico-scientific, intellectual (academic), and experiential (ecclesial) context that can be described in terms of reciprocity of science and theology without their assimilating each other. This book takes first steps toward this objective with no pretension to completing the enormous task.

The final point of this introduction is about Christ, for it is Christ, the incarnate Word-Logos of God, who is the alpha and omega of Christian theology. Science, being involved in Orthodox theological discourse, cannot avoid its encounter with Christ; from the influence of the Greek Fathers, nature, and scientific activity concerning it, cannot be seen outside Christ, through whom the meaning and purpose of all creation can be grasped. The incarnation of the Logos of God in the world as the establishment of the intelligibility of the world in its utter contingency—that is, the christological dimension of the dialogue between theology and science—recapitulates all the methodological pointers toward this dialogue, as indicated above. In this aspect, our approach to the dialogue between theology and science can be paralleled with the "theological science" of Thomas Torrance, who in many aspects attempts to employ the ideas of Patristic writers in order to argue that "neither the doctrine of creation nor the doctrine of the incarnation will allow theology to detach itself from, far less despise, natural or human science in which man is set by God to the task of exploring, and bringing to word, the order and harmony of the universe and all that takes place within it, for the universe is the sphere in which the believer glorifies and praises God the creator as well as the medium in and through which God makes himself known to man. Thus regarded science itself is part of man's religious duty, for it is part of his faithful response to the Creator and Sustainer of the Cosmos."[23]

It is through the hypostatic union of the Divine and the human that Christ recapitulated humankind and demonstrated to human beings that it is their duty to be in the center of being to mediate between the world and God and to praise the Creator through creation, by carrying out its cosmic liturgical function, which can include the mediation between theology and science.

2

Patristic Theology and Natural Sciences: Elements of History

Introduction

Two general opinions have prevailed as to the role of the church—and Christian thought in general—regarding secular knowledge at the beginning of the Christian era. One of them, still popular now, is that the church proclaimed the authority of Scripture over all aspects of human experience, rejecting freedom of investigation and any judgment on the nature of things that was in conflict with the letter of Scripture. This view, carried to its extreme, led some authors in the nineteenth century to claim that the church had been a stumbling block for the intellectual development of Europe for more than a thousand years.[1] This is a widespread view among laypeople today and probably still enjoys the sympathy of some academics. The opposite opinion has the opposite ideological purpose—that is, it seeks to promote a historical value of Christianity as the only social force able to release pagan science from its view of a divinized nature. This opinion made possible the development of natural science, which led in the end to that state of knowledge and technology we enjoy today.[2] The rise of Christianity, according to the latter writers, was a necessary condition for modern science to come into existence.

It has been argued that both approaches give a simplified view of the complicated, dynamic interaction between science and theology in the past and that therefore a more detailed analysis of their relationship must be undertaken[3] The historical dimensions of the problem of interaction of science and theology are, of course, extremely wide and embrace several subproblems. Since Christianity did not enter a vacuum, it encountered different aspects of the surrounding culture. Science, as an existing social and cultural reality, was already an important part of the Hellenistic tradition. Thus Christianity had to confront both the existing religious traditions and the contemporary secular culture, which included philosophy and its special modes, such as mathematics, physics, music, and so forth, which we now call the sciences.

On the one hand, then, Christian thought had to explain the function of Christianity with respect to the different aspects of contemporary culture; on the other hand, aspects of contemporary culture, such as the liberal arts, philosophy, and the natural sciences, had be understood and explained with respect to Christianity as a faith.[4]

This chapter outlines the views of some of the church fathers on science and its relevance to theology. The first sections address the Greek Fathers, and the second half discusses the special contribution that St. Augustine of Hippo, a Latin Father, made to the formation of the church's attitude toward science, a contribution that gave a unique flavor to the development of science in Western Christendom.

The Problem in Its Historical Setting

Between 180 and 450, the Roman Empire entered a period of general decline.[5] As a result, Greek science declined as well. Despite the fact that the Fathers of the church and some lay individuals were involved in assessing nature and the methods for its investigation, few people were engaged in active research and the renewal of the scientific component of classical culture associated with Pythagoras, Plato, Aristotle, and the Stoics. This resulted in a shift of the culture of knowledge from creativity to commentary as well as a shift from the use of original writings to the use of handbooks and compendia. In discussing the science of the Patristic period, the question inevitably arises: was there then, in fact, anything to which we would give the name *science?*

Certainly many of the ingredients of what we now regard as science were present, including a developed language for describing nature, methods for exploring it, factual and theoretical claims emerging from such explorations, and criteria for judging the truth or validity of the claims thus made. It is clear, moreover, that the resulting knowledge (in astronomy, meteorology, optics, and medicine, for example) was for all practical purposes identical to what is now taken to be genuine science.

The Fathers of the church, however, did not admire the sciences, not because they thought that scientific inquiry threatened theology nor because they were ignorant of the sciences, but because they appreciated the special nature of science and its limited ability to talk about the nature of things. An example of this attitude is provided by a passage from St. Gregory of Nazianzus (called "The Theologian") in which he explains his own view of the sciences: "For, granted that you understand orbits and periods, and . . . all the other things which make you so proud of your wonderful knowledge; you have not arrived at comprehension of the realities themselves, but only at an observation of some movement, which, when confirmed by longer practice, and drawing the observations of many individuals into one generalization, and thence deducing a law, has acquired the name of Science."[6]

The Patristic approach to nature differed from the modern approach in significant ways. For the Fathers, knowledge of nature was an integral part of the larger philosophical enterprise, and religion was a legitimate participant in the investigation and formulation of truths about the natural world far more frequently than it is today.[7]

The motivation for pursuing science in the ancient world and the institutions through which that pursuit took place differed significantly from those in place today. The government support that drives big science now would have been inconceivable during the Patristic period. Indeed, the pursuit of knowledge of nature as such was not generally encouraged in ancient society, with the exception, perhaps, of medicine and astronomy. This resulted in a general shift of interest from the world of nature toward metaphysics, law, and so forth. This decline of the study of nature was a social and economic reality not influenced by Christianity. Nevertheless, Christianity considered the study of nature an important ingredient of knowledge, one that could serve the faith.

The Fathers' position on the education of Christians was not uniform. The simplistic view that they condemned all pagan philosophy and science without qualification would definitely be false, though they did object to them for certain obvious reasons.[8] Their opinions vary from the view that a Christian can be faithful and have hope of salvation without any learning to a recognition that simple piety does not enable one to confront the enemies of the Christian faith with reasoned argument. It is also worth mentioning that in the time of the Fathers no alternative to the Hellenistic style of education existed.

Although the Fathers considered pagan literature to be inferior to the Scriptures, they believed that it could nevertheless still serve the purposes of Christian education. Gregory the Theologian reflected this approach to Christian education:

> I take it as admitted by men of sense, that the first of our advantages is education;
> and not only this our more noble form of it, which disregards rhetorical ornaments
> and glory, and holds to salvation, and beauty in the objects of our contemplation:
> but even that external culture which many Christians ill-judgingly abhor, as treach-
> erous and dangerous, and keeping us afar from God. For as we ought not to neglect
> the heavens, and earth, and air, and all such things, because some have wrongly
> seized upon them, and honour God's works instead of God: but to reap what advan-
> tage we can from them for our life and enjoyment, while we avoid their dangers.[9]

Given the similarities and the differences already noted here between ancient and modern science, are we justified in calling what the Fathers were concerned with "science"? This question is still a matter of dispute among historians. Sometimes one sees attempts to qualify the ancient scientific enterprise and scholarship of nature as science in the same sense that we use the word *science* today. But any attempt to relate science understood in this way to the faith of the Fathers would be fundamentally anachronistic. This implies in turn that if we want to explore the relationship between Patristic theology and natural sciences, we should rely on the understanding of science that follows naturally from the Fathers' writings themselves. It is critical here to remember that many aspects of ancient scientific study were deeply grounded in philosophy, which, as in our modern understanding, formed a methodological framework for the study of nature. Thus the Fathers of the church had to spend considerable effort relating Christian teaching to philosophy, for philosophy (that is, Hellenistic philosophy) claimed that it had access to truth. This presents a more serious issue, one important for the purposes of this research: the problem of faith and reason, or faith and knowledge.[10]

The problem of faith and knowledge was touched upon in one way or another by most of the Patristic writers. One outstanding contribution to this problem, however, changed all future church reactions to Hellenistic philosophy, to its methods of reasoning, and, as a result, to the natural sciences and nature itself. This influential force was the work of the great teacher Clement of Alexandria (d. ca. 211–215). Before considering his approach, however, it will help to consider what was said by other Christian thinkers before him.

The Apologists and Greek Religious Philosophy

It is probably impossible to point to a definite moment in history when the "dialogue" between Greek religious philosophy and Christian teaching began. In a sense, it is already present in St. Paul. In any case, Christian thinkers were not the first to enter such a dialogue, for the use of Greek ideas and categories for the interpretation of the Hebrew Scriptures had begun well before Christianity appeared. The Bible used by the early church was in fact a Greek translation of the Hebrew Bible, the Septuagint. Philo of Alexandria (ca. 20 B.C.–A.D. 50) prepared the way for the future encounter of the Christian Church with Greek philosophical thought through his exegesis of the Greek Scriptures.

The Christian Apologists, however, entered the dialogue with Greek philosophy in a rather instinctive, unsystematic fashion by appropriating certain intellectual resources of Hellenistic culture. Historians locate this starting point in the second half of the second century. In fact, the Apologists' approach to Greek philosophy might be described as somewhat paradoxical. On the one hand, they accepted Greek ideas; on the other, they admitted a certain hostility to them. The writings of Justin Martyr illustrate this point very well. Justin allowed that Greek philosophy contained undeniable truths and valuable insights, but at the same time he claimed that traditional philosophy was full of errors and distortions when compared with Scripture. Following Philo, Justin argued that the Greeks had actually borrowed some of their ideas from the Scriptures, which had been revealed to Moses before the Greeks had had a chance to develop their philosophy. He claimed, for example, that Plato's doctrine of creation, as formulated in the Timaeus, was borrowed from the account in Gen. 1:1-3.[11]

Justin's primary purpose, however, was to place Greek thought in its proper place in the story of Christ's revelation of God by identifying salvation history with world history. He sought to clarify some aspects of Christian teaching by fitting them into a Platonistic worldview while at the same time readjusting the latter according to the needs of the Christian faith. The fact that Justin was not a philosophical thinker of any great depth made his theology, which was essentially apologetic in its aims, both tentative and unsystematic.[12]

St. Irenaeus of Lyons (ca. 130–200) followed on from Justin but entered into dialogue with Greek thought from a somewhat different perspective, since he was struggling not so much against pagan misinterpretations of Christianity as against Gnosticism, a sectarian movement within the church. Although it was pastoral and occasional, his major work also represented a reaction against Hellenistic tradition, for in it Gnosticism was paralleled with philosophy. This was why Irenaeus's hostility to philosophy became explicit and he was happy to label philosophers as ignorant of God.[13] Christians, however, are dealing with a truth that is certain and uncorrupted by human error, that is, with the revealed truth of the Scripture.

In his struggle with Gnosticism, Irenaeus developed an approach to the relationship between God and the world that differed from Justin's approach. Irenaeus asserted that God, as the transcendent creator, does not exclude himself from his creation. God differs from every creature in his ingenerate simplicity, and this is exactly what makes God able to be present in relation to every creature.[14]

According to Irenaeus, the created world has no material cause. Its ontology, its very being, is rooted in the will of God, which is mirrored in the world. Creation is fundamentally good, and all its levels are open to divine redemption. This is confirmed through the incarnate Logos. Everything thus participates in incorruption. According to Irenaeus's teaching, this world is "generate"—that is, totally dependent on God—and is therefore also open to his continuous creative activity. The world itself is a never-ending flux of events, whose nature is whatever God makes of them. As a result, the concept of natural law is quite problematic in Irenaeus.

Science and Philosophy as Cooperating in Truth

Clement of Alexandria is considered the founder of Christian theology as understood in its modern setting as knowledge about God. Knowledge in its classical Greek sense means the transmission of facts and of statements about these facts using logical reasoning and shared language. This form of knowledge was treated as philosophy in the third century. The fundamental innovation in Clement's teaching was the transfer of the language and methods of philosophy to the realm of faith. It is through these methods that simple faith becomes a demonstrated faith and acquires intersubjective forms of expression, thereby becoming a form of gnosis, a theology.[15]

Clement understood very clearly that if he wished to achieve this goal of demonstrability, it would be unwise to disregard those achievements of Greek thought that formed the intellectual scaffolding of a still-pagan society. Historically, he was the first Christian writer who insisted on a positive evaluation of ancient culture and philosophy as an important heritage of use to Christians.[16]

Clement's argument for the usefulness of philosophy and sciences is based upon his understanding of truth as something that embraces all, that includes all particular kinds of truth. Truth is one, and it is God's truth. That is why, according to Clement in *The Stromata, or Miscellanies,* philosophy is characterized by investigation into truth and the nature of things.[17]

When he discusses philosophy, Clement thinks of it as a kind of integrated truth that is hidden in every particular form of philosophical activity, but he does not identify philosophical truth with divine truth (*Strom.* 1.6). Rather, it is a partial truth. Truth is not attainable from within philosophy, though philosophy can contribute to the comprehension of truth, "not as being the cause of comprehension, but a cause along with other things, and co-operator; perhaps also a joint cause" (*Strom.* 1.6). In a similar way, Clement argues that there is only partial truth in the sciences: "In geometry there is the truth of geometry; in music, that of music; and in right philosophy, there will be Hellenic truth" (*Strom.* 1.6). Clement claims that the Greeks, through the gift of reasoning granted to them by God, approached this truth but did not manage to collect together the divided truth and to find its source in the Logos of God: "Barbarian and Hellenic philosophy have torn off a fragment of eternal truth from the theology of the ever-living Word" (*Strom.* 1.13). Thus the function of philosophy is to be understood as that of a cooperating cause leading to knowledge of the truth. A person who uses philosophy to attain truth by bringing together its divided parts and making them one "will without peril, be assured, contemplate the perfect Word, the truth" (*Strom.* 1.13). Clement then argues that philosophy is useful for Christians as a kind of training in order to attain truth, but that "philosophy is a concurrent and co-operating cause of true apprehension, . . . a preparatory training for the enlightened man; not assigning as the cause that which is but the joint-cause" (*Strom.* 1.20).[18]

In this respect, philosophy—considered as a means to an end and supported by faith—can lead to receiving the words concerning God. Philosophical knowledge in itself is incomplete, for "it cannot by itself produce the right effect" (*Strom.* 1.20). Clement contrasts such knowledge with the Christian teaching, "which, according to the Saviour, is complete in itself and without defect, being 'the power and wisdom of God'" (*Strom.* 1.20).

Faith as a Condition for Knowledge

Moreover, Clement declares that knowledge is possible only because of faith and that faith is a condition for knowledge of any kind. Conversely, knowledge helps make affirmations of faith demonstrable and thus, according to Clement, more scientific. The faith that is true knowledge of revelation becomes a more scientific faith when supported by philosophy, and in this way it becomes gnosis (*Strom.* 1.2). Clement emphasizes that to enable faith to overcome the lack of necessity and rigor of mere opinion, one must appeal to the methods used in the sciences. Since philosophy is "scientific" by definition, in that it represents rational knowledge, it differs from other forms of knowledge—for example, ordinary opinion. Clement uses the Aristotelian method (see *Strom.* 8) to establish (in the words of Aristotle) a scientific demonstration, which is the means of knowledge and the goal pursued by the intelligence as opposed to opinion (*Strom.* 8.1). This is a demonstration in a truly Aristotelian sense and is similar to syllogism, in which from established premises a new proposition is deduced that has the same certainty as the premises despite the fact that the new proposition was not certain before the syllogism was carried out. The difference, according to Clement, is that "to draw conclusions from what is admitted is to syllogize; while to draw a conclusion from what is true is to demonstrate" (*Strom.* 8.3).

This approach to demonstration is then used by Clement to justify his further claim that one needs faith in order to employ first principles of any kind. Indeed, in cases where some truth is already established, demonstration will mean that "we try to find an argument which, by starting from things already believed, is able to create faith in things as yet not believed" (*Strom.* 8.3). This kind of demonstration cannot be applied, however, to the ultimate principles that constitute the basic premises of any demonstration: "Should one say that knowledge is founded on demonstration by a process of reasoning, let him hear that the first principles are incapable of demonstration" (*Strom.* 2.4). Since knowledge is based on demonstration emerging from the first principles that cannot themselves be demonstrated, knowledge itself cannot be demonstrated. This in turn implies that the very possibility of any knowledge at all requires the acceptance of first principles, which means faith in them. In this way, knowledge depends on something that is not knowledge; this is faith. The difference between knowledge and faith thus becomes very clear: "For knowledge is a state of mind that results from demonstration; but faith is a grace which from what is indemonstrable conducts to what is universal and simple, something that is neither with matter, nor matter, nor under matter" (*Strom.* 2.4).

It is faith, therefore, that allows one to formulate the first principles in a proper way and to perceive things that are not seen in the course of demonstrable knowledge. Demonstration, then, follows after faith, but not the other way around. The Greeks, according to Clement, participated in the truth that comes from the Logos, but they did not see any of the spiritual meaning of this truth because they did not have faith (in the Logos of God) and thus could not have access to the only true demonstration, which is supplied on the basis of the Scriptures. This is why a demonstration based on opinion cannot qualify as divine—only as human, that is, as mere rhetoric—whereas a demonstration based on reasoned knowledge produces faith in those who wish to learn of God by examining the Scriptures. Clement calls this faith that is supported by philosophical methods a considered faith (that is, a gnosis), and, according to Clement, it forms the subject matter of theology. Clement has clearly formulated a methodological principle that allows one to treat sciences and philosophy as two different ways of knowing that cooperate in truth. Whatever science and philosophy can offer to theology can easily be incorporated by the latter to deepen and extend faith within the boundaries of the church's definitions.[19] This attitude to science and philosophy could remove all modern concerns about the relationship between science and theology.[20]

For Clement, knowledge—that is, scientific knowledge—is not possible without faith in some first principles; true knowledge is spiritual knowledge, for the ultimate meaning of objects and ideas is sustained by the Logos of God, and the modes of communion with the Logos are opened through Christian faith. The result of historical developments in the stream of so-called modernism and postmodernism has been the removal of any spiritual insights from scientific discourse and its rationality. Faith as the expression of belief in unity of orders in the universe, provided by the Logos, has been nearly eliminated from the diverse, extremely specialized scientific fields we see today. Can Clement's understanding of philosophy and the sciences provide the key to a new—and yet premodern—methodology for mediating between science and theology?

The Interpretation of Nature

Within this frame of thought about philosophy and science as activities that cooperate with the truth of Christian theology, this section outlines the place that nature, its investigation, and its interpretation occupied in the thought of the Greek Fathers. The concern here, however, is not to use the various bits of knowledge accessible to the Fathers in order to describe their biblical exegesis or Christian teaching. Rather, the discussion focuses on the Fathers' attitude toward nature seen as part of creation, distinct from God, as well as their attitude toward research in the natural sciences.[21]

The Greek Fathers did appreciate and value the natural world. Of course, they looked at nature through the prism of the knowledge available to them. They did not propose any research programs or participate in any actual research, for they were bishops, not scientists. Nevertheless, they interpreted nature and its knowledge through their faith and through their vision of the world in its relationship to God. They were looking for indications of the presence of the divine in nature, but they never allowed their thought to degenerate into pantheism. They firmly maintained the fundamental Christian claim that the transcendent God of the Scriptures created the world ex nihilo but that God is present in the world through the divine *logoi* (purpose and end) of all created things.[22] It is because of this that the Fathers clearly understood that any scientific knowledge, that is, any knowledge that relates to created nature, will never be complete and that one never arrives "at a knowledge of the realities themselves."[23]

Thus the Fathers considered it their primary task to interpret scientific knowledge theologically in terms of purpose and end, thereby completing and perfecting scientific discourse. In other words, they wished to make scientific knowledge understandable in Christian terms.[24]

The Fathers found that they could easily accommodate themselves to any partial view of nature with no fear of losing their orthodoxy and the integrity of life in Christ. It is true, however, that the hierarchical vision of nature through the intelligible patterns of creation and their *logoi* had a selective effect: Plato's view of the world would prevail for a thousand years among Christian thinkers, until Aristotelian philosophy, via Islam, found its way back into Europe in the twelfth century.[25] The Fathers' treatment of science made their position rather Platonistic in that any particular knowledge was thought of as serving the ideal of an ultimate knowledge. This position—a vision of science in the perspective of "heavenly" things—was the object of criticism and accusations for many centuries.[26]

The wholeness and integrity of the Fathers' vision of science, metaphysics, and theology are particularly articulated in their treatment of the laws of nature as laws of God as well as in their understanding that the relationship between the sciences and theology can only be established on christological grounds.

The Laws of Nature

The Fathers considered the laws of nature to be the physical aspect of the natural law, and they innovatively introduced this idea into the heart of the faith of the Jews, who believed that every phenomenon, such as the growth of trees and animals, took place because of God, not because of an impersonal "force." The Fathers, for their part, claimed that the laws of nature responsible for such growth were established by God at the origin of the world. They emphasized that each moment of growth is not caused by a separate act of the divine will, but that the will of God lies behind the movement of nature. That is why, according to the Fathers, any change in nature can be justified on the grounds of the laws that were established by God at the point of creation: God's command at the moment of creation becomes a law of nature.[27]

Two points are important here. First, when seen from a modern perspective, the view that the laws were established at the point of creation does not imply that God "set the clock in motion" and then let it run on its own. This would be a form of deism. Having creating the world, God still participates in it through his *logoi* and grace, guiding nature as a whole to its final end. Second, the laws of nature (for example, mechanical or thermodynamic laws) are not a matter of necessity. They could be different, as could the structural units based on them. This is why, since the Fathers' time, it has been said that the world and the laws of nature are contingent: they are dependent on God.[28]

All laws of nature "are included in the one law which proceeds from the counsel of God."[29] This does not mean that no contingencies exist in the world's happenings apart from the original act of creation. Some contingent events happen as manifestations of our free will; others take place because of the accidental actions of the external bodies. However, nothing in the writings of the Fathers indicates that they perceived separate interventions of the divine will in nature apart from the initial establishment of nature's laws at the point of creation.[30]

Inorganic matter and living creatures other than humans are treated by the Fathers as irrational beings; it is only humans who can resist necessity because of their rational faculty, which enables them to know things and to make decisions based upon this knowledge. Gregory the Theologian acknowledges this rationality by saying that human knowledge of things is "ordained by God."[31] This, he argues, is the difference between humans and the rest of nature. The rationality of humans, made in the image of God, corresponds to the rationality in nature, which is established by the Word, or Logos, of God. In contradistinction to Greek philosophers, the Fathers of the church rejected the idea of a spontaneous coming together of the elements. In their view, God is the cause of existence and the source of its maintenance by his providential power.[32]

The laws of nature, the Fathers say, are providential, for they indicate the purpose of existing things and the way these things receive their most favorable outcomes.[33] In other words, all knowledge of natural phenomena is incomplete if it is not seen from the perspective of the final causes mysteriously present in the natural world's deep structure. It is this structure—that is, the hierarchy within nature—that enables humans to view nature teleologically and to conclude from partial knowledge to the whole and from the lower natural order to the higher. This view of nature is one expression of the Platonistic tendency in the Greek Fathers.

The Transfiguration of Nature

Despite their appreciation of nature, the Fathers could also see nature's evil. But, for them, the cruelty and suffering in nature were never dissociated from human sin. This is why, when the Fathers argued for the restoration of human nature through eliminating the divisions in human nature and bringing it back into union with God, they never forgot about nature as a whole. They always felt responsible for the imperfections in nature, for the irrational creatures that had become involved in the chain of original sin. Nature—all its elements, trees, and animals—is to be transfigured through man's mediation between the divisions in the created realm, as well as between the created and the uncreated, between this world and God.[34]

The Fathers found justification for this view of nature's ultimate "future" in the Scriptures. One of their sources can be found in Rom. 8:19-21, where St. Paul says that "the creation will be set free from its bondage to decay and will obtain the freedom of the glory of the children of God." St. Irenaeus of Lyons makes a similar assertion, this time based on a text from Isaiah 11: "The wolf also shall feed with the lamb, and the leopard shall take his rest with the kid; . . . and they shall do no harm, nor have power to hurt anything in my holy mountain."[35]

The restoration of animals and matter to union with God will come about through the salvation of man, for it is only humans who can change the order of things in nature through their own perfection, leading ultimately to union with God, to deification. The restoration of sensible nature means not its destruction but rather its transfiguration, which changes only the outward appearance of things. Origen describes this in his De principis: "If the 'form of this world passes away', it is not by any means of annihilation or destruction of the material substance that is indicated, but the occurrence of a certain change of quality and an alteration of the outward form."[36]

This idea referred not only to the restoration of a person's body but also to changes in the natural environment, that is, to restoration of the earthly paradise. According to St. Maximus the Confessor, the distinction between Paradise and the rest of the created earth is connected with ontological differences in the creation.

These differences led to the fall of humans, that is, their preference for sensible realities rather than for God.[37] In a truly ingenious way, Maximus links the restoration of Paradise with the contemplation of purposes and ends in the perceptible realm of creation.

From Uniformity in Nature to the Logos of God: St. Athanasius

St. Athanasius of Alexandria, in his fundamental christological writings, argues for the uniformity of the created world—the principle that makes it possible to apply the same method of knowledge to objects on different scales of space, time, complexity, and order—for the world was created by the Word (Logos) of God and everything exhibits God's presence, the principle of which is Christ, who is both God and human. Athanasius argues that it is through God's Logos that God gave an order to the universe so that it is comprehensible by man; it is in this comprehensibility that humans can know God from *within* creation: "God knew the limitation of mankind, you see, and though the grace of being made in His image was sufficient to give them knowledge of the Word and through Him of the Father, as a safeguard against their neglect of this grace. He also provided the works of creation as a means by which the Maker might be known."[38]

In *Contra gentes*, Athanasius makes use of such astronomical examples as the regular motions of the sun and the moon, the stars, and the sunrise to infer that there is a consistent order in the universe in which opposite motions and differentiated objects "are not ordered by themselves, but have a Maker distinct from themselves who orders them."[39]

He insists that the order among things is not self-produced but is maintained by God by means of uniting, balancing, administrating, ordaining, and reconciling created things (*Contra* 36.1–3, 37.1). He claims that if things in the universe were to exercise the power of ordering themselves, we would see "not order, but disorder, not arrangement, but anarchy, not a system, but everything out of system, not proportion but disproportion" (*Contra* 37.3). In another passage, Athanasius uses the existence of life on earth to conclude, in a similar fashion, that there exists a principle of "arrangement and combination" in the world that is ultimately granted by God (*Contra* 37.4).

The genius of Athanasius affirmed that order in the universe (by which he did not mean the order or design arising from an already created matter) is underpinned and sustained by the Word of God as the transcendent creator.[40] Athanasius means by the order of the universe not an epistemological construction (as Kant would affirm later on), but an ontological rational order whose existence has its ground in something other than the things that are ordered, that is, in the very being of the reason or Word of God (*Contra* 40.1).

This fundamental argument in favor of the rationality of the universe proceeds not from the principles of existence of the created things, which provide only for the existence of particular things in their multiplicity, but from the Word (Logos) of God, who unites all principles of existence (that is, the *logoi* of things) in himself in a harmony and order that penetrate into creation and are contemplated as the order and rationality of the universe. Athanasius writes:

> But by Word (Logos) I mean not that which is involved and inherent in all things created, which some are wont to call the seminal principle (*logos spermatikos*), which is without soul and has no power of reason or thought, but the living and powerful Word of the good God, the God of the universe, the very Word which is God, Who while being different from things that are made and from all creation, is the One own Word of the good Father, who by His own providence ordered and illumines this universe. (*Contra* 40.4)

Athanasius anticipated the possibility of skepticism as to the existence of the Word of God, the same skepticism that caused so many problems for Kant at the end of the eighteenth century. Kant argued that no demonstration of the existence of a creator of the world from the order and design of the universe was possible. Athanasius, however, insisted that such a demonstration was possible "from what is seen, because all things subsist by the Word and Wisdom of God, nor would any created thing have had a fixed existence had it not been made by reason, and that reason the Word of God, as we have said" (*Contra* 40.6).

It is through this inference of the existence of the Word of God from the created order that one can know that God is, for it is the Word of God who orders the universe and reveals the Father. At this point, Athanasius draws a clear connection between order in the created world and the concept of the incarnation of the Word of God. It was not enough for God just to create an ordered world to teach humankind about the Father: "Creation was there all the time, but it did not prevent men from wallowing in error."[41]

It was the role of the Word of God, the Logos and only Son of the Father, who by God's ordering of the universe reveals the Father, "to renew the same teaching" through his incarnation, thereby using another means to teach those who would not learn from the works of creation about God.[42] One particular aspect of the incarnation of the Word of God serves to justify a principle of uniformity and order in nature and thus make science developed on earth applicable to all aspects of the cosmos. Christ, while being incarnate God in the flesh at a given point of the history of salvation and in a particular point of the physical universe, did not cease to be the Word (Logos) of God:

> The Word was not hedged in by His body, nor did His presence in the body prevent His being present elsewhere as well. . . . The marvelous truth is, that being the Word, so far from being Himself contained by anything, He actually contained all things Himself. Existing in human body, to which He Himself gives life, He is still the Source of life for all the universe, present in every part of it, yet outside the whole;

and He is revealed both through the works of His body and through His activity in the world.[43]

This affirmation of the unique position of Christ in the world, where the incarnate Son, Christ, though being in body locally at a given point in the vastness of cosmic space, is still co-inherent at every point in space because he is in everything as the Word of God, provides an implicit principle of order in the universe that ensures that every place in the universe, as a place of the "presence" of the Word, is co-inherent with the place where God is bodily incarnate, on earth.[44]

In the view of the Christian scientists of the time, this implied that there was a uniformity in the laws of nature (which were known from their experience on earth) throughout the whole of the cosmos. This intrinsic rationality in the world, according to Athanasius, is maintained by the creative Logos of God, which is not an immanent principle of the world but rather the transcendent artificer of order and harmony in created existence, an existence thus contingent on the transcendent rationality of God. As a result, for Athanasius, both realms in creation—the empirical (visible or perceptible) and the intelligible (invisible)—as well as the common principle of their creation, order, and harmony, are encoded in the Word (Logos) of God (*Contra* 3.44).[45]

Two implications of this theological development for physics were realized by the Christian thinker John Philoponus of Alexandria (d. ca. 570). He recognized that any true order in the universe must be universally valid and inferred from the colors of the stars that the same laws govern the stars and bodies on earth.[46]

Philoponus also tried to understand the created order from the distinction between the uncreated and the created light in the theology of creation. According to him, we explain the visible order in terms of the invisible, that is, in terms of either physical or moral laws. The laws involving the intelligible order of the created world, which has a derivative existence, point back to the ultimate foundation of all order in God.[47] This example is an important argument for the possibility of demonstrating the presence of the *logoi* of created things scientifically by analyzing the interplay between empirical and intelligible reality.

St. Maximus the Confessor on the *logoi* of Creation

The problem that arises is how to demonstrate the presence of the Logos from within the created realm. The clue to this demonstration can be found in Maximus the Confessor's theology of the *logoi*. According to Maximus, it is the divine Logos (Word of God) that holds together the *logoi* of created things (that is, their immutable and eternal principles).[48]

Maximus considered the contemplation of the *logoi* of created things to be a mode of communion with the Logos leading ultimately to mystical union with God. The fundamental aspect of this communion is that, because it is exercised through the purified intellect (nous), the contemplation of the *logoi* is not the same as either empirical perception or mental comprehension. It is a mode of spiritual vision of reality in which the ontological roots of things and beings have their grounds beyond the world. This Christian contemplation of creation as if it were "from above" or "from within"—and not through external sensible or internal mental impressions—is significantly different from what is now normally accepted as taking place in scientific experience.

Indeed, science usually thinks of itself as starting from experiments and measurements, from things that constitute our sense of ordinary reality, though sometimes mediated by experimental apparatus. There is, however, another aspect of all scientific investigation that involves the shaping of contingent empirical findings into a theory. This requires access to symbolic language (for example, mathematics), which makes it possible for us to talk about the entities behind the outcomes of our measurements. This takes place regularly when, for example, physics talks of elementary particles, fields, global geometry, the totality of the universe, and so forth. All these "objects" are known to us only through their effects and are representable in our minds only with symbolic images. In other words, their physical existence is affirmed in terms of their symbolic images. We understand at present that this way of looking at reality corresponds to what we call human rationality. The source of this rationality is hidden in the mystery of the human hypostasis, the human person.[49]

The human person, made in the image of God, "is not identifiable with the body, or the soul, or the spirit. It arises from another order of reality."[50] In other words, "the transcending character of human hypostasis . . . cannot be manifested within the relationship between body and soul—for they form one nature—but only in relation to something which is not of human nature, i.e. superhuman."[51]

It is only because of the existence of this divine dimension in human beings that it is possible to infer from nature to God. Only because of this dimension can we hope to unveil the divine intentions behind created things through the principles and ideas that are introduced into science by means of human rationality.[52]

According to Maximus, the divine Logos is present in all things, holding their *logoi* together. Thus the world is filled with the divine reality, and humans, in accordance with their *logos,* can have knowledge of the *logoi* of things. Maximus expresses this thought in a characteristic, quite modern way when he speaks of the presence of the divine in the structure of the created world: "Indeed, the scientific research of what is really true will have its forces weakened and its procedure embarrassed, if the mind cannot comprehend *how* God is in the *logos* of every special thing and likewise in all the *logoi* according to which all things exist."[53]

Maximus contends that people know things from nature in their differentiated mode—that is, they see creation as divided into parts—and that this perception always confuses them. The natural contemplation of things means the knowledge of the principles of existence of those things in their differentiation. The fundamental step, which is made at this stage of mediation, is to contemplate all sensible creation in its oneness through finding that all the *logoi* of sensible things can be united in one divine Logos, which constitutes the principle of creation. To achieve this contemplation, people must be detached from sensible creation so as to see things spiritually. Maximus compares this kind of contemplation of natural things with the angelic knowledge of sensible things, for angels know the *logoi* of sensible things directly, "from above." Because the incarnation, according to Maximus, takes place both in the words of the Scripture and in the *logoi* of things that are held together in the universal Logos, spiritual ascent through the contemplation of the *logoi* of creation leads finally to the Logos-Christ. The knowledge of things of the world thus acquires all the features of participation in the Divine: "On the account of the presence of the Logos in all things, holding their *logoi* together, the world is pregnant with divine reality, and knowledge of it—through the rational quality of humans, their own *logos*—is itself a kind of communion with God, a participation in divine things through the aims and purposes that are recognized in creation."[54]

The incarnation thus gives expression to the cosmic importance of Christ, for through the differentiation of things and their *logoi*, in which Christ the Logos is present, one can contemplate their unity in the one Logos of God and through them ascend with the incarnate Christ to the Father. This movement into the spiritual contemplation of the unity of things, their purposes and ends, can be qualified as communion with God through nature, something that is possible only because of the incarnation and through the gift of divine grace to humans. The natural contemplation of the different *logoi* in the one Logos thus manifests the exodus of humans from this world to God, as the truth of the whole of creation is revealed by and in the Logos of God. Maximus treats all of this mystagogically, that is, as a liturgical process on a cosmic scale: the "cosmic liturgy."[55]

It is characteristic of Maximus and of the Greek Fathers in general that they could transcend spiritually the material world, the world of nature, in order to contemplate its *logoi* and through this contemplation praise the creator of the natural world. Afterward, they could come back to nature and see it in a new light, from the perspective of its ends and purposes, from the perspective of Christ the Logos. For the Fathers, nature was empty before Christ. Its true meaning was opened only through the mystery of the incarnation of the Logos of God. But the Fathers, though worshiping the uncreated through nature, were always aware of the danger of pantheism, for the passage between the material and the spiritual (as the easiest mental image of the uncreated) was made with such ease that the fundamental distinction between them could be confused. The Fathers never worshiped nature, only its creator. This is why when we speak of the "cosmic liturgy" of Maximus as a form of mediation between heaven and earth, we must remember that overcoming the divisions in the creation on the moral and existential level does not imply the elimination of the differences in creation on the ontological level. Praying to the Creator does not remove the distinction between God and the creation. This safeguards the position of the Fathers from pantheism. God and nature are not identical, but one may seek access to nature in order to find God.

Detachment from Nature and the Love of Nature

Though fascinated by the natural world and appreciating its great beauty, the Fathers clearly understood that if the mind were to be distracted by the puzzles of nature and to consider them as ends in themselves, then the knowledge of nature would itself become an obstacle in trying to know God. Thus a tension was created between the appreciation of nature and the danger of being trapped by its investigation. On the one hand, the natural world is accepted and affirmed, while, on the other, it is renounced as having no meaning without its spiritual ground. The necessity to rise above nature in order to find God was always experienced as the difficulty of being detached from a natural world that at the same time was highly appreciated.

In the contemplation of the *logoi* of creation, the Greek Fathers found an ingenious way of resolving this tension, freeing themselves from the demands of nature, on the one hand, while enjoying nature, on the other. They never experienced any fear of nature, which was the creation of a God "who loves mankind." Their detachment from the material world provided a paradoxical freedom to treat this world in a way that never subverted their spiritual vision of reality, that is, their faith. The secret of the Greek Fathers' freedom to enjoy nature was their detachment from it. Their spiritual vision of nature freed them to love and appreciate nature without condemning its created origin and without fearing its demands, for the natural world, like all of creation, is good because everything done by God through his Word (Logos) is good.

The Latin Church and the Natural Sciences

This section discusses the role of Latin Christianity in establishing the position of the church with respect to science. The Latin case is extremely important because its approach to science predetermined, in a way, the whole subsequent development of philosophy and science in the West, which ultimately led to the scientific achievements we face now. Some authors claim that St. Augustine of Hippo (354–430), the most influential and prolific Latin writer of the fifth century, should be considered the Father who most influenced the seventeenth-century Cartesian revolution in philosophical thinking and who anticipated certain aspects of modernism.[56]

Augustine contributed his own ideas on the role of philosophy, science, and education in the life of a Christian. His primary thesis, which became the predominant view of science in the cultural context of Western Europe until the end of the Middle Ages, was that science was important and indispensable for exegesis and the defense of the Christian faith.[57] At the same time, Augustine developed the so-called handmaiden formula, according to which the natural sciences inherited from the classical tradition have no intrinsic value. Instead, they acquire value extrinsically, since they are useful tools, serving as "handmaidens" to Christian theology and the church.

For our purposes, it is crucial to grasp that through his writings Augustine transmitted to later generations this vision of science, which he inherited from Classical Greek thought and which was later transformed into a systematic scientific enterprise carried out by the new European universities and academia. Although Augustine does not represent the whole story of the Latin Patristic encounter between science and religion, he did lay the foundations of the Christian attitude to science that later made it possible for Roger Bacon (ca. 1220–92) to continue the Augustinian approach to natural sciences as the handmaiden of theology, albeit in an elaborate, systematic way that corresponded to his own era, historically removed from Augustine's by almost eight centuries. Bacon's activity led ultimately to "legitimization" of science as a Christian activity and to the creation of the European universities and an extended system of education. The transition from Augustine to Roger Bacon, though not a straightforward, continuous process, meant that the science of the Classical tradition was transmitted to Medieval Europe. It is in this aspect of the history of science that the church played a fundamental role.[58]

From a historical point of view, it is interesting to note that the Western world, as it evolved intellectually toward the acceptance of science as a part of the educational norm in a Christian society, incorporated only those aspects of the relationship between science and theology that were developed by the Latin Fathers. The panorama of views from the Greek-speaking Christian world was nearly forgotten. One explanation for this can be found in the difference of language itself. The Western church fathers of the Patristic period and the Christian authors of the early Middle Ages were forced to rely on the derivative, Latinized version of the Classical Greek tradition. Moreover, the Latin Fathers generally knew this tradition only in the "thin" form, that is, from secondary sources and compendia. Philosophers such as Plato and Aristotle were not read in Greek at all in the Western world and thus were nearly forgotten, until the twelfth century, when a more complete version of the scientific portions of the Classical tradition was introduced in Western Europe through translations from Arabic versions into Latin, along with extensive Islamic commentaries. Not long afterward, many of the same texts were translated into Latin from the original Greek, to which Western Europeans had finally gained access.[59]

However, this return to the Classical Greek sources, such as the philosophical writings of Plato and Aristotle, did not bring about a revival of interests in Greek Fathers and their attitude to the natural sciences. The numerous writings of the Byzantine theologians were, if not ignored, at least disregarded as significant for the establishment of a "new" approach to science and education in Western Europe. After a gap of nearly eight centuries, Roger Bacon and his followers—and later, St. Thomas Aquinas—appealed only to the authority of Augustine on such issues as faith and reason, science and its role in exegesis, and so forth, and paid little if any attention to the Greek Patristic and Byzantine thinkers who contributed, as we have seen, nontrivial ideas on the importance of natural sciences and the significance of nature for Christian theology. This represents a problem for historical research that has yet to be addressed.

The aim here is to understand the specificity of the Latin Christian attitude toward natural sciences and its differences from the Greek Patristic views on nature, which were considered earlier in this chapter. This difference, which was only minor in the Patristic period, led ultimately to the large-scale differences about the relationship between science and theology that exist at present between Eastern Orthodox theology and Western Christianity in its various forms.

St. Augustine of Hippo and the Natural Sciences

The immediate problem that Augustine still faced three hundred years after Clement of Alexandria was how to react to the non-Christian philosophy and liberal arts that were still widely studied in the culture surrounding the expanding Christian Church. Like Clement, Augustine argues that philosophy, which was so important for the art of reasoning and for defending faith, must be not condemned, but Christianized. Philosophy should be seen from the perspective of faith, for there is no understanding without faith. When faith is achieved, however, it becomes necessary to understand what one believes.[60]

Augustine saw faith as a necessary condition for reason to lead to understanding. However, he was cautious—and even negative—in his attitude toward pagan learning in general. Even when treated only as a matter of curiosity, pagan learning is still potentially dangerous, he explains in his *Confessions:* "For in addition to the fleshly appetite which strives for the gratification of all senses and pleasures . . . there is also a certain vain and curious longing in the soul, rooted in the same bodily senses, cloaked under the name of knowledge and learning."[61]

Augustine declared that his personal study of the liberal arts and sciences was of no use for him, since it did not help him to find and praise God. It was because of this that pagan learning, when it did not serve the purpose of knowledge of God, was not to be appreciated: "And what did it profit me that I, the base slave of vile affections, read *unaided,* and understood, all the books that I could get of the so-called liberal arts? . . . So, then, it served not to my use but rather to my destruction."[62]

Like his Greek predecessors, Augustine argues that pagan learning, if it does not serve the purposes of faith—that is, if it is not understood through the eyes of faith—leads nowhere, because, taken as it is in itself, it does not provide its purposes and ultimate meaning. The aid to this learning means the acquisition of faith in God, who is the provider of all abilities to learn, as well as the content of learning.

It does not follow, however, from the fragments just quoted that Augustine denied any rational activity, and in particular philosophy, of the Classical culture. We have seen that the major thesis of Augustine is that understanding, rational explanation, and philosophical activity all have meaning only if they are grounded in a life of faith. Augustine makes a clear distinction between knowledge that originates from the senses, that is, from sensible experience, and that of the intellect. The latter was not so much affected by the bodily affections and was worthy of being included in the armory of a Christian as a means of defending the faith and arguing with one's enemies. He writes in *On Christian Doctrine:* "There remain those branches of knowledge which pertain not to the bodily senses, but to the intellect, among which the science of reasoning . . . [which] is of very great service in searching into and unravelling all sorts of questions that come up in Scripture."[63]

Elsewhere, Augustine warns that one should be cautious when reasoning about religious matters. The problem does not lie in applying reason to such issues as the Trinity, for example, but in avoiding false reasoning. One should not abandon reasoning altogether if some particular form of it is false.[64] In order to avoid false reasoning, reason must be grounded in faith.[65]

All this points to the fact that Augustine was relatively favorable to rational forms of knowledge and philosophy. Like Clement of Alexandria, he argues that there are many positive aspects in Classical philosophical thought and precepts of morality, which are well adapted to Christian truth. Also like Clement, he believes that those fruits of wisdom that the Greeks placed in the service of philosophy were not invented by them "but dug out of the mines of God's providence which are everywhere scattered abroad."[66]

Augustine's main appeal to Christians is to convert these achievements of Greek thought to their proper Christian use: "If those who are called philosophers, and especially the Platonists, have said aught that is true and in harmony with our faith, we are not only not to shrink from it, but to claim it for our own use from those who have unlawful possession of it."[67]

One particular thought of Augustine's must be mentioned here. He applies a typological analogy to the relation between the Christian faith and pagan philosophy by comparing the people of Israel, who took vessels and ornaments of gold at the time of the exodus from the Egyptians (who could not know how, in the future, all these things could be turned to the service of Christ), with the Greeks, who invented philosophy and the liberal arts (not knowing that they, too, could be turned to the service of Christ): "For what was done at the time of the Exodus was no doubt a type prefiguring what happens now."[68]

Augustine not only sees the problem of the relationship between Christian faith and non-Christian philosophy in its historical dimension but also assigns it some theological features. For him, the full meaning of this relationship can be understood only after the incarnation of Christ. Thus, according to Augustine, the true meaning of philosophy can be achieved only through the Christian understanding of its role as a gift of reason given to humans by God in order to praise God and his creation. This makes Augustine's position close, in general terms, to that of the Greek Fathers, who, as discussed above, interpreted science in the perspective of Christ.

Science as the Handmaiden of Theology in St. Augustine

It is clear that Augustine appreciated rational thinking and philosophy in those aspects that were required by religious thought, that is, when reason was applied to problems and objects that had religious relevance. It is interesting to understand Augustine's treatment of philosophy when it was applied to natural objects with no obvious religious significance. How did he treat empirical research in the material world in which we live? The brief answer is that Augustine did not value these investigations highly. For example, while writing on the shape of the heavens in his *Literal Meaning of Genesis*, he warns numerous writers against discussions on this topic in terms of the natural sciences because "the sacred writers with their deeper wisdom have omitted them . . . for they knew the truth, but the Spirit of God, who spoke through them, did not wish to teach men these facts that would be no avail for their salvation."[69]

Thus, according to Augustine, the writers did this for a purpose: "Such subjects are of no profit for those who seek beatitude, and, what is worse, they take up very precious time that ought to be given to what is spiritually beneficial."[70]

Does this mean that Augustine encouraged Christians to proclaim an intentional ignorance with respect to natural phenomena and the attempts to explain them? When speaking about such borderline questions as the cosmological issues involved in the Genesis narrative, Augustine follows the way of caution: saying too much about the meaning and nature of material things is worse than saying nothing. Christians' ignorance of the natural sciences must not be considered alarming if they know but one thing: the world of nature is created by God. In other words, Augustine tacitly admits that the empirical investigation of nature is possible, since things that are observed are created exactly in such forms as they are perceived by a researcher. From his point of view, any further theoretical investigation into the ultimate causes of things has no value. He confirms this in *On Christian Doctrine*: "I think, however, there is nothing useful in the other branches of learning that are found among the heathen, except information about objects, either past or present, that relate to the bodily senses, in which are included the experiments and conclusions of the useful mechanical arts, except also the sciences of reasoning and of number."[71]

Augustine, then, stresses the usefulness of the knowledge of natural facts if they are compiled in a systematic form to provide the minimum of information that Christians should know in order to understand things that are mentioned in the Scriptures.[72] This quite modest assessment of the utility of the natural sciences for Christians is associated, among other factors, with Augustine's concern about the use of scientific arguments in the interpretation of Scripture by those Christians who did not sufficiently understand scientific matters. Knowledge was better than ignorance in any case, but undeveloped knowledge could be worse than ignorance, because, by being used in ecclesial arguments, it could damage the reputation of a Christian in the eyes of a nonbeliever. Augustine writes:

> Usually even a non-Christian knows something about the earth, the heavens, and the other elements of this world . . . and this knowledge he holds to as being certain from reason and experience. Now, it is disgraceful and dangerous for an infidel to hear a Christian, presumably giving the meaning of Holy Scripture, talking nonsense on these topics; and we should take all means to prevent such an embarrassing situation, in which people show up vast ignorance. . . . If they find a Christian mistaken in a field which they themselves know well and hear him maintaining his foolish opinions about our books, how are they going to believe those books?[73]

This brings us back to the thesis already stated: Augustine affirmed that, for a Christian, it is enough to believe that all natural things are created by God.[74]

Nature viewed from this perspective must not be loved, for there is nothing to admire in the creation.[75] It is the Creator who must be praised and worshiped. Nature, which, as a part of creation, is finite in its essence, must be used only for spiritual and eternal purposes: "This world must be used, not enjoyed, that so the invisible things of God may be clearly seen, being understood by the things that are made, that is, that by means of what is material and temporary we may lay hold upon that which is spiritual and eternal."[76]

Natural philosophy thus receives its justification—and, in a sense, sanctification—through its special function with respect to theology: it is its handmaiden. Augustine develops this thesis through his exegetical work in which he uses the natural sciences to interpret Scripture. In his *Literal Meaning of Genesis,* Augustine tries to make a consistent interpretation of Scripture using the cosmology and physics of the Classical tradition.[77] As noted earlier, the status of science as the handmaiden of theology played an extremely important role in the Western church's support of scientific research and education in Europe after the twelfth century.[78] One might also argue that this attitude toward science was, in the end, responsible for the development of scientific thought in the direction of Cartesian dualism, and ultimately to the separation of science and theology.

Seminal Reasons and Natural Law in St. Augustine

From the simple observation that nature, especially in all its living forms, is still in a state of unfolding variety and development, Augustine faced a serious problem: how to reconcile this natural fact with the scriptural affirmation of the completion of God's creative activity "in the beginning." Augustine distinguishes two kinds of creatures: those that were fixed in their form in the work of God during six days (for example, angels, the days themselves, earth, water, air, fire, stars, and the human soul) and those that were created in their "seeds" and still had to develop. The latter were only *preformed* at the "time" of creation; for Augustine, these include all living things, be they plants, animals, or even humans. At the time of creation, they all existed *invisibly* and *potentially* as things whose reality was caused by their future. Augustine uses the term *rationales seminales* (usually translated as "seminal reasons"), a Latinized form of the Stoic expression *spermatikoi logoi.*[79] These hidden seeds in the world created by God are compared sometimes with the causes, which contain everything that is to be unfolded in the future.[80] Augustine writes: "For the Creator of these invisible seeds is the Creator of all things Himself: since whatever comes forth to our sight by being born, receives the first beginnings of its course from hidden seeds, and takes the successive increments of its proper size and its distinctive forms from these, as it were, original rules."[81]

The nature of these seminal reasons, or seeds, according to Augustine, is twofold. On the one hand, he argues, these seeds already exist in the elements of nature.

Although invisible, they are present in a hidden form in the created world. On the other hand, he understands them as the principles of activity in nature, ideas in a Platonic sense, which underlie physical existence and form its pattern. Augustine compares them with the numbers that bring into the elements the efficacious forces that were planted in the works of God before he completed his work of creation. From this point of view, the original creation was complete in itself, even though these forces showed their effects later, for they all were hidden in the elements themselves. In this case, God no longer creates, though he is still at work, for he keeps all things in being by his power and causes the seeds to reach the full development he established for them "in the beginning."[82]

This Augustinian view of the seminal reasons—as created and fixed preexistent principles of all unfolding processes and things—has a serious impact for natural sciences, for it denies strongly any possibility of creative evolution in nature and transformation of the species.[83] In fact, Augustine's doctrine does not explain the appearance of anything new through the unfolding of as yet undeveloped aspects of living nature; on the contrary, everything is created at the beginning of all time and nothing fundamentally new can come into existence after this, for the existence of everything was planned before and the surface of appearances contains only things developed from the "old" seeds. That is why it is true to say that God created all things "simultaneously."[84]

In contradistinction to transformation of species, the seminal reasons account for the stability of species; they represent the principles of stability rather than of change. Augustine's doctrine goes along the lines of his other arguments that rule out any real efficacy in human activity or in that of other beings. Whatever people do that leads to the further unfolding of natural phenomena—for example, when they cultivate plants—they still do not invent or create anything new but rather appeal to the hidden inner forces in nature, to the initial seeds, which from the beginning contain all power and potency to develop in the visible creation according to God's plan.

Thus, in the Augustinian universe, any scientific discovery of evolving processes does not provide evidence for the creativeness of nature itself. What we treat as novelty is just the appearance of something old and preexistent in the seminal reasons. The whole scientific enterprise thus leads us to an endless witnessing of the unfolding of the initial seeds that points back to the *creatio ex nihilo* itself. An infinite advance in scientific development thus means no more than a never-ending unfolding of the plan of creation, which, being "simultaneous" in the sense that it is God's action, is potentially infinite and eternal in its historical incarnation.

This theory of the seminal reasons in Augustine can be used to justify his attitude to science as the handmaiden of theology. Indeed, in his view, science cannot lead us to any independent knowledge of truth in creation, apart from producing indications of the presence of the initial seeds, which are brought into existence by God. That is why, on the one hand, the natural sciences and empirical research, taken in themselves, are of no real use for a Christian. They cannot provide any evidence for the presence of the Divine for an uneducated person, though scientific investigation can be useful if understood theologically and in light of its function as illustrating the presence of the seminal reasons in creation. It can serve theology by finding traces of God in the created world.

One can make an analogy with mechanics by comparing the seminal reasons with the initial conditions that are implanted in nature to launch its growth according to various dynamic laws. The seminal reasons themselves do not possess temporality except in a hidden, latent form. It is important to realize, however, that Augustine's seminal reasons not only play the role of the initial conditions for things that evolve but also predetermine their dynamics, that is, the particular features of their growth and development, their temporal flux. This allows one to argue that Augustine's concept of the seminal principles leads to the notion of natural law.[85]

If we take Augustine's notion of the seminal reasons seriously, we should make a clear distinction between what we can know about God's plan in the "continuous" creation through observing the unfolding of these reasons, and God's intention at the original act of creation as a whole. The latter is contingent and free from the necessity that we are apparently able to uncover in the world. Augustine anticipated this distinction: "For it is one thing to make and administer the creature from the innermost and highest turning-point of causation, which He alone does who is God the Creator; but quite another thing to apply some operation from without in proportion to the strength and faculties assigned to each by Him, so that what is created may come forth into being at this time or at that, and in this or that way."[86]

One can thus treat the causation that originates from the nature of things, assigned to them by God, as *natural law*. This differs from causation of the *creatio ex nihilo* type. There is no reduction of the former to the latter and, theologically speaking, causation at the "point" of contingent creation cannot be affirmed in terms of a description of the natural world. Nor can one say that natural law can be explained. It can be detected, but its ultimate origin and causal nexus constitute a theological ideal rather than a subject for scientific inquiry.

In concluding this section, it should be stressed again that the idea of seminal reasons was invoked by Augustine not to solve a scientific problem but rather to address difficulties in his exegesis of Genesis. He did not intend to make his theory of seminal reasons subject to empirical confirmation. Augustine never supposed that the seminal reasons, or seeds, were the object of experience. As mentioned before, he thought of them rather as Platonic ideas that can only be grasped by the mind. Still, it is interesting to realize that Augustine's speculations on seminal reasons were indirectly supported by empirical observations of the everlasting unfolding of the natural world. This justifies the intuition that Augustine used a one-way inference from empirical facts to speculative propositions on the underlying nature of these facts. The strength of this argument can be seen in the fact that Augustine attempted to use the idea of numbers—that is, mathematical ideas in their extreme form—in application to such entities that cannot be observed and empirically verified. This makes his attempt similar to modern theoretical physics, which speaks sometimes about unseen particles or fields in terms of their symbolic images, using the language of mathematics. The reality of the seminal reasons thus can be asserted as on a par with the reality of mathematical ideas. Augustine used the adjective *eternal* with respect to the seminal reasons, though they can also be described as "immutable" ideas. They are different, however, from the *logoi* of Greek Patristic thought, which are uncreated and originate in the divine Logos of God. At the same time, it is through the intelligible domain of the created realm that their presence in the world can be shown.

The Differences between the Greek and Latin Treatment of Nature and Science

This chapter has focused in particular on a most intriguing outcome of the historical developments of scientific enterprise in the Christian world: the difference in attitude toward nature and science that can be observed in Greek Patristic thought and the Latin tradition. This difference would appear to be ultimately responsible for the striking divergence in the understanding of the problem of science and religion in the Eastern church on the one hand, and in modern Western Christianity, on the other. At this point, I will try to highlight these differences, though with no pretension to being complete.[87]

Both the Greek and the Latin Fathers had to address the issue of natural philosophy and science in their theological reflections. In doing this, they inevitably transmitted the science of the classical Greco-Roman tradition down through the centuries. This transmission should be regarded as one of the major contributions made by the Christian Church and its theology to the future development of the scientific enterprise.

This transmission of Greek philosophy and science was naturally accompanied by a change of function as they took their place in the system of Christian thought. The Fathers' strong preference for Platonic philosophy continued to influence the development of science until the twelfth century, when the writings of Aristotle became fully available in Western Europe and were accommodated by Christian thinkers.

Christian theology itself, which was heavily imbued with Greek metaphysics and cosmology, took the shape of the unique synthesis of faith and philosophy that we now call now the Patristic synthesis. The Fathers' "conversion" of Greek philosophy, and their use of it in theology, was not the choice of a "handmaiden" for the theological enterprise. It involved an authentic creative synthesis of human thought with the Christian's mystical experience of God.

The classical image of nature was de-divinized by Christian thinkers, who approached it in a new way. Nature was freed from the Hellenistic gods who inhabited its elements and was secularized in the sense that, instead of worshiping nature, the Fathers worshiped its creator. They treated nature as good and beautiful, since it was the good creation of a good God. The meaning of nature, its purposes and its ends, was formulated in Christian doctrine from the perspective of Christ. Thus the unfolding of natural processes and knowledge of them acquired definite Christian features, for nature was treated in a sacramental fashion, that is, in the light of the incarnation of God.

What distinguishes the view of science in the Patristic era from that of the present day is that when the Fathers talked about science theologically, they dealt with the scientific laws and symmetries, which reflected an essentially Platonic understanding of the world, rather than with the particular empirical outcomes of these laws, which manifested the deviation from the Platonic symmetry in the concrete empirical situation. The complex outcomes of physical laws apparent in nature (that is, the empirical situations when the symmetric pattern of the Platonic laws were broken) became the subject of thorough scientific analysis only later, when Aristotelian philosophy and physics began to dominate Western European thinking. It was much easier for the Fathers to think in terms of Platonic regularities in nature than to investigate the particular empirical situations that are, in fact, the outcomes of these laws. Today, it is understood that neither the laws alone nor the outcomes of the laws can provide an adequate description of nature. This is why the Platonic approach to science was insufficient for its advance and why the Fathers—and the civilization they represent—did not contribute to empirical research, which generally deals with the *outcomes* of the underlying laws. Nevertheless, this was not the main reason for their lack of contribution to science. They were bishops, not scientists, and were primarily concerned with the theological issues that arose as they sought to defend their faith. Thus they felt called to make use of science but not to develop it.

Nevertheless, it is important to understand why nearly similar views on the nature of scientific activity among Greek and Latin Fathers influenced their successors in completely different ways, leading to an outburst of scientific activity in the Western Christian world while having no significant impact on the development of science in Eastern Orthodox Europe. Two conclusions may be drawn. The first relates to the historical significance of the handmaiden formula that was strongly articulated by Augustine but never seriously developed among the Greek Fathers.

In the thirteenth century in the West, Roger Bacon followed Augustine's strategy in employing sciences for learning and for services to theology and the church.[88] To avoid undesirable theological conclusions, Bacon sought to cleanse the sciences of all error and to make them a faithful handmaiden of theology. Bacon's major work, the *Opus maius,* is an apology for the new learning. In it, he builds his arguments on the basis of Augustine's *On Christian Doctrine,* using the Augustinian notion that philosophy, when properly understood and practiced, can contribute to the unfolding of scriptural truth. Bacon managed to claim—and to demonstrate—that nearly everything can fit into the handmaiden formula. He went to great lengths to see that his claim for the handmaiden status of philosophy and the various sciences was justified and systematic, covering nearly all sciences, including linguistics, mathematics, astronomy, and geography, in order to convince the reader that all can qualify as the handmaidens of theology, thereby justifying their religious utility. Bacon strongly advocated that any knowledge obtained through experiment must be confirmed in order to qualify for handmaiden status. For this reason, he called for the pursuit of "experimental science" as the methodology of such confirmation. It is important to remember that in his advocacy for the utility of natural sciences for theology, Bacon was, in fact, concerned mostly with the proper positioning of natural sciences vis-à-vis theology, rather than with any possible threat that the sciences could pose to theology. He was a philosopher, not a theologian like Augustine, and thus sought to salvage the natural sciences rather than to interpret them theologically.

The work of Roger Bacon and the success of St. Thomas Aquinas in incorporating Bacon's teaching into Christian doctrine resulted in a strengthening of the hand-maiden formula that overcame opposition to the new learning, leading to the establishment of new universities in Europe and a new intellectual climate within Christian culture. Although the handmaiden formula was important for promoting experimental science in general, it never seriously influenced the course of development or content of any particular science. Through the approach to science as the handmaiden of theology, initiated by St. Augustine and transmitted in the Western church, science entered Western Christian culture and acquired a position of prominence that it has not yet lost.

The second conclusion is theological. St. Augustine's theological position differed from that of the Greek Fathers on at least two dogmatic points. These were later transformed by St. Thomas Aquinas in a way that laid the foundation for the scientific revolution of the seventeenth century. It was Augustine who introduced the view that physical, material nature was separated from the divine not only ontologically but also in terms of God's grace. On the one hand, Augustine argued, the material universe should be understood in the light of Christ. On the other, however, the same universe cannot participate in the life of the Divine. As a result, knowledge of finite things in the universe has no theological relevance, since through this knowledge one cannot participate in the Divine. It was this stance that made it possible for Augustine to put forward his handmaiden formula for science. Scientific knowledge can be used for various passages of Scripture, for example, but even when treated in terms of its purpose and end—Christ—it still cannot provide any insight into the presence of the Divine in the world.

The concept of nature in Augustine has a very specific status. Nature, or the natural state, corresponds to the world created by God before the fall, when all things were brought into being according to their seminal reasons, which Augustine treated as ideas in the mind of God.[89] Creatures in this prefallen state receive grace from God, a grace that does not belong to their natural state, because they receive it extrinsically. Created beings have no ability to participate in their seminal reasons (ideas), since these ideas are not intrinsic to the things that are created in their image. Even in this prefallen state, all creatures, including humans, are separated from God and are deprived of any participation in God's energies. In the actual, fallen world, the gulf between God and the created, according to Augustine, is unbridgeable. The natural world, including humans, has no chance to participate in the grace of God, even extrinsically.[90]

Here we clearly see that the Orthodox doctrine of the Logos of God, who is the source of the *logoi* of all things visible and invisible and the center of the divine uncreated energies and grace in the whole world, was drastically narrowed in the sense that apprehension of the *logoi* and access to grace were strictly conditioned by the boundaries of the established church. This meant that the natural world after the fall, in Augustinian thinking, was separated from the unceasing activity of the Holy Spirit and from participation in the Divine. Thus nature in itself lost its sacramental quality. It is this development of Augustinian thought that led ultimately to the recognition that nature is governed by its own natural law, which has nothing to do with grace. Philip Sherrard has described this perspective as the "desanctification of nature."[91]

Despite the fact that Augustine himself never treated his view on nature as its desanctification, he definitely developed an argument on nature and its knowledge from a theological position that did not incorporate the whole of the idea of the Logos and participation in the *logoi* as developed in the Greek Fathers. This prevented him from seeing nature as a sacrament, in the light of Christ and his incarnation, and not as something somehow abandoned by God at creation. For the Greek Fathers, nature was a manifestation of God, a revelation of God's loving activity through the divine *logoi* in a world that is good. It was through God's works in nature, where the Holy Spirit is always active, that the Fathers were able to enter into communion with God. Knowledge of nature was, for the Greek Fathers, a part of the fullness of their liturgical experience, an experience that gave meaning to science and made it capable of leading people to a knowledge of the *logoi* of created beings. If the Greek Fathers saw scientific activity as a mode of the liturgical experience, understood through participation in the creative energies (and divine *logoi*) of God, then Augustine saw science as no more than a handmaiden of theology devoid of deeper spiritual meaning.

The liturgical vision of science has advantages as well as disadvantages if the problem is considered within the framework of the dialogue between science and religion. The liturgical understanding of science, which in philosophical terms implies its vision through the eyes of Christian Platonism, does not provide any scientific, investigative methodology, since the treatment of nature has a highly speculative character and makes use of hierarchical structures and mathematical laws. Science, however, when understood in this way through the prism of its place in the whole of humankind's experience, does acquire a sacred quality and receives its justification in terms of higher spiritual realities. The scientific enterprise as a whole thus becomes indispensable for our better understanding of the meaning of this world as seen in its relationship to God.

The Platonistic approach to science, however, as mentioned earlier, does not deal with the outcomes of physical laws and with broken symmetries. The development of an experimental science requires that we see nature in its variety, not only as highly symmetrical and organized but also as complex and full of disorder. The revival of Aristotle's philosophy and his ideas on the nature of scientific inference in Western Europe during and after the twelfth century led to the establishment of an empirical science that had no immediate implications for theology. Science was no more than a handmaiden of theology. This in turn led eventually to the divorce of science and theology and the mutual incomprehension that we sometimes see today.

It is difficult to say exactly why Greek Patristic and Byzantine theology had no significant impact on the development of new learning in Europe after the twelfth century. This lack of influence is commonly attributed to its inherent Platonism, which was always suspected in both Greek and Latin circles of being essentially pagan. Perhaps a certain antipathy to the Greek East, with its Platonizing tendencies, after the Great Schism of 1054 also made it easier to accept in the long run the new wave of Aristotelian philosophy introduced to Western Europe by Arab scholars in Spain.[92] Whatever the cause, in Western Europe an Aristotelian philosophy was absorbed by Christian thought, replacing the largely Platonistic theology of the Christian East and leading to the differing attitudes to science that we see today.

3

What Makes Theology Unique among Sciences: The Patristic Vision versus Modern Understanding

Theology as Experience of God: Patristic Vision

The *Concise Oxford Dictionary* (1990) offers the following definition of theology: it is "science of religion, especially Christian." Since this definition employs the term *science,* one wonders whether theology is a science in a sense similar to physics, biology, psychology, or sociology. Historical evidence shows that this definition of theology as a particular subject, which can be taught and studied, is not exactly what the church fathers meant when they used the term *theologia.*

Theology is not a scriptural term; it does not appear in either the Old Testament or the New Testament. The Apologists of the second century treated this term with some suspicion, for at the time it was thought to involve speculations about pagan gods, similar to those from Greek philosophy. The term was introduced and legitimized in the Christian context by Origen and by Clement of Alexandria, who is considered by some authors to be the founder of theology.[1] Clement inserted philosophy into the realm of faith in order to establish a more "scientific and exact faith"—to Clement, a theology, or the demonstrated faith, that is, gnosis.

Considering that the term *theology* was introduced into the Christian context by Clement, no uniform, general definition of theology existed for the Greek Patristics. The Fathers were united in their view that theology is the organized exposition of the Christian doctrine, but they expressed their approach to it differently. A sharp contrast to Clement's discursive definitions of theology, for example, is Evagrius Ponticus's famous affirmation that theology is prayer: "If you are a theologian you will pray truly and if you pray truly, you are a theologian."[2] This remark makes the invaluable point that truth, which is a subject of a theologian's inquiry, is accessible only through personal participation in this truth through prayer—prayer that forms the living experience of truth, and it is only through prayer that the experience of truth is possible. In the quote above, Evagrius develops the ideas of his teacher St. Gregory the Theologian (Nazianzus) that the necessary condition to be a theologian is to live an ascetic life, to be virtuous and go through moral purification.[3] More categorically, theology is not possible without purification (*katharsis*); the reference to this dimension of theology can be found in the New Testament: "Blessed are the pure in heart, for they shall see God" (Matt. 5:8).

Elsewhere, Evagrius employs the notion of communion in the context of prayer: "Prayer is communion of the intellect with God"—that is, theology is communion with God.[4] This aspect of theology is especially emphasized by St. Maximus the Confessor. According to Maximus, theology is the last and the highest "stage" of spiritual development in man; it is the accomplishing mode of a Christian's experience of deification. Maximus interprets this experience as a liturgical one, exercised by man in the world before God. As a culmination of this "cosmic liturgy," man receives in grace God's communication, that is, the knowledge of the Holy Trinity in *theologia*.[5] Maximus writes: "When the intellect practices the virtues correctly, it advances in moral understanding. When it practices contemplation, it advances in spiritual knowledge. . . . Finally, the intellect is granted the grace of theology when, carried on wings of love beyond these two former stages, it is taken up into God and with the help of the Holy Spirit discerns—as far as this is possible for the human intellect— the qualities of God."[6]

It is clear from this passage that theology for Maximus—that is, the knowledge of God as he is in himself—is granted only in the mystical union with God, at the last stage of deification, which is not an instant act but is preceded by a long spiritual development (*katharsis*). This highest state of union with God was granted to saints—for example, to Moses, who, on the Sinai mountain, entered the mysterious darkness of God, and to apostles at the mountain of the transfiguration.[7] Developing this insight by Maximus, St. Gregory Palamas argued later that it is the saints who are the only true theologians, for only they received the full communion with God: "Through grace God in His entirety penetrates saints in their entirety, and the saints in their entirety penetrate God entirely."[8] By the virtue of the saints and the Fathers, theology acquires, so to speak, an extended historical dimension, because "the Fathers are liturgical persons who gather round the heavenly altar with the blessed spirits. Thus they are always contemporary and present for the faithful."[9] This is why Patristic theology is the living, incarnate Orthodox faith, which never ages and is always present in the mind of the church. Patristic theology transcends its historical title as the theology of the ancient Fathers and cannot be dismissed from the modern theological discourse as old and outdated.

We see that this approach to theology, based on the personal and ecclesial experience of God, makes it clear that authentic Patristic theology radically differs from what is understood by the term *theology* among modern academics. Borrowing the concise definition of theology from the glossary of *The Philokalia,* the main source of Eastern Orthodox spirituality, we find that this definition differs indeed in comparison with the one quoted earlier in this chapter: "Theology (*theologia*) denotes . . . far more than the learning about God and religious doctrine acquired through academic study. It signifies active and conscious participation in or perception of the realities of the divine world—in other words, the realization of spiritual knowledge."[10] Theology is the spiritual knowledge that is attained through *communion* and *participation* and is a *gift* bestowed on extremely few people.[11] Theology, according to this definition, is not a theory, or a science with a definite subject, prior to investigation. On the contrary, theology is the mode of existence with God in which knowledge of God is the unfolding of one's own experience of life in God.

According to *The Philokalia*'s definition, in order to receive a gift of *theologia* one must be nearly a saint. How, then, can one be a theologian if one is not a saint? How can theology be communicated and taught if it involves a personal experience of union with God? Gregory Palamas suggested that those who have no direct experience of God but who trust the saints can also be regarded as true theologians, but at the lower level.[12] This means that in order to be a theologian in this lower sense, one must be able to read and trust the saints and the Fathers of the church. This implies, however, one's participation in the life of the church, whose living experience (that is, historical experience of the saints and fathers) constitutes its tradition and its theology. This participation is attained through communion with Scripture and through the church's sacraments, that is, liturgically. Theology, as a personal experience of participation in truth, which is affirmed by the church, thus constitutes communion with God.

The notion of truth being involved in a theological context makes the experiential dimension of theology even more vivid because—as far back as Ignatius of Antioch and Irenaeus of Lyons—truth was linked with life, understood eucharistically. This innovative view proclaimed the eucharist as a principle of existence, understood as life. The eucharist became a principle of truth, as a principle of immortality. Since in our everyday lives we are subject to decay and death, life in the church, understood as the acquisition of the ecclesial hypostasis in our nature (that is, incorruption and immortality), is achievable through the eucharist, keeps us alive, and provides us hope of immortality.

Christ is the center of the eucharist and the principle of life. As Irenaeus of Lyons writes: "For it was for this end that the Word of God was made man, and He who was the Son of God became the Son of man, that man, having been taken into the Word, and receiving the adoption, might become the son of God. For by no other means could we have attained incorruptibility and immortality, unless we have been united to incorruptibility and immortality."[13]

Proclaiming the truth of Christ as the truth of incorruptible and everlasting life, Irenaeus justifies his view by appealing to the eucharist, which, according to him, establishes his doctrine: "Our opinion is in accordance with the Eucharist and the Eucharist in turn establishes our opinion."[14] In other words, it is the eucharist itself that forms a principle of truth: namely, that participation in truth is attained only through the eucharist. Theology thus is seen as life in Christ, life in unceasing communion with God, life through participation in building the body of Christ (the church), whose being is sustained from the eschatological future. Theology thus is not only *the* way but also *the* reality of God conferred to the person in an ecstatic rapture, in the form of the blessings of the age to come.[15]

Another important aspect of the Orthodox view of theology is that theology, and the truth that it proclaims, is inconceivable without the presence of the Spirit of God.

Here, the charismatic dimension of theology surfaces, making it inseparable from the liturgy. We experience the presence of God in the eucharist as the presence of his Word (Logos) in either written or spoken form, but we also know that God is present because we experience that presence in the Spirit. "For where the Church is, there is the Spirit of God; and where the Spirit of God is, there is the Church, and every kind of grace; but the Spirit is truth."[16] This indicates that the only theology that is true is that which receives its fulfillment in the Spirit. *Charisma* as another aspect of theology thus means that the knowledge of God is revealed to us by Christ and through Christ: "No one has ever seen God: the only-begotten Son, who is in the bosom of the Father—he it is who revealed God to us" (John 1:18). This indicates in turn that theology is not just our searching for God but rather God's self-revelation to us, God's charismatic manifestations, where we receive knowledge of God from God in response to our quest, which is faith. God grants to the person this knowledge because the person is known by God through the communion of faith (see Gal. 4:9). The charismatic nature of theological knowledge is distinctive, when compared with anything in science, because the knowledge is bestowed upon us by God, by the triune hypostasis, who wants us to know him and who is the active center of theology, understood as an "outflowing" and a "shining" from God. The charismatic dimension of theology leads naturally to the conclusion that truth affirmed by theology has strong ecclesiological connotations.

What is indispensable for the presence of the Spirit in the eucharist, as a communion event, is the particular *structure* of the eucharistic gathering, that is, the Christian community around the bishop.[17] This implies that church dogmas cannot survive as truth outside communion events and, as a consequence of the structure of the latter, outside the community. Truth in theology depends on the community. It is because of this that the church historically has expressed its faith officially through the councils of bishops as leaders of the eucharistic communities and not through academic theologians. This measure prevented the conceptualization of truth, making it an abstract philosophical idea.

We see thus that even this lower level of theologizing, which is available to all "who trust the saints," requires an enormous effort of participation in the church tradition, for the experience of communion with God through ecclesial life will condition a person's claim to be a theologian.

The Inevitability of Mysticism in Theology

It is now appropriate to ask what is the relationship between an "experiential" mode of theology, discussed in the previous section, and theology as verbal expression of the church's dogma, that is, a set of formulas that can be transmitted and taught to everyone. For the early church, in which experience was empirical, using ordinary language and dogmatic affirmations became a necessity both for Christian instruction and for the defense of the church's ecclesial truth against enemies and heretics. But in all circumstances, theology, as a set of definitions, had meaning for the early church only in the context of mystical experience, because knowledge of dogmas does not provide any ground for their genuine understanding, which can come only from experience of them. Thus contemporary writers from the Christian East are eager to defend this "ancient" view of theology in the modern context, where the experiential dimension of theology is often forgotten and is replaced by formal knowledge and the art of arguing.

The Russian Orthodox theologian Vladimir Lossky reminds us that

> the eastern tradition has never made a sharp distinction between mysticism and the-ology; between personal experience of the divine mysteries and the dogma affirmed by the Church. . . . Far from being mutually opposed, theology and mysticism sup-port and complete each other. One is impossible without the other. If the mystical experience is a personal working out of the content of the common faith, theology is an expression, for the profit of all, of that which can be experienced by everyone. . . . There is, therefore no Christian mysticism without theology; but above all, there is no theology without mysticism. Mysticism is . . . the perfecting and crown of all theology: as theology *par excellence.*[18]

Bishop Kallistos Ware talks about the danger of separating mysticism from theol-ogy: "Just as mysticism divorced from theology becomes subjective and heretical, so theology when it is not mystical, degenerates into an arid scholasticism, 'academic' in the bad sense of the word."[19]

It is worth stressing again that theology in its spoken or written form is able to create an environment such that every person *can* experience God, but it does not provide any direct means of this experience. The direct experience comes only from personal participation in ecclesial and liturgical life.

The modern Greek Orthodox theologian Christos Yannaras develops a similar thought. The Eastern Christian tradition of theology has a different meaning than that in the West today: to the former, theology is the gift of God, the fruit of interior purity of the Christian's spiritual life, based mostly in living the church's truth empir-ically, that is, through what is experienced by the members of the church body directly. The language, terms, and expressions were introduced to express the eccle-sial experience, but the verbal and written word about God is intrinsically linked to the vision of God, with the immediate vision of the personal God.[20] Theology there-fore is not a theory of the world (that is, a metaphysical system) but is "an expression and formulation of the Church's experience . . . not an intellectual discipline but an experiential participation, a communion."[21]

One should admit, however, that articulating the experiential dimension of theol-ogy is not a prerogative only of the modern Orthodox theologians. The Scottish the-ologian T. Torrance, in his arguments for the objectivity of theological knowledge, talks about the *dialogical* dimension of theology as participation in the relationship with God: "Theological knowledge is not reflection upon our rational experience or even upon faith; it is reflection upon the object of faith in direct *dialogical relation* with that object, and therefore in faith—i.e. in conversation and communion with the living God who communicates Himself to us in acts of revelation and reconciliation and who requires of us an answering relation in receiving, acknowledging, understanding, and in active personal participation in the relationship He establishes between us."[22]

Lossky, Yannaras, and Torrance affirm that the key element of the proper approach to, and understanding of, theology is personal experience. This experience, received as a gift of grace, is active since it assumes participation, communion, and transfiguration, which lead ultimately to a vision of God. Theology implies personal involvement and personal experience in a way the other subjects do not. As theologians, we cannot be detached from—and objective (in an ordinary sense of this word) with respect to—what we study. If we remain outside the subject, we cannot understand it properly; in the words of Diadochos of Photiki: "Nothing is so destitute as a mind philosophizing about God when it is without Him."[23] To theologize *truly*, one must be part of the experience.[24] Given this view, is it possible to teach theology, and if so, what are the means of doing so? Despite its purely experiential and mystical nature, theological teaching, as the exposition of Christian faith, must be expressed through language. What, then, is the foundation for theological teaching as an expression of the church's mystical experience in words? How is this teaching possible at all?

The answer is theological in its essence, since it relies on the mystery of the incarnation of the Word of God (Logos) in the words of Scripture, in nature, and in Christ. God revealed himself through his Word in the world; it is because of this that humans are endowed with language and other faculties in order to witness the presence of the incarnation in the world. The Word of God can be thought, painted, and sung.

If teaching in words is possible in principle, how then can we teach (as we do with different university subjects) the experience of ecclesial life, the experience of knowing God through personal participation? This probably can be done through learning about and teaching the experience of saints, who are, according to Gregory Palamas, the only true theologians and who must be trusted. Not everyone can be a theologian, not everyone can teach theology, and theology cannot be taught to everyone, any subject.[25] The trust in saints assumes two things: asceticism and education. A person who learns theology must be educated, tested, and involved in purification.[26]

Theology involves human language and reason, which is employed in its ultimate limit and requires an extreme vigor in its exercising. But theology does not depend simply on reason. Faith, personal faith, enters in: "Faith is the substance of things hoped for, manifestation of realities unseen" (Heb. 11:1). Faith is not a psychological attitude; it is a state of communion with God that provides "an ontological relationship between man and God."[27] It is worth recalling that, according to Clement of Alexandria, knowledge is based on the first principles, which are not demonstrable; the acceptance of the principles forms faith in them. In this, knowledge depends on something that is not knowledge, and this is faith. In other words, one must believe in order to know.[28] Augustine affirms a similar thought: that belief has to come prior to understanding. If one does not believe, then one will not properly understand.[29]

It follows, then, that the student of theology cannot be detached from what is studied; one needs faith and participation in the *object* studied. This indicates that theology has a distinctive position because of its subject matter (that is, God): to know something of God, one must participate in God. This knowledge cannot be objective (in the sense of modern rationality) because it depends on how one is involved in the subject; one's knowledge is *relational* with regard to what is studied, since the subject of the study is accessible only through one's personal communion with God, that is, in one's experience. As will be explained later, dogmas and verbal theological formulas provide only the limits of human experience of the divine; they never substitute for or exhaust the experience itself.

Since theology, as activity, demands participation in the subject that is to be comprehended, it inevitably presupposes that there is a genuine object of the theological knowledge; participation in something is not possible if it does not exist as object. In other words, the "rationality" of theology, in philosophical parlance, is that theology's subject matter (its object) is God, and theology as participation is possible as long as it has its object in which one can participate. In this view, all nontheological, a priori assumptions have no meaning for theology, for theology is driven by its own object, God (see John 1:18; Gal. 4:9). This is why true theology is open to the infinite self-disclosure of its object.

From the preceding view, it can be argued that theology establishes a special understanding of objectivity, different from that prevalent in modern scientific discourse—namely, that objectivity means detachment from the object. In order for an object to be revealed as it is in itself, one should remove all passions and emotions involved in the inquiry, to suspend one's activity and any subjective influence on the object. In other words, one must shed any a priori assumptions that can influence the vision of the object. This is supposed to be possible because reason can separate itself from attachments in order to be detached from the finite object.

However, theology involves the spiritual intellect, which makes it possible to exercise direct cognition of metaphysical realities and the Divine. Thus no prior assessment of attachments to the object is possible, for the intellect itself is revealed only through its relationship with the Divine, which means that any imagined detachment of the intellect from its object would represent the immediate cessation of its function. Because of the attachment of the spiritual intellect to its object (God), we can achieve an objective knowledge of the object, of God. The difference between the commonly accepted objectivity in science and that in theology can be described as the difference between, on the one hand, detachment from all presuppositions about the object, which is required by scientific objectivity, and, on the other hand, the impossibility of detachment from the object in theology, understood as experience of participation in the Divine. In the words of Thomas Torrance: "It is sheer attachment to the object that detaches us from our preconceptions, while we detach ourselves from our preconceptions in order to be free for the object, and therefore free for true knowledge of it."[30]

Knowledge of God can be said to be objective and true—that is, not accidentally subjective and individual—because it is the engagement with God that disengages one from any attachments that could eventually distort the vision of God.

Theology as Unique

One can see that the Patristic understanding of theology and its treatment of possible knowledge of God removes the "problem" often addressed in modern Western sources as the relationship between truth of revelation (that is, truth in "revelational theology"), and those truths established by reason from observing the natural world and brought to its limit ("natural theology"). The truth of revelation, in its Patristic sense, can be attained gradually through participation in the ecclesial reality of the Christian mysteries; any genuine knowledge can be achieved only if this suprarational knowledge—that is, faith—is established. This implies that the conclusions of reason taken in and of themselves can never constitute ultimate, genuine knowledge; rather, they represent relative truths. The reason can achieve a glimpse of "genuine relative knowledge" only if it conforms itself to the truths that transcend the natural order. This transformation means that the reason participates in the activity of the *spiritual intellect,* which is able to know truth by direct intuition and through participation in the orders that transcend nature.[31]

This explains why the division and tension between revelational theology and natural theology that are so often referenced in modern discussions on science and theology do not constitute a problem from the Patristic perspective. The reason, and natural theology, which employs this faculty, cannot provide any access to true knowledge if it is considered separately from the spiritual intellect, which not only provides a direct intuition of the divine but also justifies the activity of the reason itself. The Orthodox theologian P. Sherrard, analyzing the Patristic understanding of faith and reason, concludes: "The idea that the reason in itself may attain to anything more than a most relative kind of knowledge does not occur [in Patristic thought]; nor does the idea that the reason may operate independently of the truth of revelation and faith, its conclusions being valid in one sphere, where the truths of revelation valid in another."[32]

St. Isaac the Syrian affirms a similar thought on the function of reason. He talks explicitly about the limits of reason, stating that the knowledge that is accessible to reason can be thought of as legitimate and true only if it deals with the *finite* things in the natural world: "Knowledge adheres to the domain of nature, in all its ways. . . . Knowledge is not able to make anything without materials. Knowledge does not venture to step over unto the domain which lies outside nature."[33] This is why accurate designations can be established concerning only earthly things. This is not the case, however, if reason trespasses the boundaries of its legitimate sphere and attempts to discuss things not of this world. In this case, it is "faith [that] makes its course above nature," such that "knowledge is united to faith and . . . lifted up from the service of earthly things towards the place of its creation, acquiring also other things," that is, toward the things of the age to come.[34] These things do not possess a true name and can be apprehended only by simple cognition, which is exalted "above all perceptibility," all signs, forms, colors, and composite denominations.[35] Therefore, when "knowledge elevates itself above earthly things and . . . faith swallows knowledge, gives anew birth to it, wholly spiritual," the fathers use any designations they like concerning this knowledge, for no one knows their real names.[36]

One can then infer from St. Isaac that theology, understood as faith, is unique in its subject matter. Science discusses earthly and visible things, those of the present age and natural world (that is, created reality). Theology, on the other hand, discusses things of the age to come, transcendent reality, the uncreated.

This means that however exhaustively scientific reason inquires into the origins of the universe, it cannot infer from this knowledge to the knowledge of God. The theologians, without claiming that they know the mind of God, at least exercise talking about it. This is exactly what Isaac means when he says that the Fathers used any designations when they talked about God. In this way, the theologian uses human language and concepts that are derived from the sensible world. It is appropriate to compare this thought with Athanasius of Alexandria's caution against using the language with respect to humans and God: "Terms must be taken in one way through their reference to God and understood in another way in their reference to men."[37] While theologizing, however, the theologian employs these concepts with respect to what is beyond the sensible world, beyond language itself, beyond the intelligible world and concepts. It is because of this that when the theologian attempts to talk about God, he cannot produce precise definitions or descriptions of what he means. He exercises an enormous freedom that involves any means for expressing his faith and his personal experience but still remains within certain boundaries.

Church's Definitions as Boundaries of Faith

Despite the previous discussion, one must not be confused here with what is meant by the dogmas when referring to the Councils of the Church, which produced many verbal and written statements described as "definitions." What we today call "dogma" was for the Fathers a "definition" (Gk. *horos*, literally "a limit, boundary, horizon").[38] In this context, the definitions of the church function as a fence, setting a limit around the Christian mysteries and excluding certain false interpretations while—and this is fundamental—not claiming to explain the mysteries themselves. At this point, we come back to our previous observation that acquaintance with the dogmas does not provide knowledge of what is actually stated in the dogmas, that is, the experience of the Christian mysteries. This means that any abstract theology, which is based on philosophical speculations around the dogmas, is not *theologia* in the Patristic sense, for what it is lacking there is precisely the experiential dimension and personal involvement in ecclesial life that fills dogmas, as boundaries of faith, with living truth. Dogmas as constituting the traditional doctrine "can be apprehended and understood only in the living context of faith. . . . Faith alone makes formulas convincing; faith alone makes formulas live."[39] "Theology, and even the 'dogmas' present no more than an 'intellectual contour' of the revealed truth, and a 'noetic' testimony to it. Only in the act of faith is this 'contour' filled with content."[40] This is why J. Zizioulas affirms that "credal definitions carry no relationship with truth in themselves, but only in their being doxological acclamations of the worshiping community."[41]

The dogmas formulated by the church councils, despite being formulated in ordinary language, transcend this language; they also transcend the historical reality of those places where they were set up as the definitions of the historical church communities. It is through the charismatic events at the church councils that dogmas acquire the features of the communion, universal for all church communities. The incorporation of the dogmas into the structure of the communion hypostasizes in dogmas the element of truth: "Dogmas, like ministers, cannot survive as truth outside the communion-event created by the Spirit."[42] This last remark points toward another aspect of the experiential nature of theology: its close bondage to the communion as the only true relationship with the subject matter of theology (God).

One must not, however, diminish the importance of an *epistemic* dimension in theology. Its presence in theology must not mislead us about the true foundation of this dimension: since theology is to go beyond concepts and is to support contemplation, there is no sense in building up or constructing a fixed theology for the sake of the construction, be it even philosophically consistent and an aesthetically attractive enterprise. According to Lossky: "A theology that constitutes itself into a system is always dangerous: it imprisons in the enclosed sphere of thought the reality to which it must *open* thought."[43] Lossky stresses here an interesting and important point—despite the fact that theology cannot avoid rational, systematic thinking, the very form of thinking must be open to novelties of the reality at which this thinking aims, that is, the reality of the Divine. Torrance argues, from a different perspective on the same topic, that theological statements operate with essentially *open concepts,* that theological inquiry must operate with an *open* epistemology, so that it is impossible to set in advance any particular philosophy of knowledge that could constrain a theological discourse, making it just a prison for an attentive soul.[44] It is because of this that any theological inquiry, while being made with application of the reason, must still be deeply rooted in faith and experience of God, for only the inexhaustible "objectivity" of God, God's potential "infinite intelligibility," prevents reason from being constrained by the dogmas of philosophical systems. It is in this sense that "theology is never a self-explanatory discipline. It is constantly appealing to the *vision of faith.*"[45] On the other hand, Christian dogmas, being only the boundaries of faith (not epistemological delimiters), never prevent the analytical soul from expanding its theological inquiry into the depths of faith, readjusting its epistemology to the needs of the religious experience.

Apophaticism of Orthodox Theology

As the definitions of faith, dogmas never exhaust the experience of the religious life, for although revealed, God is never totally and exhaustively revealed. For the living community of the church, the limits set through dogmas are fixed points of truth, which means that members of the ecclesial community cannot change or deviate from these definitions. However, being faithful to these definitions does not restrict church members in their experiential unfolding of the living truth of the church, which is always a mystery; to be a Christian means to follow a *way* of life that leads to truth, not just to follow a theoretical notion of truth. Knowledge of truth is not exhausted in its formulation. To the Eastern Orthodox tradition, this is the *apophaticism* of knowledge of God, the freedom within the horizon of the church's definitions that helps to separate and distinguish truth from its distortion and falsification.

The apophatic dimension of theology thus points again toward its distinct and unique position among other—let us say, scientific—ways of knowledge. While employing discursive reason in its dogmatic formulations, theology also has to rely on symbolism, paradox, and antinomy. It uses poetry and images, music and liturgy, to manifest itself internally in the ecclesial life, which externally is circumscribed by the dogmas. It thus can be seen here that some human faculties are involved in theological understanding that do not assume the discursive reason at all.

It sounds paradoxical, but it is true, that theology admits the inadequacy of the mind and the tongue in expressing the significance of what it studies. St. Basil the Great expressed this thought in one of his letters: "No theological term is adequate to the thought of the speaker, or the want of the questioner, because language is of natural necessity too weak to act in the service of the objects of thought."[46] Theology appeals to other forms of reflection, which are more suitable for capturing what theology attempts to express, namely, the mystery. The mystery should be understood in religious terms, as something that is revealed to us by God, but never exhaustively revealed. As Scripture says: "We see in a mirror in a riddling, enigmatic way" (1 Cor. 13:12). Naive, cataphatic thinking is tempted to make God conceivable, expressible, and visible, to create the idols full of deception. Liturgy and prayer are indispensable tools for recognizing this deception and destroying such conceptual images by bringing us ontologically to the mystery of the Divine in its incomprehensible grandiosity.

This function allows us to reaffirm that theology is unique and distinct from other sciences. Science, dealing with the mysteries of the world, never talks mysteriously; rather, it aims to formulate the concepts and their content in discursive terms, employing reason and ruling out any attempts to make scientific judgments intuitively and inarticulately. It is interesting to observe, however, that in those modern scientific fields where discursive reason has difficulty creating a coherent vision of reality, mysticism is coming through the back door, in numerous speculative and competing interpretations, which are similar to endless attempts to catch the ultimate truth in words and formulas that are not adjusted for expression of this truth.

The Faculty That Makes Theologia Possible and Its Role in Discursive Theologizing

To discuss this topic, we must inevitably enter the field of theological anthropology, for the model of the human being, as it was developed by Patristic writers, contains in itself the answer to what makes *theologia* possible. The Patristic model differs from the modern, widely accepted understanding of the human person as a being endowed with a reasoning brain, consciousness, will, and emotions. The early Fathers considered the human person not only in the light of the dualism between body and discursive reason (*dianoia,* or intellect in its contemporary sense, the mind). They made a subtle distinction between *dianoia* and *nous,* in which the latter stands for the faculty of apprehending truth, which is superior to discursive reason. The notion of *nous* cannot be easily translated into modern English because the understanding of humanity has shifted since the era of the Greek Fathers. Thus the meaning of the term *nous* as it was used in Patristic anthropology must be carefully explained in modern terms, which have no direct reference to the Patristic lexicon. It can be broadly explained in modern language as spiritual insight or as intellect beyond which logic cannot be used; instead, the intellect (reason) experiences silence, which gives way to *nous,* or spiritual intellect.[47]

Dianoia (reason, mind) functions as the discursive, conceptualizing, logical faculty in man. In other words, *dianoia* employs such particular cognitive operations as dissection, analysis, measurement, and the use of mathematics. It works by either induction or deduction. The function of *dianoia* is to collect information about objects that are *outside* itself, be it data derived from sense observations or received through spiritual knowledge or revelation. In all cases, the limits of *dianoia* are outlined by its ability to draw conclusions (by syllogistic deduction) and to formulate concepts (by induction).

Dianoia is similar to object-oriented thinking, which by definition aims to obtain knowledge of an object, posed in thought as an external object, by means of the logical formulas "A is B" or "A is not B." *Dianoia* thus can grasp objects that are given in experience as either sensible or intelligible entities, which can be related to the reason through the syllogism; this constitutes the *rational* mode of knowledge. This is why *dianoia* is the cognitive faculty used in scientific research. Historically, the acquisition of syllogistic structures in the natural sciences led to modern science.[48]

At the same time, it has been clear, since the early Fathers, that *dianoia* can be applied only to things that allow rational thinking, that is, to things of the created world. Maximus the Confessor comments thus: "Created beings are termed intelligible [that is, they can be grasped by the reason (*dianoia*)] because each of them has an origin that can be known rationally [that is, discursively]. But God cannot be termed intelligible, while from our apprehension of intelligible beings we can do no more than believe that He exists."[49]

Maximus agrees with Isaac that rational thinking (that is, *dianoia*) cannot be used in *theologia,* in the immediate vision and experience of God. The glossary of *The*

Philokalia explains this point by qualifying knowledge based on the *dianoia* as the knowledge of a lower order than spiritual knowledge: "It does not imply any direct apprehension or perception of the inner essences or principles of created beings, still less of divine truth itself."[50] The apprehension in the latter sense is made possible only by *nous* and is beyond the scope of reason.

This distinction can help us understand the apophaticism of Patristic theology from the anthropological and psychological points of view. Apophaticism can be understood as the inability of the reason (*dianoia*) to have any direct apprehension of God; at the same time, apophaticism means that any rational discursive definitions of God as truth are inadequate—that is, the rational concept of truth is not possible. The *dianoia* as a passive organ, or faculty, of the whole human cannot participate in things that are inquired into; it cannot, as taken in itself, provide communion with truth.[51]

In contradistinction to *dianoia*, the *nous* works by direct apprehension. Its subject matter is not simply outside itself. It does not reason from premises to conclusions by strict logical steps; rather, it apprehends the truth through a kind of inner vision. *Nous*, according to *The Philokalia*'s definition, is the "highest faculty in man, through which—provided it is purified—he knows God or the inner essences or principles of created things by means of direct apprehension or spiritual perception."[52]

According to St. Maximus: "The intellect [*nous*] is the organ of wisdom, the intelligence that of spiritual knowledge."[53] The Fathers made a clear distinction between knowledge in the ordinary sense, as the knowledge of things, and spiritual knowledge, which by its function transcends the natural realm and aims to apprehend intelligible realities and the realm of the Divine: "It possesses the capacity for a union that transcends its nature and that unites it with what is beyond its natural scope. It is through this union that divine realities are apprehended, not by means of our own natural capacities, but by virtue of the fact that we entirely transcend ourselves and belong entirely to God."[54]

This aspect of transcendence exercised by the *nous* closely resembles what many religious people would simply call *faith*. Faith, for many, is a gift of God's grace, which should not be discussed or positioned in the whole hierarchy of human faculties. One can assume that the *nous* provides conditions for faith to be intentional: one who wants to find God through reason can do it, theoretically speaking, by developing one's *nous*. At the same time, it is clear that the exercise of rational faculties in order to develop the *nous* requires one, in a sense, to deny the rational faculties that one starts with. This is an important observation, for it asserts that if the *nous*, by its constitution and function, is the denial of the priority of the relational, discursive mind, then the *nous* is ultimately the ground of the *dianoia*, for the *nous* manifests itself in the otherness of the *dianoia*. Faith sometimes is juxtaposed with knowledge. In our context, this juxtaposition means one of *nous* with *dianoia*.

The *nous* thus provides a foundation for reason to infer from the created things to the existence of God, that is, to experience the foundation of all things in their otherness (that they are created and they have a creator). This inference constitutes faith in the existence of God (which is more than any logical proof) and is granted to a believer by God himself: "Faith is true knowledge, the principles of which are beyond rational demonstration; for faith makes real for us things beyond intellect and reason (compare Heb 11:1)."[55] Faith, whose organ is *nous,* allows us to transcend general conditions of knowledge imposed by mind and reason with respect to things of this age. This transcendence makes it possible to "see" not only the intelligible realities but also the underlying principles of existence of all things (that is, their uncreated *logoi*) leading to God.

So how is *theologia* possible? The answer so far is that *theologia* as experience of God is possible because humans have the faculty of *nous,* which allows them in principle to have the experience of God and to be in communion with God. It is clear for any careful reader that the logic of our argument is based, in fact, on the acceptance of the Christian Patristic model of the human being, which means in turn that the question of why theology is possible is in itself the theological question, for Christian anthropology is a part of Orthodox theology. In other words, to justify the existence of *nous,* we should appeal to theological anthropology, which calls for another, similar question as to why theological anthropology is possible. To avoid this closed circuit in rational thinking, the only feasible way out is to assert that, theologically speaking, it is impossible to detach the question of the faculties involved in theological knowledge from theological anthropology at all. They go side by side together. For ultimately our attempt to give a discursive description of the human faculties involved in theology, as well as anthropology, demands that both have the same source in the integrity of the human person and the integrity of religious experience. The nature of this experience can be investigated only by abstraction from the experience itself, by the dissection and analysis with which the *dianoia* is so successful.

It is important also to realize that the affirmation that *nous* makes *theologia* possible assumes, in fact, not only that this faculty is present in human composite but also that *nous* is related to the essence of the human person, to that individual, distinct link that a person has with God and which makes one person different from another. This clearly indicates that there is something in *nous* that transcends the natural aspects of the human person (the body and soul). The *nous* refers rather to *hypostatic* properties in people, which transcend what is naturally differentiated. In Patristic thought, body and soul constituted the natural composition, which is held in human hypostasis. St. Maximus compares human composite with Christ. The unity of body and soul in Christ is purely hypostatic (that is, nonnatural), whereas in humans the same unity is not only hypostatic but also natural.[56] It is exactly this unity that, according to St. Maximus, constitutes a person. The hypostasis of humankind (being not only of human nature) is rooted in the Logos of God, that is, it is itself *enhypostasized*. This implies that human nature—that is, the unity of body and soul (which are both co-hypostasized, meaning they both have the same hypostasis)— assumes the personal relationship to God.

Nous as a mode of human existence has a close relationship to human hypostasis; it is understood by some Fathers as the divine part of humans. As a faculty, *nous* is associated with the contemplative part of man and is primarily responsible for man's relationship to God. As mentioned earlier, *nous* is the "organ" that makes faith possible, for *nous* is connected with prayer, hope, and love for God. On the other hand, *nous* is identified by Maximus with the totality or wholeness of man, with the mode of human existence known as what Maximus calls "the inner self" (or the person, in modern parlance).[57] Realizing one's potential toward full existence makes a challenge for *nous;* if humans succeed in this—that is, if they manage to establish ultimate personhood, to make "a monk of the inner self"—their *nous* will fit for *theologia*, for the mystical contemplation of God to the extent that is possible for humans.[58]

What in Theology Can Be Related to Science?

The question now is, what is the meaning of the dialogue, or mediation, between theology (understood Patristically) and science (which represents an opposite to theology) as knowledge of particular things achieved through discursive reasoning and clearly articulated in scientific language? Is it possible to relate the experiential mode of theology, requiring personal participation in the mysteries, with the objective knowledge obtained from scientific research, the knowledge that is universal in terms of languages and their material references, accessible to the majority of an educated population, at least in a popularized form? The negative response to this query would be quite obvious if one did not make a distinction between the ever-living mysticism in the church (the *theologia*), on the one hand, and the verbal and written tradition of transferring its experience through the church's earthly history in *economic theology*.

As above, our ability to talk of God, to read God's Word, and to express our convictions in religious and philosophical language is grounded in the incarnation of the Logos of God. It is the confession of the incarnation that allows us to witness to the transcendent God in his immanent revelation to us in Christ. The reality of our knowledge of God (in an apophatic mode) and the possibility of our personal participation in God's mysteries is granted by Christ, who, by unifying the divine and the human, made it possible for us to be theologians in two ways: (1) to experience God directly, apophatically; and (2) to think, talk, and write about God, to express our knowledge of God cataphatically. Christ, who revealed God in the world through his immanent, *economic* activity, witnessed at the same time God who is transcendent to the world; that is, Christ witnessed for the knowledge of God as God is in himself through *theologia*.

The gift of theology (both *theologia* and *economia*) thus has its origin in the incarnation of the Word and is active in us through the Holy Spirit. By receiving this gift, this revelation of God, we have to adapt our thought and language to it. For this we need wisdom, which will never let us sink in the endless attempts to express verbally the mystery of theology. The wisdom we need comes from faith in the incarnate Word of God, which is Christ: "God has spoken to us finally through His Son" (Heb. 1:2). According to Lossky: "For the theologian the point of departure is Christ, and it is also the point of arrival."[59] Christ is theology. As the unity of divine and human,

Christ transferred upon us a twofold experience of God: God in Himself, who opened his mystery to Christ the Son and about whom we know from the Son, and also through the natural order, of which Christ the Son is a part. Acting in the natural order, God revealed himself by creating the world through his will and the love of the Holy Trinity, in order for his Son to be incarnate and to profess the message about the Father through this order. This is why the roads of the natural sciences, which study the *economic* activities of God in the created world, could constitute a mode of theological experience.

The Greek Fathers of the fourth century made a clear distinction between *theologia* and *economia,* which were based on two different aspects of the church's life. On the one hand was the direct experience of the Trinity, with no references to the activity of God in the world. On the other hand was the philosophically developed teaching on the incarnation, salvation, the church and its mysteries, the second coming of Christ, and so forth. The Fathers called this latter teaching *economia.*[60]

The distinction between *theologia* and *economia* is not absolute, for any discussion of the activity of God in the world (that is, God's economy) assumes that we believe in God as maker of this world, a belief that comes first; this belief, sustaining the empirical life of the church, is in itself mystical theology (*theologia*). G. V. Florovsky expressed this thought in the context of a discussion of St. Athanasius's distinction between the essence of God and God's will. According to Athanasius, the ontology of the created world is rooted in the will of God, so that a radical difference exists between theology of God as God is in himself and theology of the willing activity of God in the world: "θεολογια in the ancient sense of the word, and οικονομια must be clearly and strictly distinguished and delimited, although they could not be separated from each other. God's 'Being' has an absolute ontological priority over God's action and will."[61]

Later in the history of Patristic thought, the distinction between God as he is in himself and God's revealing activity in the world was expressed in a different language, one that made a distinction between the essence of God and his *energies* as the processions of God beyond himself toward creation. This ontological distinction reveals the difference between *theologia* and the realm of God's economy through energies, which is the subject matter of economic theology. Whereas *theologia* deals with the aspect of unity in God, economic theology is interested in "distinctions" of God, or God's processions beyond himself, that is, God's energies. This leads in turn to the distinction between apophatic and cataphatic theology. St. Dionysius the Areopagite saw the contrast between negative and positive theology in the distinction between unknowable essence of God and self-revealing divine energies. The energies occupy a middle place in theology: on the one hand, they belong to theology of the Trinity as it is in itself (that is, they are transcendent); on the other, they enter economic theology, because it is in God's energies that God manifests himself in the creation (that is, God's energies are immanent.)[62]

It is much more nontrivial to demonstrate that economic theology, starting its discourse from the activity of God in the world (that is, in its cataphatic mode), leads (through an apophatic stage) necessarily to a trinitarian theology. If one infers scientifically from the created order to God, one should legitimately ask on what grounds all claims on the nature of the Divine will have any reference to the Holy Trinity, whose essential being transcends its own economy. This points again to the thought that ultimate and true theology must be mystical, for any discursive ascension from our knowledge of God's economy through God's creation of the world and God's incarnation will demand the confession of belief in the Trinity, implying an apophatic thrust.[63]

The distinction between *theologia* and the teachings of economic theology can be seen through the *logos* of human being, or human hypostasis, which assumes the differentiation between the spiritual intellect—as ability to experience God directly (this provides the ability of *theologia* in man)—and that of the reason—based on logic and discursive description of the realities visible and invisible (which are employed by economic theology).

Later in history, the distinction between *theologia* and *economia* disappeared, and the term *theology* was substituted for knowledge both of God and of God's relationship with the world. As follows from the discussion above, the experiential approach to theology (theology as worship or liturgy, as participation in the mysteries of the church, corresponding to the Patristic use of the word *theologia*) is missing from most modern discussions of science and religion. This gap is linked to the fact that theology, as understood in modern Western usage, represents mostly economy, the teaching on the relationship between God and the world. It has acquired different names in modern academic usage, including systematic theology, natural theology, and theology of nature. It is this spectrum of theological discourses that the modern dialogue with science employs. Nobody risks talking seriously about the engagement of science with mystical theology. Thus what are the consequences of forgetting the mystical dimension of theology for the modern dialogue with science? If this happens, theology and science can be leveled and compared. One example of such a comparison can be found in J. Polkinghorne's attempt to draw analogies between the formation of christological concept and modern quantum theory.[64] It is the fact that Christology is linked to the mystical dimension of theology, whereas quantum mechanics deals with the realities of this world, that makes the comparison devoid of any constructive outcome.

Christ-Event as the Foundation of Theology

Here we must rearticulate the role of the Christ-event as the major ontological reference in the church's experience and theology. As discussed earlier, the church had an empirical focus in the beginning of the Christian era and had to commend itself to the systematic exposition of its doctrine in order to defend itself against enemies and heretics. What, then, was that *element* of the church's experience that was indispensable for the church and which kept it alive and *invariant* during its empirical mode?

The phrase "church of Christ" refers to the historical initiation of the church's mysteries in the *event* of the meeting of humanity with God in Jesus Christ (we call this meeting the *Christ-event*). This implies that, despite the fundamentally mystical aspects of church life, there was a point where the mysteries, including the mystery of the church itself, were revealed to man. Thus the church (as the gathering of the faithful in order to *commemorate* this event) is constituted by the initial, and historically real, *communion-event*, the meeting with the incarnate God Jesus Christ in physical space and time. This event is unique in time as well as in space.

A mind outside Christian faith can question on what grounds is it reasonable for the church to consider this single event in history as the foundation of its claim that through this event man received knowledge of truth (Christ as Alpha and Omega), such that by its very constitution it transcends history (that is, time and space). If such a mind invokes a natural, scientific view of the realities of things, it refers to their stability and endurance in space and time,[65] which guarantees that these things can be accessed by different observers, or participants, in different places and at different times. It is because of this that a scientific mind, being restricted in its vision by things in space and time, can hardly understand the grounds of the church's claims that the reference to the Christ-event—as a single happening in the fixed historical past (two thousand years ago) and in a fixed place (Palestine)—constitutes the foundation of the integral Christian experience as a totality seen in different ages and places. On the other hand, if the Christ-event as a historical meeting of man with God could happen repeatedly and predictably at different times and places, then the meaning of all claims of the church as to the divine origin of this communion-event would be undermined by a simple observation—that this event is, in fact, a part of the natural order, and that any claim for its transnatural meaning would be only a matter of a collectively established opinion, based on either mystical piety or superstition.

There is a fundamental difference between the status of the Christ-event, understood as initiating the church's history on earth, and any natural event that could lead to explainable consequences in its own future. A good example is the idea of the big bang in cosmology as an initial event in the remote past of the universe that, according to modern physics, predetermined the necessary (not sufficient) background for the display of all consequent events in the long history of the universe, including its present state. The reality of this initial cosmological event thus is based on a strong belief that there is a correspondence between this initial event and its remote consequences that we observe here and now, based on the laws of dynamics, which drive the evolution of the universe. Can, then, the Christ-event be considered an "initial condition" for the "dynamics" of the Christian Church?

The *outward* impression the Orthodox Church produces is that there is no dynamics at all. The appearance of the church in the world and the church's message and liturgical life are all nearly the same as they were centuries ago. This sharply contrasts with the *inward* contemplation of an intense dynamics in the life of the church, accumulated and expressed in the church's written and unwritten tradition of the vision of God and in its liturgical and worshiping experience.

The internal dynamics in the church's life can be seen only as the realization of the plan of humankind's salvation, which has been initiated through creation of the world and the incarnation of the Logos of God in flesh. But this dynamics is not based on natural laws. This means that the inward dynamics of the church—her prayer and theology—escapes, from a purely scientific mode of inquiry, leaving a curious mind only with mystery.

How is this internal church dynamics, independent of any natural laws, preserved in the ever-changing historical conditions of the social world? On the one hand, we talk about "the tradition," which sustains the life of the Orthodox Church. The tradition acquires here an ontological status (that is, the church exists as tradition, and tradition exists in the church). On the other hand, we would be right to guess that the church's dynamics, initiated by the Christ-event, is sustained through the continuous presence of this event in the life of the church—presence understood not only through the historical memory of an empirical meeting with Jesus Christ but also as a never-ending effort to build the church as body of Christ (in other words, the church understood not only as historical reality but also as eschatological reality). Christ, after the resurrection and ascension, left us with the memory of the meeting with him, conceived later by the church not only historically but also eucharistically and eschatologically, as an act of communion with God in his kingdom.[66] But this communion is ontologically different from what is meant by involvement through natural law and causation. The absence of causal dynamics, which is so essential for things in the empirical world, is replaced here by the activity of the divine agency, the Holy Spirit.

This leads us to the important conclusion that the dynamics of the church's life, being in its outward impression unchanging and uniform in time, is, in its inward ontological grounds, atemporal and eschatological, that is, open to the endless source of its unfolding fulfillment in the body of Christ. The Christ-event is conceivable as constitutive for the church only if it is treated as eschatological reality. This is why it is not considered the foundation of the history of the church in the past but rather is treated as building the church's history in the reverse order, that is, by coming from the future kingdom. When the church commemorates the Christ-event in the eucharist unceasingly, it invokes the name of God in his kingdom; in doing so, the church transcends space and time to experience the presence of Christ (the Christ-event) in the eternity of his kingdom.[67]

It becomes clear now that when we said that the church lived its first centuries empirically, we did not mean that its experience was based on an attempt to reproduce the Christ-event literally as the meeting with Christ in physical space and time. The church employed a perception of the reality of God that did not rely upon its stability or repetition in space and time. The church's stability in physical space and time has been since then her function as the worshiping community, scattered across the world, and the preaching of the apostolic message of God, which could not be expressed and referred to by anything other than the historical Christ-event; in its essence, this message of truth has been coming through the ages from the realm of God.

This means that the earthly church sketches only the visible boundaries of her continuous existence. Her experience and the inward mode of existence unobservable from the perspective of space and time thus form her communion with God in his kingdom. It is known to the members of the eucharistic communities, whereas it is obscured for those who do not *participate* in the church's mysteries and who are inquiring about religious matters only out of vain curiosity.

Our theological inquiry experiences here an antinomial difficulty in its attempt to reconcile the dualism of the Christ-event as historical and eternal, temporal and everlasting, visible and spiritual. There is no stability or spatiotemporal repetitions in our meeting with Christ; this event was historically unique, but, paradoxically, it belongs to eternity as a part of God's plan of salvation for humanity. This problem was tackled by the Greek Fathers, who had to adjust the biblical vision of truth with the Classical Greek tradition's approach to truth. Greek ontology placed the question of truth in a cosmological context, that is, truth was a locus of the Greek cosmos, interpreted as the unity of the intelligible principles of being (*logoi*); the mind, which could comprehend these principles (*nous*); and being itself. It is because of this *cosmic* view of truth that history was problematic for the Greeks. History itself does not bear any reality and truth; it must be explained in terms of its *logos*. All truth is beyond this visible world in the world of ideas, which are eternal in their essence but conceivable by human beings. If one could not find a corresponding *logos* of a historical happening, it was equivalent to explaining it away, just to dismiss history. It is easy to realize that both approaches—that is, either explanation of history in terms of the *logoi* or its dismissal as unreal—are similar in saying that there is no place for truth in the flux of historical events.

The Fathers of the church had to demonstrate that truth, because it is ultimate in its essence, can operate in history without ceasing to exist as ultimate truth, and that this truth is the historical Christ, who is at the same time the Son-Logos of God and the Alpha and Omega of history. The historical flux (despite being seen outwardly as taking place in the empirical world, which is subject to corruption and decay) is thus understood as containing in its every moment truth eternal, which is not subject to change.

What, then, is the truth of theology, which expresses in different ways our experience of God? The truth of theology is Christ himself. What we should understand, then, is the nature of our participation in the Christ-event as participation in a *reality* that, on the one hand, consists of our memory of the historical happening in Palestine two thousand years ago and, on the other hand, manifests the condescension of God to man, which we believe endures throughout the ages and places. Our constant participation in this event forms the communion with God that sustains our existence as Christians. This leads us to the understanding that the truth of theology, its acting ontology, is the proclamation of our existence—that is, that theological ontology is in its essence an existential ontology.

Modern science could easily dismiss any arguments on the importance of the Christ-event, arguing that there is no necessity in this event, for the necessity, if it were present, would be rooted in natural laws. From a sheer scientific point of view, there is no underlying law for the Christ-event; it is seen as a contingent happening in history, representing the outcome of historical and social circumstances rather than anything fundamental and ontological. But the history of events fits with great difficulty into the general scheme of natural law. It is this inevitability of thinking of the Christ-event in both historical and transcendent rubrics that allows us to affirm that in order to understand the Christ-event, one should participate in it, that is, live with Christ and in Christ liturgically.

The stability of the church's experience or, in different words, the ontological references of her *theologia* are thus rooted in two inseparable modes of the church's existence: her tradition and her worship, because it is in the liturgical reality that the church experiences the stable presence of Christ.[68] The liturgy and the communion make the church and her theology because as long as the eucharist exists, the church exists (and vice versa).[69] Christian worship is exactly that element of the visible, empirical practice of the church which is stable in time (worship does not cease at any time) and invariant in space (the church and its worship is everywhere in the world). It is because of this stability that we affirm that liturgy constitutes such a stable pattern in the church's life, which can be treated as the church's ontological reference, that is, the constitutive element of the reality, which the church experiences and treats as theological truth.

Science and Theology "Compared"

When science in its philosophical arrangement is co-related to theology, it is often assumed that both terms of this relation—science and theology—are uniform terms, that is, their subject matter as well as their methodologies, if not similar, at least allow them both to be considered within a conceptual system wider than the two combined. Put differently, some Western trends in science and theology assume that there *is* a subject called science, which is concerned with the natural world (and does not need any justification from nonnatural agencies), and that there *is* a subject called theology, academic theology, whose subject is God and God's relationship with the world and humankind. Then the quest for the relationship between the two subjects is seen as a different, third subject, which by assumption is able not only to grasp knowledge of both science and theology but also to judge their relationship. It is not difficult to imagine, then, that a variety of different outcomes of the relationship between science and theology is possible, because everything becomes a matter of a chosen ad hoc methodology of mediation between science and theology that is "above" both terms and relies on metascientific and metatheological ideas.[70]

This approach to science and theology becomes possible only because the discursive reason, detached by its ambition from its own spiritual foundation (the spiritual intellect), believes that it is able to ascend above both science and theology and to conduct a comparative analysis of the two from within an intellectual frame that is wider than those in science and theology. Such a frame can be chosen from the variety of philosophies. This assumption contains in itself the premise that science and theology are uniform both epistemologically and ontologically—that is, it assumes that the philosophical foundations of science and theology, if not identical, are uniform. The naïveté of these assumptions can be grasped easily if one refers to our previous analysis of theology (as *theologia*) and its obvious dissimilarity with science. The very fact of such a straightforward approach to science and theology points toward the danger that ambitious reason will have to face if, forgetting its own spiritual grounds, it tries to judge with authority those aspects of human experience whose nature transcends reason's capacity. As far back as the fourth century, the Latin Patristic writer Hilary of Poitiers criticized those who applied the logic of their natural reason to things that instead demand "infinite comprehension": "They measured the omnipotent nature of God by the weakness of their own nature, not that they exalted themselves to the heights of infinity in their conjectures about infinite things, but confined infinite things within the boundaries of their own power of comprehension and made themselves the judges of religion."[71]

Such a noncritical reason should probably seek some support from the spiritual intellect. The difficulty that discursive reason experiences in establishing an authoritarian position with respect to science and theology can be characterized as an assumption about a *symmetry* between science and theology. In fact, this symmetry between science and theology can be established only if science receives its treatment and justification from theology. When we criticized the scheme of the relation between science and theology, in which both are treated as uniform terms, we naturally meant economic theology in its academic version—that is, when it is separated from its experiential grounds, from *theologia*. Such a detachment of economic theology from the *theologia* either has sense as an empty abstraction or is just a fallacy, for, as analyzed earlier, it is *theologia* as a direct experience of God in personal or ecclesial modes that is the foundation and sense provider for economic theology. This means that all truth affirmed by economic theology is derived epistemologically from the immediate intuition of God through the mystical experience of the church, that is, from theology in the Patristic sense, in which faith in God must be present all the time to initiate and to sanctify the reasoning.

It is easy to realize then that the *realities* proclaimed by economic theology all have their deep foundation in the life of the transcendent God-Trinity, in God as he is in himself. If economic theology makes serious claims of the presence and activity of God in the world and, then, as follows from our previous discussion, the grounds for this activity are not confined by the limits of created realities—visible (empirical) and invisible (intelligible)—but rather have their origin in the relationship with the God-Trinity, then the last thought can be rephrased to say that the *ontology* of God's manifestations in the world is relational upon God's mystical existence in himself. It is because of this that economic theology is always open-ended with respect to the manifestations of God's willing and providential condescension to the world. All affirmations that economic theology makes about the presence of God in the world can thus be seen as confirmation of the fundamental theological intuition that the world has its own foundation in God, who creates the world, but who is still transcendent to the world. The neglect of this understanding in the dialogue between science and theology, when economic theology is put on a level with science and both are treated by discursive reason with no reference to the spiritual intellect, represents a theological fallacy rather than a philosophical mistake. It follows thus that the dialogue between science and theology is not possible from a nontheological perspective, for thinking about theology (if it is understood Patristically) is itself the activity of theologizing—that is, it is theology.

Spiritual Intellect and Mediation between Theology and Science

We now draw attention back to the role of the human faculties involved in theology and science. It is quite clear that the main faculty involved in scientific research is reason (*dianoia*), understood in Patristic thought as an analytical part of the human soul. Reason exercises rational, or object-oriented, thinking, based on laws of logic. By its constitution, reason is not in a position to grasp either the inner essences (the *logoi*) of things or the Divine. Reason needs the help of the *nous* to advance its ability to comprehend spiritually the *logoi* of created things. To do this, a person requires not so much training in the use of the logical abilities of reason but an advance in spiritual life, which means the development of the faculty of *contemplation* (in the modern context, this term would correspond to the faculty of imagination and conceptual intuition). Contemplation's function is to go beyond the outward appearances of sensible things or intelligible entities to the attentive soul and to "see" behind them the *logoi* of things or ideas.[72]

Some Fathers would call this *natural contemplation*. However, there is not a smooth, logical transition from the appearances of things and their ideas through the reason to the natural contemplation of their *logoi*. Because, as discussed earlier, the latter relies on the help of the divine part of man (that is, ultimately on the help of God), the Fathers stress that the contemplation of the *logoi* in creation belongs to the work of the Holy Spirit in humankind's sanctification and deification.[73] Knowledge of the *logoi* is the divine gift.[74] Thus natural contemplation represents a mode of spiritual knowledge available to man that is not yet *theologia* but that, according to the Fathers, forms the condition for man to receive true knowledge of God through mystical union with God—that is, to receive *theologia*. But any further advance toward the fulfillment of *theologia* (which, in theological anthropological language, means the transfiguration of human nature, its deification, the acquisition of the ecclesial hypostasis) has no direct reference to rational faculties of the human soul (this feature of *theologia* makes it fundamentally different from any kind of *gnosticism*, be it the ancient heresy of the early church or some novel gnostic movements, such as New Age). Thus there clearly is an ultimate frontier in all attempts of the discursive reason to discover God from within the created world.

When all outward impressions of things and ideas given to reason are exhausted, interpreted rationally, and explained logically, reason comes to a clear awareness of its own limited nature, such that it cannot exalt itself beyond its own rationality and logical insufficiency. But before this happens, there is a long road for reason to exercise its curiosity and to attempt to explain things that are not explainable. This reminds us of the apophaticism of *theologia* as an inability to constitute the concept of truth and the insufficiency of reason to reflect upon the mystical experience of the *logoi* or the Divine. The natural contemplation of the *logoi*, which is to expand reason beyond its legitimate domain, requires the nonanalytical transition from the faculty of reasoning to the act of faith in God (employing the *nous* for this purpose), which will persuade the reason to accept its own limit in the search for the Divine, if it exercises the standards of object-oriented thinking. If this happens, reason will have to change its own logic and to transcend itself, thus negating the validity of logic as general conditions of knowledge in favor of "spiritual knowledge," whose "logic" is different and relational upon the object of spiritual knowledge, the source of the *logoi* of creation, the divine Logos. This logic, which is (in contradistinction to discursive logic) deeply imbued with faith, can be exercised only in the Spirit; that is, it must be voluntarily sanctioned by God himself.

It is important now to realize, however, that the logical approach to the transition from discursive thinking to natural contemplation can be demonstrated discursively, because it is an ascension from the created realm to its grounds, which are manifested in the otherness of this realm. This demonstration, which is by its function the exercise of logic in its extreme, leads to the understanding that something lies in the foundation of the things or ideas in the created realm. The detection of this foundation brings us further to a purely logical conclusion—that the things and ideas that are given to the reason through outward impressions, have in their depth a nonworldly ontology, that is, they are relational upon God. The mediation between theology and science thus requires the understanding in immanent, rational terms how to identify this threshold between the created things and ideas, on the one hand, and their ultimate essences, which are not from this world, on the other hand. The problem of the relationship between theology and science is how to give a rational account of knowledge beyond the limits of the experience related to this created world, either sensible or intelligible (this is exactly what can be called in the spirit of Torrance a "theological science"), by using concepts established by rational thinking in this world. The purpose of this is not to claim that rational thinking can apprehend fully knowledge of the uncreated; rather, the purpose—modest in its aims—is to direct the reason toward what is beyond it, toward what is novel and cannot be grasped in terms of the usual. This mediation between the world where science is an efficient mode of description and the uncreated realm of the Divine, being only directional in its nature and not pretending to say too much on what is the Divine, provides—in the words of Torrance—"the medium of transcendental reference" to God.[75]

The mediation between science and theology can thus be understood as the development of transcendental references to God from within the faculty of reason, but in such a way that reason exercises its function at its extreme, transgressing intentionally its own limits and leading the thinking to paradox or antinomy that points toward the otherness of the reason itself, as well as to the otherness of those ontological references that reason tries to establish. In doing this, reason operates with strange concepts that have a dualistic constitution: on the one hand, they are formed by rational thinking rooted in this world; on the other, because they are directed toward God, they are fundamentally open-ended, for no logical restriction exists on the nonworldly side of these concepts. This incomprehensible, open-ended intelligibility of the Divine makes reason unable to think anymore, for the intelligible entities become nonrational or, more precisely, transrational; reason enters the domain of *learned ignorance:* it knows that it knows something, but it cannot express what it knows.[76]

It is intuitively clear that when we refer to the exercise of reason in its extreme, in trespassing the legitimate limits where it can function correctly, we implicitly refer to such a philosophical situation where reason itself must be criticized (a well-known example of such a situation is Kantian transcendental philosophy). What is important for us here is that philosophy must inevitably be used if one wants to direct reason to its limits. Varieties of philosophical systems exist where philosophical theology plays a concluding part. All of these systems exercise reason in order to create a consistent synthesis with a transition from the world to God. The questions that naturally arise in the context of our research are the following: Can the ideas of the God of the philosophers be useful tools in mediation from science to theology? And, what particular philosophical system would be more suitable for the purposes of the synthesis of science and Orthodox Christian theology? To answer these questions, a review of Orthodox theology's attitude to philosophy is in order.

Orthodox Theology and Philosophy

We have already discussed that Christian theology, being enclosed in the boundaries of the church's definitions (Christian dogmas), does not prevent an attentive soul from exploring faith in God through its analytical mode (reason). The only caution that has been clearly articulated since the early church fathers is that reason, in its attempt to ascend to an understanding of the Divine, will have to readjust itself throughout the process not by following a predetermined epistemology of its own but by allowing itself to be involved in open-ended development, which is guided by the infinite intelligibility of God revealed through *nous.* This evolving reason will have to be deeply rooted in faith in order to find adequate ways of absorbing the knowledge that is provided by the experience of God.

Previous sections focused on the difference between reason (*dianoia*) and the spiritual intellect (*nous*). We can approach this difference now from a slightly different angle: the ability of reason to follow a flexible epistemology of the experience of God is exactly rooted in *nous.* What does this mean from a philosophical point of view? If we, together with Torrance, accept that theological statements operate with essentially open concepts, concepts that are not constrained by this-worldly logic and references to space and time, and which are open to change in the face of God's intelligibility, we say that the open-ended epistemology of theological inquiry not only assumes the removal from this epistemology of any references to the space and time of this world but also assumes that object-oriented thinking, which is based on the ordinary logic of propositions such as "A is B" or "A is not B," must be completely abandoned.[77] The way that reason functions with respect to the open experience of an infinite God should acquire the features of the relational logic rooted ontologically in the reality of the Divine.

What philosophical system, then, can demonstrate the shift from the logic associated with object-oriented thinking to that of relational logic, in which the object of inquiry cannot be predicated at all? The following section will show that the demonstration we are seeking is possible and can be developed in the framework of apophatic theology by employing a particular philosophical approach as a starting point. Is it essential that we use a particular line of philosophical arguments to demonstrate the need for a change of logic in theology? Can other philosophical trends to be useful for theology? In order to respond to these questions, we should briefly discuss the ontological aspects of the transition from worldly logic to open, "illogical" epistemology.

When we affirm that theology can be adequately expressed in a conceptual frame only if this frame is not fixed, and is therefore subject to changes and developments, which are driven by its subject matter (the Divine), we also affirm that fundamental ontological differences exist between this world and the realm of the Divine. It is exactly this different ontology of the Divine that demands a development of *open* epistemology, any suitable epistemology that will be a part of the dynamics of approaching the Divine, guided by faith and kept within its boundaries. This poses, however, a serious problem for the development of such a new, open epistemology; most classical philosophical systems are monistic, and correspondingly their epistemology could be applied effectively only within the world. The same problem will arise in any attempt to mediate between theology (dualistic in its nature) and science (monistic by its aims and construction). We have pointed out that attempts have been made to remove this problem: the discursive reason (*dianoia*), if it is detached from its roots in the spiritual intellect (*nous*), is tempted to level theology and science in order to eliminate ontological differences in their systems and then to compare them as uniform terms.

An alternative to this approach would be to develop a consistent system of ontological dualism, which, in the manner of any existing philosophical theologies, could offer the conceptual basis of Christian faith. In the latter case, the mediation between science and theology would become a hierarchical relationship, in which science, being monistic, would be a lower term in the unified philosophical and theological synthesis, which is "dualistic." This was the tendency of the early church fathers, rooted in their affinity to Platonism. Agreeing in general with their line of thought, we still should make clear one point to make our view coherent with what we said before on open epistemology. Even if we accept that the philosophical frame of thought suitable for theology and its mediation with science should be dualistic, it does not imply that epistemology, built upon this system and operating from within our human capacity, should be fixed (that is, conceptually, the system of ontological dualism would be developed once and forever).

The fundamental feature of ontological dualism is that it affirms that the ontology of this world is relational upon the realm of the Divine, which implies that the epistemology that is to grasp this dualism is relational in turn upon a "limitless eternity of God" and demands an "infinite comprehension" of things by which God is known in the world. To say that theology, philosophically, is a dualistic system is equivalent to saying that one needs open epistemology in order to express this dualism—that is, that any philosophical form of expression of the Divine through the capacities of our creaturely reason is relational not upon the fixed categorical boundaries provided outwardly by the relationship between subject and object but on the Divine itself, entering into the human person through *nous*. This means that when we quote "ontological dualism" in a theological context, we simply set the boundaries of our philosophizing about God. This is similar to Christian dogmas understood as boundaries of faith: they never exhaust faith in terms of a personal encounter with God. Similarly, "ontological dualism" is just a delimiter, which states clearly that no monistic philosophy can hope to express, conceptually, divine truth. The dualistic frame provides the freedom of search, the openness of intellectual expressions of faith, which never constitute a closed, accomplished vision of God, for all of these will exercise an attempt to break the monistic ontology rooted in the ontology of the world. This makes clear that the dualism between God and the world is another expression of the apophaticism of Orthodox theology, which implies in turn that all philosophical systems have a similar weight in their utility in theology—that is, there is no particular philosophy that would better fit the purposes of theology than any other. Thus what particular language of philosophy must be employed is not so important, since its role is mostly to express in rational terms the experience of God, not to propose any ontological schemes for God's being.

There is no risk of using philosophy in theology if one follows the rule of apophaticism that concepts never exhaust truth. Lossky highlights this point, referring to the Fathers of the church: "The question of the relations between theology and philosophy has never arisen in the East. The apophatic attitude gave to the Fathers of the Church that freedom and liberty with which they employed philosophical terms without running the risk of being misunderstood or of falling into a `theology of concepts.'"[78] Lossky's conclusion seems similar to the results of our discussion above: "There is no philosophy *more* or *less* Christian."[79]

This observation provides us with a valuable methodological rule on mediation between science and theology, namely, that *any* suitable philosophy can be used as a methodological tool for such mediation. Since there is no fixed subordination between Eastern Orthodox theology and philosophy, one is free to employ any philosophical models and schemes to reveal the relationship between theology and science, as long as such schemes fall under two "dogmatic" requirements: they must be both dualistic and open-ended. This would require following the spirit of theological apophaticism, which simultaneously sets the boundaries of the dialogue between Orthodox theology and science and secures us from any danger of substituting scientifico-philosophical ideas in place of the living God of Orthodox faith.

Orthodox Theology and Science: Epistemological Formula

It should be clear from the previous analysis that, theologically speaking, it is impossible to build an accomplished, fixed epistemology that could serve theology once and forever. This points to a fundamental methodological conclusion that, with reference to the ontological dualism between God and the world, we are actually saying only one thing: that the ontology of this world is relational upon God. The only way to express this philosophically, using the categories of thought from this world, is to say that the experience of this relational ontology transcends the norm of creaturely rationality, involving in itself the process of multilogical, irrational, or open-ended thinking, which those who like clarity and simple logic would call mysticism. Indeed, the open-ended epistemology exactly resembles mysticism from the point of view of a person trained in the rigorous logic of propositions. This merger of the open-endedness of theological discourse with mysticism indicates what we have already denoted as the apophaticism of theology, that is, an inability to express adequately the experience of God by using concepts and logic employed by reason.

It is interesting to note that the very existence of an opposition of dualism *versus* monism, in the mediation between science and theology in human thought, is possible only because of the position of humans as microcosm, that is, as the only beings capable of mediating between the sensible and the intelligible, between the created and God. Humans are the only creatures who are able to think in a twofold way—on the one hand, to think in classical Hellenistic terms bounding oneself to the necessity of the world, and thus denying its own freedom from the world; on the other hand, being spiritually advanced, to long for freedom from this world, looking for its source beyond the world in God. It is this aspect of humankind's mediating position between the world and God (humans as *zoon theoumenon*) that makes mediation between science and theology possible at all. It follows, then, that, without faith in God, reason cannot even see the problem of science and theology. It is only through faith that the problem of how to reconcile monistic science with theological dualism can be tackled in a way that preserves the rigor of scientific method in its search for contingent truth as well as the profession of faith in God as an ultimate ground of this truth. This makes the mediation between science and theology a plausible and justified undertaking.

When we affirm that theology must rely on open epistemology—that is, apophaticism as to the inability to have an accomplished conceptual presentation of the Divine—we inevitably promote the same view in relation to the mediation between theology and science. In other words, the logic that has to be developed in relation to such a mediation should depart from its naive version (such as when science and theology are related to each other in such concepts as friendship, compatibility, complementarity, assimilation, and confrontation). What kind of logic must replace these naive choices? To construct a new epistemological formula of the relationship between science and theology, we here undertake a case study by appealing to a particular passage in Lossky's *Mystical Theology of the Eastern Church*. This passage states precisely and clearly what to expect from theology in its relation to science. Our analysis will allow a provisional justification of the methodology of mediation between theology and science.

Lossky proposes his formula in the context of the discussion of an attempt by Father Pavel Florensky, one of the original Russian theologians of the twentieth century, who was also a scientist, to build a joint scientific and theological venture. In response to Florensky's attempt, Lossky states that any new cosmology and actually "any scientifically defensible synthesis *has no real value* for Christian theology, which *is able to accommodate* itself very easily to any scientific theory of the universe, provided that this does not attempt to go beyond its own boundaries and begins impertinently to deny things which are outside its own field of vision."[80]

Any straightforward, naive interpretation of this quotation could create the wrong impression that there is not and cannot be any mediation or dialogue between Eastern Orthodox theology and science; however, this is only a surface impression. When Lossky says that science "has no real value" for theology, this statement, despite its outwardly negative tone, has a positive meaning for our discussion, because it declares that there is *no conflict* between science and Orthodox theology. This is an inspiring beginning in our search for relationship between science and theology, if one hopes to avoid confrontation and to establish mediation between the two. What Lossky probably means here is that science is not able to engage any conflict with theology or to add anything new to it that could change its dogmas, that is, the boundaries of its experience. Lossky does not spell it out, but he assumes that since the subject of science is rooted in the created world, it is hardly to be believed that science could advance theology as the experience of nonworldly things. Since true theology is the way toward mystical union with God, Lossky argues that any reference to the natural sciences has meaning for theology in the following sense: "The cosmology, or rather cosmologies, of the Fathers, have only been mentioned here in order to single out from them certain theological ideas which have their place in the doctrine of union with God."[81]

This is why, in the second part of the same quotation, Lossky states that Orthodox theology "*is able* to accommodate itself" to any scientific theory. In doing so, he tacitly admits that the relationship between science and theology is possible. However, this relationship follows a special type of logic. It assumes that, despite the fact that any advance in science does not change anything in the primes of theology, theology incorporates any scientific novelty into its conceptual structure with no loss of its truth and meaning as experience of the live God.

One can observe some dialectics in the relationship between science and theology deduced from Lossky's quotation. On the one hand, nothing from positive knowledge of the world can disturb or amend the personal mystical experience of God in this world. God as he is revealed to us through faith is not accessible by science or by any type of comprehension based on the logic and faculties bounded by the created realm, which is not God. On the other hand, scientific knowledge can be properly treated by apophatic theology in a sophisticated manner (for example, the Patristic approach to science) when nature and science receives its interpretation from its purposes and ends—that is, science could acquire some features of theological inquiry.

One can formalize this dialectics in the form of antinomy on science and theology:

Thesis: Science *has no real value* for Christian theology.
Antithesis: Christian theology *is able to accommodate* itself to any scientific theory.

If one considers the thesis and antithesis in this antinomy as symmetrical propositions, it is no wonder that the antinomy will look like a contradictory statement. It has been known, however, since Kant that the genuine meaning of antinomies is not to formulate simple puzzles but, on the contrary, to point out serious epistemological problems dealing with the limits of applicability of the concepts entering the antinomies—in our case, the limits of science in its relationship to theology. This antinomy touches also the difference between science and theology in terms of their different, but at the same time overlapping, ontological references.

Let us first clarify that there is no symmetry between the thesis and antithesis in this antinomy. If one treats the thesis in isolation—that is, as not a part of the antinomy—it is natural to arrive at a principle of complementarity of science and theology: that they operate in different domains. Science conducts its inquiry within its own logic and methods in the realm of contingent nature, searching for a pattern in the created order, whereas theology makes its inquiry in the transcendent ground of this order by using rational thinking and religious experience to contemplate the otherness of this world and acquire the vision of the Divine.[82] The principle of complementarity makes the dialogue between science and theology meaningless, and even impossible.

The disadvantage of this approach is that one loses the chance of an interpretative treatment of science by theology (and vice versa) as well as a reflection upon both science and theology as two modes of human experience that both flourish from the common source, the human's *nous,* the divine part in man.

The antithesis states that Christian theology can easily accommodate itself to any scientific theory. This statement opens a way to treat all theories of the world order as activities that look, in a historical perspective, as existing in their own right; but, if they are understood anthropologically, they originate from the same source in human beings, their spiritual intellect. If we accept that both theology and science manifest two modes of spiritual activity of human beings, it is hardly possible to also accept that these two modes lead to contradictory views on the nature and meaning of humankind and the universe as God's creation. This is why an understanding of the meaning of science would benefit if carefully treated within a broader theological context (one that relies on open epistemology). Only in this case can Lossky's statement, made implicitly in the thesis that any scientific synthesis cannot affect theology, indeed be interpreted in a positive sense—that is, nothing in science (as only a component of a much broader experience) can be in opposition to the wholeness of this experience that is theological by definition.

It does not mean that everything in science has a genuine theological meaning. Theology is dealing, rather, with questions of ultimate reality and the meaning of all that exists in its transcendent ground in God. Science, on the contrary, has many worldly insights and technological implications, which are useful for man's earthly existence but have nothing to say about the meaning of nature and its origin. There are several fundamental issues in science, however, that deal either with the total aspects of the world or with the principles of life and knowing that could challenge theology and thus need to be placed in the focus of the dialogue between science and theology.

One should stress, however, that science in the proposed treatment is not subordinated to theology. Scientific activity takes place in the realm of contingent nature, and its aim is not to produce philosophical models or theological ideas as inferred from knowledge of facts in this realm but to investigate nature. The fact that theories can have theological meaning can be revealed only from beyond science, by a kind of external introspection, when scientific theories become a subject of philosophical or theological contemplation. This is why, instead of subordination of science to theology, we treat the antithesis as a theological judgment about scientific activities, treated as man's endeavor of seeking knowledge of God from within creation.[83]

The positive evaluation of the thesis comes in a paradoxical way from its purely negative assertion that "science has no real value for theology." Indeed, if one excludes interaction between science and theology, this in turn prevents conflict. The further implication of the thesis could be to reverse the formula in order to say that theology has no real value to science. Fortunately this reversion is not possible, for, as is well known, scientific theories have deep roots in metaphysics and implicit theological principles.[84]

The antithesis, in its positive affirmation that theology can "accommodate itself to any scientific theory," affirms, in fact, that there is essentially no difference among different branches of science as related to theology; all of them have the same weight when compared to theology (this is similar to our previous conclusion that there is no particular philosophical system that fits better with Christian faith than the others). All sciences have a common principle (*logos*, the underlying principle of their functioning, structure, object of interest). This principle can be formulated so that all varieties of the scientific discourse have a similar relationship to theology: the latter can accommodate itself to them. Or, in different words, all varieties of the sciences have common metaphysical ground (monism), which makes them all similar with respect to theology (which is nontrivially dualistic in its essence). The existence of this principle makes impossible the reversal of the thesis—that is, making the claim that theology has no real value for science—because the *logos* of science is that it is methodologically and epistemologically rooted in philosophy and theology (scientists can think of the world because the world is endowed with intelligibility, and humans have access to it through *dianoia* and *nous*).

It can now be easily understood that the antinomy, constructed from the quotation from Lossky, is not exactly an antinomy in classical form, such as that of Kant, for example. There is an asymmetry between the thesis and the antithesis that is based on the difference of their ontological references. The thesis can be treated as a statement that the subject domain where science and theology can meet is void. In mathematical symbols, the thesis can be written as $S \cap T = 0$. The antithesis can be written in a symbolic form as the proposition $S \cup T = T$—that is, that the subject domain of theology is wider than that of science; the scientific domain is a subset of the realm of theological inquiry in both the ontological and the epistemological sense. It is easy to observe, then, a formal contradiction between the thesis ($S \cap T = 0$) and the antithesis ($S \cup T = T$). The fallacy originates from a wrong conclusion that the *thesis* implies that science and theology operate in two distinct subject domains that are different not only methodologically but also ontologically. The antithesis demonstrates that this is incorrect, because it explains that the ontological references in both science and theology, being different, do not exclude a relationship between science and theology, for the subject domain of science is not outside that of theology but is just a subset of the latter. This means that the symbolic formula for the thesis must be corrected as follows: $S \cap T = S$; hence it removes a contradiction with the antithesis $S \cup T = T$. Both the thesis and the antithesis lead us to a simple formula that theology incorporates science epistemologically and ontologically: $S \in T$.

The antinomy based on the passage from Lossky is resolved now by recovering a proper meaning of those ontological references that are present implicitly in Lossky's statement. One can now reformulate this antinomy as an "antithetical" proposition:

Thesis: Science *has no real value* for Christian theology in the sense that its subject domain is narrower than that of theology, and science cannot affect theology in its concerns with things that transcend scientific inquiry.

Antithesis: Christian theology *is able to accommodate* itself to any scientific theory, because the ontology of the subject domain of theology is broader than that of science and contains the scientific domain as its subset. Theological epistemology is *open,* that is, it is able to incorporate any particular scheme science uses in its methodology.

A kind of dialectics in the relationship between science and theology, which we develop here, may probably upset "hard-line" scientists, who can argue that the scientific method (because of its incredible efficiency in knowing things and transforming them) has every right to be free from employing the ideas of transnatural causes in order to prove some truth about the world. Theology, in such a view, is always redundant or superfluous because it makes things more complex. The problem, however, as we have said before, is that those aspects of scientific theory that have relevance to the dialogue with theology are based on many tacit philosophical presuppositions (which are often not spelled out clearly in theories themselves). This indicates that the scientific enterprise always exists in a wider social and cultural context, which is dependent on the dominant philosophical and theological views of reality and which penetrates science, influencing the outcomes of its quest.[85]

Any scientific inquiry is carried out under the rubric of rational thinking, which has a limited domain of application (an epistemological horizon) that predetermines its ontology. It is always difficult for science to transcend this horizon and to judge its ontological statements from outside, from an epistemological frame that transcends the world (into the realm of existence not embraced by science), because this "outside" is not identified by science as a comprehensible, objective reality.

The belief in a *single* reality, as the only reality, which is comprehensible by rational inquiry, constitutes the philosophical position of science known as ontological monism. It does not actually matter whether this monism is rooted in empiricism or dogmatic rationalism (in different terms: objective realism [materialism] versus idealism). The crucial feature of monism is its belief in the self-sufficient and self-explanatory nature of the world, which is ontologically necessary and does not assume anything from beyond in order to sustain its order and the cause of its existence.

Science never questions how to free itself from the necessity of that ontology, which forms a basis for any research. It is simply impossible, because science cannot make an ecstatic exit from its own monistic boundaries in order to evaluate itself from a broader epistemological perspective—that is, science is not able to develop an awareness that the world has no *grounds* of its being in this being (the world is not *causa sui*). If this were to happen, science would cease to be just an exploration of the outward world; it would transform into a metascientific (philosophical) enterprise conducting a quest for general principles of the knowledge and foundations of the world. These principles that structure our reason cannot be deduced from science in any chain of empirical causation (the old Kantian assertion).

As soon as philosophical scientists realize that science cannot overcome the monistic ontological necessity in its epistemology and ontology on its own, they will become prepared to start thinking of the breakthrough beyond its boundaries by appealing to open epistemology, aiming to identify the ultimate references of the actual content of scientific knowledge in the otherness of the world.

The gradually growing self-awareness by the scientific mind of its limitedness rooted in a monistic view of the world should lead in the long run to an understanding of the difference between science and theology, for theology's primary aim is to transcend the world and affirm in an apophatic way the things that are not subject to ordinary grasp. Science and theology thus stand as two different philosophical systems: (1) *ontological monism* of the world in science and (2) *ontological dualism* between God the creator and the world in theology. This points out from a different perspective that any straightforward mediation between science and theology is philosophically problematic and brings us back to the problem of the relationship between theology and philosophy. As we have seen in the previous section, this problem constitutes a special issue. Science, as a counterpart in the dialogue with theology, cannot enter this dialogue in a "pure scientific" mode; it will be inevitably interpreted in a wide cultural, linguistic, and social context, in a way that puts the global perception of science into metascientific perspective. Philosophy thus plays the role of a linguistic and conceptual mediator between the rational patterns of science and the open-ended apophaticism of theology. The mediation between science and theology can be attempted, therefore, only from within theology, and, as will be argued later, can be achieved as a mode of theological knowledge or, in broader terms, as a mode of Christian religious experience. Such a mediation can employ any possible philosophy within its capacity to mediate between dualism and monism, as well as by being not an a priori set of logical rules but an open-ended epistemology following the ways of apophaticism.[86]

In this chapter, we formulated an epistemological formula for mediation between science and Orthodox theology based on the assumption that the domain of theology, as a cognitive expression of belief in God, is broader than the domain of science, which explores a subdomain corresponding to the created world. That is why the mediation between science and theology is in fact an inseparable part of the undivided experience of personhood as communion with being and God. The task is to make the experience of mediation between science and theology clearly formulated in categories of thought; the apophaticism of the Orthodox theology grants us the freedom to employ any philosophical ideas and schemes to develop the methodology of mediation.

4

Toward a Theological Methodology of Mediation with Science

Philosophy and Apophaticism

As established in chapter 3, mediation between theology and science requires the use of philosophical language, not as the highest capacity of reason, which transcends both theology and science, but rather as a tool to express both the differences and the similarities between the two. Theology and science, seen in abstract philosophical definitions, constitute two different but related ontological systems. Simply saying that philosophical expression of theological views can be characterized as ontological dualism will not express the meaning of theology in full, for God, being transcendent to the world, still exercises his will in order to overbridge the gulf between himself and the world and to become known to men. The transcendence of God implies God's immanence to the world, although the being of God in himself will always be a hidden and mysterious essence.[1] This means that no simple philosophical formula exists to describe the relationship between God and humankind, between God and the world.

The philosophy thus required to express this mystery must undergo a change in which ordinary logic is replaced by a "logic of a mystery" (called an open epistemology chapter 3). This demand can easily be comprehended if one remembers that any formal theological statements, in whatever language they are expressed, never exhaust the truth about God and our relationship with God, for this truth, as we discussed at length in the previous chapter, is the truth of our personal participation in the Divine—direct knowledge of God achieved not by bypassing discursive reason, but directly, via the spiritual intellect (*nous*), whose operations cannot be expressed in simple logic.

In other words, religious philosophy, or any attempt to reduce theology to philosophy, will fail to realize that the substantial part of theology (understood Patristically)—that is, its experiential part—will be missed. This latter part reveals that any philosophical expression of religious truth has limited value; any affirmation or negation of the realities beyond this world has a mere symbolic meaning, giving no access to the divine realities in themselves. The incompleteness of philosophy

75

in its attempt to talk theologically has its origin in deep mysticism, which underlies true theology. This is a mysticism that originates not in us but in the very Word of God, which we receive as a gift of God's grace. According to St. Dionysius the Areopagite, while speaking of the living God, "we must not then dare to speak, or indeed to form any conception, of the Godhead, except those things that are revealed to us from the Holy Scriptures."[2]

It follows, then, that any straightforward scientific attempt to form a coherent view of the Divine will be deficient because it is devoid of scriptural truth. There are at least two reasons for this: first is its nonexperiential, nonhypostatic nature, which makes doubtful its realistic claims;[3] second is that science makes its statements by using affirmations as a major tool. These affirmations, treated philosophically, can approach the realm of the Divine in terms of the properties imported from the finite physical world. Formally stated, science, polished philosophically, can pretend to offer a set of cataphatic (that is, positive) statements about the attributes of God as they relate to the world in which we live. Theoretically, this set of definitions is open from its "end"; we will never stop our discursive approach to the expression of the Divine using these definitions. A serious question, typical for any so-called natural theology, arises, then, as to whether the chain of intelligible series that ascends from the world to God leads us to knowledge of really existent being or, alternatively, produces only an intellectual ideal of what is sought as the Divine. It is at this point that the deficiency of the cataphatic approach to the Divine reveals itself: all attributes that one wants to predicate of God are constructed with reference to aspects of this world; in other words, they are conditioned by something that is outside God.

The Fathers of the church conveyed a different message, asserting that true knowledge of God cannot be achieved by attempting to make a syllogism, referring God to anything beyond God. St. Maximus the Confessor, for example, formulates the mystery of God as follows: "God is one, unoriginate, incomprehensible, possessing completely the total potentiality of being, altogether excluding notions of when and how, inaccessible to all, and not to be known through natural image by any creature."[4]

God is presented here as the principle of existence, which does not allow one to use any definitions based on worldly ontology, that is, taken from outside God. It is impossible to talk about God in terms of God's origin because there is nothing beyond God that could determine God's origination with respect to anything beyond God. This is why God is atemporal, beyond time. God is not accessible to us as part of a causation from one thing to another in time; in addition, any natural (that is, creaturely) image of God is inadequate.

Maximus articulates here that relational logic cannot be applied to affirm anything about God if one attempts to do so through a series of causations starting in the created world, for the category of *relationship* cannot be invoked in order to predicate on God.[5] Maximus writes: "No origin, intermediary state or consummation can ever be altogether free from the category of *relationship*. God, being infinitely beyond every kind of *relationship*, is by nature neither an origin, nor an intermediary state, nor a consummation, nor any of those things to which it is possible to apply the category of *relationship*."[6]

In a different passage, Maximus clarifies his point by making an interesting link between the employment of the category of relationship and affirmations of the created things as existing in space and time: "Ages, times and places belong to the category of *relationship,* and consequently no object necessarily associated with these things can be other than relative. But God transcends the category of *relationship;* for nothing else whatsoever is necessarily associated with Him."[7]

Relational logic can be applied to all things that are in space and time as well as to our (human) relationship with God. But since God is beyond any relationship, our participation in God does not affect God's being; in other words, our intellection about God does not provide us with any knowledge of God as he is in himself. As we will discuss below, the being of God is relational being, based on the communion of love of the persons of the Trinity. Still, despite being a relational being, God is not involved in any relations with things that follow the creaturely logic.

The paradox we face here is that the logic of references based on the principles of discursive reasoning can point toward God's existence, but it will never succeed in affirming anything about God as he is in himself. We are in relationship with God, but this relationship does not allow us to penetrate God's mystery, if we only use the rational ability (*dianoia*) to predicate about God. This is the basic assertion of the apophaticism of Orthodox theology, its truly mystical nature.

The mind always faces the difficulty of meeting the opposite outcomes of its own judgments about God, such as the recognition that God (that is, the Holy Trinity) is a relational being but the relation asserted here has nothing to do with the relationship of God to creation—that is, to anything that is beyond God—for the latter relationship cannot condition or influence God's essence. At this point the mind stops in front of an intellectual mystery, a kind of antinomy, which demands for its solution that one transcend the ability to think discursively to the spiritual intellect (*nous*), which alone is capable of resolving the paradoxes and having a direct vision of God.

Even God's very existence is not self-evident if one attempts to grasp it by reason. In another passage, Maximus writes about knowledge of God: "God is not accessible to any reason or any understanding, and because of this we do not categorize His existence *as* existence. For all existence is from Him, but He Himself is not existence. For He is beyond existence itself whether expressed or conceived simply or in any particular mode."[8]

This mode of vision of God, called apophaticism above, is quite different from what is meant by abstract "theologies," which are based on deductions from scientific and philosophical theories. Theology is dualistic in terms of not only its ontological references but also its method because of being rooted, on the one hand, in the ecclesial experience and Scripture and, on the other hand, (as the system of knowledge) in the human ability to think philosophically, using categories and logic. It is apophatic not only in its experiential dimension but also in its philosophical setting. The latter does not mean that theology values philosophy only as *negative philosophy,* or, in different words, that philosophy in its function tells us everything about the world and its unity, that is, about everything that is not God. As mentioned repeatedly in previous chapters, philosophy was an indispensable tool for the Fathers of the early church, who had to defend the Christian faith in the Greek world, a world whose mentality and psychological makeup "was incompatible with obscure mysticism and naive sentimentality" ascribed to the Christians.[9] The Greek mind demanded to express the Christian mysteries in its own language, a demand that constituted a great challenge to the Christian thinkers. The Fathers never dismissed philosophy as a divine tool to accommodate faith in a concrete culture, and it is their success in creating a synthesis that history has not known since.

While employing the language of philosophy, Christian theology's apophaticism is always honest in doing so—that is, it clearly states that philosophy has been used as a tool, exercised in its extreme, to express the transcendence of human experience beyond the world, using the language and philosophical rules that are inferred from this world. For the Fathers, who used philosophy to express the relationship between God the creator and the world, it was not an easy task. The Greek philosophical ontology, being monistic, circumscribed the orders of the sensible and intelligible and, being closed in itself, did not provide enough means to express the dualism between the Divine and the world; in other words, the ontology of the world is relational upon and rooted in the internal life of God. The Fathers employed philosophy in theology not to reason about God but rather to explain faith and its demonstration by using philosophical language, providing what, since Clement of Alexandria, has been called gnosis, or demonstrated faith. Since faith implies the ecclesial experience and scriptural tradition, this employment of philosophy was justified. Theology, assimilating the philosophical language but being at the same time faithful to the spirit of the Scriptures, developed an apophatic culture of reasoning that, with no threat to dogmas (treated as the boundaries of Christian faith), allowed one to exercise any faculty to express this faith.

Realization of this apophaticism in philosophical terms creates a difficulty for reason. On the one hand, as V. Lossky writes, apophaticism "is, above all, an attitude of mind which refuses to form concepts about God. Such an attitude utterly excludes all abstract and purely intellectual theology which would adapt the mysteries of the wisdom of God to human ways of thought."[10] On the other hand, the human mind, has to undertake a "journey to the inarticulate," to something that cannot be known from our everyday experience and cannot be expressed in ordinary language. The mystical and discursive are united in apophatic theology understood along these lines.

In philosophical abstraction and in methodology, the apophaticism thus can be understood as two modes. First is the direct mystical experience of God, which transcends the world and can hardly be expressed through the earthly system of references. The second mode is based on knowledge that starts from the world, and then, when the knower through the extreme exercise of the knower's faculties reaches the limit of the world, the knowledge denies itself, pointing toward its nonworldly foundation. This apophatic knowledge of God can bring the person who exercises this knowledge to a direct experience of God at whatever moment. This implies that intellectual, apophatic knowledge of God, be it through the world or through direct cognition, is ultimately grounded in the experience of God.

The same can be said about the affirmative way of ascending to God, despite the fact that this way is always connected with the world.[11] The deduction from the world, which is always a term in all chains of affirmation, to God, who is the creator of the world, still assumes some direct and prior vision of the Divine, as the cause of the world and who is outside the world.

But this means that the apophatic way of knowledge of God includes the cataphatic and that cataphatic knowledge is dependent upon the apophatic. By no means do we want to claim that the cataphatic, positive way of knowledge of God is not important for theology. Rather, the cataphatic way of knowing God from the created world is insufficient if it is taken in itself, that is, if an awareness of its dependence on the apophatic mode in theology, either intellectual or experiential, is lost.[12] In the latter case, the infinite chain of affirmations of the Divine, which is produced by discursive reason, leads to the idol of the abstract god of philosophers, which, in Kantian parlance, functions rather as the demiurge, an architect of the universe, than the almighty God-Creator of the world, who is beyond the world.

If, however, cataphatic reasoning is not detached from its ultimate apophatic foundation—that is, if the affirmations on the nature of God are imbued with faith and refer to the experience of God—it can be a valuable tool in our attempt to mediate between science and theology. This is because scientific knowledge, by its own nature, is cataphatic, as all philosophical generalizations of science are built as affirmations.

The difficulty of making a clear-cut demarcation between the apophatic and the cataphatic ways of theology was experienced by the Fathers; when necessary, they used either negative or positive ways of talking of God and God's revelation, always finding a resort in the personal experience of God when any reasoning and talking could not proceed further, and would use allegories and poetry, music, and art to symbolize this experience.[13]

The following section spends more time on the question of how to employ the interplay between the apophatic and cataphatic approaches to make use of some theological inferences from science. The cataphatic approach will be used to demonstrate that predications of God, made from within some scientific theories, are useful for theology. These predications are based on an a priori theological assumption that any cataphatic inference to the Divine has sense if and only if it is placed in the wider scope of theological apophaticism, which is present explicitly or implicitly with its dualistic ontology and such human faculties that allow one to express this dualism epistemologically.

Scientific Monism and Apophaticism

When theologizing scientists attempt to speculate about God, they never recognize explicitly and honestly that everything which is affirmed by numerous scientific theories is circumscribed philosophically by what can be described as monistic "realism." That is why their ambition to mediate with theology, whose ontology is, strictly speaking, nonmonistic, should be carefully justified. Since the following sections will discuss ontological monism, a brief mention of monism in the context of the cataphatic/apophatic approaches to knowledge of God is needed here.

The monistic ideal of knowledge has been known since Classical Greek philosophy. This view maintained that the world is ontologically self-sustained and, epistemologically, fully explainable from within itself, with no need for appeal to any entity or agency that does not belong to the world, for example, the transcendent God.

One particular realization of the monistic ideal is naturalism, which is defined, for example, as "a species of philosophical monism according to which whatever exists or happens is *natural* in the sense of being susceptible to explanation through methods which, although paradigmatically exemplified in the natural sciences, are continuous from the domain of objects and events. Hence, naturalism is polemically defined as repudiating the view that there exists or could exist any entities or events which lie, in principle, beyond the scope of scientific explanation."[14] Naturalism can be purely methodological, that is, it does not make any ontological claims in general, leaving this issue to philosophy and claiming its own relevance only to what it can justify. Proponents of this kind of naturalism, as it is concerned with religious issues, can be idealists, materialists, atheists, or theists. One strong representative of methodological naturalism in modern cosmology is Stephen Hawking. Hawking states straightforwardly that he is a positivist and that he does not demand that his cosmological theories correspond to reality, for he does not know what reality is.[15] At the same time, when in his famous phrase "What place, then, for a creator?" he attempts to dismiss God as an original cause of the universe from scientific explanations, he exhibits himself as a naturalist of a methodological kind.[16] One can see a logical contradiction in this position, for in denying God, Hawking denies not only the idea of God but also God's ontological reality. In this case, the many critical commentaries by religious thinkers with respect to Hawking's claim make sense.[17] Otherwise—that is, if God in Hawking's thought is just a hypothesis (as he himself states, Hawking does not know what reality is; thus he does not know what the reality of God is)—there would be no serious clash with the living religious tradition, which affirms the God-Creator ontologically.

Those who follow ontological naturalism—that is, materialism (in all its forms: reductive, nonreductive, and so forth)—have no interest in theology. Their major strategy is to defend naturalism with the argument that all levels of complex reality are described by science with no need for nonscientific insight.

What does it mean, then, to predicate about God if one positions oneself in the framework of monism/naturalism? The theistic methodological naturalists could attempt to mediate with theology in scientific terms, paying no attention to the onto-logical differences between theology and science. This, however, makes the method-ological theistic naturalism quite problematic. Does it really mean that one can infer to the Divine by using intelligible series of causation if one constrains oneself to the boundaries of philosophical monism? The Kantian response, based on Kant's cri-tique of the physico-theological argument, would be negative. Using our terminol-ogy, one could state that the chain of cataphatic statements of God will never lead us to the otherness of the whole series of definitions, leaving us only with the idea of the good architect of the universe, not its creator.[18] According to Kant, any attempt to predicate to God from the world leads to the antinomian difficulty of reason, which, if one remains bounded by the monism, cannot be resolved, leaving the idea of God an empty logical form, that is, a form with no content.

As we will see later, Kant's skepticism, with respect to the methodology that derives the notion of God from the world, is ultimately based on the fact that his phi-losophy exhibits some features of monism. This means that one who wants to make theological inferences from the order and harmony of the world must either ignore Kantian objections to this attempt or develop a suitable method to overcome the dif-ficulty pointed out by Kant.

Many writers on science and theology who argue in favor of "theistic insights" in science use the observations of complexity in the universe (including different forms of life on earth) as well as the existence of conscious observers to make an inference either to the "Mind of God" or just to the notion of God (in a vague sense).[19] How do they deal with the possible objection to their claims raised from the perspective of the Kantian criticism? The usual position is to not pay too much attention to the "old-fashioned" Kantian critique of classical theism or to consider it as an erroneous one.

It is amazing, however, to discover that some modern theologizing scientists, who argue for God through a deep intellectual insight into the modern scientific world-view, invoke for their defense an argument similar to what we used above to justify the cataphatic approach to reasoning about God (that is, that cataphatic theology has its foundation in the apophatic mode of theology, in the direct mystical experience of God). An example of this comes from J. Polkinghorne, who offers a kind of contem-porary theistic argument, deeply rooted in evaluation of the scientific experience as a whole. For example, from a claim made upon observation of scientific research—that the world is the carrier of values at all levels (cataphatic proposition)—Polkinghorne makes an inference similar to the classical axiological argument for the existence of one true God, who is sustainer of the value in the universe and who is "worthy of worship."[20] We observe here ascension from the world to God, which is performed in a cataphatic way, when the reality of God is associated with the value present in the universe. In this case, value (hypostasized as a universal attribute of all created things) acquires the status of one of God's names. Affirming this name (which is meaningful only in the context of the apophatic, immediate vision of God), Polkinghorne exercises an extreme vigor, and a truly theistic insight, when he states immediately afterward that the vision of God as a provider of value is "confirmed by our worshipping experience, mediated through public liturgy and private prayer."[21]

What a fascinating apophatic conclusion! Indeed, in order to see God through the value present in the universe, one should have an immediate vision of God through one's personal participation in ecclesial and liturgical life. We observe here that despite logical difficulties with the ascent from nature to its creator, the vision of God can be expressed as an *existential* claim, based on the experience of God, rather than on any advanced abilities of arguing. In this, we observe the interplay between cataphatic knowledge of God (through reasoning) and the apophatic, experiential mode of contemplation of God, which are both present in the context of the modern dialogue between science and theology. It is not surprising to discover that the relationship between *theologia* (apophatic theology) and *economic* theology (cataphatic theology) is reaffirmed in a nonobvious fashion by some authors in the modern dialogue between science and theology; this is an inevitable consequence of any *true* theologizing (including its contemporary form), which is, according to Evagrius Ponticus, true prayer.[22]

We see thus that the argument from the world to God exercised by Polkinghorne overcomes the antinomial difficulties of reason (as they were formulated by Kant), when the latter tries to articulate the transcendent God by replacing de facto the faculty of reason by that of *nous* (in other words, the difficulty of understanding in predicating on God is removed by implying the direct cognition of God by the *nous* through worship and liturgy).

As we have clearly seen before, the inference to God made from the cataphatic set of definitions drawn from the world can be useful for theology if and only if it is accompanied by direct, apophatic experience of God. This latter mode of experience restrains our thinking about the Divine from being absolutized—that is, it forbids us from substituting the concepts that we employed cataphatically in the place of the spiritual realities they are to describe. This means that if we want to demonstrate that the spiritual insights drawn from the scientific theories are really theistic (that they offer the vision of the transcendent God-Creator), we must know how to express discursively that the cataphatic inferences co-relate with their apophatic foundations (this would be to follow the ways of the apophatic/cataphatic dialectics, which we consider below). Alternatively, if the latter is not possible, we should appeal to our direct intuition of the Divine, rooted in faith (this is exactly what was done in the Polkinghorne case analyzed above). In the latter case, there will be a lack of demonstrative power; all words will be helpless, for any proclamations on the presence of the living God originate from the *silence* of thought, or "mystical ignorance," understood by Maximus the Confessor as contemplation of the "division that divides creation from God."[23] This is the contemplation that allows one to grasp the *logos* (principle) of the world, namely, that the world has its ground in its *otherness*.[24]

The above example of Polkinghorne's theistic inference represents exactly what was said by Maximus: to conclude from the world to God, one must transcend the division between them. A kind of transcendence, which we observed in Polkinghorne's case, is done by a simple act of "re-cognition" that God who is affirmed in words is ontologically confirmed through religious experience, but in a complete *ignorance* (that is, ignorance understood in an apophatic theological sense).[25] The monism of the world is broken, but mystically, rather than discursively.

Antithetic Dialectics and Antinomial Monodualism

A more serious question emerges if we want to make demonstration of the presence of the threshold between the world and God more scientific, that is, more philosophical and formal. This would require a different tool, one based, as mentioned before, on the more elaborate dialectics of the apophatic and cataphatic, which will enable us to reinterpret Kantian antinomies in terms of their ontological references. Despite the negative nature of apophatic reasoning, such reasoning tacitly contains a positive core, which is inseparable from the antithetic structure of thought that unites positive and negative propositions about God.

The antithetic dialectics of cataphatic and apophatic propositions about the Divine was developed in a more complete form by St. Maximus the Confessor, who advanced some ideas of his intellectual and spiritual forerunners Dionysius the Areopagite and Evagrius Ponticus. When discussing the apophatic theology of Maximus, L. Thunberg makes a distinction between an ignorance based on the inadequacy of our knowledge of God in comparison with that of other objects of understanding (which was discussed by Dionysius) and an ignorance based on the naked inadequacy of the mind in relation to God as the supreme object of its desire (which was defended by Evagrius).[26]

Dionysius's apophatic attitude is developed in its extreme: the nature of God is inaccessible to humans, and they are not able to arrive at knowledge of God outside the negative way. For Dionysius, negative theology implies an ascending tendency toward higher and higher attributes, which must be understood as a gradual transcendence. When one starts from the ideas of the world, the more one ascends to the convergence of these ideas toward God, the more one loses the ability to use discursive reason, images, and parables to affirm God. Dionysius believed that the high attributes of God cannot be treated simply as nonaffirmation; rather, they are achievable through mystical contemplation and thus represent a "superaffirmation," a real knowledge in a sense of *theologia*. Thus Dionysius establishes a kind of dialectic through a combination of positive expressions about God (based on the use of analogy) and negative predications (because of God's impenetrable nature). This leads to antithetical affirmations, such as unintelligible intellect, superdivine divinity, and so forth, which are not nonsense and are above pure negation. This paradoxical attitude indicates that, in the end, this is a matter not of subject and object in the mode of discursive thinking but of mystical union.[27]

It is interesting, however, that the antithetical arrangement of positive and negative predications about God in Dionysius is highly affirmative. This means that the opposition in thinking about God, who is treated as *being* through his relationship to the world, as well as *nonbeing*, because of his radically different nature in comparison with the world, retains its importance and relevant certainty within the realm of the relationship between God and the world. The Divine, being either affirmed or negated from within the world, thus is revealed only through its immanence to the world. If one tries to lift this dialectics beyond this relationship, everything becomes uncertain, dissolved in the fog of the inarticulate.

The alternative, which is expressed in the theology of Evagrius, regards the mind (identified with man's *rational* faculty) as fallen from an original *contemplative* relationship with God and obscured by the flesh. Consequently, according to Evagrius, the mind has to break away from the sinful dependence of the body in order to return to its perfect communion with God. But this means that this purified knowledge of God (in the naked mind) is different from all other kinds of knowledge. It is the naked mind that contemplates God and the Trinity, and its nakedness implies that nothing is left in the mind but the divine reflection itself. This is opposite to Dionysius, because with Evagrius the divine reality is revealed within the very self of humankind. It is interesting that here we have another form of immanentism, that of divine presence in the mind.[28]

The ethos of apophatic theology was pushed forward by Maximus the Confessor, who followed the thought of neither Dionysius nor Evagrius but learned from both of them.[29] Maximus's position is of particular interest to our analysis, since his profession of ignorance in relation to God is not a formality but a constructive way of revealing that God *is*. According to Maximus, what we can understand from natural contemplation and through manifestations of God's creation is merely the fact *that* God is—not *what* he is, because God is above all that we know. Since the *logoi* of creation can be detected by man, it is believed that God does exist, but no more than that. Contemplation of the *logoi* of creation (which is an advanced stage of religious spiritual development) proclaims the meaning of existence for things themselves and thus provides an indirect knowledge of God. It is, however, essential for Maximus that he is interested not in apophatic expressions as such as the right way to God but rather in the maintenance of a strict transcendence and a gulf between God and the created world. According to Maximus, the method of negation does not bring us to its goal, for nothing can be defined through negation. The negative way is therefore not more effective than the affirmative (cataphatic) way, since the essence of God remains inexpressible. Maximus states that God is above both cataphatic and apophatic definitions. God is not close to anything else that is or that is expressible, nor is God close to anything else that is not or that is not expressible:

> If you theologize in an affirmative or cataphatic manner, starting from positive statements about God, you make the Logos [Word of God] flesh, for you have no other means of knowing God as cause except from what is visible and tangible. If you theologise in a negative or apophatic manner, through the stripping away of positive attributes, you make the Logos spirit or God as He was in His principal state with God: starting from absolutely none of the things that can be known, you come in an admirable way to know Him who transcends unknowing.[30]

Finally one can say that Maximus professes a certain *dialectic* of affirmation and negation. He says that affirmation and negation are opposite to each other and yet go well together. He explains this as follows: "the negations show *what* God is not, while the affirmations tell us what it means to say that the being thus negated *is*. And, on the other hand, the affirmations tell us *that* this being is, or what it might be, while the negations tell us what it means to say that the being thus affirmed *is not*."[31] Two passages from Maximus's *Two Hundred Texts on Theology* illustrate how this dialectics works. In the opening of the first passage (1.4), Maximus invokes a set of negative statements about God (highlighted here in italic type): "God is *not* a being either in the general or in any specific sense of the word, and so He *cannot* be an origin. *Nor* is He a potentiality either in the general or in any specific sense, and so He is *not* an intermediary state. *Nor* is He an actualization in the general or in any specific sense, and so He *cannot* be the consummation of that activity which proceeds from a being in which it is perceived to pre-exist as a potentiality."[32]

According to the logic of Maximus, the negations show what God is not: the existence of God is not the mode of existence on the level of substance typical of the world. Because of this, God is not the origin of the world; God is not a potentiality of the world's existence; and God is neither the actualization nor the consummation.

In the second half of the same passage, Maximus makes affirmations about God that show us what it means that the being, which is negated in the first half of the passage, *is* (affirmations appear here in italic type): "On the contrary, He *is* the author of being and simultaneously an entity transcending being; He *is* the author of potentiality and simultaneously the ground transcending potentiality; and He *is* the active and inexhaustible state of all actualization. In short, He *is* the author of all being, potentiality and actualization, and of every origin, intermediary state and consummation."

According to this part of the passage, God is the creator of the world (being transcendent to the world and existentially distinct and free from the being of the world). God is the creator of the natural states of origin, impasse, and consummation.

In passage 1.10 from the same text, Maximus follows the inverse logic. He starts with affirmations about God, telling us what the being of God *is:* "God *is* the origin, intermediary state and consummation of all created things. . . . He *is* origin as Creator, intermediary state as provident ruler, and consummation as final end. For, as Scripture says, 'All things are from Him and through Him, and have Him as their goal' (Rom. 11:36)."[33]

Then Maximus explains what it means to say that God thus affirmed *is not:* God *is not* the origin, intermediary state and consummation of created things in an immanent sense, but he *is* "as acting upon things *not* as acted upon, which is also the case where everything else we call Him." This implies that God, being the origin of all created things in temporal flux, is transcendent to all things, that is, God's being can be understood as the negation of those things that he brought into existence.

This example demonstrates that any attempt to catch the mystery of the Divine, which is initially given to us in living experience, by discursive thinking and to express this mystery in the form of a proposition such as "A is B" (where A stands in this case for the notion of God), must be declined, for it is inadequate with respect to what we mean by God. In other words, the algorithm of object-oriented thinking, which follows the pattern "A is B," is not applicable in theology, for God cannot be an object for that type of thinking. The natural reaction to such a conclusion would be to say that the negative form of the proposition—"A is not B"—would be more suitable in order to say something about God, which is, however, still an inconceivable mystery. The difficulty with this negative proposition is that it indeed affirms that A is not B, that is, it still predicates on A, but in a negative sense. This means that the very form of the proposition "A is not B" is, in fact, different, but of the same quality as, the form of predication used by object-oriented thinking. But "A = God" is not an object. We observe here a paradoxical situation: the negative proposition "A is not B" also is inadequate for reasoning about God.

Both kinds of propositions that are logically possible, the affirmative "A is B" (cataphatic) and the negative "A is not B" (apophatic), appear to be inadequate with respect to the Divine. We thus can think of the Divine simultaneously in two equivalent ways as being (B and not B), or as not being (neither B nor not B). There is no contradiction, however, in this encounter of opposite propositions about God, for God, not being an object of object-oriented thinking at all, is above affirmation and denial. Dionysius the Areopagite formulated this principle of reasoning about God explicitly in his *Mystical Theology:* "When we make affirmations and negations about the things which are inferior to it [universal cause, Godhead] we affirm and deny nothing about the Cause itself, which, being wholly apart from all things, is above all affirmation, as the supremacy of Him who, being in His simplicity freed from all things and beyond everything, is above all denial."[34]

In a different passage, Dionysius clarifies this view further by saying that affirmation of the universal cause of things (God) does not contradict its denial: "While It [the universal cause] possesses all the positive attributes of the universe . . . yet in a stricter sense It does not possess them, since It transcends them all, wherefore there is no contradiction between affirming and denying that It has them inasmuch as It precedes and surpasses all *deprivation,* being beyond all positive and negative distinctions."[35]

Let us pay attention to the use of the word *deprivation* in this English translation of the passage. Deprivation in this context means "limitation"; God transcends all limitations posed by either affirmative or negative propositions. This is a crucial point, for the reason both kinds of propositions—"A is B" and "A is not B"—are not applicable to predication of God is that both limit God. In other words, object-oriented thinking, by its epistemological structure, limits an object at which it is aimed, as the object of knowledge. This reduces our knowledge of this object to particular aspects that are selected by the form of the propositions "A is B" and "A is not B," that is, to those special modes of A's existence that are limited by B, which enters in both cases into the relationship with A. In this situation, A is known only as long as B is known, which means that A (as it is in itself) appears to us only through its limitation by B.

One can illustrate this conclusion further by using the dialectics of J. G. Fichte.[36] Imagine that we want to create a logic of propositions that is similar to those of "A is B" or "A is not B" but in which both A and B stand for the ultimate being, which we call God. In this case, there are both the hope that we can avoid the limitation of God and the temptation to affirm that the simplest possible cataphatic predication of God (that is, "God is God") is adequate from a theological point of view, since it supposes first of all that God *is* (God exists) and that this existence can be understood as the self-identity and integrity of our notion of God (epistemologically) and the uniqueness and unity of God (ontologically).

Following Fichte's logic, we must admit, however, that this innocent affirmation means a lot and that it immediately involves the limitation of God in thought. Indeed, the proposition "God is God" assumes that there is a relation of God to himself, that is, a relation that affirms God's self-identity, or personhood. The form of this relationship that is conceivable by human reason through the proposition "God is God" introduces differentiations in the wholeness of the immediate experience of the living God. In order to define (but not to contemplate) God, discursive reasoning makes the notion of the indivisible God to be self-transcending, that is, self-differentiating through the relationship of the unity split in itself: "God is God." This self-transcendence of God indicates that there is now something in God that has not been in God before the act of self-transcendence has taken place. The clearest indication of this is the *form* of the proposition "God is God," for the form (as a special type of the link between God and God) transcends the primary intuition of God and, as a result, leads us to the affirmation that there is something in God that is not God in Himself, for the affirmation of God has a special *form*. It is not difficult, then, to understand that the proposition "God is God" manifests, in fact, the limitation of God by that something which is not God. We face an inevitable limitation that our reason imposes on God while it attempts to rationalize about God.

Pushing this thought further, we must accept then that in saying that there is something in God that is not God, we at this very moment attempt an apophatic approach to the definition of God, that is, we try to define God in terms of something that is not God because we want to explain what it means to say that the being affirmed in the proposition "God is God" *is not*. Our explanation, according to Fichte's logic, is simple: the very form of the proposition "God is God" is not God. The affirmation of God through the formula "God is God," which, as we have seen, by its form contains some elements of negation, implies thus the negation of this proposition itself, which means that the proposition "God is God" is not true. This leads us to the negative proposition "God is not God." Since we now have two propositions about God, we are tempted to follow the same logic, as we did before, and to predicate on God in terms of the coincidence of the opposites, to say that the form of a genuine proposition of God is "God is God and is not God." This is not a satisfactory result, for the form of this contradictory proposition follows the same pattern of object-oriented thinking, assuming tacitly that "God" in this proposition is an object and that one can predicate on this object both positively and negatively simultaneously, thus uniting both predications logically in one object of thought. Apophatic theology must now be considered in order to clarify this point.

The logical construct "God is God and is not God" shows that we can say nothing concrete and specific about God, except that the form of any proposition about God will look like a contradiction or, to be more precise, like an antinomy. We referred above to Dionysius, who explained clearly that theology deals not with contradictions but rather with antinomies, for the "object" that is affirmed in the cataphatic proposition (thesis) and negated in the apophatic proposition (antithesis) is, by its theological constitution, beyond the realm where the human logic of affirmations and negations works. In other words, the presence of antinomies (and this is in a complete coherence with the classical Kantian claim made more than a thousand years after Dionysius and Maximus) indicates that human reason not only is limited in arguing about something that is beyond the limits of the created realm but also is not a sufficient instrument in theology, whose subject is mystery, the "inconceivable reality" of God, requiring some alternative abilities to inquire about him.[37]

It is important to observe here that the negative proposition we deduced through our logic was tacitly present in the affirmative proposition with which we started. This indicates that one cannot separate entirely affirmations and negations present in the mode of discursive thinking based on the laws of the logic of differentiation.

In this, both the cataphatic and the apophatic ways of reasoning about God encounter each other in their limited ability to produce nontrivial statements about God. This limitation brings the two methods close to each other, revealing their unity and similar capacity for theological implications. Since both negative and affirmative propositions about God are limited, they meet each other, showing their relatedness to each other and to God. Maximus says that both methods, compared with each other, manifest the antithetical opposition, but in relation to God they show their kinship by effecting an encounter of the extremes.[38] In their opposition, they do not express anything about God, but they mark the *limit* of human knowledge. Because of the nature of propositions, they affirm God in their mutual and integrated limitation.

Two methods of reasoning, cataphatic and apophatic, bring us only to a limited result, namely, to a recognition that God *is*. We are not able to know of *what* God is, because of the limited nature of logical propositions in both positive and negative approaches; they give us only indirect knowledge of God. This indirect knowledge, by its rational construction, has a fundamental feature: in all its attempts, it is unable to overcome discursively the gulf between God as he is in himself and the created. We know that God *is* but we cannot affirm anything about him; such an affirmation, if made, would be limited by the horizon through which we search for the Divine from the perspective of the created world.

The main conclusion that we can draw from our discussion of the apophatic method in this section is that theology is antinomial in both its essence and its form. In its essence, theology is mystery: "We see [God] through a mirror in a riddling, enigmatic way" (1 Cor. 13:12). In its formal structure, as it is given to human reason, theology is constituted by antinomies. According to P. Florensky, "antinomies are constitutive elements of religion, if it is thought of by the reason."[39] Indeed, on the one hand, we have seen that the intuition of the living God cannot be captured adequately by discursive thinking in a form of judgment. On the other hand, we need knowledge of God in order for it to be reflected in the form of judgment, for the latter is the only tool that is given to human reason. The result of our attempt to predicate on God is the contradiction, a statement that unites positive and negative definitions of God, creating an abstract conception of God as unity split in itself. To overcome this abstraction and, at the same time, to keep the reflection of the living God in the form of reason's judgment, we are forced to admit that the only theologically viable option is to speak about God "through a mirror, in a riddling, enigmatic way" by overcoming the unity and division of the opposites in the cataphatic and apophatic approaches, by lifting up our thinking beyond them to an antinomial vision of God, in which reason never reaches God adequately but catches God's image through the *form* of the antinomial knowledge. The antinomial knowledge, by its form, constitutes learned ignorance.[40] The ignorance follows from the fact that the proposition about God that we construct has an antinomial form, that is, it contains both affirmation and negation; in this, the ideal of rational, object-oriented thinking to overcome the opposition is not achievable. It is important, however, to realize that the positive knowledge of God obtained through the same antinomial proposition comes from the very fact that the antinomy has the *form* such that it always contains thesis and antithesis; in other words, the antinomy always contains two statements, which seem to contradict each other.

Acceptance of this simple result—that is, an intentional escape from an attempt to make an accomplished logical synthesis of what is predicated in both positive and negative judgments in the antinomy by means of unification of their content—leads us to a stable factor of any knowledge that aims to transcend the world and to find the roots of the worldly existence in its own otherness. Such a conclusion on the nature of our ascension to knowledge of God through discursive reason forms in its turn a kind of synthesis, which we cannot, however, call *rational,* for antinomial knowledge is not rational since it does not follow the logic of object-oriented thinking. Instead, one can call this knowledge *transrational* (transcending ordinary rationality). The freedom that antithetic dialectics of affirmations and negations in theology acquires is amazingly similar to what was called in chapter 3 open epistemology, that is, epistemology that does not follow the logic of syllogism and is determined by the unfolding dynamics of the reality of the Divine, which creates a proper epistemology in order to grasp this reality. Can our conclusion on the role of learned ignorance, the antinomial nature of thinking in theology, be treated as the "pattern" of open epistemology we are looking for? We believe that the antinomial pattern of open epistemology does not make open epistemology "closed" or fixed, for the antinomial form of the antithetic dialectics tells us only one important thing: that the reality of God, inconceivable in his essence, always enters the relationship with our finite comprehension in the form of mystery, whose logical expression will be a riddle of antinomies in which God appears as affirmed and negated at the same time. The ultimate truth of God's reality, which can be experienced directly through faith and by means of the *nous*, will still be inaccessible to precise grasp by the *dianoia*, leaving only a trace of its presence, with no definite logical location "between" the thesis and the antithesis in the antinomy. Thus the form of antithetic propositions, as a pair of theses and antitheses—that is, the aspect of theological thinking we associate with the adjective *learned* (ignorance)—shapes constructively the operation of open epistemology in theology. In other words, all theological statements are always mysterious and "contradictory," leading human reason to incessant wonder between the poles of conviction and doubt. When reason tires of this wonder, it submits itself deliberately to the silence of faith, as a truly apophatic knowledge of God.

What is the major lesson of the antithetical dialectics in an ontological sense? What is affirmed and negated together in the antinomy? If we say "God," we make only a philosophical statement about being, whose reality cannot be established with certainty by discursive thinking. Still, we are far away from experiencing this God as the living God of Christian faith, for in order to have this experience we have to appeal to the spiritual intellect, the organ of faith. This means that the antinomies, even if they bring us closer to God, by themselves cannot bring us beyond a certain point. What is this point? As stated earlier, the antithetical dialectics makes it clear that our ability to predicate about God is limited. But the limited ability of the reason can be demonstrated not only with respect to the transcendent aspects of reality (God). The parallel result is that we also have limited ability to speculate about the grounds of the unity of the world as it is seen from within the world—for example, about the unity of different realms of the world, its ages, and things, as having their grounds in their own otherness. The antinomial knowledge expresses our experience of this otherness, its fundamentally contradictory nature. In fact, it is through antinomies that reason expresses the inadequacy of its attempt to grasp its own creaturely roots.

The otherness thus is given to our comprehension in the form of dualistic antinomial formulas. Thesis and antithesis express differently the same aspect of the existence of everything in the world, namely, that everything has ground in its own otherness that is in nonbeing. This aspect of knowledge unites thesis and antithesis in a single expression of the fact that the world is creation and has a creator. In this, the form of antinomies in theology—that is, the cataphatic–apophatic dualism of discursive thought—can be overcome by referring to the single ontological reference of this dualism, to the otherness of the world, the ground of its existence in the Divine. The antinomial dualism of our thought is resolved ultimately into monistic dualism, as dualism that is overcome through the unity of opposites in their nonworldly grounds.[41] But epistemological monistic dualism is still based on the ontological differences between the world and the otherness of the world, which is in God. Thus the relational ontology of the world, as contingent on God, can be adequately expressed only through the antithetical dialectics, which, while being dualistic in its form, is inherently monistic in its ontological references to the Divine.

Even this modest achievement of apophatic theology is crucial for us, because, when speaking about mediation between science and theology, we should clarify the meaning of their mutual agreement on the existence of God, that is, what it means that God *is* in theology and in science. As discussed earlier, theology proposes the antithetical dialectics of affirmations and negations of God as a tool for reason to establish the presence of the Divine in the world. Can we use the same or a similar method in the scientific discourse to infer from the created realm to God? If yes, what will be our final result, the ultimate frontier in our knowledge of the Divine, which we cannot overcome further without invoking the mystical mode of contemplation (*theologia*)? That this limit exists evidently follows from Maximus's argument that we are in a position to claim only that we know that God *is*, that there lies the limit of human knowledge. What does this limit mean from an ontological point of view? If God reveals his presence in the world, to what extent can science, treated from a theological perspective, advance its inferences of the Divine? The answer to this question would form a theological methodology of science, in which the different stages of scientific research would be given their theological status.

Theological Apophaticism and Transcendental Philosophy

Having established a general pattern for any reasoning about the Divine—its fundamentally antinomial structure, which is rooted ultimately in the apophaticism of *theologia*—it is reasonable now to ask how the antithetic dialectics can be used in the mediation between theology and science. In particular, what are the implications of the antinomial method in an attempt to make inferences about God from the created world? We return here to one particular problem of natural theology, to Kant's objections to a physico-theological proof of God. As asserted in chapter 3, any natural theology has to face the Kantian criticism. To successfully argue about God from the world, this issue must be addressed carefully, for Kant, by constructing his antinomies of reason, intended to demonstrate that no ontological claims about God were possible along the lines of physico-theological argument. This is exactly the opposite of our aim here, to demonstrate that by starting from the created domain and by using science one can affirm that God *is*.

Our strategy assumes at least two things: (1) positively resolving the antinomial difficulties raised by Kant, by using them as antithetical propositions that affirm God as the ground of the world in its otherness; and (2) showing to what particular ontological references (in the constitution of the relationship between God and the world) the antinomial structures point. The last point is particularly important, for it will be based on the distinction between God's *essence* and God's *will* (or *energeia*). The apophatic theology dealing with the direct comprehension of God forbids us to make any reasonable conclusions about the essence of God, for God is incomprehensible in his essence. As discussed earlier, this incomprehensibility is expressed by reason in the form of antinomies, which cannot be overcome if one approaches the Divine from the created realm. This is exactly the point to be made here: the antinomies, being formulated through the series of affirmations in the created world, attempt to assert God from the side of God's creation. This means that antinomial propositions about God reflect not his essential features but rather God's *willing* activity, the activity of his Word, his *energeia*. The antinomial nature of our reasoning about God from the world, whose ontology is based on the *will* of God, not his essence, point to the otherness of the world rooted in the will of God, to the ground of the willing activity of God, to his existence (that he *is*).

It should be reemphasized that the purpose here is to develop a methodology of mediation between theology and science free from possible Kantian criticism. The objective of this methodology is not to use creation to argue about *what* God is, which is impossible anyway, but, by following the rules of the antithetic dialectics applied to scientific concepts, to demonstrate *that* God is. This corresponds to the idea of Maximus the Confessor that the being (substance) of the created world is the teacher of theology: "Through it we, seeking the source of all things, teach through them that He is. Not endeavoring to know how He is essentially, for there is no indication of this in the things that are; but through it we return, as from a thing caused, to the cause."[42]

Kant's Objections to the Argument from Design

In order to make our analysis more specific, we must analyze briefly the nature of Kant's objections to the inference of God from the world, with a particular emphasis on the ontological difference between a Kantian and a Patristic understanding of God. We consider, as an example, a classical form of an argument from design, which was a subject of Kant's *Critique of Pure Reason*. The theistic argument from design in the universe is still a very popular topic in the science–religion discussions. It is often argued that the cosmological fine-tuning and anthropic principle points toward the divine purpose behind the fruitful and beautiful universe.[43]

The argument from design is especially amplified when the fact of man's existence is considered from the perspective of the vastness of the universe. What is the significance of man, whose typical spatial scale (let's say 100 centimeters) is hardly comparable with the 10^{28} centimeters used to represent the size of the observable universe? Modern cosmology states that, in order for biological life to emerge, the universe must be large and old. This leads to another question: Does the whole universe really have a plan to evolve in its vast space, and, during a long time, sustain life in a nearly infinitesimal island of physical being? In other words, does the physical universe indeed bear the pattern of design at its ontological level? Or, alternatively, is the design that we infer from modern cosmology instead the design of our intellect?

Recall from Kant that the inference from design is a natural tendency of human understanding to find order and harmony in a manifold of objects and events where the order could not exist "naturally" because of the vastness and a priori decoherence of existence. Kant himself described an attempt at this physico-theological proof of the existence of God in the *Critique of Pure Reason* as "the oldest, the clearest, and the most accordant way of common reasoning of mankind. . . . This way suggest ends and purposes, value and meaning, where our observation would not be able to detect them by itself, and extends our knowledge of nature by means of the guiding-concept of a special unity, the principle which is outside nature."[44]

The transition from observations of the universe in its varied content and unlimited extent to the intellectual assumption that the universe is built with some determinate purpose is based on an observation of *contingency* applied to the order of the universe. From observing the order that science uncovers in the universe (such as large-scale structure, cosmic coincidences, fine-tuning, and the anthropic principle), one comes next to the conclusion that this order and beauty do belong to the universe contingently, because it is hardly to be believed that the diverse things in the universe could cooperate themselves in order to fulfill the formation of the order to which we attribute purpose and design. At this point, reason appeals to some wise cause of the order in the whole world.[45]

The notion of contingency of the order in the universe leading to the accomplishing cause of the universe is applied, in fact, only to the *form* of the world, not to its *matter*, or substance.[46] The wise cause, or the concept of the unity of the world, functions as an *architect* (a demiurgic god) who is constructing the world from the given material but who is not the creator of the world, for in order to prove the latter we must prove the contingency of the *substance* of the world. The wise cause cannot be understood on purely empirical grounds. Indeed, in order to make any meaningful statements about it, one should appeal to the cosmological idea, that is, employ the concept of the world as a totality of the series of alterations.

In theory, this concept serves as an ultimate foundation for diversity of phenomena and their contingency. But the concept of the world in this sense does not deviate from the series of appearances, which regresses in accordance with the empirical laws of causality, and therefore, it assumes that the world itself is a member of this series. The main problem, however, is that by ascending through the series of empirical conditions, there is no chance to find any first beginning or any highest member (as a primary or an ultimate cause) in the series as a concluding term of the series.

At this stage, discursive reason makes a jump from the physico-theological argument for the existence of God to the cosmological argument, transferring (illegitimately, in Kant's view) the causation in the *temporal* series to the causation in the purely *intelligible* series, the completeness of which is based on the existence of an absolutely necessary being, which is free from empirical conditions.

On the other hand, according to Kant, the contingency of everything that is determined in the temporal series cannot bring us through the empirical analysis to the existence of an absolutely necessary cause that would not be contingent itself. This is why, despite the inference from design about the existence of the cause of the order in the universe made by an appeal to intelligible series of causations, one can state on purely empirical grounds that *there is no necessary cause* (being).

This paradox constitutes the subject of the fourth antinomy of Kant:

Thesis: There belongs to the world, either as part of it or as its cause, being that is absolutely necessary.

Antithesis: An absolutely necessary being nowhere exists in the world, nor does it exist outside the world as its cause.[47]

Kant uses this antinomy to make a negative conclusion with respect to all claims about the existence of an absolutely necessary being. Any possible theoretical expression of its existence would correspond to the transcendence of the understanding over the domain of the intelligible series of causation beyond any empirical and temporal determination. This would lead to the conclusion of existence of an absolutely necessary cause beyond space and time, that is, according to Kant, in a sphere of pure thought, with no reference to anything ontological.

In Kant's view, the very fact of the appearance of the antinomies indicates that the object of the antinomies (that is, an absolutely necessary being) is an illegitimate construct if one attempts to establish its references in the empirical realm. Kant argues that in order to resolve the antinomial difficulties, reason must be reinstated to its proper limits within the experiential world; it must not transcend beyond the empirical realm, thus preventing the antinomial difficulties as well as refraining from introducing illegitimate ideas, such as an absolutely necessary being.

According to such a treatment of antinomies, the construct of reason—the "absolutely necessary being"—inferred from the contemplation of the purpose and order in the world and appearing as a term in the thesis and antithesis of the antinomies, can only be considered in relation to objects as objects of thought in general, whether phenomena or not. Then the object of antinomies is sought by reason as the unconditioned unity of all possible predicates. This cannot be found in the stuff of empirical perfections but has to pass beyond the conditioned. It thus objectifies the indeterminate goal of its search as an *ideal*.[48]

Despite the fact that an object of an ideal of reason is referred to as the "primordial being" (*ens originarium*), the "highest being" (*ens summum*), and the "being of all beings" (*ens entium*), all these terms do not signify the objective relation of an actual object to other things; rather, they signify the relation of the *idea* to concepts. That is why Kant emphasizes that we have no knowledge as to the existence of such a being.[49] This unconditional completeness through all predicates ascribed to the object of the ideal leads to the concept of God taken in a transcendental sense. Kant asserts that there is no way to prove the existence of this God within speculative reason.[50]

The Kantian approach in general manifests a kind of immanentism that originates from his conviction that the only knowledge that is possible is established within the epistemological horizon constituted by the forms of sensibility and categories of the understanding, which form by definition the references to the phenomenal world. Whatever transcends this horizon cannot be objectified as existent ontologically, for, by definition, whatever is beyond space and time is not *objective* and, hence, real. The constructs or ideas of things, which are outside the horizon—the wise cause of the universe and transcendental God, for example—play only a regulative function in ordering the data; they reflect the integrity of human intelligence rather than the integrity of the cosmos and thus of God. In this sense, according to Kant, the argument from design cannot be a proper theistic argument for the God-Creator, for it manages to demonstrate the contingency of only the form of the world, not its substance.

Kant, in his negative assessment of the transcendental arguments for the existence of God, revealed a methodologically weak aspect of all theistic inferences from the contingent creation, namely, their attempts to find a foundation for the world, its *substance*, in the world itself. Kant demonstrated that this is impossible to do. The ground for the world order is represented to the discursive reason as an ideal, which is constituted as the intelligible reality, that is, the reality of transcendental thought. Kant treated this reality as a subjective one in the sense that it is deprived of an ontology, independent of human thought. Despite the many ingenious findings of his philosophy, the transcendental ideas, as forming principles of unity of knowledge and reality, do not acquire any independent ontological status—for example, in a Platonic sense. This happens because the very question of a transcendent origin of the transcendental ideas—that is, the ontological grounds of the ideas themselves—was foreign to the spirit of Kantian philosophy. This is why we can assert that the ideas in his philosophy are immanent to the world, as being produced by humans, if we think of humanity in a transcendental sense as a collective of subjects endowed with two forms of sensibility and twelve categories of the understanding.[51] This point makes Kant's philosophical system suspiciously monistic, different, for example, from that of Platonism, in which the place for the ideal could be the world of ideas, distinct from the world of empirical things, and also distinct from the mental world, derivative from the physical one. For Kant, however, it was difficult to imagine that the intelligible domain could be hypostasized by a transcendental subject as a distinct ontological realm, which could easily accommodate the ideas of the reason, and of the ideal in particular.

Kant's implicit monism stopped him from finding a truly theistic argument from design, namely, that the foundation of the world (its ground) has an ontology distinct from the ontology of the world itself; that the ideal, being by its constitution only the intelligible image, forms together with the varied empirical world a basic dichotomy in creation (that is, the *difference* between the sensible and the intelligible). This difference, if treated Patristically, points toward the basic constitution of the world as created out of nothing, and ultimately to a common principle of being, that the ground for the empirical and the intelligible is in their nonbeing, in the will of God.

One can state now that the problem for all "classical" forms of the argument from design is connected with an attempt to justify the design of the world without breaking the closed ontology of the world. The breakdown of this closed ontology requires a philosophical change such that the foundation of the world must be sought in its otherness. This implies that the methodological approach to an inference of God from design in the science–theology dialogue must be radically changed in order to make possible the *demonstration* of the existence of the transcendent ground for the world from the world design.

A historical example of such a breakdown of the closed, monistic ontology of the world can be found in the Christian Patristic theologians, who struggled with the monistic Hellenism of the pressuring culture and who by their genius developed a theological synthesis between the Gospel message and the Greek culture, which never existed before.

Patristic Response to Kant: From Monistic Substantialism to Relational Ontology

Ontological "substantialism" as a philosophical platform can be traced back to Hellenistic thought, in which the fundamental issue of any philosophical inquiry was being, which constituted a principle of unity of all things existing separately. The meaning of the word *being* can be connoted with such terms as *substance* and *essence*. Being, according to the Greeks, was a concluding term of the world, but at the same time it was a principle of harmony among existent things, a principle that is characterized by the word *cosmos*. Nothing, according to the Greeks, could escape from the ontological unity of being; even God was in the world. This was the manifestation of the closed nature of the Greek ontology, its fundamentally monistic character.[52]

Observed from this ancient perspective, the meaning of the Kantian critique of the arguments for the existence of God at the end of eighteenth century could be easily interpreted as a demonstration of the inability of human intelligence to break the closed ontology of the world (as it was in the Greeks) and to find the grounds of this ontology beyond the world (that is, in God). This is because Kant was arguing that any reference to an absolutely necessary being as the cause of the world was an unjustified transcendence of the understanding beyond its legitimate realm of sensible experience, toward the world of intelligible forms, with no hope to hypostasize ontologically (that is, not only in thought) that being, which has been stated as God.

Kant's critique does not leave a chance to infer from the world to God, because his philosophy is a monistic transcendental phenomenalism, in which the phenomena are circumscribed by the transcendental experience such that the experience does not provide an access to reality as it is in itself, that is, to genuine ontology. Any attempt of the understanding to find substance behind the experiential data through an intelligible synthesis is, according to Kant, a vain activity, for there is no gateway to reality in itself apart from the way of experiencing the effects of this reality, as it appears to us through a "prism" of transcendental human perception. According to Kant, any claim about an ultimate reality, as inferred from the experience, is an incorrect epistemological conclusion.

In spite of all this, modern scientific advance has on its agenda substance (matter, ultimate fields, particles, and so forth); it rejects the Kantian critique. Science introduces the notion of ultimate reality on the level of *constructs*, conceptual realities that express rationally the aspects of observable empirical things that are not seen but whose existence is inferred in the chain of logical causations. Scientists sincerely believe that there are objective references corresponding to their concepts, which, by their constitution, transcend the experiential domain. This belief in the existence in themselves of entities that stand behind scientific concepts constitutes the difference from the Kantian position, for conceptual realities in science are considered ultimately to have the same ontology as empirical data.[53] We observe here a kind of an extended monism that incorporates intelligible realities. This, however, in contradistinction to Kant, makes the task of separating the worldly aspects of existence from those associated with the *energeia* of God even more difficult, for there is a risk of ontological identification of some aspects of the extended notion of the world—for example, its intelligible pattern and order—with the Divine. The Christian theistic position would be threatened by this kind of "theistic" insight. This results in the fact that the extended but still monistic scientific substantialism is not able to detect that the ontological basis of the world is beyond this world, that is, in its otherness, in the nonbeing of the world, in the God-Creator who *is*. What, then, is the place for the inference from the world to God in modern scientific attempts to bridge science and Christian theology?

In order to justify the inference from the world to God and to make it a useful instrument in the science–religion dialogue, one should adopt a different methodological approach, one that is ultimately based on breaking the monistic trend and its view of the world, and which will fit properly into the methodology of the theological monodualism discussed above. This requires one to shift from monistic substantialism in philosophy to the view of relational ontology of the world, as created by God through his *will* and his Word.

It is in Patristic thought that the idea of Greek substantialism was eventually removed from the search for truth and ontological monism was broken. This shift was associated with two fundamental steps: the first was the employment of the concept of hypostasis as *ousia;* the second was the identification of the hypostasis of a being with *person* (Gk. *prosopon*) in the theology of the God-Trinity.[54]

The introduction of the hypostasis into the heart of being makes this being existence—that is, the ontology of being becomes an existential ontology, based on the relationship of those hypostases that are involved in this being. But this implies the whole transformation of the idea of substance; substance acquires a relational character.[55] The difference between the substantial and the hypostatic properties of God made it possible to break the closed ontology of Greek philosophers in order to develop the theology of the Trinity. The break was explicitly achieved by Athanasius of Alexandria, who made a distinction between the notion of substance and the will in God. He argued that to be, to exist, does not mean to *act*. In the context of the trinitarian discussions of the fourth century, this distinction had a fundamental implication: the ontology of God as Trinity, with its internal life, is based on the *substance* of God, whereas the ontology of the created realm, of the world, is based on the *will* of God. Because the substance of God and God's will are distinct in God, the ontology of the uncreated realm and that of creation are different.[56]

This manifests roughly the ontological dualism between God and the world that has been affirmed earlier; it states in simple words the essence of the philosophical position of theology.[57] There is a difference, according to theology, between the Creator, God as he is, and the created, which is dependent on the will of the Creator but is ontologically distinct from the world of God.[58]

Athanasius expressed his vision of ontological dualism as follows: There are two modes of existence, radically different and totally dissimilar. On the one hand is the being of God, eternal and immutable, "immortal" and "incorruptible." On the other hand is the flux of the cosmos, intrinsically mutable and "mortal," predisposed to change and corruption. With respect to the created world, Athanasius used such adjectives as *impotent, precarious, unstable, mortal,* and *liable to corruption.*[59] J. Zizioulas rephrased Athanasius's assertion by using the term *otherness:* "Between God and the world exists an *otherness,* founded on the fact that the world's being is based on the will, not the substance of God."[60]

In modern, rather technical philosophical terms, one can repeat the same thought: there are two incompatible (incommensurable) modes of existence. Creatures have their own mode of existence: they are outside God. Creatures cannot "coexist" with the eternal God. The "beginning" of temporal existence and existence in time is the manifestation of the "nature" of created things. The world has a beginning because it is *contingent,* and it moves toward an end that has been designed by God. The two modes of existence, the Divine and the creaturely, can be respectively described as *necessary* and *contingent,* or *absolute* and *conditional.*[61]

The fundamental, final step in setting up the ontological priorities in the Christian concept of God and God's relationship to the world was made by the Cappadocian Fathers, who identified the hypostatic properties of God's existence with personhood. The ontological primacy of person over substance shaped the Christian ontology in a way that had never existed before. The trinitarian vision of God has an enormous impact on the understanding of a person, as a theologizing and philosophizing being, in created existence, which is hypostasized by God through an unrepeated and unique existential link of every person with God. The Chalcedonian definition emphasizes the unity of the humanity and divinity in Christ. But this also indicates a fundamental change in the approach to a human person in the Christian context, in comparison with the Hellenistic dualism of body and soul. Christ's humanity, being complete by comprising a spiritual soul and body, does not prevent him from being the incarnate Word—that is, Christ is not a human person in the ordinary understanding of this word. Rather, Christ is a divine person, the Son coeternal with the Father. The human person "is not identifiable with the body, or the soul, or the spirit. It arises from another order of reality."[62] It is the existence of this divine dimension in human beings that makes it possible to infer from nature to God. It is exactly this understanding of human being as the unity of *natural* (body, soul, reason, and so forth) and *personal,* achieved by Patristic theology, that enables us to overcome the Kantian implicit natural monism and to infer from the world to God through the divine dimension in the person. It is the person, through an ability to be in communion with God, via a spiritual intellect (*nous*), which is granted as a gift to know God from within the created world, who establishes the meaning of reality and the criteria for its truth. For without communion with God, the reality, articulated by persons in the created realm as knowledge of events and objects, theologically speaking, has no being at all.

Using the Kantian language, knowledge is possible only because of man's *natural* ability to sense, to think, and to contemplate. The difference between the Patristic vision of knowledge and Kant's is, however, enormous. The knowledge achieved by the person is in its content a hypostasized form of ontological reality, articulated by the person through the person's link with God; it is not a subjective impression and mental construction, because this knowledge is not dependent on only the natural in man. According to Kant, however, knowledge of the appearances of things does not guarantee that these appearances bear any ontology, because for Kant man is capable of affirming only *natural* things, given within the horizon of man's faculties, based on the body and the soul. To affirm the genuine underlying ontology, human being has to transcend its naturalness; this is exactly what is achieved through the experience of personhood. For Kant, it was impossible not only to affirm God (because one would transcend beyond nature in doing so), but also to accept an independent ontological existence of conceptual realities (that is, constructs in science), which, being a part of nature, require one to have a soul in order to access them, a soul that together with the body forms a composite hypostasis of the human person.

The difference between the Kantian view of ideas and their relation to the empirical realities and the theology based on Patristic ideas refers ultimately to the ontological differences in understanding the whole creation. Patristic theology confesses a twofold ontological dualism: between God and the world and, in the created domain, between the sensible and the intelligible.[63] The concept of this dualism is linked by the Fathers to the Christian idea of creation of being out of nothing. According to T. Torrance, this idea "represented a far-reaching epistemological revolution, for it meant that the whole universe of invisible and visible or celestial and terrestrial realities was regarded, while creaturely and not divine, as nevertheless permeated with a unitary rational order of a contingent kind."[64] Both the empirical and the intelligible—for example, the ideas—do belong to the created order, but both, despite being united in their otherness with respect to the Logos of God, who ordained the world by intelligibility and rationality, are ontologically different.

This means that the ideas and constructs in science, which are the subjects of human reflection, do possess an independent ontological reality that, however, differs in comparison with the ontology of sensible things.[65] It is only a person that can mediate between these two realms in creation because it is only through personhood that one can hypostasize the sensible domain and intelligible domain in creation, as distinct ontological realms.[66]

Kant disagreed with this, saying that the intelligible forms are not objective, because they are beyond space and time; they have no ontological significance. Because his ontology is based on sensible, spatiotemporal experience, it is clear why, for Kant, the physico-theological argument could not have any profound theological meaning: the order and harmony of the universe, its wise cause or architect, all are treated as merely mental constructs, as ideas with no ontological references independent of the human mind. Thus they do not provide a base for a theistic inference for the God-Creator, based on the observation of the basic dichotomy in the created domain, the dualism between sensible and intelligible.

In contrast, for the Patristic mind the design-like argument (as an inference from the world to God) can have an ontological significance, not so much in the sensible domain but, rather, as an intelligible pattern of the empirical world, which is objectively present in the domain of intelligible forms and which has an independent ontological mode of existence. The fundamental result that follows from the latter is that this argument cannot provide any evidence for God as he is in himself (this is similar to the Kantian claim), because God as substance (*ousia*) is separated from the creation. However, the argument can be used for evidence of the *willing* activity of God in the creation—that is, to point to the will of God, who created the world and made it intelligible by his Word—by identifying the fundamental ontological *difference* in the created realm between the sensible and the intelligible.[67] This difference, being a constitutive element of *creatio ex nihilo,* provides the contemplative mind, the *nous,* with the vision that both the empirical order and the intelligible order have a common root in their otherness, in the fact that they both are created; thus it can establish the knowledge of the underlying and forming principle of creation, its *logos.*

If we return to the initial point of our discussion in this section—a possible Patristic response to the Kantian denial of the theistic inference to God the creator from the structures of the visible world—we should admit that from a Patristic view of the creation as constituted by the dichotomy between empirical and intelligible (Christian Platonism, not Classical Platonism), all difficulties of the reason, expressed in term of Kant's antinomies, receive new expression.

Let us analyze again the fourth antinomy of Kant quoted earlier. It is stated in the thesis that there *is* an absolutely necessary cause of the world, which is in the world. The Patristic view of the created realm would suggest reading the thesis through Platonic eyes. Indeed, the inference from the order and harmony of the empirical world leads the reason to claim that there is a principle of the integrity of the visible order that is treated as the cause of this order; this principle, being deduced not by the syllogism from the structure of the world but, rather, through the inference from the variety of the visible to the intelligibility of its order, constitutes itself as an intelligible entity, as an idea of the cause of the universe which, by its constitution, belongs to the intelligible realm in the created. This is why the proposition made in the thesis can be treated by a Christian Platonic philosopher as the inference from the empirical world to the intelligible world (which exists ontologically, not only mentally, in contradistinction to Kant), that is, as an expression of the dichotomy between the empirical and the intelligible in creation.

When Kant argues for the antithesis, he tries to make a connection between an absolutely necessary cause, assuming that it exists either in the (empirical) world or outside the (empirical) world, with a temporal series of causation in the world: he argues, for example, that "this cause, as the highest member in the series of the causes of changes in the world, must begin the existence of the latter and their series."[68] It is exactly at this point that we disagree with Kant, for, from a Platonic point of view, the temporal series of causation in the empirical world cannot be caused or uncaused ontologically by an absolutely necessary cause, which is the idea of reason, existing in itself (that is, independent of any empirical causations) in the intelligible world. The link between the two is established by a human person, who, according to its hypostasis, embraces both the empirical and the intelligible worlds and is able to catch the interplay between the temporal series and the idea of its ultimate term. A person, then, can hypostasize both separately—empirical series as well as an absolutely necessary cause—treating them as two ontologically distinct entities. In this, the antithesis, in analogy with the thesis, affirms the interplay between the two worlds, which is successfully identified by reason as a part of the constitution of the whole created being.

The antinomial nature of the proposition about an absolutely necessary cause points, as established before, to two things: (1) no positive (cataphatic) definition of this cause is possible (our ignorance about this cause is expressed exactly by the antinomial difficulty); and (2) the very form of the antinomy provides some positive knowledge about an absolutely necessary cause of the world, namely, that it always appears in reflection together with the empirical series of the world in the form of antinomy. This points out that the Kantian antinomies can be treated as antithetical structures of discursive reason, leading, as understood earlier, to the affirmation of its ground in the otherness of both terms of the antinomies, that is, the empirical world as well as the intelligible world (which is represented in the fourth antinomy as an absolutely necessary being). In this, the antinomies, understood theologically, point toward the ground of the world in its *differentiated* constitution (the empirical and intelligible), to the principle of creation of the world by God out of nothing, to the *logos* of creation.

The *logoi* of Creation and the World

This section will explain that the Kantian antinomies, if seen through Christian-Platonic eyes and treated with reference to the dichotomy in the creation, can be used as a tool for affirming the presence of the *logoi* of creation.

The dualism between God and the world articulates the distinction between God's essence, which is not accessible to man, and God's creative activity in the world, manifested through God's *energies* and described through his words, the *logoi*. According to V. Lossky, the doctrine of energies expresses itself as an antinomy: "The energies express by their procession an ineffable distinction—they are not God in His essence—and yet, at the same time, being inseparable from His essence, they bear witness to the unity and the simplicity of the being of God."[69] The Word of God was hypostasized in the world through the effected events that we call nature.

It is the ontology of God's activity in the world (which is distinct from the existence of God in his essence) that is rooted in the *energeia* of God, or the *logoi*, which, being themselves not from this world, form and sustain the existence of all things visible and invisible in the world. The distinction between the essence of God and God's energies leads to a fundamental antinomy in human knowledge about God, which is expressed in the words of St. Gregory Palamas, quoted by V. Lossky: "We attain to participation in the divine nature, and yet, at the same time it remains totally inaccessible. We need to affirm both at the same time and preserve the antinomy as a criterion of right devotion."[70] The antinomial form of our discursive arguments about God becomes inevitable in one's attempt to predicate on God from within the created world.

Some similarity exists between the concept of the *logoi* of created beings in the theology of Maximus the Confessor, which we have referred to many times in this text (see, for example, chapter 2), and the concept of the energies that was introduced in Patristic theology by Gregory of Nyssa and Dionysius the Areopagite and developed later by Gregory Palamas. In his *Mystical Theology of the Eastern Church,* Lossky interpreted the *logoi* in Maximus's theology as uncreated energies in the sense of Gregory Palamas. Despite an ongoing discussion about a possible lack of sufficient evidence for this interpretation as well as some differences between the two concepts in terms of their function in theology, we employ their similarity here for the purposes of uniformity in considering the concept of the *logoi*, which plays an important role in our search for mediation between science and theology.[71] In other words, while discussing the *logoi* of created things, we will assume some analogies between them and the divine energies. To elucidate these analogies, we now must discuss further the nature of the *logoi* of natural being.

The *logoi* of natural created beings, which are the forming principles and ideas of the sensible and intelligible worlds, are our primary interest here. On the one hand, we apprehend these *logoi* as existing through the links with their common source, the divine Logos; on the other hand, the same *logoi* can be considered with respect to the world, which is constituted by them. This latter inquiry into the nature of the *logoi* is exercised through "natural contemplation" (philosophically speaking) of the created being and thus represents a subject of theological ontology.[72]

The whole created world is seen, then, as manifesting the different intensities (condensations) of the incarnation of the Logos, which is mysteriously hidden in God's *logoi* under the surface of the created being.[73] The task of ontology is to contemplate these *logoi*, that is, to establish the fact of their existence with respect to sensible and intelligible things and then through generalization to establish their unity with respect to the common source of their existence, the divine Logos.

The important point, which was raised by Maximus, is that the *logoi* have a complex relationship to the Divine (the Logos of God) and to the concrete created world in the multitude of its manifestations. On the one hand, according to Maximus, the *logoi* are preexistent in God. On the other, God called them to realization in concrete creation to show the continual presence of God and the Logos in Creation. One can assert, then, in an antinomial fashion, that the *logoi* are both *transcendent* to and *immanent* with the created world. As immanent, they manifest the divine intentions and principles of every single nature, that is, of every object, law, and intelligible image. They actually manifest the *existential purpose* of everything: "As realized in the existence of things, they materialize in the created order."[74] One can say that the *logoi* are realized in the existence of things, but they are not themselves created or part of the created order; in other words, their "material" manifestations through sensible things and their intelligible images do not condition them from within the creation, for they are in themselves beyond the created, and the ground of their immanent manifestations is in the transcendent side of their rootedness in the divine Logos.

One observes here, however, a kind of dialectics that argues that the *logoi*, by having their source in the Logos of God, do not dissolve in this Logos—that is, their unity, being in Logos, does not eliminate their individuality. In other words, it is God-Logos who preserves the *logoi* in their unity; at the same time, the *logoi* are fixed in the Logos as they are, that is, they are in the unity, which is split in itself: "The *logoi* are thus not identical with the essence of God, nor with the empirical forms of existence of the things of the created world."[75]

A geometrical analogy—that of the radii and the center of a circle—has been used since Neoplatonism to describe the relationship between the Logos, who is the center of a circle, and the *logoi*, which represent the radii of the circle, originating from the center and terminating on the boundary, which imitates the created realm. This analogy can help illustrate the twofold nature of the *logoi* as transcendent and immanent: the *logoi* as the radii of the circle have their origination in the center of the circle, which is paralleled with the Logos of God. In this, they are transcendent to the world. On the other hand, all radii in the circle terminate on the circumference—that is, in the things created—thus the *logoi* face the world in their immanent mode, turned out from the Logos to the world. Every radius has two points: the beginning and the end. In their "beginnings" (in the divine Logos), the *logoi* are transcendent; in their "ends" (their manifestations in the world), they are immanent. Any *logos* itself represents the unity of the transcendent and immanent with respect to the world, but in no way does it belong to the world. The world is held by the *logoi*; thus one can argue about the presence of the *logoi* in the world, but not in an ontological sense, for the *logoi*, being uncreated, do not share the ontology of the created things, visible and invisible. Still, the ontology of the created things is relational upon the uncreated *logoi*.

To elucidate the asymmetry in the relationship between God and the world (described previously as monodualism)—which we affirm through the twofold nature of the *logoi*, that is, that human knowledge of God can be advanced only through contemplation of the uncreated energies of God, not God's essence—we appeal to a different "geometrical analogy," which arrives from the Greek term *diastema* (Gk. διαστημα). In Classical Greek geometry, this term meant the distance between two points; in music, the interval between two notes. In theology, the term was used by St. Gregory of Nyssa to characterize the created world as extended in space and in time. Gregory used this term in a negative sense to predicate about God by affirming that there is no *diastema* (in the spatiotemporal sense) in the being of

God. It is more important for us here to point out a different use of the term *diastema*, which Gregory applied to describe the theological distinction between God and the world. This distinction contains in itself a kind of a dialectics that is present in the relationship between God and the world, a dialectics that is asymmetrical: on the one hand, there is the *diastema* between God and the world, which is unbridgeable from within the world; on the other hand, God knows the world, which God created, through the *logoi*, which the Logos uses to cognize the world. The *diastema* in this case can be represented by an asymmetrical, one-way extension in relationship between God and the world. Yes, there is a basic *diastema* if one attempts to cross the gulf between the word and God from within the world; however, there is no extension, no *diastema*, in the divine condescension to the world. It is worth quoting P. M. Gregorios, who describes the usage of the term *diastema* by Gregory of Nyssa as apophatico-cataphatic antinomy:

Apophatic:
"There is *no* way, conceptually or ontologically, to pass from the *ousia* of the creation to the *ousia* of the creator."
Cataphatic:
"In the other direction, that is, from the creator to the creation, there is no *diastema*, since the whole of creation from the beginning to an end and from boundary to boundary is permanently co-present with the creator."[76]

This passage elucidates our understanding of the transcendence and immanence in the *logoi* of created things. Indeed, the contemplation of the immanent aspects of the *logoi*, which is considered by the Fathers a phase of one's spiritual development, means thus the "knowledge" of the Logos of God in his energies, not in his essence. The transcendent aspects of the *logoi*, which constitute the ground for the immanent mode contemplated by humans, are rooted in the otherness of God's willing activity in the world. This otherness is exactly what is inaccessible to any creature. The participation of man in the energies of God, that is, the contemplation of the immanent modes of the *logoi*), which was defined by Gregory as the principle of existence of all creation, does provide the knowledge that there is a transcendent ground for existence of the *logoi*, but *what* this ground is remains the divine mystery.

From a formal point of view, the antinomy just quoted manifests the pattern of the theological thinking described above as antinomial monodualism. Dualism between God and the world is affirmed in the apophatic part of the passage, and monism (as panentheism) is affirmed in the cataphatic part of the same passage.

The geometrical analogy of the Logos and the *logoi* as the center and the radii of a circle can be accompanied now by one important detail, which reflects an asymmetry in the relationship between the Logos (the center of a circle) and the world (the boundary of a circle): they are connected by the *logoi* (the radii) in only one direction, from the Logos to the world. In other words, the *logoi* meet the world on the circumference; this meeting provides one with the knowledge that there are *logoi*. But no movement is possible in the opposite direction from the circumference (the world) toward the center of the circle (the Logos).

The one-way *diastema*, however, which is present in the thought of Gregory of Nyssa, does not prevent humankind, and in fact all of creation, from participating in the Divine through the *energeia*. In other words, according to Gregory, in order to overcome the radical ontological dualism, which is just a different expression of the *diastema* from the world to God, participation (Gk. *metaousia*) in the energies of God, not knowledge of God, provides a way to assert that God *is* by a simple fact of the *existence* (of everything) and that it is God who sustains all levels of existence, empirical and intelligible.[77] The different orders in the universe are all dependent on the single reality of the energy of God, manifested through different *logoi*. All levels of reality in created being do participate in the energies of God; thus all of them carry an ontology relational on the energies of God, or God's *logoi*.

It is in this context that created matter, as a theological problem, receives some interpretation. Since everything in the created world depends on the energies of God—physical bodies, particles, planets, human bodies, and human senses and intellect—it is self-contradictory, theologically, to argue that God is not present in some aspects of nature, that is, that nature is freed from God, de-divinized. Indeed, the Fathers of the church affirmed that a fundamental distinction exists between God and the created, so that God is not creation in the pantheistic sense. On the other hand, by affirming that the ontology of the created world is relational upon God's energy and will, and that the latter is manifested in the creation through the *logoi*, the Fathers saw God present *in* nature while being distinct from nature. In this sense, any attempt to excommunicate the presence of God from nature contradicts the very view of matter as a manifestation of the energies of God. The denial of the presence of God in nature would reduce everything to nothing.

Humanity and the whole creation do participate in the energies of God across the basic *diastema*, and it is through this participation that humans form the image of matter: matter is the energies of God, made palpable to our senses and to our intellectual grasp. It now becomes clear how humankind can participate in establishing nature, together with God. It is through Christ, the Logos of God, who created all things, and granted man the chance to participate in matter as an effected event because of his composition of body, mind, and intellect (*nous*), that humankind knows matter and that matter knows itself through humankind. Ultimately, humans, as a divine image, were granted reason in order to be in a dialogical relationship with another reason, the reason of God. As God hypostasizes his words in effected events (in nature), humans can participate in the effected events, contributing through the dialogue with God toward the formation of nature.

It is important to stress that Christianity understands the dialogical relationship with God as the dialogue with the person whom we know through the historical name of Jesus Christ. The name Jesus manifests the personal hypostasis of God—that is, the meeting with God is an event of relationship, a call out of nonbeing into being (Rom. 4:17). Thus the formation of matter and its knowledge is a dialogical relationship of the hearing and articulation of God's words in human thoughts and words. Matter understood as a logical possibility is not possible as reality without the hypostatic existence of those who affirm the existence of matter and, in so doing, bring matter, as hypostasized existence, out of nothing. This results in the outstanding conclusion, which was reached by the Greek Fathers, that nature is empty before Christ—that is, that its full theological meaning becomes comprehensible only through the hypostasis of the Logos of God, through Christ. The makeup of matter, its existence as hypostasized in the effected words, the *logoi*, contemplated and participated in by men, is shaped by the incarnation of the Logos of God. Matter and nature in Orthodox theology receive their ultimate ontological foundation, their hypostasized existence and meaning, from Christ as the Alpha and Omega of everything in the created world. Humankind made as an image of God constitutes such a matter, which started to be able to know itself (where matter acquired the hypostatic properties).

The fact that we can sense matter does not imply, however, that the deep source, or the possibility of its sensation, is also disclosed to human being easily. The awareness that the *logos* exists in the human composite hypostasis, which is similar to the *logos* of creation of all things, and that it is this similarity that makes it possible for humans to participate in the *logoi* of creation through knowledge of things, represents an advanced stage of human cognitive and spiritual capacities. This kind of awareness differs from simple cognition by the senses to an enormous extent, for material nature itself is seen now as a sacrament, in which humankind is gifted to participate. Indeed, if one accounts the presence of the Logos in all things, holding their *logoi* together—that is, that the world is pregnant with divine reality—then the knowledge of it, which is exercised through the rational qualities of man, through his own *logos,* is itself treated as a kind of communion with God, a participation in divine things through the purposes and ends of things that are recognized in creation.[78]

One must make, however, a distinction between knowledge of the *presence* of the principles of creation—that is, that there *are* the *logoi* that hold the creation—and the *contemplation* of the *logoi* as a special stage of an advanced spiritual development. If the former is probably accessible to discursive reason (through scientific research, for example), the latter requires one to have made an advance in religious contemplation, which is sustained by one's participation in ecclesial life. When both knowledge of the existence of the *logoi* and their contemplation are combined in one human person, then science definitely can be said to participate in the contemplation of the *logoi* of creation. On average, however, it would be a modest task to demonstrate only the presence of the *logoi* in created being.

On the relation of knowledge of the *logoi* to knowledge of the Logos, which holds them together, Maximus the Confessor asserts that the contemplative activity reflects the convergence of the *logoi* to the divine unity and the unifying intention of God and the Logos. The Logos is itself the many *logoi*, but then the *logoi* may be said to be the one and only Logos, although what we know of them and their variety does not

106   Light from the East

exhaust what is contained in the Logos. Thus there is no complete identity. In addition, what we know about the *logoi* can contribute only to our knowledge of the Logos as the common source of their differentiated inhabitation in the created world. In other words, knowledge that the *logoi* exist does not provide itself the inference to the divine Logos, as the personal God of Christianity. The latter requires one to advance in apophatic mystical theology, that is, in religious life in God.

The *logoi* of Creation and Antinomies

Because natural contemplation of the *logoi* is not entirely based in discursive thinking, it is important to try to formulate an algorithm of demonstration of the presence of the *logoi* (not their contemplation) in the rubric of a purely discursive analysis of scientifico-philosophical affirmations about created nature. In a way, this task is quite paradoxical, for we are trying to discover through analysis of worldly things their *logoi*, the presence of the uncreated principles of the existence of created beings, which manifest that the ontological grounds of the worldly things studied by science are beyond the world and that everything in the world is rooted in its otherness. This is why these transcendent principles, if they exist, are present in scientific or philosophical arguments only in a hidden, mystical way. They can be revealed only from an a priori theological perspective and expressed in an apophatic and paradoxical way.

As established previously, a typical example of paradoxical thinking that points toward the transcendent source of that which is affirmed or negated has an antinomian structure. It consists of a cataphatic proposition (thesis) and an apophatic proposition (antithesis) with respect to the same notion. Remember that, for Kant, it was natural to claim that the presence of an antithetical structure in thought indicates that this thought is in trouble, that it speculates about notions that are beyond the legitimate sphere of application of the thought. Kant denied the ontology behind the notions that are affirmed or negated in the antinomy and thus claimed that the source of the difficulty is associated with a fallacy of the mind but is not inherent in the nature of things. For Kant, any notion that was not experiential (that is, empirical) was a product of intelligible causations and thus was not ontologically real.

Theology, in contradistinction to Kant, offers a different understanding of the antithetical structures of knowledge, one based on a basic dichotomy in the created realm, that is, on the *difference* between the sensible and the intelligible domains in creation. As established earlier, the thesis and antithesis of the antinomy demonstrate that the ontology of the empirical domain cannot have its ground in the intelligible domain, and vice versa, the ontology of the intelligible domain cannot have its ground in the empirical domain. The further step is based on the mediation between sensible and intelligible, which, in the theological terms of Maximus, corresponds to the ascension to a mystical knowledge of God.[79] Performing the mediation between the sensible and the intelligible in man's creaturely state of existence and with the whole human nature, one comes to the conclusion that there *is* the *logos* of all creation and that there *is* a principle of creation. There is no way, however, to develop this principle further because of the one-way *diastema* between God and the world. To understand this principle, one would have to be immanent to God. The transcendent gulf between God and creation prevents us from knowing why God created at all. The principle of why God overbridged the gulf between himself and all that can be created is a mystery and is hidden from us in God as he is in himself.

How, then, can the contemplation of the presence of the *logos* of creation be formulated discursively? Maximus approaches this by using his idea of humankind as microcosm. As a microcosm, humankind "recapitulates the universe in himself," that is, it is able to communicate with the universal *logos* of the world at large, the macrocosm.[80] The basic point for Maximus is that there is a parallel dichotomy in humans, one of sense and mind, that resembles the ontological difference in creation between the sensible and the intelligible.

The position of humankind as *microcosm* implies that by their senses humans are linked to the sensible world, to empirical things, whereas the human mind provides access to intelligible entities. Since humans are consubstantial to both kinds of reality in creation, they are able to mediate between sensible and intelligible. This composite nature of humans does not violate their unity because there is an underlying and forming principle of humans, their *logos,* which binds their elements together. Maximus explains this as follows: "As a compound of soul and body he is limited essentially by intelligible and sensible realities, while at the same time he himself defines these realities through his capacity to apprehend intellectually and to perceive with his senses."[81]

It is exactly this point—the human ability to hypostasize both sensible and intelligible realities as different, on the one hand, and at the same time united with respect to humans as a source of their hypostasization—that makes the mediation between the sensible and the intelligible in humankind itself possible without violation of its *logos.*[82]

As mentioned before, creation as macrocosm is formed also by the fundamental principle of being: macrocosm has the foundation for its being from nonbeing; it is created, and the constitutive principle of this creation is the *difference* in creation between sensible and intelligible. This means that humankind's mediation between its elements as microcosm does not violate these elements but holds them together; this is true not only for microcosm but also for macrocosm, being at large. The mediation between constitutive parts of creation, between the sensible and the intelligible, does not violate their ontological difference (*diaphora*) because it does not violate their different *logoi,* which all preexist in God.

Finally, the universal *logos* of creation must be accessible to humankind, and at the same time it must remain a secret, the divine secret (that is, although we can detect the presence of the *logoi,* we do not know their ultimate meaning and purpose). Maximus treats the antinomial difficulty, based on this one-way *diastema* between God and the world, by appealing to the principle of creation of the world out of nothing in accordance with which "the whole of creation admits of one and the same undiscriminated *logos,* as having not been before it is."[83] L. Thunberg reexpresses this thought more clearly: "The divine principle which holds the entire creation together is that it should have non-being as the ground of its being."[84] This helps give the discursive explanation of what it means to detect the *logos* of creation: detection of the presence of the *logos* of creation from within the created domain means the understanding that every object in the created realm, be it intelligible or sensible, has one and the same transcendent ground of its existence in its nonexistence (nonbeing) or its otherness. This formula implies that the principle of creation is one that states the limit that divides creation (in its being) from its nonbeing. Given this, can antinomies of discursive reason, invoked when it attempts to predicate on the ultimate reality, help detect the presence of the principle of creation in scientific thinking?

Maximus's extraordinary formula, which describes the root of the created in its own otherness, its nonbeing, can be used methodologically as follows. Starting with the antinomial difficulty with respect to some aspects of created things, we separate through them two dimensions in the composition of everything, namely, its empirical display in contradistinction to its intelligible mode, revealing thus the fact that both the intelligible and the sensible have their own *logoi*. To overcome the negative aspect of the antinomy, the spiritual reason refers, then, to the common source of both aspects of the existence of the thing, which is beyond both intelligible and spiritual aspects of its being, in its otherness, or nonbeing. In doing so, the reason asserts that there *is* the *logos* of creation of this thing and of any things at all. The achievement of the reason can be summarized in two points: (1) creation is contingent upon the uncreated (nonnatural) source, and (2) the composition of creation (the dichotomy between the sensible and the intelligible) points toward the common principle of creation. Again, reason is able to assert only that it detected the presence of the *logos* of creation—*that* it *is*, but not *what* it is. Detection of the *logos* of creation through the antinomy changes completely the negative tonality of the antinomy, pointing thereby to the fact that the very form of the antinomial proposition contains the affirmation of the transcendent source of the references in thesis and antithesis, which unites them both in a single unity, the *logos* of creation.

The mediation between intelligible and sensible creation, which leads man to the knowledge that there *is* the *logos* of creation, reflects, so to speak, only an epistemological participation in the universal *logos*—that is, it results only in a dispassionate knowledge of its existence, with no ontological effect on either man or creation at large. The contemplation of the *logos* of creation, on the other hand, is a liturgical process in which, through mediation, humankind holds the entire creation together in its relationship to the divine Logos, the Creator.[85] This brings humans to the frontier of natural knowledge, to the contemplation of the *logos* of creation itself, beyond which there is only the mystery of the transcendent gulf between creation and creator, which is the beginning of genuinely theological knowledge in the mystical sense of apophatic *theologia*. One must caution, then, anyone who attempts to ascend to God through natural knowledge by using discursive reason: there is an absolute limit in this ascension leading to the detection of the *logos* of creation. The overbridging of this limit (that is, the mystery of creation, one-way *diastema*), is impossible without the grace of God, which can be granted to humans as a gift through their participation in ecclesial life.

Hypostatic Dimension in Theistic Inferences from Creation

Before turning to specific scientific problems, in order to demonstrate how the antinomial monodualism works in discovering the *presence* of the *logoi* of creation, we must discuss in what sense the detection of these *logoi* can provide further inference to the Divine Logos, the Second Person of the Holy Trinity, by whom the *logoi* of all things are embraced. Can scientific research, if it is subjected to theological inspection, provide us with *pointers* to the presence of God in the world personally or, in different words, hypostatically. For the presence of the impersonal *logoi*, if it is established, does not indicate that these *logoi* are inherent in the hypostasis of the Logos of God. We need some "extra" insight in order to extend theistic inference from the created universe to what is specific for Christian faith, namely, that God who is affirmed is the community of Love among the Persons of the Holy Trinity. For otherwise, using the words of Basil the Great, "if we have no distinct perception of the separate characteristics, namely, fatherhood, sonship, and sanctification, but form our conception of God from the general idea of existence, we cannot possibly give a sound account of our faith. We must, therefore, confess the faith by adding the particular to the common."[86] In our case this particular is the personality of the Logos of God who is in intricate relationship with the world he created, and which should be pointed at.

Orthodox theologians never separated the arguments for the evidence about the intelligibility of the universe rooted in the Logos of God from the context of the living faith in the incarnation of the Logos in Jesus Christ, through whom the creation of the world by the Holy Trinity has received new assertion, dictated not so much by the observed necessities of the created world, but rather by the logic of Divine Providence and God's plan for the salvation of man and the universe, revealed through Jesus Christ. This is the reason why our expectation of the utility of modern physical science for making the inferences about God is very reserved in general, for if physics is detached from the experience of the living God of Christian faith, its assertions about the Divine, which always play in this case the role of transcendent references, will only end in the idea of the philosophical God with no correlations with God, who condescended to the universe and took human form in order to reveal the truth about himself as well as about the place of human beings in the immense cosmos. Thus the reality of the living God can never be achieved through cosmological gnosis as such unless the latter is sanctified by human faith and ecclesial life, in order to become the manifestation of the relationship between human beings and God, the relationship which inevitably involves the universe as its term.

T. Torrance has argued persuasively, by reference to Patristic thought, that natural theology is possible in the Christian context if its subject is driven by the reality of God himself, both revealed in faith in Jesus Christ, as well as detected through scientific knowledge as the boundaries of the worldly references, pointing toward the almost incredible contingent intelligibility of the universe, rooted in the Logos of God. This implies that the rationality of human reason and inferred rationality of the universe, especially when they pretend to affirm some truth about their own foundations, have sense only as conceived in the light of the intelligibility of the Logos of God who conferred the intellect on human beings in order that they might contemplate the contingent intelligibility of the world. Thus all forms of intellectual arguments about the existence of God that constituted classical natural theology can have only limited value, for, using the words of Torrance, "no argument from created intelligibility, as such, can actually terminate on the Reality of God, but in accordance with its contingent nature can only break off."[87]

Can, then, the articulation of the personhood of God be achieved if one argues about the Divine from within creation? It is important to stress here that the central position of human beings in the universe plays a pivotal role in articulating the reality of the world in specific and concrete intelligible forms, which function in human beings through the intelligibility of the Logos of God who holds the *logoi* of human beings; this means that the reality of what we call the universe is articulated by human beings, and it is the same human beings who can make the inferences from the universe to God. This is the reason to suspect that the image of the universe, that is, its existence as apprehended in human hypostases, contains inevitably the image of God and his intelligibility. Physics and cosmology, then, articulate the reality of things in human hypostasis, and human beings can then be treated as cocreators of the universe who are responsible for and who can sanctify the universe by relating it to its own ground in the living and personal God. It is through this insight that we articulate a nontrivial ontological conviction that the universe exists *inwardly* through human consciousness, the potentiality and possibility of which is rooted in the Logos of God, whose image all human beings experience hypostatically through their individual *logoi*.

The detection of the hypostatic presence of God in the world thus becomes a task of understanding nature not in abstract terms as "objectively" existent matter (substance), but as "nature" existent in the personality of God himself, that is, as having its ultimate origin in the person of God. How, then, can this hypostatic dimension of the universe, as inherent in the Logos of God, be revealed by scientific research?

One of Patristic theology's achievements was to articulate the difference between "natural" and "hypostatic" existence, which shaped the concept of nature and matter as being closely linked to the concept of hypostatic, personalized existence. That is why any reasoning about the universe involves human agency. It is the same human agency which provides the arguments for God's existence from observing the created world. This implies that these arguments are shaped by the limits of human creaturely existence, and they can be addressed in words and thoughts developed within created human nature which is inherent hypostatically in the Logos of God. Here we need some further clarification.

The Universe as "Hypostatic Inherence" in the Logos of God

The meaning of the term *hypostatic* comes from the Greek word *hypostasis*, which was used in the Patristic theological context in order to underline the "personal," active as well as intransitive dimension of existence as different from impersonal substance (*ousia*) or nature (*physis*). The difference was articulated in Patristic thought in the context of the trinitarian and christological discussions throughout the fourth to seventh centuries. *Ousia* (as related to universals, families, or species) tends to be used with regard to internal characteristics and relations, or metaphysical reality (in this it almost identical with *physis*), whereas *hypostasis* regularly emphasizes the externally concrete character of the substance, its empirical objectivity, and the existential aspect of being, expressed through the realization of freedom, movement, and will. It is important to stress that though every individual substance moves and is moved, the personal element in the realization of the potentiality of the substance is not included in the concept of substance itself, that is, the hypostatic aspect of individual existence is not immanent to what is included in the substance.

The difference between *ousia* and *hypostasis* can be elucidated in the Christian doctrine of *creatio ex nihilo,* which asserts that the world was created out of nothing as an ecstatic act of interpenetrating love among the persons of the Holy Trinity. In Patristic theological language there were different expressions of this belief. It was affirmed that the world was created by the will of God and this implied that the ontology of the world was rooted in God's will, but not in his essence (*ousia*) (Athanasius of Alexandria).[88] This entails that God is present in the world, not ontologically (i.e., on the level of the world's substance), but rather relationally and personally, on the level of his loving kindness to the world, expressed through his will and realized by his Word. It is affirmed since the times of the Gospel of John that it is the Word-Logos of God, the second person of the Holy Trinity, who entered the world by creating it and preparing his incarnation in Jesus as the meeting of the uncreated Divine with created humanity. It is at this point that the cosmological mystery of the presence of the ontologically transcendent God in the world acquires christological (and anthropological) dimension. For the presence of God in the world cannot be understood without the *hypostatic mystery* of Christ as a locus of the divine and human.

Nature or substance (in its self-realization, which is accounted for by God's will as creator) can be divided and shared while the *hypostasis* of a particular being is indivisible. The reality of substance (i.e., its transcendence) is made available to human beings because of God's economy, which relates independent creation to the Creator through communion; that is, substance becomes evident and real only in *hypostases,* that is, in what is indivisible. In a theological context *hypostasis* is similar to *prosopon,* that is, person in modern parlance. This implies that the nature of things becomes evident if it is *personified.* The *hypostasis,* then, is seen as the foundation of being, for it is that in which nature exists.[89]

The distinction between nature and hypostasis allows one to articulate the unity of all creation in two different senses. On the one hand, all varieties of sensible objects share the same nature (e.g., the same elementary particles). On the other hand, if one considers the world in relationship to its creator, then natural existence acquires the features of existence for someone, that is, the Creator, who is not an impersonal substance or essence of the higher order (in which other individual substances participate), but who is the personal God. Thus when Christianity affirms that the world was created by the Word-Logos of God and that through the Logos everything was made, it effectively affirms that the natural existence of the world is existence in the personhood of God, that is, in his *hypostasis;* this means that whole creation is brought to unity in the hypostasis of the Logos and that the link between God and the world is nonnatural (i.e., nonontological, nonphysical, nonbiological, etc.), but *hypostatic,* which, can be expressed as the *relationship* between the Divine and the world in the personhood of God. The creation of the world and its existence have sense, then, only in relation to the person who is acting as the creator and provider of meaning of the existence: there cannot be impersonal creation as well as existence.

The universe, however, being created by God, is not capable of knowing that it has its creator, for impersonal physical objects are not hypostatic creatures: they have no ability to contemplate their own existence and relate it to their ultimate source. Thus the intelligibility of the universe and its meaning are accessible only to hypostatic human beings, who are created in the Divine image, and whose hypostasis is capable of personifying objects in the universe, that is, making the universe self-conscious of its own existence and origin. Maximus the Confessor strongly argued that man as a person cannot be isolated from the fact that human nature has its hypostasis in the Logos and it is in this sense that it can be said that human nature is itself *enhypostasized.* In other words, it is *hypostatically inherent* in the Logos; this means that a personal relationship with God cannot be excluded from human nature and is identical with fully realized human existence.

The term *hypostatic inherence* refers theologically to the Greek words *enhypostatic* or *enhypostasis,* which were introduced into heology by Leontius of Byzantium in the context of christological discussions of the sixth to seventh centuries, and whose meaning (appropriate for the purposes of our research) in Greek Patristic usage can be described as: "being, existing in an hypostasis or Person," "subsistent in, inherent."[90]

One can refer to a theological view of "participation" in the Divine in order to illustrate the idea of "hypostatic inherence" of the universe in the Logos of God. When it is said that created beings know about God, it means that they *participate* in God through a mode which is distinct from his essence (uncreated energies, for example). However, the very ability to *participate* in God is willed by God himself, for it is God who brought into existence participating beings; the knowledge of why this participation is possible at all is concealed by God from participating beings and known only to himself.[91]

It was natural, then, for Maximus the Confessor to argue that "everything that derives its existence from participation in some other reality presupposes the ontological priority of that other reality";[92] he meant the priority of the Logos of God with respect to all other created things which do participate in him.[93] The "hypostatic inherence" of the universe in the Logos of God can then be interpreted in Maximus's words as the Logos's eternal manifestations in different modes of *participation* by created beings in him. This participation takes place in spite of the fact that the Logos, is eternally invisible (i.e., ontologically distinct from creation) to all in virtue of the surpassing nature of his hidden activity.[94] But this *participation* does not assume any ontological causation; for to participate in the Logos means to be made by the Logos a participating being, that is, to be made as a being in the hypostasis of the Logos himself. This implies that existence through participation in the Logos is subsistence in his personhood, that is, the *inherence* in his hypostasis. In short, one can say that hypostatic inherence in the Logos is the same as *participation* in his person.

Another example, which illustrates what the existence in a hypostasis or person means, can be brought from a sphere of theological anthropology, which asserts that "man is hypostasis [personality] of the cosmos, its conscious and personal self-expression; it is he who gives meaning to things and who has to transfigure them. For the universe, man is its hope to receive grace and to be united with God."[95] The universe as *the expressed and articulated existence* is possible only in human hypostasis, that is, it acquires some qualities of existence if it is reflected in the personality of humanity. Using the words of Maximus the Confessor, every intellection about the universe inheres as a quality in an apprehending being.[96] The universe thus acquires qualitative existence in the being who apprehends it.[97] The link between the universe as articulated existence and the apprehending being is not ontological, but rather hypostatic or personal. A Patristic theologian would say that existence of the universe as the articulated existence is *hypostatic* existence, that is, the universe is *enhypostatic*.

Can, then, hypostatic human beings, because of apprehension of the universe as inherent in the Logos, interact with the Logos and change him? Maximus the Confessor has already prepared a response to this by saying that the Logos, who is beyond intellection, unites himself to human intellection, which is purified from any manifold and temporality, and makes it his own, giving it rest from those things which by nature change and diversify it with many conceptual forms they impose upon it.[98] This means that human intellection of the universe does not affect the Logos, which is beyond intellection. The link between the Logos and the world is not subject to temporal change and instability of nature, which human intellect operates with. The world is in the hypostasis of the Logos of God from ages to ages, so that the Logos experiences the world as being in rest from his works, "just as God did from His (Gen. 2:2; Heb. 4:10)."[99]

One should not think that the ideas about "hypostasis" are some outdated relics of the old tradition, which have no links with modern philosophical development and its fusion with theology. For example, the term *hypostasis* was used by a contemporary French phenomenological philosopher Emmanuel Levinas in a very special way that will be useful for elucidating our thought.[100] Levinas puts a stress on the difference between the *transitive* existence of beings, through relationships, for example, and the absolutely *intransitive* element of one's own *existing* as freed from intentionality and relationship. The *existent* and its *existing* do not coincide in every creature.

For if, according to Levinas, the existent "contracts"[101] its existing, it forms an *event* which he calls *hypostasis*. One can say that the hypostatic existence of human beings, as *existents* (and of the whole humankind), is the event of contracting by them their *existing*. What will happen, then, if we consider the situation when the *existent* cannot contract its own *existing*, but can be *existent* in the *existing* of the other? Are we still obliged to talk about the "event" of hypostatic existence? For example, some physical object has no inclination to perceive its own existence. This means that it is *existent* without its own *existing*. But, at the same time, the same object can be articulated in the *existing* of a human being, so that it contracts its existing in the other, that is, in human being. A human being, being itself a hypostatic event, makes the contraction of an *existent* physical object its *existing* in the apprehension of human being an *event*, so that the "hypostatic inherence" of a physical object, in the knowing subject, has some features of temporality and emergence, which follow from the *event* of human hypostasis. The situation drastically changes if the existent receives its existing from the Logos of God whose hypostatic ever-being is not involved in any chain of worldly relations and events; in this case the "hypostatic inherence" as contraction by the universe of its existing in the hypostasis of the Logos of God has no features of emergence and temporality. This is the reason why we do not want to express the existence of the universe in the person of the Logos of God, in order to deliver the reader from the temptation to think about the universe as "personalized" by the Logos. Personalization is an emergent notion usually applied to something which has already been in existence. This is why the Greek term *enhypostasization* would be more appropriate for us in order to affirm that "the universe is enhyposta-sized by the Logos of God." We express this thought by using the language of "hypo-static inherence" in order to make it easier for a modern reader to comprehend the term; by so doing we avoid the danger of affirming the link between God and the world in emergent terms.

The creation and existence of the universe thus can be seen as enhypostatic in two senses: (1) the universe as mere nature exists in the hypostasis of the Logos; (2) but the very knowledge of this, that is, the transcendence beyond substance from within the universe, can only be achieved if nature is contemplated in the human hypostases (which in turn exist in the hypostasis of the Logos). The universe thus acquires the features of its *hypostatic inherence* in a twofold sense: in the Logos of God who brings the matter into existence through His effected words, and in hypostatic human beings, who through analysis and differentiation of this matter lead the universe to self-awareness of its purpose and end, that is, to realized existence in God and for God. It is in this sense that one can argue that human beings are cocreators of the universe: the universe is brought into being as the meaningful and self-conscious existence in the personhood of humanity. The universe, as articulated existence in the human hypostasis, can be treated in turn as the hypostatic event, contingent upon the human phenomenon, which constitutes an element of God's economy for salvation.

One then concludes that the link between the Logos of God and the universe is hypostatic, that is, the universe is seen as *hypostatic inherence* in the Logos of God. But this signifies that once the universe is apprehended by us in its connection and unity with the primordial ground of the Logos, it becomes for us something greater and other than "only the universe," because the specific "worldly" character of the universe is overcome without the universe itself being "removed" or "eliminated." The meaninglessness of the universe, its pure factuality and impersonality, its indifference to the Divine truth, are overcome. This signifies that the presence of God in the world can only be detected through manifestations of the enhypostatic mode of the world's existence.

A word of caution must be said if one attempts to treat the notion of the *hypostatic inherence* in terms of the bilateral relationship between God and the world. We stress the Patristic belief that God is hypostatic being but the world is not. Since the link between God and the world is hypostatic (as we have argued above), any bilateral relationship between God and the world would only be possible if the world as such exhibited hypostatic features. Then the bilateral relationship between God and the world might be understood as the relationship between two persons: God and the world. But it is exactly at this point that our position states clearly that the created world as such is not hypostasis at all, it has a mode of existence which is inherent in the hypostasis of the Logos of God, and that is why the relationship between the Logos and the world is established through the one-way *diastema*, that is, as the permeation from God to the world, but not vice versa.

The claim of the so-called generic panentheism about the bilateral relationship between God and the world, as seen though Patristic eyes, runs the risk of affirming something similar to the old Patristic idea of *perichoresis* (co-inherence) of God to the world. Certainly this similarity must be analyzed with caution, for it must not be understood as analogous to the trinitarian formula of co-inherence as interpenetration and mutual indwelling of the persons of the Trinity (it would be a theological nonsense to affirm that created nature is capable of interpenetrating the Divine).[102] It can rather be paralleled with *perichoresis* in the christological context as the interchange and reciprocity of the human nature with the divine nature in Christ. Then by analogy, one might affirm panentheistically the *perichoresis* of the Divine and the created in a sense of "interchange" and "reciprocity" (bilateral relationship) between God and the world. But even in this, so to speak "weak," form of the *perichoresis,* panentheism must not forget the origin of this *perichoresis,* i.e. that it proceeds from the personhood of the Divinity, not from the matter of the world. The Divine, having once permeated through the world, bestows on its matter an ineffable *perichoresis* with itself. The interchange or reciprocity of the Divine and the created is ultimately initiated and held by the hypostasis of the Logos of God. One can see again that the process of the Divine permeation of the world is one-sided and entirely determined by the Logos himself. This has been demonstrated by God through the incarnation of the Logos in Jesus Christ.

The world as such has no hypostasis of its own and cannot initiate and sustain the *perichoresis* to the Divine. It is possible, however, to speak about hypostatic agencies in the world, i.e. human beings, through whom the world acquires some personal qualities, in the sense we have explained above. Human beings can initiate the interchange between the world and God through the apprehension of the created universe, so that the world, being articulated by human beings, is related to God as its uncreated source. Any panentheistic claim, then, about the world which is brought to godself must be understood in the context of human deification and involvement of the world in the transfiguration, which brings it back to the union with God. But all this is initiated by the Logos of God, who created human beings with such *logoi* as to allow human beings to relate to God through personal interaction as well as through apprehension of the universe created by him. This is the reason why the universe, being personified by human beings, still exhibits its hypostatic inherence in the Logos of God. Human beings thus become the locus points in creation through whom the evidence of the hypostatic inherence of the universe in the Logos can be seen.

From what we have said above, namely, that the presence of God in the universe can be detected only through the enhypostatic mode of the universe's existence, it is clear that science is closely connected with the articulation of the created nature of things and their foundation in the effected words of God-Person, and it cannot be alienated from theology at all; for, by its function, science articulates the human participation in creation and through it the participation in the relationship between the world and God. This relationship is articulated by created human beings who are the inevitable part of this relationship.

Human consciousness thus cannot be alienated from physical research and its theological generalizations, being in fact a part of those equations which drive the whole universe. It is clear, then, that any knowledge of things, and their ultimate foundations (the *logoi*) must involve subjects of knowledge in the entirety of their human constitution. The theistic inferences made in this perspective have by their constitution the hypostatic dimension pointing toward the source of the personalized existence of everything, that is, to God. The mediation between science and theology then acquires a strong anthropological dimension, which manifests that both modes of articulation of God's creation—through science discursively and through religion mystically and liturgically—have a common source of origin which is the human intentional subjectivity and transcending spirituality which manifest the essence of human *being-in-the-world-with-God.*

5

Creation in Cosmology and Theology

Creatio ex nihilo and Contingency of the World

The Christian teaching on creation out of nothing, its doctrine of *creatio ex nihilo,* did not enter the cultural and spiritual environment of the ancient world in an empty background. The worldview asserted by Classical Hellenistic philosophy—that the world exists necessarily, that is, there is no need for justification of the very fact of the existence of the world—had had a deep impact. Greek thought could not cross this line of inquiry about the nature of things that was the foundation of all foundations in its philosophical meditation about the cosmos. The world, according to the Greeks, was permanent, unchangeable, and, despite all internal movements, such as the origin and decay of things, the world as a whole was in a state of "eternal return"; its cosmology was cyclic. The endurance of the cosmos of the Greeks was ontologically necessary; the premise of its existence was an absolute fact, the last resort of all possible philosophizing.

The message of the Bible and the doctrine of *creatio ex nihilo,* which was developed first in the Christian context by Theophilus of Antioch and Irenaeus of Lyons, challenged Greek philosophy and cosmology by affirming that the cosmos cannot be regarded as a self-explanatory being.[1] Rather, it is dependent on the existence of God and hence cannot be described as eternal, for its dependence on God means that the world is different from God and that its mode of existence, being different from the divine, is *finite* in all possible senses of the word (for example, temporal), for if God is infinite (apophatic definition), then the world is finite. The world is created by God and in its matter is radically different from God.

The Christian message affirmed the world's radical contingency upon God, which implied that the laws of the world established in it are contingent and do not possess a status of an absolute necessity. This implied that the act of creation of the world by God out of nothing is a "free" act of God's willing kindness to the world and, because of God's freedom, the creation is not inherent in God's own being. This produces a twofold contingency: contingency on the side of the orders in the universe, which could not have existed at all, and contingency on the side of the God-Creator, who could not have created anything at all.

The concept of *creatio ex nihilo,* which has its roots in the Hebraic tradition, was radicalized in the Christian context through the doctrine of the self-revelation of God in the incarnation of God's son, the Logos of God, and the resurrection of Jesus Christ. The meaning of creation and its order was established by the divine Logos, the Word of God, who endowed the world with a particular rationality that is contingent on God's "transcendent rationality." The notion of contingency was developed by the Greek Fathers to express the nature of the universe as created freely by God, the universe that is utterly different from God yet dependent on him.

As a result of this development of Christian thought, the dualism of Classical Greek philosophy, in which there was a separation between the intelligible and the sensible world, was overcome: the whole universe, intelligible and sensible, heavenly and celestial, was regarded as creation, not as the Divine, but also as penetrated through with a unitary rational order of a contingent kind, which can be studied only in accordance with its own nature and yet is able through the order and harmony in the cosmos to point to the creator.[2]

The affirmation of creation in the Christian doctrine cannot be made in separation from the whole context of the Christian ethos, namely, the teaching and experience of the divine plan of salvation of man. Here Irenaeus, who pioneered the development of the doctrine of creation out of nothing, considered the material creation as the precondition for God's saving work among men.[3] The creation of mankind was at the center of Irenaeus's emphasis, and he treated it as the beginning of God's work of salvation. Irenaeus emphatically argued that the world was created by the will of God (the world was created freely because of the willing kindness of God to mankind) through God's Word and that the world is made by God because of God's original plan: "As soon as God's mind conceived it [the plan of creation], the thing His mind conceived was made."[4] Despite this plan, which is rooted in the actual self-determination of God, grounded in God's *ousia,* one affirms that the world is still contingent on God; in talking about the plan of creation, one appeals to the "transcendent rationality" of God, which cannot be conceived from the perspective of the contingent world, which need not exist at all despite God's plan. We experience here an inherent apophaticism of any teaching on creation, for *creatio ex nihilo* is a fundamentally mystical concept, for it is not so much a concept about the world as it is about God in terms of his relationship to his creation. This is why the notion of the "plan" of creation, on the one hand, and the contingency of the divine act of creation, on the other hand, require for their comprehension an antinomial logic, which by its function transcends the paradox of the "plan" and contingency and does not risk arguing about God too much. This point can be elucidated by an appeal to Athanasius's distinction in God of his essence (*ousia,* substance) and his will and, consequently, the treatment of the created world as rooted in the will of God, not his essence.[5] Athanasius argued that to *be* (that is, to exist) does not mean to *act.* Because the substance of God and God's *will* are distinct in God, the ontology of the uncreated realm and that of creation are different. This led Athanasius to affirm the difference between God and the world in ontological terms, that is, that the ontology of the world is based on the *will* of God, not on God's essence.

But the creation of the world Athanasius affirms, as does Irenaeus, is essential for the divine plan of salvation: "Nothing in creation had erred from the path of God's purpose for it, save only man."[6] There was the divine plan of salvation (the transcendent rationality of God), and there was an act of free creation of the world by God's will and because of God's love (the contingency of creation). As Athanasius asserts in the quotation above, the creation was essential for God's plan to save man. In other words, the act of creation, being contingent upon God, constitutes a step in God's transcendent rational planning to save man. This makes it possible to affirm that the created world is necessarily contingent.[7]

The contribution of the Cappadocian Fathers to the problem of creation can be mentioned briefly. The first is the trinitarian theology of the Cappadocian Fathers, which affirms *creatio ex nihilo* as an act of ecstatic love of the Trinity. Because of the consensus of one will in all persons of the Trinity, and because of God's freedom, the world was created as an act of ecstatic love of God—for without freedom, there is no love. The will of God *hypostasizes* the world, making this world ontologically based on the will of God, not on God's essence.

The Cappadocian trinitarian theology can be considered as accomplishing the formulation of the ontological dualism between the *inner life* of God as the Father, the Son, and the Holy Spirit, and the creation, which is a deed of the divine *will* common to and identical in all three persons of the one God. The fundamental meaning of their contributions toward theological developments was, in fact, the overcoming of the closed ontology of the Greeks, who were monistic in their heart, either believing in the uncreated nature of matter in the world or identifying the creator of matter with some supernatural deity in the world, which is rather the architect, the worker in the created order. Christian ontology represents an immense shift from Greek philosophical monism toward an ontology of the created being, which has its own foundation in its *otherness*, that is, in God, whose mode of existence is ontologically distinct from that mode of existence of the created world.

The second aspect of the Cappadocian theology, which was mentioned in chapter 4 in the discussion of Gregory of Nyssa's teaching about the one-way *diastema* between God and the world, affirmed the radical distinction between God and the world, on the one hand, and the revealing presence of God through his energies in the world, on the other hand. Gregory's theology distinguished between the essence of God and God's *energeia*. It is in the *energeia* of God that the world has its ultimate ground. Everything in the world is formed by the divine energy, which is accessible to contemplation by human beings because of the gift of grace of God. This, however, brings another dimension into our discussion of the concept of creation, namely, the role of the Logos of God in creation, God's incarnation in the *logoi* of things and God's incarnation in flesh, in Christ.

As a preliminary conclusion, one can assert that, from a theological point of view, the concept of creation has sense as the concept of the relationship between God and the world, rather than about the world alone. This implies that if science (cosmology, for example) attempts to predicate about the creation of the universe, it can do so only from within the immanent aspects of the world, which are accessible to scientific investigation as a gift by the will of God. This means that it is doubtful from the very beginning that science can provide a model of creation of the world out of nothing that could compete with or simply be leveled to that of the Fathers' teaching about creation. Indeed, the challenge for science is to try to uncover the transcendence, present in the world, by doing research from within the world. This transcendence would point toward the relational nature of the universe and its ultimate contingency upon the reality, which is beyond nature and is in its otherness, that is, in the Divine.

It is clear, however, that any analysis in this direction can lead one only to the detection of the rootedness of the world in the will of God, or God's *energeia,* which can be technically expressed as the implicit presence of the *logoi* of creation in some scientific ideas.[8] The important aspect of such a detection is that it is possible, not only because the world is available to us in its created givenness but also because the world, being created according to the plan of God, has in its contingent appearance some features of necessity that point toward the fact that creation has a purpose and an end. Contemplated by science as the universe's order and structure, this is accomplished by God through the incarnation of the Logos of God in the *logoi* of things, as the agency that provides the guidance and sense to everything that is observed and contemplated. This means that creation in cosmology, understood discursively, refers to that aspect of the theological *creatio ex nihilo* that is associated with the hidden rationality of a contingent origin, the rationality that is inherent in God's plan of salvation of man and realized through the incarnation of the Logos of God in nature and in the flesh of Christ. This leads to the conclusion that the understanding of creation, if attempted from within science as a challenge to a theological view, should address not only the origination of the material universe, its evolution, and its sustenance but also the question of its rationality and ability inherent in humans to communicate with the universe and to contemplate this rationality. This imposes a great demand for cosmology to reflect on the nature of the incarnation of the Logos of God as a step in God's plan to create the world for the sake of man's salvation.[9]

Creation and Incarnation:
Intelligibility of the World and Scientific Advance

Since the creation of the world out of nothing was a precondition of the whole history of salvation, the Fathers of the church articulated clearly that the full meaning of creation could not be understood outside the context of the Christ-event. Indeed, when Irenaeus, for example, discusses the creation of man as made in the image of God (one should remember that for Irenaeus the making of man was a central point in the history of creation-salvation), he says that the image of God was not *shown,* "because the Word, in whose image man was made, was still invisible."[10] The Son-Logos of God through his incarnation in flesh of the created world, according to Irenaeus, recapitulates the whole creation: "God recapitulated in Himself that ancient handiwork of His which is man,"[11] and "When He became incarnate and was made man, He recapitulated in Himself the long history of mankind."[12]

Following Irenaeus's logic leads to the conclusion that the incarnation as recapitulation is the only definite thing in the affirmation of creation as a saving work of God with respect to mankind, for the sense of what God was planning when he conceived the plan of salvation becomes clear only through the Logos of God, who condescended into the created world in order to become a visible teacher to us.[13] Ireneaus emphatically asserts that the truth of the incarnation is the only "real" and is definitive.[14] He describes the dynamics of God's revelation about creation in three stages: "Through the creation itself the Word reveals the Creator, and through the world the Lord, the world's Maker. . . . Similarly through the law and the prophets the Word proclaimed both Himself and the Father. . . . Finally through the Word made visible and palpable, the Father was revealed."[15] The revelation about creation was granted to mankind in two stages: the first to provide the knowledge that there was a creator of the world, and the second, after the incarnation, to provide the meaning of creation as a precondition for the salvation history.

If we now turn to Athanasius's thought, we find some similar ideas on the role of the incarnation of the Logos of God in flesh in order to elucidate the meaning of creation. But Athanasius proceeds much further than Irenaeus, for the former not only asserts the incarnation as a pivotal element in the history of salvation but also links the incarnation of the Word of God with establishing a principle of intelligibility in the contingent creation.

Athanasius argues that it is through the inference of the Word of God from the created order that one can know that God *is* (that is, that the world is contingent on God), for it is the Word of God who *orders* the universe and reveals the Father (who is the creator with his transcendent rationality). Athanasius links the order in the created world with the incarnation of the Word-Logos of God. It was not enough for God just to create an ordered world to teach men about the Father: "Creation was there all the time, but it did not prevent men from wallowing in error."[16] It was the part of the Word of God, God's Logos and only Son, who by ordering the universe reveals the Father (that is, reveals the hidden plan in contingent creation) "to renew the same teaching" through the incarnation, using another means to teach about God to those who would not learn from the works of God's creation.[17]

There is one particular problem that we would like to discuss in this context, namely, the problem of the contingency of the created realm on God and, at the same time, the presence of elements of necessity in the created world that make the incarnation principally possible.

Starting from Irenaeus, the Greek Fathers affirmed that God created the world freely, but from his plan. It is obviously expressed in the Nicene Creed that the "Son of God, the only begotten of the Father, begotten before all ages," participated in the plan of creation and salvation before the world actually was made. At the same time, by planning the creation of the world and the salvation of man, God-Trinity planned the incarnation of the Son-Logos of God in the flesh of that world, which is supposed to be created.

The question then arises: did God plan the creation of the universe in some specially designed form in order to bring human beings into existence in such a shape as to make the incarnation of the Logos of God possible? Some Fathers (Origen, for example) are inclined to make a connection between the fall and the incarnation, while others (St. Maximus the Confessor, for example) are not. The main question still remains: if the history of salvation of man through the incarnation of the Logos in Christ and resurrection of Christ had been planned "before" the creation of the world, can we affirm that the world was created out of nothing by God's will contingently (that is, freely and because of God's love), on the one hand, and intentionally (in a shape that allows the history of salvation to be realized in this world), on the other hand? This means that the mode of existence of humanity in its fallen state, with its body, dependent on physical matter and biology, which was shared by Christ through the incarnation of the Logos, was a necessary element of the divine plan before creation. It implies, then, that the structure of the physical universe, which acts as the necessary condition for man's physical and biological existence, was a necessary element of the divine plan before creation. In this, we face the problem of the freedom in God's creation of the world out of nothing, on the one hand, and some inherent necessity underlying this creation, on the other hand. One can phrase this as the presence of "contingent necessity" in the world, which enables one to establish the *meaning* of creation as it was planned by God in his intent of salvation.

When one affirms the creation of the world by God, one means that the world, being created freely yet in its constitution contingent on God, possesses a kind of contingent rationality (this is reflected in the words *constitution* and *contingency*). The combination of the two words *contingent* and *rational* seems contradictory, for *rational* can be understood as structural and, hence, necessary. The genuine meaning of the phrase "contingent rationality" points toward the Christian assertion that the world is created by God because of God's own plan, that is, because of God's own uncreated "rationality," so that the rationality of the created world, as intelligible and comprehensible, depends on the uncreated rationality of God. This implies that any attempt to comprehend the worldly structures by exercising the faculties of contingent rationality granted to man will inevitably appeal to something that transcends this rationality, that is, to the ground of the contingent world, which is relational upon God. The world is not self-explanatory; its comprehension will always depend on some meta-level of explanation, originating from the uncreated rationality of God. This makes it possible to assert that the created realm, being contingent on God, yet contains some features of *necessity,* which means that creation is dependent on God.[18] One may speak about contingent necessity of the world, which expresses some freedom in its structures and their interactions and changes, on the one hand, and the limitedness of this freedom, which preserves the world from complete chaos and arbitrariness, on the other hand. Contingency and necessity combine to make the world unique: free in its self-expression and progression, granted by the freedom of the divine creation, and necessary, by being always dependent on the life of God, who maintains the being of the universe.

It is the concept of the incarnation of the Logos of God in flesh that clarifies the presence of the necessary dimension in the contingent creation. This dimension is associated with the intelligibility of the universe, its order and uniformity.[19] In this, the incarnation of the Word-Logos of God provides us with a "vertical" dimension to everything that is involved in temporal flux in the created existence, treated as the horizontal dimension. Using the words of T. Torrance, the supreme axis of the incarnation is provided for the direct interaction with creation within its contingent existence and structure.[20] The incarnation is not to be regarded as an intrusion into the creation or into the structures of space-time but, rather, as the freely chosen way of God's rational love in the fulfillment of the eternal purpose of the universe. The incarnation thus functions as the re-creation and deepening of the order in the universe, which is threatened by chaos and decay.

Being an eschatological act in its essence, as the affirmation of the kingdom of God, the incarnation of the Word of God establishes the goal of all movements in the universe as directed to their rest (stasis). In individual terms, it means the reaching of the union with God by involving the whole creation in the process of deification, through the liturgy of thanksgiving offered to the Father, the supreme creator and planner of human salvation.

Cosmology thus can be an instrument that helps reveal the necessary features in the contingent creation, which, theologically speaking, are associated with the creation of the universe by the Word-Logos of God. As discussed in chapter 4, the Logos is present in the world through the logoi, whose immanent function is to hold the created things, to provide the purpose and end for their existence. Detecting the presence of the logoi of creation in the world by means of scientific investigation can, in some sense, provide the evidence for creation, not in a literal sense, as an explanation of creation out of nothing in causal terms, but rather as a contribution toward the understanding of the creative rationality of the uncreated Logos of God, God's unfolding revelation to the world, which will be expressed scientifically in various forms of the never-ending advance of science.

From this Patristic perspective, one can guess that science, and cosmology in particular, cannot seriously challenge the Christian doctrine of creatio ex nihilo, for cosmology, being a worldly thing by construction, would rather attempt to "explain" the creation of the universe in terms of physical mechanism, which operates in matter as a priori given. The question about the existence of elementary matter as well as the laws that govern it cannot be properly addressed by cosmology at all, for the laws that manifest a particular existence do not justify the existence itself. In other words, the laws of nature provide us with some reference to the necessary aspect of contingent creation, as creation exercised according to the divine plan. It does not provide us, however, with the tools suitable for the explanation of the contingency of the world itself, that is, why the world was created in this particular shape but not in another.

Science, and particularly cosmology, can challenge the *ex nihilo* concept in a disguised fashion—namely, when it claims that there will soon be the end of science, that is, that the ultimate theory of everything is nearly built and there will be nothing to explain further. This claim was made, for example, by S. Hawking in his famous speech of 1980 titled "Is the End of Theoretical Physics in Sight?"[21] The claim was later repeated by Hawking in his book *A Brief History of Time,* when he affirmed that the ultimate theory will make us capable of the knowledge of the mind of God.[22] What was prophesied by Hawking is the end of scientific advance, that is, that science will come to a standstill by discovering all the laws that are to explain the universe without an appeal to any transcendent reference. This, according to Hawking, will be the knowledge of the mind of God, leading ultimately to God's redundancy, for the idea of God is not needed anymore if the world is explained from within itself, and if the laws thus found form the absolute attributes of the world and sustain its existence. The world thus is not contingent at all; it is necessary in an absolute philosophical sense. The only viable philosophy that could support this conclusion would be a scientific monism, the ancient ideal of the Greeks. If this were to happen, the Classical *ex nihilo* doctrine would be "disproved," or, more precisely, abandoned, for the world does not need to be created—it just exists according to the inherent laws.

The knowledge of these laws would make humans the divine beings, for they would know the ultimate truth. Science itself, in its accomplished form, would probably also acquire nonhuman features, for it is through *knowledge* of the ultimate truth that mankind would deify itself in a fashion that was only dreamed of by Gnostics, who were fought by the early church fathers. But the ultimate truth is not a human product. According to A. Chalmers, truth is "preordained by the nature of the world before science is ever embarked on. Science . . . if it were ever to reach this end point, so conceived, would abruptly change from being a human, social product to being something that in the strong sense, is not a human product at all."[23]

It is conceivable from what we have just said that science, being a human, social enterprise (that is, not being a divine activity), is in a state of infinite advance, an endless unfolding of the rationality of nature, which points toward its contingency, whose necessary features are being caught by science. As the deification of man is not possible through knowledge (being a kind of intellectual heresy similar to the Gnosticism of the second century), the ultimate theory of physics, whatever is meant by this, will never replace the theological doctrine of *creatio ex nihilo,* which affirms that the world is infinitely contingent on God, the presence of whose transcendent rationality can be revealed by human and social scientific discourse.

Along the lines of this approach to the problem of creation, we will now analyze what model cosmology can offer toward understanding the meaning of creation as it is conceived from within the world.

Creation in Classical Cosmology: Cosmological Evolution and Initial Conditions

We should start by recalling that classical cosmology (nonquantum cosmology), being a part of classical physics, takes for granted that the description of physical processes in the universe is made in terms of preexisting space and time. Cosmology uses Einstein's theory of general relativity to model the spatiotemporal continuum of the universe. Space and time in general relativity are relational upon matter content, so that spatiotemporal dynamics in the universe is linked to matter. This implies that if cosmology were to attempt to explain the origin of space and time, it would also explain the origin of matter in the universe. It becomes even more clear in the light of the geometrical interpretation of gravitational field developed in general relativity; to explain the origin of space-time would mean to explain the origin of all matter, including the gravitational field itself.

This presents a real challenge for cosmology, for this kind of explanation would definitely transcend physics. To explain the origination of matter and space-time from "something" that is not matter and not space-time is probably an inconceivable task for physics, which is based on the classical concept of causation. Such an explanation would require cosmology to model the transition from a philosophical "nothing" ("no-thing" in an absolute sense, not a physical vacuum) to something (fields, particles, space-time); this modeling not only is an improper task for cosmology but also demands a philosophical and theological logic, when the creation of matter and space-time would be expressed in apophatic terms, that is, in terms of its relation to a transcendent source.

Despite this general understanding, classical cosmology experiences a serious difficulty when it has to speculate about the temporal origin of the visible cosmos. This problem is inherent for cosmology, which affirms that the universe experiences global expansion. Since the dynamics of this expansion is described by the Einstein equations, for example, by the equations for the universal scale factor a, which is a function of cosmological time t, the extrapolation of the solution of this equations for $a(t)$ backward in time leads inevitably to such a point where $t = 0$ and $a = 0$. This point in the evolution of the universe is logically called the beginning of the universe, the point beyond which physics and cosmology cannot proceed, for most of the classical concepts lose their sense.[24]

If cosmological theory, by extrapolating the expansion of the universe backward in time, were to predict that all physical matter and space-time disappears at the point of the "beginning," then there would be a justified temptation to announce that the point of the beginning is the absolute *origin* of the universe in terms of both space and time—that is, no thing was before this point in terms of the cosmological time t. In reality, however, the situation is completely opposite; the values of all physical parameters reach infinity at the point of beginning: density of matter (ρ), and the curvature of space-time (R) become infinite when a approaches zero:

$$\rho \longrightarrow \infty, R \longrightarrow \infty, \text{ as } a \longrightarrow 0$$

It is because of this that the initial state of the classical universe is called the big bang or, cosmologically, the singularity. Both matter and space-time experience extraordinary behavior at this point, which is hardly to be described by physics, and there is no ground to claim that there was *nothing* at the singularity. On the contrary, all physical quantities are infinite (that is, indefinite) there, so that no particular specification of the initial state is possible; all hypotheses leading to these infinite values will be untestable and useless even in terms of their heuristic function.

The appearance of infinities in cosmology is inevitable if one assumes the classical forms of matter in the universe, such as radiation and dust.[25] As discussed before, cosmology with classical forms of matter leads to a series of problems, which can be overcome if one invokes the presence in the universe of "nonclassical" matter, such as quantum fields described in modern parlance either as "inflaton" (ϕ) or "cosmological constant" λ. In these models, the dynamics of the universe is driven either by decaying inflaton ϕ or cosmological parameter λ. Formally, inflationary cosmology succeeds in removing the singularity at $t = 0$ and placing it in the asymptotic limit $t \longrightarrow \infty$, so that the problem of the beginning of the universe is converted into the problem of its preexistence in infinite time. The preexistent vacuum state decays in time, driving the evolution of the universe to its present state. The only advantage of this model is that the average energy of the vacuum state, which is given by λ, is finite at all times, including the limit $t \longrightarrow -\infty$, so that inflationary cosmology allows one to avoid a bizarre conclusion about the apocalyptic state of matter and geometry at the big bang.[26] It can clearly be seen that if one talks about "creation" of the universe in this case, this is the production of matter not out of nothing but out of matter described either by ϕ or by λ, whose preexistence is postulated.

In both cases—cosmology with classical matter as well as inflationary cosmology—physics fails to explain the nature of the initial condition for equations that drive cosmological evolution. The dichotomy between the laws of dynamics and the initial conditions that fix a specific outcome of these laws acquires some unique features in cosmology. Since we can speculate on the nature of these conditions only from within our universe by extrapolating backward the properties of the observable universe, the "knowledge" of the initial conditions thus achieved does not tell us anything about the genuine nature of these conditions, as if there were special physical laws responsible for these conditions, separated from us in the past and not being similar to laws of dynamics. Being bounded by the universe in which we live, we cannot know the laws of the initial conditions of the universe; for this would require us to transcend the universe, which is impossible.

The ideal variant for cosmologists wishing to describe the creation of matter in the universe would be to construct an initial state such that the total energy of matter would equal zero and that this requirement would be a meta-law, imposed on the matter of the future universe in the preexistent space and time. This kind of a model was offered by Tryon and was treated later from a philosophical point of view by Isham.[27] The major feature of this model is that the universe originates in preexistent space and time as a result of a fluctuation of the physical vacuum (a physical state of quantum matter in which the values of all observables of particles are zero). Geometrically, the development of the universe can be presented as a future light cone, whose apex is positioned completely arbitrarily in preexistent space and time.

This constitutes a philosophical difficulty with this model: it is impossible to specify and justify why the universe originated at a specific point of space and time. In this theory, the spontaneous creation of the universe (as a result of a fluctuation) could occur anywhere and at any moment of time. This means that the variety of different universes could originate at different locations of the preexistent space-time, driving cosmology to face the serious problem of the mutual influence of different universes. Definitely, this kind of model has nothing to do with creation out of nothing in a theological sense, for space, time, the meta-law, and the quantum vacuum are all assumed to be preexistent. It is reasonable to talk about the *temporal origination* of the visible material universe rather than about its creation out of nothing.

It is interesting to note that the first "scientific" ideas on the origination of the universe in preexistent space and time were proposed by Newton, who intended to reconcile the biblical account of creation, in which the world had to have a beginning, with his view that time could have neither beginning nor end. Newton asserted that the visible universe was brought into existence by God in the past, which is separated from us by finite time, but that this took place within the absolute and infinite space and time. The creation of matter is detached in his model from the creation of time. We see here a fundamental difference from general relativity, where space and time are relational upon matter, so that the split in origination of matter and time becomes theoretically inconsistent.[28]

The logical difficulty with this kind of model is connected with our inability to locate the moment of time where the universe originated, from outside, by transcending the universe itself, into its imaginable preexistent "before." One cannot know whether the big bang was preceded by a "big crunch" or not. We can argue about the absolute beginning of time within the visible universe by extrapolating its expansion backward in time, but this will never allow us to claim scientifically that there either was or was not preexistent time "before" our universe came into existence. This situation was described by Kant in terms of his first cosmological antinomy:

Thesis: The world has a beginning in time and is also limited as regards space.

Antithesis: The world has no beginning and no limits in space; it is infinite as regards both time and space.[29]

In modern terms, the thesis corresponds to the view that the universe as we know it is unique and that the big bang is an absolute beginning of the universe as well as of time and space. There are no reasonable arguments about existence of anything beyond our universe and "prior" to the big bang; the latter is the absolute beginning of being. Any attempt to speculate about "outside" and "before" the universe would be, in the spirit of the Kantian philosophy, an ambitious attempt of reason to depart from the empirical series of causation, corresponding to the visible universe, toward purely intelligible series, which have no ontological significance.

The antithesis corresponds to the model of the universe with preexistent time and space, in which the visible universe is one particular realization of a potentially infinite number of existing universes, corresponding to different initial conditions at different moments of preexistent time. Because of the impossibility of locating the point of origination of our universe in preexistent time, and hence of making this point special, one cannot claim that there is no time and space beyond the visible universe. It can originate at any moment of preexistent time so that that could be, potentially, an infinite time before the visible universe came into being. All points of preexistent space and time are equivalent; space and time are uniform and infinite.

One can look at the same antinomy from a different perspective. For example, the thesis can be treated as an affirmation that the visible universe is unique, whereas the antithesis can be treated as the opposite—that is, that the visible universe, being finite in terms of its temporal past, is one particular representative out of the ensemble of the universes with different boundary conditions (that is, in different moments of their origination in preexistent time). In this setting, the antinomial nature of any propositions about the origination of the visible universe in preexistent time becomes evident: on the one hand, we cannot transcend our universe in order to assert scientifically that we are a part of the big ensemble of the universes; on the other hand, nothing can stop us from making a Platonistic assumption that there is the ensemble of the universes, which we cannot verify empirically but can affirm through an intellectual inference. In this case, the whole meaning of the antinomy reveals itself as predication about two ontologically distinct realities, the empirical visible universe and the Platonic ensemble of the universes.

The presence of such an antinomy in cosmology with preexistent time points, as understood before, to the fundamental ontological difference (*diaphora*) in the created realm, which is inevitably invoked by reason when it tries to speculate about the origins of the world. The antinomy analyzed here points toward the conceptual and ontological difference between empirical time in the visible universe and Platonic-like time in the preexistent but conceptual universe. The attempt to explain the origination of the visible universe out of an ensemble of possible universes can then be interpreted as a *conceptual* causation from the world of ideas to the empirical world; this, according to our previous conclusion, indicates not the creation of the universe itself but, rather, a special aspect of differentiation as its constitutive element—the *diaphora* between empirical and sensible.

One can draw a preliminary conclusion that all models of origination of the universe in preexistent time will never explain the origination in empirical, scientific terms, and that, instead, they will indicate a problem of the dualism between the evolution of the observable universe (which follows the laws of dynamics, testable in principle) and its initial conditions (which are untestable in principle and which constitute instead the realm of metaphysics, or the physics of ideas). As E. McMullin commented, the spontaneous, uncaused origination of the universe, such as that proposed in Tryon's model, strictly speaking cannot be a "creation" in a proper sense, for the cause of creation (that is, a creator), which must be outside the chain of spatiotemporal events in the universe, cannot be present in the physical theory. This means that the desire to justify "the creation" in cosmology, as causation in a rather philosophical sense, leads the scientist beyond physics into the realm of philosophical ideas or even theology.[30]

The unsatisfactory nature of the assumption that the universe was created in (pre-existent) time was recognized as early as the Patristic writers, who defended the concept of creation of the world *ex nihilo*. Basil the Great, in his *Hexaemeron* ("The Commentary on Six Days of Creation"), distinguishes between the creation of the intelligible world with no temporal flux and no spatial dimension, and the creation of the visible universe together with "the succession of time, for ever passing on and passing away and never stopping in its course."[31] Basil asserts that the meaning of the biblical phrase "In the beginning God created" must be understood as "in the beginning of time," that is, that God created the visible world together with time and it was the beginning of time in the visible world.[32] To articulate the atemporal nature of "the beginning of the world," and to remove any causation at the beginning in terms of time series, Basil affirms that "the beginning, in effect, is indivisible and instantaneous . . . the beginning of time is not yet time and not even the least particle of it."[33]

Augustine, in his *Confessions* 11, addresses the problem of the origin of time directly, affirming similarly to Basil, while using quite contemporary words, that "the way, God, in which you made heaven and earth was not that you made them either in heaven or on earth. . . . Nor did you make the universe within the framework of the universe. There was nowhere for it to be made before it was brought into existence."[34]

The last sentence is a proper theological reaction to any cosmology with preexistent time. If we attempt to talk about creation of the universe out of nothing in cosmology, it means that we cannot use for this the cosmological models in which the visible universe originates in the universe "at large," preexistent with respect to the visible one. Similarly, Augustine asserts that the universe was not created by God in time but was created with time.[35] Augustine affirmed the creation of the universe and of time within it as the only consistent expression of the Christian affirmation of *creatio ex nihilo*. The *nihilo* could not be something; it could not have any attributes of the created things. Rather, it must be absolute philosophical no-thing. In particular, it is not in time and space.

It is clear, then, that if cosmology hopes to challenge the theological teaching on *creatio ex nihilo,* it must at least refuse any models of the universe with preexistent time. In other words, time itself must be explained as a result of cosmological theory. This sounds suspicious at first glance, for any physical theory assumes time as a necessary background in which the dynamics and change take place. A reasonable starting point in this attempt, however, is to find such models of the universe in which the initial state will manifest a singularity similar to global space, so that it will not require any assumptions about preexistent time. The initiation of the visible universe takes place at this singularity, so that empirical time originates at this singularity and the universe can be said to be created not in time but in the preexistent space of the singularity.

If one assumes that there is a variety of initial conditions at the global spatial singularity, then the "physics" of this variety is very problematic again. One can produce very exotic theories about the global initial space, but they will have a limited impact for the verifiability of this theory in the visible universe, whose initial conditions are posed only in a tiny domain of the global surface. This is why any proposal for the nature of a global singularity that covers all possible initial conditions would be untestable by definition, even with all the information available in the visible universe.[36]

At any rate, the model of the origination of the visible universe from the global space-like singularity assumes that there was a finite time back when the observable universe came into existence and started to develop to its present state. Time was brought into existence together with the universe, and the problem of the positioning of our universe in preexistent time is not present in such a scenario. At the same time, if the global singularity is assumed to be in existence prior to what we call our universe, it is difficult to assert that the universe was created out of nothing, for the point of origination of the universe is positioned at the initial singularity, which is not nothing in a theological sense but is preexistent space. It is clear, then, that one can apply the same argument, which we used before in the context of an antinomial proposition similar to the first antinomy of Kant, in which the word *time* is omitted. From a philosophical point of view, the difficulty of predicating on the origin of the universe in terms of different initial conditions in space is the same at it was before for models with preexistent time.

This implies that the next logical step would be to attempt to modify the theory in order to remove all preexistent entities, such as time or space, and to construct the model of the universe in which space and time would originate together with matter. Can this be done in cosmology?

To make clearer what kind of problem we face here, let us compare the dynamics of the particle in classical mechanics, on the one hand, and the dynamics of the universe in general relativity, on the other hand. The difference can be understood easily from the diagram in figure 5.1:

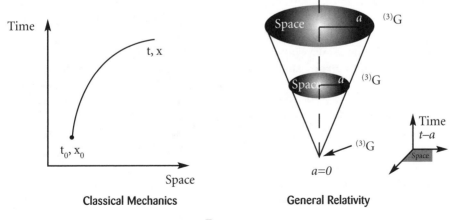

FIGURE 5.1

At the left-hand side, we have a trajectory of a particle in a configurational space, which describes the transition in preexistent space and time from the original point (t_0, x_0) to some arbitrary point (x, t). At the right-hand side, we have a cone, whose vertical axis corresponds to what we call time, and two perpendicular dimensions to space. The fundamental difference between classical mechanics and general relativity is that there is no preexistent time in the latter case. Space in general relativity is a relational concept; its dynamics follows the dynamics of matter, and it is a three-dimensional space $^{(3)}G$, which is the dynamical variable in relativity and cosmology. Time emerges in relativity as parameter, which describes the change of the three-space $^{(3)}G$; it can be, for example, the changing radius of the section of the cone perpendicular to its vertical axis in figure 5.1. It is clear that there is no direct analogy between classical mechanics and general relativity theory, for the internal dynamics of $^{(3)}G$ can be described as "evolution" in the continuum with the dimension larger than $^{(3)}G$, that is, in space-time $^{(4)}G$ only postfactum, or when the global dynamics of $^{(4)}G$ is defined. The fact that time is not a preexistent entity but is defined by the dynamics of space $^{(3)}G$ can be easily understood if one realizes that the spatial sections of the complex $^{(4)}G$ can be drawn arbitrarily with respect to the vertical dimension of the graph, thus also defining the time variable arbitrarily.

The common feature of both the classical description of dynamics of a single particle and the evolution of 3-space $^{(3)}G$ is that both have a "point" of the beginning. In the case of space-time, it means that the three-space $^{(3)}G$ has a zero radius—for example, a zero radius of the universe, beyond which theory cannot be extrapolated and all concepts such as space and time lose their sense. From this point of view, one could argue that this is exactly the point at which space and time come into existence, at which they are created. The problem, however, typical for classical dynamics as well as for cosmology, is that there is a dichotomy between the laws of dynamics and initial conditions; there is a variety of solutions corresponding to the dynamical equations that drive the evolution and that contain a conical singularity, as presented in figure 5.1. The theory cannot select a particular solution that would be unique and would correspond to the visible universe.

We thus face a problem of how to remove this initial point from the solutions. In classical mechanics, it is impossible to do it at all, for time and space do preexist and form a background for development of a system. The initial condition corresponds to a choice, made by an observer when that person starts to follow the evolution of a particle. In the case of relativity, the situation is much more exciting, for the beginning of time corresponds to some particular properties of space, when the radius of the universe is zero, for example. This point forms a problem for classical physics, for all physical observables approach infinite values in the vicinity of this point; classical physics collapses at the singularity.[37] At the same time, as was proved by S. Hawking and R. Penrose, the singularity in classical general relativity is inevitable. The presence of the initial singularities in general relativity leads to the impossibility of formulating in physical terms the initial conditions of the visible universe. The dichotomy between the initial conditions and the laws of the evolution of the universe becomes unbridgeable in classical general relativity. If this is true, and we cannot specify in physical terms the "laws" of the initial conditions of the universe, we cannot not fully answer the question of the nature of the visible universe. In this case, a deistic temptation enters the cosmologist's mind; one appeals to a deity who did set up the initial conditions and the laws of the universe but then left the universe to its own devices. Physics and cosmology provide us with the understanding of the laws of the evolution of the universe, but they do not teach us what was God's choice in setting up the initial conditions.

In theology, which advocates that the created order is contingent on God (radically different from God) and that the laws of the world are free from any inherent necessity, originating from God, it would be very ambitious to pretend to uncover the "laws" that stand behind the initial conditions of the universe. This is because with the knowledge of these laws—that is, knowing that the initial conditions of the visible universe are conditioned by something that is ontologically necessary—we would enter the domain of the divine reason and attempt to apprehend God's intentions in creating the world. This is, however, hardly to be achieved in cosmology on its own, so that theology enters the scene of speculation at this point.

Some cosmologists argue for the possible comprehension of the laws of boundary conditions of the visible universe in principle. Hawking, for example, appeals to the history of science to argue that this history eventually uncovers the underlying order of things and events that seemed to be incoherent and arbitrary before. He believes that the same kind of order can be found in the extreme physical situation at the cosmological singularity: "There ought to be some principle that picks out one initial state and hence one model, to represent our universe."[38]

This belief should in a way contradict the result on inevitability of the singularities in cosmologies with all pathological features of the theory, which we mentioned above (infinities of all classical physical variables). This, in turn, provides us with an argument that the "law" of the initial conditions must be nonclassical, different and new in comparison with what is known from general relativity. These laws, if they exist, should avoid the problem of temporal beginning, which has its root in the asymmetry between space and time. Indeed, the conical space-time of the universe has one particular feature, which makes the whole geometry $^{(4)}G$ singular: its boundary is formed by a conical surface plus a singular point, the apex of a cone. The new nonclassical laws of the singularity, if they exist, must change our view on space-time of the universe as a singular cone. This means that the geometrical presentation of the evolution of the visible universe, as presented in figure 5.1, must be replaced by something with a different, nonsingular boundary. In this case, the problem of the beginning of time, according to the proponents of the laws of the initial conditions, would be explained away and no theistic references would be necessary order to explain the "temporal origin" of the world. How successful is this program?

Elimination of Real Time in Quantum Cosmology

It must be explained first of all that when Hawking advocates the existence of the laws of the initial conditions—that is, that the new physics of the singular state of the universe can be developed—he, in fact, assumes that the whole of cosmology must be transformed from being a classical view of the universe into the so-called quantum cosmology. The latter "theory" represents an as yet unfinished synthesis of general relativity and quantum mechanics applied to the universe as a whole. This synthesis is a big issue in modern physics and needs to be subjected to a long philosophical scrutiny, which is not a topic for this book.[39] The very possibility of this synthesis is based on fundamentally nonclassical physical ideas that, it is believed, can contribute to the attempts at challenging the *creatio ex nihilo* concept scientifically. Our interest thus will be in the analysis not of the logical consistency of the synthesis between cosmology and quantum physics but, rather, of some of its concepts that can indirectly contribute to the theology of creation of the world out of nothing, understood Patristically.

The challenge of quantum cosmology is to provide the "laws" of the initial conditions of the visible universe, that is, to describe the state of origination of the universe in such ontologically necessary terms as to condition the emergence of time in the universe. This means that in no way must time be an ingredient of these laws. At the same time, quantum cosmology does not deny the presence of space in these laws. In other words, space is considered a more fundamental ontological reference than time. The visible universe is in space and in time; the state that is prior to the visible universe cannot be in time, but it is accepted that it can be in space. The existence of space, which is devoid of temporality, is considered as existence forever, with no need for an explanation of "when" this space came into existence. The timeless state of the universe (as a pure space) can be considered an initial member in a series of temporal causation, which itself is beyond time.

The conceptual transition from classical to quantum physics can be understood as a change of the description of physical objects as having some given positions in space—for example, let us say x, y at a given moment of time—to the description of the dynamics of objects in terms of the so-called wave function Ψ, which is a function of x, y and is subject to evolution in time according to the Schrödinger equation. It is important that the coordinates of the particle cannot be observed precisely, as occurs in classical mechanics, but one talks about the probability of the particle to be found in the vicinity of the point x, y, which is described by the square of the modulus of the wave function $p(x, y) = |\Psi(x, y)|^2$. In general, p is a function of time, and its evolution is completely determined by the Schrödinger equation, subject to our knowledge of the initial distribution of probabilities p_0 at some moment of time t_0. The evolution described by the Schrödinger equation is reversible—that is, knowing the initial state, one can predict all other states in the evolution of a particle, and, vice versa, one can restore the initial condition if the state of the particle is known afterward. In this sense, the evolution, even in quantum mechanics, is ahistorical; no novelty is generated in the system since it started its development from the initial state. The specificity of the system is thus determined by the setting of particular initial conditions that are not subject to dynamics. The most considerable conceptual change when one enters the sphere of quantum physics is that the description of physical processes is done in terms of the wave function Ψ, which is not a physical observable in principle. As a mathematical object, it belongs to the abstract Hilbert space, whose ontology is obviously detached from the empirical world and represents, rather, the world of Platonic forms.

The synthesis of quantum physics with general relativity, especially in its application to cosmology, leads to a novel feature of the resulting theory that did not exist in the quantum physics of micro-objects. Indeed, as mentioned in the previous section, relativity experiences some difficulties with the introduction of time. Time is not a natural parameter in the theory; rather, it is an epiphenomenon constructed upon the primary dynamical variable, which is three-dimensional space $^{(3)}G$. This means that if one wants to construct a quantum state of the whole universe (that is, to describe this mathematically by the wave function of the universe), this function will not be a function of time explicitly; rather, it will be the function of three-geometry ($^{(3)}G$) and matter (some field for example, which we denote as φ), which is linked to geometry according to general relativity. The state of the universe is thus described by the wave function $\Psi[^{(3)}G, \varphi]$ which is defined in the superspace of all possible three-dimensional geometries as well as all possible states of matter. Time is not present in this "frozen" formalism.

In a quasiclassical domain, where the function $\Psi(t)$ follows from a Schrödinger equation with time t, the evolution of the universe follows a simple, *reversible* dynamics. This means that if one can predict the state of the universe at t_2, knowing its state at $t_1 < t_2$, that is, $\Psi(t_2) = U(t_2, t_1)\,\Psi(t_1)$, then one can reverse this formula and predict the past state of the universe (at t_1) if one knows it at present (at t_2), for example, $\Psi(t_1) = U^{-1}(t_2, t_1)\Psi(t_2)$, where U^{-1} is the inverse transform that exists because the evolution is reversible. Now quantum cosmology says its decisive word in order to construct a wave function Ψ that would be unique and would satisfy the required boundary conditions. Since we want to find such a solution, which corresponds to the initial state in terms of time t, there must be such a solution $\Psi(t^*)$ for which dynamics toward the times less than t^* would not be possible—that is, the transform U^{-1} could not be constructed and applied to $\Psi(t^*)$. This would be by definition the "origination" solution, which allows its quasiclassical continuation only for t that is greater than t^*. This solution would correspond to such a state of the universe, which would not be itself in time. It nevertheless would provide us with the conditions for emergence of time as flowing in one particular direction from the "moment" of its origination.

As mentioned before, the solution for Ψ, which provides a conical singularity of a type as depicted in figure 5.1, and where the initial point of space and time (the apex of the cone) corresponds to the beginning of space and time together, is not a good candidate. This is because it represents a space-time with a boundary, which is the surface of the cone plus the point of origination. Thus the desirable solution for $^{(4)}G$

in the quantum domain should, rather, correspond to the geometry where the four-dimensional space-time has only one three-dimensional boundary. At first glance, this kind of solution does not relieve us from the presence of time, for the boundary of four-dimensional space contains a temporal dimension. The crucial step that has been taken in order to overcome this concern is a conceptual change in views on the asymmetry between space and time, which is an attribute of the macroscopic experience. In simple words, one can say that time was considered an extra-dimension of four-dimensional space. The important feature of this new time is that it is not a real time, not a time of our everyday experience. Rather, it is a mathematical abstraction of time, such that it makes an imaginary time (in a sense of complex numbers) to be principally unobservable and nonmeasurable. The trick is simple technically but is not so convincing philosophically.

The idea to geometrize time in a modern physical context and in terms of a rigorous mathematical language dates back to the developments of special relativity, in which the unification of space and time in one complex was achieved through the concept of the *interval* between two events, which is usually treated as a metric (that is, the device that allows one to measure distances between any events in space-time, which is known as Minkowski space). The interval between two close events is usually presented as

$$\Delta s^2 = c^2 \Delta t^2 - \Delta x^2 - \Delta y^2 - \Delta z^2,$$

where c is the speed of light. There is an asymmetry between the temporal variable t and the spatial variables x, y, and z in the last formula, which has a deep philosophical meaning—namely, that despite being united into the complex with space, time is still fundamentally distinct from space, for the presence of time with a different sign in the formula for the interval makes it possible to talk about the motions of particles in time and about the evolution of physical systems in time in general. For example, according to the principle of special relativity that the velocity of physical objects cannot exceed the speed of light c, all physical motions are possible only if $\Delta s^2 > 0$. This makes the graphical presentation of the propagation of signals in space asymmetric by definition, for it is only the motions within the light cone (defined as the loci of the equation $\Delta s = 0$) that are allowed in physics, which treats space and time as *real* measurable entities. In other words, if one treats time t as empirical time corresponding to our subjective experience of temporal flow, time is different from space physically and mathematically. Space-time as a whole, depicted with the help of the Minkowski diagram, is nonuniform, for there are regions in space-time, which are prohibited for physical processes. This implies that the very abstraction of unifying space and time into one Minkowski space must not mislead anyone about the empirically evident difference between space and time.

It is clear, however, that the formal trick of introducing a new imaginary time $\tau = ict$, where i is a complex (not real) unit with a property $i^2 = -1$, allows one to rewrite the metric Δs^2 in the form

$$\Delta s^2 = -\Delta \tau^2 - \Delta x^2 - \Delta y^2 - \Delta z^2,$$

where the new temporal variable τ enters the metric of space-time on equal footing with space. If one introduces the notation $\tau = x_4, x = x_1, y = x_2, z = x_4,$ then the form of the interval becomes (up to the minus sign) Euclidean:

$$-\Delta s^2 = \Delta x_1^2 + \Delta x_2^2 + \Delta x_3^2 + \Delta x_4^2.$$

Time $\tau = ict$ acquires in this formalism the features of an extraspatial dimension, so that the difference between the temporal nature of imaginary time τ and space disappears completely. If now someone recklessly identifies the ontological status of the imaginary time τ with that of the real empirical time t, the temptation would be great to claim that there is no distinction between space and time in general and that, using the words of H. Minkowski, "space by itself, and time by itself, are doomed to fade away into mere shadows, and only a kind of union of the two will preserve an independent reality."[40] The philosophical danger of this claim, which, as we will see later, Hawking makes in his quantum cosmology, will be a subject of our special attention in the next section.

Now we must elucidate further how the geometrization of time—its actual removal—happens in Hawking's model. The transition to imaginary time, which leads to the conceptual change of the whole theory, is dictated in quantum cosmology by two reasons: (1) It attempts to provide the description of the initial conditions of the universe with no reference to anything beyond the universe, which could condition the initial conditions from outside; thus it is believed that the initial conditions of the universe could be inferred as a part of a theory. And, (2) in calculating the main object of quantum description of the universe (that is, the abstract wave function), which is supposed to provide as a solution the geometrical configuration of the universe, the method, used by Hawking, involved the so-called path integral, the mathematical object, defined on the set of all possible universes (this set is called superspace, for the elements of this superspace are all imaginable three-dimensional spaces). This mathematical method, however, imposed a serious constraint on the form of those metrics (spaces), whose paths should appear in the integral. As Hawking writes: "It seems, therefore, that the path integral for quantum gravity must be taken over nonsingular Euclidean metrics" (that is, over the metrics with imaginary time).[41] One should remember this statement for our further analysis, for it illustrates a remarkable inference in theoretical cosmology: the purely mathematical requirement for consistency and the nonsingular nature of calculations lead to a choice of the set of geometries with no obvious reference to the physical world. As Hawking expressed this in *A Brief History of Time*: "To avoid the technical difficulties with Feynman's sum over histories, one must use imaginary time."[42]

The crucial point now is to formulate proper initial conditions for the space-time of the universe, assuming that the universe in not pseudo-Euclidean (as depicted in figure 5.1), but Euclidean—that is, that time and space are equal and "there is no difference between the time direction and directions of space."[43] There are two "natural" (mathematical) choices: the infinite Euclidean space, which incorporates time, and the compact (finite in volume) space, which does not have a boundary. Hawking provides some reasons in favor of the finite (compact) space, which constitute the essence of his and J. Hartle's "no-boundary proposal," which states that the path integral involved in calculation of the wave function of the universe must be taken over all *compact* Euclidean metrics.[44] This removes the problem of the initial conditions in the universe because, logically, the condition that is supposed to condition the initial state of the universe now reduces to a tautological statement that the universe must be initially with no boundary. In other words, the term *initial* loses its ordinary sense, for there is no special location in the universe that could be taken as an 'initial' boundary: there is no boundary. This opens a way to a new, interesting situation in physics, the removal of the problem of boundary conditions in general. This implies that the classical solutions of the cosmological models with nonphysical infinities in the singularities no longer threaten physics, so that one could be tempted to say that the collapse of physics at the cosmological singularity, which has been discussed by J. Wheeler in so many papers, is overcome.[45] There is no breakdown of physics at the edge of the universe, and hence there is no need to appeal to the "laws" of the boundary conditions, which, according to classical cosmology, would manifest the transcendent plan of the divine design rather than anything physical following the laws and logic of the visible universe.[46]

If the no-boundary proposal is implemented in theoretical calculations, it leads to a wave function of the universe as a function of the radius a of a three-dimensional section of the four-dimensional compact space, which incorporates an imaginary time. The radius a of $^{(3)}G$—that is, a three-dimensional section of the compact (with no-boundary) $^{(4)}G$—satisfies the Einstein equation that involves the distribution of matter in the universe. The radius of a three-dimensional compact space a can extend indefinitely from zero to infinity. There is, however, a threshold in terms of a, which marks a radical change in the behavior of the wave function of the universe. Indeed, if the energy density of matter in the universe is nonzero and constant, ρ for example, then the maximum radius of the closed three-dimensional universe $^{(3)}G$, as a boundary of $^{(4)}G$, will be equal to $a_{max} = \sqrt{3/\rho}$. The wave function of the universe increases exponentially in terms of a if $a < a_{max}$ and oscillates rapidly in terms of a if $a > a_{max}$. In order to illustrate the meaning of this transition in behavior of the wave function, let us make a simple analogy: consider the Schrödinger equation for a particle whose energy E is constant, but negative. It is easy to show that the so-called stationary solution of this equation has a simple oscillating form $\Psi = Ce^{(iE/\hbar)t}$. What will happen to this solution if time t is imaginary, that is, $t = -i\tau$? It is clear that the solution will change to $\Psi = Ce^{(E/\hbar)\tau}$, acquiring the features of an exponentially growing function.

This analogy suggests that the transition in the behavior of the wave function of the universe corresponds to the transition from the quantum state of the universe as a four-dimensional compact Euclidean space (with imaginary time being a spatial dimension) to the classical evolving universe, whose geometrical structure corresponds in general to the curvilinear cylinder (a special case of this kind of a cylinder is presented in figure 5.1 as a conical space-time) where its vertical dimension corresponds to real, empirical time. The change from the quantum state of the universe to the "classical" universe, whose evolution leads ultimately to what we observe as the present-day visible universe, is accompanied by the transition from imaginary time to real time.[47] Hawking proposes to present this transition graphically in the form shown in figure 5.2:

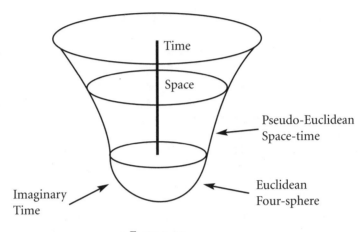

FIGURE 5.2

This transition is supposed to describe the "creation" of the visible universe. There is not, however, any point of creation, or origination of the universe, for it originates from space, which has no temporal properties (space simply exists). Thus it should be emphasized once more that the creation of the visible universe in Hawking's model is not creation as "origination"; rather, it is a transition (in a sense that will be established later) from atemporal (timeless) Euclidean space to space-time, in which time is distinct from space and where one observes the temporal flux of events.

The major achievement of the scenario proposed by Hawking is the elimination of the singular states in the history of the universe, where the physical laws break down. The absence of temporal dimension in the boundary state of the universe removes the problem of preexistent time and offers a response to the paradoxes connected with the creation in preexistent time. One should remember, however, that the validity of this response is contingent on the belief that that the world has an imaginary temporal dimension, that is, that the world is fundamentally nonempirical (as will be said later, nonphysical). Hawking suggests that if "the so-called imaginary time is really the real time, and that what we call real time is just a figment of our imaginations," then the entire universe is compact, with no boundary, so that the vision of the universe as having a beginning in the past (as well as the problem of original creation in general) is just an illusion of human consciousness.[48] Hawking's attempt to elucidate the meaning of the word *reality*, as he uses it, leads him ulti-mately to confusion, for, according to him, mathematical theory is just a model and there is no meaning in questions about the "reality" of time, whether it is imaginary or real: "It is simply a matter of which is the more useful description."[49] There is a positive asset of this quantum cosmology, however: the prediction/explanation of the behavior of the universe that when it gets off the quantum realm (that is, becomes classical), it will be like inflation of space. Inflationary cosmology is the popular model nowadays that is capable of solving some puzzles of the classical big bang cosmology.[50]

The model of inflationary cosmology, proposed by Hawking, resonated not only in professional physical and mathematical circles but also among philosophers and even theologians. This is because Hawking himself concludes his exposition of the "history of time" in the universe in a theological manner, stating that "the idea that space and time may form a closed surface without boundary also has profound implications for the role of God in the affairs of the universe."[51] Immediately after this "theological" claim, he exposes himself as a deist by asserting that one needs the idea of God in order to describe the initial conditions in the universe and to set up the laws of the universe.[52] Finally, in order to refute deism, Hawking proposes to take his scenario of the "evolution" of the universe with an imaginary time not only as a model, which helps with explanation of observations, but also ontologically: "If the universe is *really* completely self-contained, having no boundary or edge, it would have neither beginning, nor end: it would simply be."[53] The ultimate manifestation of Hawking's triumph as a "religious thinker" is in his concluding phrase, which has caused so much agitation and controversies in scientifico-theological circles: "What place, then, for a creator?"[54]

Our response to Hawking's proclamation will be established along two different lines. One line is critical, based on the analysis of logical and philosophical internal inconsistencies of the theory, which, by the virtue of public opinion established through the media, is treated as a picture of the real world. Our criticism will not repeat extensively what has already been said about this model in other sources; it will simply clarify some points and make further references to other papers. The sec-ond line is constructive for the purposes of this book; we will attempt to treat Hawking's model as regards its usefulness for theology, especially Orthodox theol-ogy. In this case, our task will be to interpret Hawking's model theologically, that is, to intentionally depart from Hawking's grounds of thought and to look at his model as something that is natural and nearly obvious for a theological mind. In doing so, our major task will be to clarify one particular point: that Hawking's way of thinking represents a stable pattern of any possible scientific attempt to affirm or deny God from within the created universe.

It should be repeated here that interpretation of Hawking's model through the eyes of Eastern Orthodox theology has nothing to do immediately with what Hawking embedded in this quantum cosmology's meaning and formalism. Rather, we follow here the prescription of the theological methodology of science that we proposed earlier. The positive aspect of our evaluation of Hawking's model is that it can be used in theology for a particular demonstration of how far in the direction of the Divine one can lift up one's theistic insight, if one attempts to make an inquiry about God by using science.

Some General Comments on Hawking's Model

When S. Hawking published *A Brief History of Time* in 1988, it had a significant impact on the development of the dialogue between science and religion.[55] As demonstrated earlier, Hawking proposed a concept of the universe in which the classical cosmological understanding of the origin of the universe as an origin in time was replaced by a view that the visible universe represents a special phase of a generally atemporal scheme of being, which does not contain any reference to the "first moment" of origination of the universe. This view led Hawking to claim that the problem of the creation of the universe in a theological sense can be removed, for the universe simply exists and does not require any ground in its existence from "outside"—that is, it does not need a creator.

In fact, if we analyze thoroughly not only particular phrases quoted by different authors outside of the overall context of Hawking's thinking but also the place of Hawking's claims in his overall philosophy, we will find that Hawking, being an idealist of a positivistic kind, makes his claims on "no place of a creator" in a manner that does not provide any evidence that his claims refer to anything ontological (that is, hypostasized as existing in either empirical or intelligible reality). If our analysis is correct, then we can assert that the point of view Hawking follows is just a matter of his personal opinion, with no serious implications for theology understood as the experience of the God-Creator.

Hawking builds his cosmology on the grounds of positivistic (according to his own definition) methodology, in an approach that never makes inquiries as to the ontological meaning of those "realities" that are present in cosmological theories. He describes his understanding of the meaning of cosmological theories as follows: "Theory is just a model of the universe, or a restricted part of it, and a set of rules that relate quantities in the model to observations we make. *It exists only in our minds* and has no other reality (whatever that might mean)."[56]

If one reads this passage straightforwardly, one will be puzzled by the emphasized part of this quotation, for it follows from it that cosmology, being a theoretical enterprise, does not provide any realistic vision of what the universe is actually but, instead, supplies only the symbolic means for the description of what we observe here and now. If cosmology exists only in our minds, it is similar to any kind of science fiction, with the only difference that it pretends to describe the entire universe in a coherent way, which will be consistent with what we observe in the sky. If one follows this view consistently, one must admit that such notions as the universe as a whole (for example, the big bang) are just mental constructs and have no independent ontological status apart from their remote effects in the present-day universe.

Summarizing in different words, cosmology as a theory dealing with the remote temporal past as well as with remote parts of its space has no ontological references, according to Hawking. All its claims have a status of conventions useful for understanding the observable universe in terms of unobservable entities, such as equations and concepts. A particular cosmological theory is valued for its quality to provide a more effective description of our observations; there is no sense in asking whether the constructs that constitute the theory referred to anything we call "real"; they matter simply as useful tools of description and no more.

Later, Hawking reaffirms his positivistic approach to cosmology by juxtaposing it with the Platonism of R. Penrose.[57] According to Hawking, Penrose is worried about the reality of those concepts that are involved in quantum cosmology, whereas it does not bother him: "I do not demand that a theory correspond to reality because I do not know what it is."[58] This last remark makes Hawking's overall philosophical position controversial.

Indeed, if cosmological theory does not provide any evidence for ontological references of cosmological constructs (such as cosmological fluid, global space-time, the wave function of the universe, and the big bang), then any predication about God (in a positive or negative sense) as the absolute cause of the temporal beginning of the universe, as inferred from a cosmological theory, has only a rhetorical sense. This is because the construct of the early universe that Hawking proposes as a "true" theory of the state of the universe that preceded one we observe now is just a construct, not an ontological entity. This implies that if Hawking wants to use the beauty and elegance of this construct to deny the existence of the God-Creator (the original cause of the universe), he tacitly levels both constructs, "the universe" and "God," making them uniform terms of the logical alternative, which, according to Hawking's logic, must exist only in his mind. If this is true, one then immediately recognizes that the "God" that is meant by Hawking in his famous phrase "What place, then, for a creator?" is just a concept, an idea of God, a mental symbol of an uncertain deity. If Hawking thinks about God (as a genuine positivist) as a construct, then he can dismiss one construct (God) in favor of another (timeless universe). But this operation of reason has no implication whatsoever for theology, which, as discussed in chapter 3, deals with the experience of the living God, who is ontologically present in the world, but not with any false, conceptual idols of God, which are strictly refused by apophatic theology.

But if Hawking believes that he can dismiss God in an ontological sense, then we should admit (by virtue of his philosophical inconsistency), first of all, that he falls into contradiction with himself, for there is no chance of comprehending the existence of the living God while resting on a positivistic view of nature. In the concluding chapter of his book, Hawking exposes his controversial thought by making a correct distinction between two questions in cosmology: (1) "What is the universe?" and (2) "Why does the universe exist?" He assumes that his response to the first question is provided by his arguments throughout his book—that is, the universe has such a particular structure, which follows from the laws of physics and a special no-boundary condition (we remember that this is a positivist's statement). But in the second question Hawking inquires not into the particular temporal origin of the universe but into the fact of the very existence of the universe. Why does the universe, which is described by the Hawking model, exist at all? This question by its essence is an ontological question, a response to which cannot be made on positivistic grounds. Hawking's hope is associated with his vision of a complete theory of the world, which "would be the ultimate triumph of human reason—for then we would know the mind of God."[59] It is still unclear whether the knowledge of "the mind of God" in the last quotation is just a mental construction of a positivist scientist or whether Hawking is speaking about knowledge of God through ontological communion with God.

The dream of the final theory as a principle that could explain the structure of the universe in self-sufficient terms, without appeal to its contingency upon a transcendent source, assumes that the advance of science in its unfolding of nature must stop at some stage, so that the ultimate knowledge will give a divine power into the hands of human beings. This could make a real challenge to the *creatio ex nihilo* concept, for knowing the laws of the universe in full would imply no necessity for a transcendent creator. This implies that Hawking's claims of dismissal of a creator of the universe in a sense of an original creation have a much more moderate impact on theology in comparison with his beliefs in the final theory, be it purely positivistic or not.[60]

It is obvious that positivism in science is hardly likely to be consistently compatible with genuine theology, which affirms the real and living God through communion with God's energies while God remains yet transcendent in his essence. As discussed before, theology, even in its exposition of Christian faith in concepts and linguistic formulas, is ultimately rooted in the mystical experience of God, which is not just hallucination and spontaneous perception but a systematic way of life and faith, receiving its evidence through the presence of the Spirit in the church and the community.

Despite the preceding criticism of Hawking's philosophical presuppositions, the goal here is to demonstrate that Hawking's model of creation of the universe out of nothing, which by no means dismisses the Christian dogma of *creatio ex nihilo,* can contribute in a sophisticated way to the Patristic understanding of the theology of creation out of nothing. This assumes that we undertake a theological interpretation of Hawking's model and that we intentionally depart from a positivistic treatment of cosmology in favor of a Platonic vision.

The line of thought here resembles to some extent the arguments raised by W. L. Craig in his serious critique of Hawking's model and its philosophical appraisal.[61] Craig reveals a valuable distinction that is tacitly present in Hawking's book between the attempts to refute God as the original cause of the universe, on the one hand, and God who is similar to sufficient reason in the philosophy of G. W. Leibniz. We entirely agree with this distinction in general, assuming that it has sense only if Hawking thinks of God in both cases as ontologically real. The major problem, however, is Hawking's ontology in general. The positivistic tone of his claims makes his analysis trivial and nonproductive; if the constructs Hawking employs are nonrealistic, there cannot be any problem with his "pseudo-theological" conclusions, which are also nonrealistic. The attempt to criticize Hawking on the grounds that the mathematical constructs he involves in cosmology are "physically unintelligible"[62] is also nonproductive, for Hawking states clearly that these constructs have no ontological references to anything in reality, for he does not know what reality is. What, then, is the meaning of all Hawking's speculations on the universe and God? Hawking does not provide a clear answer. Craig, however, argues in his paper that despite Hawking's "defunct positivism," he is leaning toward scientific realism by "ontologizing" the mathematical operations, which, according to Craig, leads to metaphysical absurdity.[63] Craig demonstrates persuasively, and we agree with him completely, that the abstractions and ideas Hawking develops in his model of the universe have no immediate references in terms of physical realities and that they are inconceivable as physical entities. This, according to Craig, "contradicts Hawking's realist expressions and intentions."[64]

This is the point where our attitude to the Hawking model differs considerably from that of Craig. Craig builds his criticism of Hawking by assuming that he managed to demonstrate the realistic nature of Hawking's pretensions in cosmology (realistic in a sense of "physical realism"). Then he successfully uncovers all contradictions between this realism and the nonphysical ideas involved in Hawking's cosmology. But this feature of Craig's criticism is obvious for any philosophical scientist, especially a cosmologist. Since all cosmological models dealing with the early universe, or its initial conditions, can be tested only in their remote effects in the present-day universe, most cosmological models have a provisional and rather methodological character with no serious hope of being tested in a visible future. That is why, for any sensible physicist, Hawking's theory and his model of the universe have, first of all, purely a theoretical and heuristic meaning, which implies that all constructs that Hawking invokes have an ontology of mathematical ideas only. Hawking himself does not recognize that he, in fact, follows instead a Platonic pattern in pursuit of truth about the universe; on the contrary, as we have seen above, he openly distances himself from Platonism.

The question then can be posed as to whether Hawking, from the point of view of an external philosopher, is a consistent Platonist. Here Craig's criticism will be quite appropriate in order to affirm that Hawking is not a consistent Platonist, for he is attempting to attach to his constructs immediate physical meaning, which, as Craig has demonstrated, leads to serious philosophical problems and which makes all of Hawking's claims on the nonexistence of a creator of the universe theologically unjustified.

It will be argued later in this chapter that Platonism is tacitly present in all of Hawking's reasoning and that the Platonic treatment of Hawking's model is the only viable option if one wants to save the content of this model from accusations of ontological inconsistency and physical unintelligibility. This option is denied by the positivist Hawking and is not recognized in Craig's realistic apology. The vision of

Platonic ontology behind all of Hawking's constructs can potentially save his theory, giving this theory a chance to contribute in a tricky way to the theology of *creatio ex nihilo*. But in no way does the Platonic treatment of Hawking's model justify his claims for the nonexistence of a creator. On the contrary, his model provides an interesting theoretical tool, which, if it is treated along the lines of Patristic theology, allows one to identify its theological meaning as an affirmation of the constitutive elements of creation and to point to a creator.

The task now is to analyze the key concepts employed by Hawking, in order to make a distinction among them in terms of their ontological nature: what is empirical in his model and what is intelligible, what is the meaning of the mixing of the empirical and the intelligible that takes place in his model, and how can this interplay between empirical and intelligible be treated by Patristic theology in order to make use of it in the theology of creation.

In exercising the theological treatment of Hawking's cosmology, we follow the scheme of mediation between science and theology that we have developed earlier. We are fully aware, however, that we intentionally interpret the theory in philosophical and theological terms that are not present in the theory itself. The meaning of our analysis is not to assess the value of this theory for theology but to articulate an idea that any scientific theory, attempting to argue on the origins of the world (including Hawking's, as an example), will tacitly contain similar features of the dualism between the empirical and the intelligible, and that any theory will be inclined to overcome this dualism in favor either of empiricism (positivism) or of idealism (for example, Platonism). The problem from a theological point of view is not simply to overcome this dualism but to identify through its analysis the presence of the otherness of the dualistic universe in the theory, which points toward God as the ground for the universe both empirical and intelligible.

Imaginary Time in Quantum Cosmology and Timeless Time in Christian Platonism

The various critical comments about Hawking's claim of no place for a creator within scientific cosmology, which are present in philosophical and theological literature, are unanimous in one particular conclusion: that the model of quantum cosmology, suggested by Hawking, in no way dismisses the Christian doctrine of *creatio ex nihilo*.[65] Neither four-dimensional Euclidean space nor matter present in the universe represent *no-thing* in a philosophical sense. One can also add that the laws of mathematics, which allow one to formulate the no-boundary proposal, are also a part of the created order, so that if one assumes that these laws are working in the early universe—that is, that they do preexist the universe—this fact probably indicates that mathematics itself is God's creation, so that the model itself does not change the status of the *nihilo* concept. This point brings us to the main theological stance of this book: the intelligibility of the universe because its ontology is relational upon the Word-Logos of God, whom we know in the creation in God's energy and through God's *logoi*, which manifest the incarnation of the purpose and end of all creation in every particular thing. Hawking's model is just an inquiry into the providential activity of God through the creation; the inquiry, based on communication with the *logoi*, implies that the meaning of Hawking's model can be understood only as some particular indication of the unfolding of the *logos* of creation to mankind.

Hawking's model provides an interesting example of the deconstruction of the temporal order of being in order to remove its temporal origination or, speaking philosophically, to make this being unoriginate, that is, unconditional with respect to temporal flux. As mentioned earlier, Hawking was heavily criticized for ontologizing the universe with the deconstructed time. This criticism is justified only if one assumes seriously that Hawking's model can be correlated with physical reality. In fact, however, Hawking's desire was to remove time as a condition under which the visible universe exists. By removing this time, he hoped to relieve the universe from time and to produce an "apophatic-temporal" model of existence, in which the apophatic stands for the unoriginate. Definitely his intention, as seen from a theological point of view, is quite clear. The difficulty, however, is that the "removal" of time in Hawking's model is not exactly what apophatic theology would expect from this procedure; for the geometrized time, time as space, is not exactly the *apophatic* deconstruction of time; rather, it is a disguise of time under a different *name*. But any name, even if it attempts to speak of the timelessness in an ordinary sense, is by definition cataphatic, and, as a result, it participates in the predicating of the ultimate reality from the side of the created. This indicates to us that the "apophaticism" used by Hawking to deconstruct the empirical temporality of the universe is not perfect enough. The genuine deconstruction of the cataphaticism in cosmology with the aim of raising it up to the theological level would correspond to the removal of all fundamental units of physical description or subjecting them to the relational status with respect to "realities" that transcend physical being. This kind of program was suggested many years ago by J. Wheeler, who was probably the only physicist who realized in full that the construction of the physical world is contingent upon the *meaning*, the intelligibility, that is not established on the impersonal level of particles and fields but originates from the community of human persons, observer/participants, whose rationality and ability to hypostasize the reality is rooted in transphysical agencies and which ultimately form the basis for the world as we understand it.[66]

This is why it is worth considering Hawking's model as a model of the created order (but definitely one radically different from that associated with the empirical temporal order), with an ultimate aim to formalize our intuition about the relation of this model to the contemplation of the *logos* of creation. The nature of the difference between the order in the universe with an imaginary time and the universe involved in temporal flux can be expressed theologically as the basic dichotomy in creation between the intelligible and the empirical. We intend to rearticulate the notion of the basic *diaphora* (difference) in creation in terms of temporality.

Recall the distinction between phenomenal reality and transcendent reality that was developed in Neoplatonism and was often used by Christian theologians to contrast the created and the Creator. At the same time, Christianity, through adapting and interpreting Neoplatonism, made a distinction between the intelligible and the empirical (phenomenal) in creation. This implied that the term *transcendent* in the Christian context was referred to the uncreated, whereas both the intelligible and the empirical were treated as immanent with and constitutive for creation.

Neoplatonists made a distinction between *time* and *eternity* that was based on the distinction in relationship between eternity and the intelligible universe, on the one hand, and between time and the visible (empirical) universe, on the other hand. In the Christian context, it can be affirmed that the realm of the intelligible has no time (in an empirical sense)—that is, it is timeless, not eternal—for it is still created, so that it has a beginning in a logical sense and cannot be called eternal in the same sense as one asserts the eternity of God. The empirical realm (the world of senses) is always in a state of temporal flux of events and the creation of novelty; from this perspective, one can use the Neoplatonic terminology to speak about timeless time of the intelligible created domain as *transcendent time*. In this context, the adjective *transcendent* stands as a contrast to empirical time, which is measured by the flow of events.

What, then, is the meaning of timeless time (or transcendent time) at all if it is detached from empirical, living time? The response to this question can come from the observation that since all sensible things, involved in temporal flux, are "mirrored" in the intelligible realm through the immanent aspects of their inner essences (*logoi*), the flux of these things itself can be "mirrored" in the intelligible world as a definite *structure* (for example, a logical structure), so that this structure would represent itself as "frozen time," as time with no succession or happenings of events, as a serial order stripped of process. This "frozen time" is called timeless time or transcendent time.

There is an interesting distinction, made by Proclus, between transcendent time as "unparticipated" time, on the one hand, and empirical time as "participated" time, on the other hand.[67] Transcendent time is a fixed "monad" in distinction with empirical time; it can be thought as a number (in a Pythagorean sense), the number of cycles of the Hellenistic universe. The temporal flux of the empirical world proceeds according to this number—that is, temporal time is derivative from transcendent time. The ontological status of transcendent time is determined as its participation in the *ousia* of an intelligible being, which is timeless. Proclus used such adjectives as *eternal, fixed,* and *unified* when he referred to transcendent time. If one appropriates transcendent time as a feature of the created realm, it would be more suitable to use the adjectives *timeless* and *immutable* with respect to it.

Proclus considered time an integral concept that unites both aspects of one and the same being. He treated time as a two-sided unity: on the one side, time is in itself (that is, there is time's inner being, which is stable, immutable, and timeless); on the other side, outwardly, with respect to the empirical world, time reveals itself as the temporal flow of events and things. The former aspect of time is unparticipated time; the latter is the time that participates in transcendent time.

Coming back to quantum cosmology, it is not difficult to catch some similarities between Hawking's model of the universe and that of Neoplatonism. Indeed, Hawking's attempt to distinguish between the reality of imaginary time of the quantum universe and the reality of empirical flowing time, which one experiences in a macroscopic visible universe, is based on his assumption about human cognitive faculties. He asserts that what one experiences as real time is just a "figment of our imagination."[68] This is similar to the Neoplatonic distinction between two sides of the same time as unparticipated and participated time. Indeed, the imaginary time in quantum universe is undivided and unified time, which is, in fact, just a spatial dimension, given in its whole span across the Euclidean universe, and is described by some number, a radius of this universe, for example. This is the inner aspect of time; it is transcendent timeless time (timeless in a sense that the order of things in this time is not identifiable as the flow of events in real time). The outward aspect of this time, which is accessible to human perception, corresponds to temporal flow in pseudo-Euclidean space-time. It is because of human intellectual ability that one can speculate that the empirical time can be thought of as imagination of transcendent time; thus one can assert that the empirical time indeed participates in transcendent time (but we know about this only through an intellectual inference).

In analogy with Pythagorean metaphysical mathematics, one can argue that the wave function of the universe, which contains implicitly all information about the entire structure of the universe as a spatial and temporal continuum, can be considered a monadic property of the universe—that is, as an intelligible totality that is conditioned only by the laws of mathematics and by the metaphysical (nonempirical) no-boundary proposal. The visible universe, as a domain in the empirical part of the created realm, is predetermined somehow by the wave function in the quantum domain. In other words, the monadic wave function of the universe, as a part of the intelligible, contains, according to the ideology of quantum cosmology, the ground for a particular realization of the visible universe. We do not want to pursue this idea in order to claim that the ontology of the visible universe is rooted in the ontology of the intelligible transcendent time and presented monadically as the wave function of the universe. This would be the desire of Hawking, probably in his ontologizing of the imaginary time, and it is exactly the issue for which he was seriously criticized.[69] Our interpretation, rather, follows a dualistic approach based on the basic dichotomy within the created world, that is, the *diaphora* between sensible and intelligible creation, with no desire to ontologize the imaginary time universe as existent on the same footing with the empirical universe. On the contrary, the comparison of quantum cosmology with the Neoplatonic treatment of time convinces us that the quantum Euclidean universe in Hawking's model is an intellectual construction—that is, its ontological status corresponds to an entity from the intelligible realm of the created world.

This makes Hawking's rhetoric on the place of a creator in the universe unsound. Indeed, the four-dimensional space of the Euclidean universe, being by its epistemological status an unobservable entity, can only be hypostasized by the reason as intelligible reality. The straight relation of this intelligible reality to the visible universe, which is made along the lines of the positivistic rhetoric of Hawking, is inconsistent.

One more note on the similarities between Hawking's model and Neoplatonic views on time is in order. There is the distinction between the so-called first and second creation that can be found in Neoplatonism. The first creation is the creation of eternity itself, whereas the second creation is the creation of time. In Hawking's case, it is difficult to talk seriously about his quantum, Euclidean universe as eternal and endless time, of the "greatest time," for in terms of imaginary time, the universe is finite. It is certain, however, that an order in imaginary time is the timeless order from the point of view of real time. In this sense, it recalls the difference between eternity and "the whole time" in Neoplatonism.

The wave function of the universe can be said to encapsulate the whole time rather than eternity. Indeed, as we have seen before, the wave function satisfies the equation that does not contain time at all; time appears later as an internal parameter, derivative from some particular spatial degrees of freedom. But since by itself the wave function represents conceptual reality—that is, it is an object from an intelligible creation—one cannot say that it describes in any plausible way *eternity*.

In analogy with Neoplatonists, who assert that the whole time is unity, which is fixed numerically (in a Pythagorean sense), and that the flowing time is derivative from the whole time—that is, its activity (*energia*) is caused by the whole time—one can see in Hawking's model a similar tendency of thought (embodied in modern mathematical formalism). This thought is that the genuine ontological time is imaginary time, and that the wholeness of this time for us human creatures, whose senses adjusted rather to the pseudo-Euclidean temporal flow, is manifested either in the abstract idea of the wave function of the universe (which, in fact, contains as a variable the variety of different geometries containing in a codified form the wholeness of their own times) or in the image of the four-dimensional Euclidean sphere. The *energeia* of this timeless transcendent time (imaginary time)—that is, the "transformation" of the "whole time" into the temporal flow in real time—corresponds to the transition from intelligible timeless time to the empirical time accessible to our senses.[70]

The major question, then, is, what is the status of the transition from imaginary time to real time? Either this transition is physically real—that is, the timeless Euclidean universe is ontologized as physical reality (which seems to be Hawking's claim when he argues as a physicist)—or this transition is purely subjective—that is, it plays merely a methodological role in justifying some observable data with no serious reference to the concept of reality that stands behind the scientific constructs involved (this is again Hawking's claim when he reveals himself as a positivist).

With no further comments on this internal inconsistency of the quantum cosmology of Hawking, which we have already touched on in a previous section, and with the reference to Craig's criticism,[71] we are inclined to interpret the transition from the intelligible Euclidean universe to the visible universe not as "physically objective" or "psychologically subjective" but, rather, as an ontological differentiation between the intelligible and the sensible universes, which is identified by spiritual reason. The fundamental difference of this interpretation from the original Hawking model, as well as from that model's critiques by other writers, is that the model of the intelligible Euclidean universe with imaginary timeless time (let us denote this universe as IU, intelligible universe) and the visible universe with real, empirical time (denoted as VU, visible universe) are both hypostasized by human reason as two ontologically *different* realms of the created order. The transition

$$IU \longrightarrow VU \text{ (fig. 5.1)}$$

which stands in quantum cosmology for the explanation of the origination of the visible universe from the quantum domain and which corresponds to the diagram in figure 5.2 receives a completely different interpretation as seen from within Christian Platonism.

The reader should remember that figure 5.2 is a typical picture reproduced in many books on quantum cosmology and its philosophical commentaries. It explains in visual terms what the model based on the no-boundary proposal attempts to say—namely, that the visible universe (VU) associated with pseudo-Euclidean structure (that is, with clear distinction between time and space) does originate from the timeless Euclidean region (IU), in which time is spatialized, being an imaginary spatial coordinate.[72] The Euclidean universe, not being in time, possesses existence with no point of origin: it just exists. The visible universe has its origin as the transition from the quantum domain to the classical domain. Both universes, IU and VU, are assumed to be on the same ontological footing in quantum cosmology, so that the diagram is supposed to present the process in the physical realm.

According to our interpretation, however, the diagram in figure 5.2 corresponds to the transition between two ontologically distinct domains, so that their linking together in one single complex, as is done in the diagram, has no more than an allegorical sense, for it unites together two ontologically different entities. The transition (5.1) then has meaning not as a causal transition from one physical stage to another but as a logical indication of the *difference* in the created domain between what is given to us as the visible universe and what is thought of as the intelligible explanation of what is visible.

The comparison of Hawking's model, which affirms the universe as a closed one with imaginary time, on the one hand, and which provides the mechanism of the emergence of the visible universe involved in temporal flux, on the other hand, with the Neoplatonic model of time as a dialectics of transcendent timeless time and flowing time, has for the purposes of our analysis the following significance.

The Neoplatonic dichotomy between transcendent and empirical time is rearticulated in the Patristic Christian context as the polarity between the intelligible and the sensible realms of creation. In other words, from a Christian perspective, the ambition of quantum cosmology to describe by using Hawking's model the *creatio ex nihilo* is unsound because, in fact, it describes rather the "origination" of that part of space-time that we associate with the visible universe, out of the timeless realm, which by its own genetic status represents an intelligible world, rather than anything physical, if one intends to ontologize it. If we refine this thought further, we must admit that Hawking's model proposes a scenario of some "changes" in the created universe (be it the intelligible or the empirical universe)—that is, in the universe that is contingent upon the Divine—through the mathematical and physical laws. The fact of this contingency is not reflected at all in quantum cosmology, which, by its methodological design, is monistic, attempting to explain the structure of the universe from within itself. The contingency, on the contrary, if someone were reveal its presence in the cosmological theory, would mean identifying the transcendent elements in the model, which point to the ground of the universe and its immanent physical and mathematical laws, which is beyond the universe and its laws.

If we use Christian Patristic terminology, we should say that the ontology of the universe, be it visible (classical) or intelligible (quantum), is relational upon the *energeia* of God and is manifested in the *logoi* of creation of all things. This implies that our next step in the analysis of Hawking's cosmological model is to understand what it actually says in terms of the universe's contingence upon the intelligibility of the Logos, which can be contemplated through the *logoi* tacitly present in our vision of the universe. This leads us again to the question as to what is the meaning of the distinction that appears in Hawking's universe between the spatialized, imaginary time-universe, where time is effectively closed and finite, and the pseudo-Euclidean space-time of the visible universe, where the linear history of events (the irreversible flow of events) is contemplated by us.

One possible answer comes from the distinction between the Greek vision of the closed universe, in which there was no actual flow of time, and special dates in history. As discussed in chapter 3, history was always problematic for Greek cosmology; history was considered an illusion in an endless cyclic return of the world. The Hellenistic universe is characteristically non-Christian, for it has no beginning and no end. This means that the cosmology with imaginary time is in serious conflict with Christian eschatology, as the progressive movement of time (*kinesis*) to its rest (*stasis*). The biblical view of time, in contrast to the Neoplatonic treatment of time, does not start from the universe as enclosed (that is, the universe existing as a totality, for example, as a four-dimensional spatial continuum); rather, it reflects the awareness that time is the succession of the individual events connected with the divine *economy* in the world, starting from creation and leading to the incarnation and resurrection toward the final goal of the union with the kingdom of God. This biblical understanding of time does not allow any *theory* of time, that is, some kind of laws of time, which underlie its empirical appearance through separate events. This is in strong contradistinction to the Neoplatonic view that the whole time can be described in spatial, overall terms. It is clear now that Hawking's model—if one treats this model ontologically (that is, accepts that his imaginary time is real, so that the universe is closed)—stands for the ideal of Greek cosmology and provides the "schemata" of history as the sequence of possible events stripped of the temporal flow.

If, however, we look at quantum cosmology as a model initiating the classical universe, with, rather, a linear flow of time, the whole evaluation of Hawking's model can change. For in this case, whatever was in the quantum temporal world can be treated as a kind of "typology" of what should happen later in the development of the universe in real time. It is important to realize, then, that the reference to the quantum state of the universe as to the "past" loses its strong sense, for from the "typological" point of view, the history of the visible universe can be treated as initiated not from the imaginary "past" but from the eschatological "future." This implies that the "transition" from the quantum universe to the empirical classical universe, as depicted in figure 5.2, assuming intuitively that time is flowing to the top of the diagram, can be easily reversed as an upside-down diagram, in which time is flowing down from the future.

The analogy that we used while talking about the quantum universe as the concise image of the history of the universe in real time must not be transferred straightforwardly into the theological discourse, for we must remember that both the quantum universe and the classical historical universe are created and contingent upon the *energeia* of God, so that no simple analogy between the timelessness of the quantum universe and the eternity of uncreated God in his kingdom can be made. What we wanted to articulate is the created nature of the universe, which is *differentiated* into the intelligible and the empirical. From this perspective, the intelligible quantum universe as "giving origination" to the visible universe neither exists in the "past" nor in the "future" of the visible universe; rather, it exists as the parallel, intelligible creation, which is hypostasized by the human person, participating in the effected words of God. In this, the whole meaning of Hawking's model changes completely, leading us to the conclusion that this model can hardly deal with the *creatio ex nihilo* itself but rather with the constitution of the latter through the hypostasization of the difference in the created world by the effected words of God.

Quantum Cosmology:
Diaphora in Creation versus Creation out of Nothing

In order to proceed to our main conclusion on the meaning of Hawking's model from a theological point of view, we should refine the Patristic notion of the *difference* in creation, whose issue, as argued below, is implicitly present in quantum cosmology and other branches of physics.

In order to appreciate the importance of this notion in Christian doctrine, we recall the words in the beginning of the Nicene Creed, in which we affirm our belief "in one God, Father, Almighty, Maker of heaven and earth, and all things *visible* and *invisible*." What do we mean then by things *visible* and *invisible*? Are these terms purely "technical" words, with no deep theological foundation, or do they express the dichotomy in creation, its division into two distinct realms, which are both important in the context of religious belief? If the words of the creed mark an ontological difference between two realms of the created being, what would be a proper theological explanation of this dualism? If these two questions are attended to theologically and philosophically, one can hope to respond to the dualism in creation affirmed in the creed from a scientific perspective.

The affirmation from the creed reflects the Christian understanding of the *creatio ex nihilo:* God created the world out of nothing in such a way that there was an initial distinction between two realms, the realm of intelligible forms and the realm of sensible reality. The intelligible realm is understood simply as the spiritual, intellectual level of created being. A good way of referring to this realm is as the *noetic* level of creation or *kosmos noetos* (this expression was used by Greek Fathers, whereas St. Augustine called it created wisdom made by the Word of God).[73] On this level, God formed the angels, who have no material body. But this level contains also intellectual images of sensible reality, that is, ideas. This makes the noetic realm reminiscent of the world of Platonic ideas (which are created in a Christian context).[74] Ideas as intellectual images of sensible reality are inevitable ingredients of scientific theories, such that it is arguable that scientific ideas have an immediate relation to the noetic realm, which complements the sensible realm, the material universe, with its physical, chemical, and biological forms of matter and life. The objective existence of the intelligible realm lies in the fact that it contains the community of living minds, that is, from the experiential aspects of humankind's existence and its ability to think, rationalize, memorize, and symbolize the sensible creation in intelligible forms. The only thing not so easily grasped by the empiricist or positivist type of thinker is that the world of intelligible forms has an ontology that differs from the ontology of the sensible realm. It is exactly at this point that some modern scientific theories of the universe follow the naive assumption that their mathematical constructs have the same ontology as the objects that they purport to describe.

Despite the dualism proclaimed in the Nicene Creed, there is a unity between the two realms of created being that is explained by the mystery of creation as whole; in other words, both the intelligible and the sensible are united in their common ground in the Divine, both realms being contingent on God. The dichotomy in creation in general is manifested clearly in the constitution of humans, whose hypostatic origin in God unites the bodily and mental functions. It is because of this that only humans exist on two levels of reality, and only humanity can be a mediator between these levels and hence be a witness of their ultimate unity, as the unity of God's creation.[75]

If one attempts to formulate the concept of *creatio ex nihilo* in cosmological terms, in terms of the traces of creation in the world, one can argue that there is a kind of structure that is imprinted in the created world through the difference between intelligible and sensible. In other words, the distinction between the sensible and the intelligible can be used to affirm that the world is created (that is, its ontology is relational on God). The Greek Fathers used the word *difference* as a cosmological, theological term to articulate the *creatio ex nihilo* from within the world.

This term comes as the translation of the Greek word διαφορα (*diaphora*) and has theological reference in christological discussions in contradistinction to the Greek word διαιρεσισ (*diairesis*), which means "division."[76]

We, however, are more interested here in using the term *diaphora* in a wider, "cosmological" sense as characteristic of the general difference of being. Dionysius the Areopagite first used the term beyond the christological context, applying it to the differences of all things in creation.[77] Maximus the Confessor followed him and used the term as a characteristic of created being, its constitutive and distinctive feature. The *diaphora* is the ontological feature of the created being. This implies that the difference in creation will never disappear. The *diaphora* plays a constructive role in creation because it provides a common principle of all created things: all things are differentiated in creation, and at the same time, the principle of their unity is that they are differentiated. In particular, it provides a common principle for the unity of intelligible and sensible creation through its constitutive meaning in the *creatio ex nihilo*. From this perspective, the issue of the *creatio ex nihilo* can never be separated from the issue of differentiation in creation between intelligible and sensible; the *diaphora* in God's creation is an established order, the principle of variety and unity in creation, which is distinct from the Creator. This principle as imposed on the created realm through creation by Word-Logos is the *logos* of creation itself. This *logos* was confirmed in Christ.

The immediate implication of the ontological category *diaphora* in creation, as applied to a scientific quest for the *creatio ex nihilo*, is that any physical or cosmological model trying to imitate the *creatio ex nihilo* in scientific terms should deal with the fact that it is not enough just to produce a reasonable scenario of how the empirical visible (sensible) universe came into being from "nothing"; one must realize that there is a "parallel" creation of the invisible world, the world of intelligible forms or the noetic realm. But the theory of creation of the noetic realm would be quite problematic because it assumes a theory of meaning, or a theory of the intelligence, that is responsible for the models of the sensible creation in physics. Some attempts to incorporate the formation of intelligence into the global genesis of physical reality, based on the transcendent applications of quantum principle, have been made in numerous papers of J. Wheeler.[78] The importance of this attempt is rooted in an explicit appeal to factors of modern scientific discourse that transcend the boundaries of "normal," established physics. This demonstrates in turn that while providing the genesis of the physical picture of the world, one needs to appeal to realities that are not quantifiable in the rubrics of physics. One needs philosophy or even theology.

Indeed, the creation (understood theologically) of meaning for things sensible is the work of the Logos through God's uncreated *logoi*, which, by definition, constitute the principles of existence and meaning of all things, including intelligible forms themselves. But the *logoi*, being uncreated by their ontological essence and being transcendent and immanent with respect to the world, are not accessible to scientific inquiry, for contemplation of the *logoi* relies much more on spiritual intellect than on discursive thinking. The latter is able only to establish the presence of the *logoi* in scientific research, to affirm that the *logoi* of things *are,* but not *what* they are.

Science therefore can responsibly argue only for "half" of creation (the empirical realm), assuming that the meaning of this half is provided from outside, from the noetic realm, which is not itself a subject matter of science (but rather of philosophy and theology). This is why the maximum that science can claim in the analysis of the genesis of the world is that it found the mechanism of differentiation in creation between empirical (sensible) and intelligible (noetic) as seen from the sensible perspective. This results in the fact that the *creatio ex nihilo* is accessible through science only up to the extent of ontological differentiation in creation, not as theological creation out of nothing. This idea can be illustrated with the help of the diagram shown in figure 5.3:

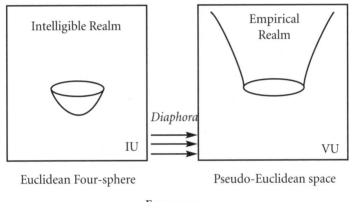

FIGURE 5.3

The contemplation of the ontological difference in creation leads one, however, through the mediation between the sensible and the intelligible (as discussed in chapter 4) to the discovery of the common principle of existence for both the sensible and the intelligible realms, the *logos* of their creation (that is, that the *logos* of creation *is*).

The discovery of the existence of the *logos* of creation requires one to follow the antinomial pattern of demonstration that was discussed in chapter 4. To reveal this pattern in the context of quantum cosmology, we should revise some steps in its logic in light of its interpretation along the lines of Christian Platonism used above.

The pivotal idea of cosmology is to explain the observable cosmos. The idea of the universe as a whole is invoked in cosmology in order to operate mathematically with equations applied to the universe beyond the horizon of its visibility for us. Yet it is assumed that the universe, being a uniform and isotropic continuum of matter and space-time at large, is subject to a scientific grasp. This universe as a heuristic idea can be denoted as *VU*, visible universe. The specific features of this universe are supposed to be explained in terms of simple principles of unity, providing the explanation for the whole variety of things in the universe, which seems to be completely contingent at first glance. The contingency of the observable universe becomes a final target of cosmology, which hopes to replace the contingency by some "necessary law" that itself will need no further explanation. In quantum cosmology, it is believed (as discussed earlier) that this kind of law should exist, and the law is sought in the remote past of the universe, when classical physics must be replaced by a quantum description of matter and space-time. This implies that the universe that we observe here and now as a contingent state of affairs was not so in the past—that is, it followed a pattern of behavior that excluded the contingency of its further evolution and, consequently, its appearance to us as it is.

The fundamental difficulty with this attempt is that the law of the initial conditions of the universe, discussed before, does not belong to the temporal series of causations in the visible universe VU—that is, by definition it transcends the universe VU. In Hawking's model, this transcendence is achieved explicitly by breaking the ordinary temporal series of causations in the VU and by appealing to the modified state of affairs, which does not contain time (that is, to the Euclidean four-dimensional space, which, being beyond temporal flux and not subject to any origination, yet initiates in a tricky way the "classical" universe, the universe VU, with the temporal flux). This *primordial* universe was qualified previously as the intelligible universe and denoted as IU. The invocation of the intelligible object IU to "explain" the empirical universe VU can be subject to a criticism analogous to the Kantian critique of the physico-theological argument for the existence of God. Since IU cannot be found as an element of the empirical series in VU, its invocation as an explanatory element has sense only as a construct. This means that IU, which is to explain the structure of the universe VU, in fact departs from the field of empirical realities and the temporal series in the universe VU by acquiring the properties of the pure constructs. This is the logic of the transition in quantum cosmology from VU to IU: $VU \longrightarrow IU$. The logic is quite natural, for one ascends from the variety of data to a unified principle that is to explain this data.

The situation changes completely, however, when the transition from VU to IU is reversed, that is, when the quantum universe is now treated as a level of reality that is more fundamental than VU, giving rise to the visible universe from the underlying quantum structure.[79] According to the logic of quantum cosmology, the transition $IU \longrightarrow VU$ describes the actualization of the visible universe VU out of IU; however, we must understand it, in view of our interpretation of the quantum universe IU, as a causation in a conceptual space. This implies that the mechanism that actualizes the universe VU out of IU is itself seen by us also as a construct whose ontology is, however, the intelligible one.

We observe here a kind of intellectual inversion, from causation in the temporal series ($VU \longrightarrow IU$) to causation in the purely intelligible series ($IU \longrightarrow VU$), the completeness of which is based on the existence of an absolutely necessary cause (that is, the quantum universe). This jump in reflection is based on an inability to build the empirical content of the concept of the unconditioned condition (IU) in the series of empirical causes. According to Kant, however, from the structure of the visible universe *VU*, one cannot conclude via the empirical analysis to the existence of such a necessary cause (*IU*) that would not be contingent itself. This is why one can state that there is no absolutely necessary cause or being that would explain *VU*. This means that the quantum universe has no ontological references in the empirical realm. It exists as an intelligible object, which functions in thought only as the purpose of the logical justification of the theory of the visible universe *VU* as a contingent state of affairs involved in temporal flux. Hawking, as we have seen, believes, however, that *IU* has the same physical ontology as *VU*, and that is why the causation that brings *VU* into existence out of *IU* is sought as a physical law (we mentioned before that Hawking claimed that there must be laws of the initial conditions in the universe).

The clash between the realistic treatment of *IU* promoted by Hawking despite his generally positivistic metaphysics, on the one hand, and the opposite claim on the same treatment following from a simple Kantian analysis, on the other hand, leads us to an antinomial puzzle. This puzzle points to the only justifiable formula for dealing with the situation: to treat Hawking's intention to justify the visible universe as originated from quantum level—that is, the transition *IU* ⟶ *VU*—as an antinomial reasoning, which is similar to the Kantian reasoning on an absolutely necessary being briefly expressed in his fourth antinomy.[80] The antinomy about the origination of the visible universe out of intelligible quantum universe can now be formulated as follows:

Thesis: There belongs to the world the quantum universe (Euclidean four-sphere) *IU*, which provides the boundary condition for the visible universe *VU* and whose existence is absolutely necessary for the visible universe *VU* to exist; this is a causal condition for *VU* to be as it is.

Antithesis: There nowhere exists the quantum universe *IU* in the world as the cause of the visible universe *VU* (there is no connection between *IU* and *VU*: they belong to the different ontological realms—intelligible and empirical—correspondingly).

As mentioned above, Kant would use this antinomy as a negative conclusion about empirical evidence for the existence of an absolutely necessary being as a cause of the visible universe *VU*. His argument probably would be that the quantum universe *IU* belongs to the intelligible realm and does not have an independent ontological being (*ousia*), apart from the thought, which brought the ideas of *IU* into being. This Kantian denial of substance behind the idea of a necessary being (that is, its ontological existence in the intelligible world) leads ultimately to the denial of any theoretical evidence of the existence of God, of the possibility to ascend to God through the observation of his *economy* in the created realm. This is an inevitable result of the Kantian agnostic monistic substantialism. The need to overcome this monism, as we have seen before, leads us naturally to a change in the anthropology of a subject of knowledge, understood now in terms of personhood. It also leads to our previous epistemological assertion that any reasoning on the underlying causes of the created being brings us to the antinomial monodualism as a natural and inevitable result of inherent apophaticism in the attempted knowledge of God from within creation, as well as the fact that the epistemology is fundamentally open about God. This means not that we think of antinomies as puzzles for human reason, as something that is fallacious on its own, but rather that we consider an antinomy as a natural difficulty in relating the ontology of the sensible world to the ontology of the intelligible world and vice versa.

The main lesson we have learned from the Kantian analysis of antinomies and his skepticism about the proofs of the existence of God is that antinomies reflect an epistemological situation such that we cannot find the ontological ground of what is affirmed or negated by thesis and antithesis in the created being. The resolution of the Kantian antinomies in a theological perspective comes from the observation that antinomy reflects the process of mediation between the sensible and the intelligible realms, which is performed by humankind and leads ultimately to the detection of the presence of the common *logos* of the two realms in creation, the immutable and uncreated principle of their differentiated existence (that is, the *logos* of creation).

We now clearly understand that the presence of antinomies in the cosmological discourse, in which one attempts to speculate on the creation of the universe out of nothing in a theological sense, points to the fundamental difference in the contingent creation, that is, the *diaphora* between the intelligible and the sensible realms. It makes it possible for us to guess whether this tendency of a split in theory between empirical realities and their conceptual images, if taken in its extreme, will always lead a scientist to the detection of the ultimate frontier in attempting to synthesize the variety of physical experience in a single principle of unity, namely, to the unbridgeable ontological *diaphora* in the created domain. The mediation between intelligible and sensible, which is theologically justifiable within Christian anthropology and whose manifestations are clearly seen in modern scientific advance, reflect, rather, the unification of the divisions in creation (that is, the division between intelligible and sensible realms) that take place not ontologically but on the level of cognition.

The antinomial structure of the proposition about the causation between the intelligible quantum universe and the visible, combined with our analysis of the intelligible ontology of the quantum realm with an imaginary time, leads us finally to the conclusion that quantum cosmology is dealing with differentiation in the contingent creation (that is, with the basic *diaphora* in creation), rather than with *creatio ex nihilo* in a theological sense. Since the presence of the difference between the intelligible and the sensible reflects a general tendency and specific feature of all scientific attempts that try to provide the genesis of the attributes of the empirical universe in a single unified theory, it becomes evident that these scientific models can be theologically interesting in terms of their particular schemes that allow one to detect the presence of the *diaphora*.

The antinomy formulated above in the context of Hawking's model can be now rephrased as an affirmative proposition on the constitution of creation: God, creating the world out of nothing, sets up the difference between *IU* (quantum universe with a compact topology of a four-dimensional sphere and imaginary time) in the realm of intelligible creation, and the visible universe *VU* in the realm of sensible creation. Interpreted from this perspective, Hawking's model can be seen as an attempt to describe this *diaphora* between *IU* and *VU*, as it is seen from within the *VU* (that is, in terms of physics and mathematics). This thought can be illustrated with the help of the diagram in figure 5.4:

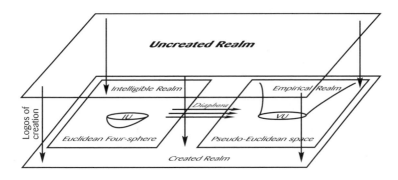

FIGURE 5.4

As argued earlier, the *diaphora*, being a constitutive element of the *creatio ex nihilo*, provides the indication that there *is* the *logos* of creation, that is, the transcendent source of the whole contingent creation. This is the common *logos* of both *IU* and *VU*; the meaning of what we say about the presence of this *logos* can be expressed in the formula that both *IU* and *VU* have nonbeing as the ground of their being.[81]

This leads us in turn to the conclusion that quantum cosmology, and Hawking's model in particular, provide the tools to reveal the relational ontology of both the intelligible (mathematical) and the empirical (visible) universe. This means, in turn, that the models of creation out of nothing in physical cosmology can be used in a theologically mediated way as indications of the divine rationality, which yet stands behind the contingent creation.

6

Irreversibility of Time
and the *logos* of Creation

Irreversibility of Time and Eternity

This section contains some theological reflections on the problem of irreversibility of time in modern physics. We will discuss only this particular aspect of the phenomenon called "time," understanding its property to be in a flux leading toward novelty and to the endless unfolding of the reality of the world. This means that we will intentionally avoid discussing the notion of time in the context of the theory of relativity and its geometrical representation by Minkowski space.

Special relativity does not solve the problem of flowing time. In its extreme, geometrized form, it treats time on equal footing with space and treats the whole space-time as eternally existing. The universe that corresponds to this picture is called the deterministic "block-universe," a "frozen being" in which one has only the rearrangement of events, no true becoming.[1] The problem here is similar to that touched on briefly in the previous chapter: how to explain the emergence of macroscopic irreversibility from microscopic reversible dynamics. This is a matter of continuing scientific debate, and only a few scientists have tried to address this issue by revising the foundations of classical physics. One of these scientists is I. Prigogine, and his collaborators in Brussels and Austin, whose approach to the riddle of time's arrow we will discuss later in this chapter.

It is typical for the block-universe view to assert that the division of time into past, present, and future is an illusory one and that all events in the universe are given at once, but in a Platonic sense. In this case, it is understandable why there is no flow of time and novelty in this universe: its time, according to the terminology referred to in chapter 5, is transcendent time, which somehow incorporates all events that are experienced by human beings as distinct in time. This makes it possible to suspect that the block-universe is not a model of the real visible and empirical universe but, rather, is an attempt to represent the totality of all possible empirical experience of time through a pattern existing in the intelligible realm. The problem, then, is how to link the intelligible frozen time with the empirical flow of time. It has analogies with what we have discussed in the context of Hawking's model of the universe with imaginary time in the previous chapter, so the whole issue of the source of time's irreversibility can have some theological implications.

The debate over the block-universe thus reveals an interesting point in nearly all discussions on the nature of time, namely, some inevitability in the appeal to the Platonic vision of time as an image of timelessness and eternity, in order to justify the empirical time. Indeed, the supporters of the block-universe perceive the eternal reality of Minkowski space-time as an essential ingredient of relativity theory. This manifests an interesting, but predictable from a philosophical point of view, split of the whole being into the empirical and intelligible realms, if one attempts to address the problem of time. We will show below that some sincere attempts of modern physics to solve the riddle of irreversibility of time strictly within a physically realistic ontology cannot be sustained. To justify this point, we intentionally reduce the whole spectrum of problems around time to one in particular—to time's irreversibility, or, to be more precise, to the problem of the source or foundation of this irreversibility. In other words, we concentrate our quest for the source of irreversibility and the arrow of time, assuming that this source exists somehow. Our aim thus is to understand the *nature* of the reality of this "source." The result of this search will lead us to the conclusion that the "source" of the macroscopic irreversibility of time transcends not only the empirical world but also the Platonic world—that is, it originates from the split in the created realm, from the basic *diaphora* between the sensible and the intelligible. One can anticipate, then, our conclusion that the problem of the irreversibility of time cannot be seriously discussed by physics on its own but requires one to employ philosophy and theology to address this issue adequately.

Indeed, even in the context of the Platonic block-universe, assumed as existing eternally, there is a theological question about the ground of its existence—that is, what is the sufficient reason for its existence? It also can be approached as an issue of the contingency of the block-universe (treated either realistically or Platonically), that is, the nonworldly grounds of its existence. The very structure of the block-universe (with no becoming), if it is considered as an arena of God's actions in the world, would be very destructive for Christian assertions about salvation history and for Christian eschatology in general. This is why, from a theological point of view, the question of becoming and its ultimate origination in the mystery of the *creatio ex nihilo* is important in our discussion here. We want to assert once more that we do not discuss time here as a background of God's economy in the world; rather, we discuss the origin of temporal flow as linked to the Christian concept of creation. It makes our interest here much closer to the problem of time and contingency.

The definition of time, its meaning and logical expression, can be presented in many different ways. On the one hand, it seems psychologically evident to speak about time and to pretend to know what it is, appealing to time not in terms of its underlying essence but rather to empirical events, which are in time and which describe time in terms of things that are themselves not time. Time is usually described in notions that are finite and contingent in all possible senses. The problem, however, if we long to understand the ultimate source of the irreversibility of time, is to justify the definition of time in rubrics of thought that transcend the immediate surface of temporal appearances of things and refer to the realm of the unconditioned and the necessary.

Time can be seen as a fundamental, all-encompassing entity that has to justify everything diverse, concrete, and contingent in the empirical realm by uniting all of them in time. This shows, therefore, that there is something in time that originates not from the empirical world. We can only perceive the empirical world through the mode of temporal experience, so that any hypothetical removal of time in reasoning about experience would mean its negation, that is, the affirmation of its nonbeing. Time, however, is not reduced only to its temporal manifestation in experience, which consists of specific and distinct phenomena that in their diversity do not exhaust the essence of time, leaving its intuitively asserted unity and undivided foundation beyond experience itself.

This tells us in turn that any possible philosophical definition of time as the sum of events contains some negation of the temporality of time, pointing thereby toward the realm that is beyond the empirical expression of temporality itself. In Kantian parlance, we can say that the origin of that *temporal* time, which we know through the immanent form of sensibility, is itself beyond the world, which is known to us in temporal terms. The Russian philosopher N. Lossky comments on a similar thought: "Time is a condition for the world to fulfill its task for the sake of which it was created."[2] There are two points in this comment where we find that time, understood as materialized in the world, has its foundation beyond the world. First, time is understood as a condition for the underlying and forming principle of creation (its *logos,* which is uncreated itself) to be realized in the world, but this condition (time) is revealed to us only in its immanent form of the temporality of the world and its history. Second, one can argue that by projecting itself into the domain of the created, the forming principle of creation (*logos*), which initiates time in order to fulfill the task of creation, does not exhaust itself; it is still beyond this world and is the ground of creation and time. Despite this theological treatment of time, it indicates that one comes to similar insights on the nature and origin of time in modern scientific inquiry.

To understand this better in general terms, not yet employing specific scientific theories, it would be useful to rephrase the theological insight into this problem in modern terms. We understand time, which is experienced as a temporal order of events. In other words, our experience is possible only as experience in time. That is why the problem of the foundation and origin of time can be understood in a twofold way. If one adopts the notion of time as a directed and irreversible flow of events, one could try to give justification for its irreversibility in *local* terms, that is, as some physical cause that *coexists* logically and physically "simultaneously" with the displayed aspects of irreversibility. In this case, the irreversibility, being an immanent aspect of time, is caused by some deep underlying physical processes and may be explained from within the same level of reality (that is, the same ontology as temporality itself) with no appeal to the idea of the transcendent cause of time. Prigogine and his collaborators follow this methodology in order to tackle the mystery of the irreversibility of time.[3]

This methodology has two problems. One will be analyzed later in this chapter, where it will be shown that an attempt by Prigogine to find the source of irreversibility of time in some deep level of physical reality leads him, in fact, beyond empirical physical reality into the realm of conceptual spaces with different ontological properties and criteria for their existence.[4] This adds to our previous assertions that the source of irreversibility of time has its ground in the nonempirical realm. The theological analysis that we apply to Prigogine's ideas will help us to reinstate the problem of the irreversibility of time to its proper theological status in the context of the concept of creation out of nothing.

The second problem is that if Prigogine's attempt were successful and the arrow of time were to be explained, this could bring his supporters to claim that there is no need for any nonworldly agency in order to describe the irreversibility, and in a sense the description of temporal flux would be monistic, needing no justification for either its "beginning" or its "end," because the irreversibility destroys any ontological significance of the unknown past and indefinite future. This would imply that any speculation on the nature of the initial conditions in the universe would be fundamentally untestable. The claims of the block-universe proponents would then also be extremely unsound, for the idea of a global space-time with deterministic dynamical laws would be irretrievably undermined. It is understandable that in such a universe the permanent emergence of novelty would make it difficult to advocate the stability and intelligibility of the patterns in the universe, which represent the outcomes of the laws that drive the irreversibility. The only ultimately stable feature would be the very law of irreversibility. The problem, then, is about the origin of this law. If one believes in evolving cosmology, does it mean that these laws come into existence together with the universe? In this case, their contingent status follows from the contingency rooted in the initial conditions of the universe, which, as discussed in chapter 5, have grounds in their otherness, that is, in the realm of the God-Creator. This implies that an attempt to explain the irreversibility of time by postulating some underlying irreversible laws whose outcomes lead to the observed irreversibility—that is, to make it a part of a new law—still does not succeed in explaining away the contingency of irreversible phenomena, for these irreversible laws need to be justified, which indicates that they are contingent on their own.

It is also important to remind the reader that, in its essence, the approach to the irreversibility of time in physics is usually associated with the irreversibility of processes. In other words, one asserts the irreversibility of time not in terms of *time* itself, which is a difficult and ill-defined concept, but in terms of some physical processes whose behavior manifests the irreversibility of time. Philosophically and theologically, this approach is justifiable, for time was created together with the world, which means that it is difficult to separate a "pure" time from its manifestations in the processes. This was anticipated early, by the Jewish philosopher Philo of Alexandria, who developed a biblical exegesis through its synthesis with Hellenistic philosophy. In his account of the creation, he asserted that time cannot be separated from what is observed as change in time: "Before the world time had no existence, but was created either simultaneously with it, or after it; for since time is the interval of the motion of the heavens, there could not have been any such thing as motion before there was anything which could be moved."[5]

Time discloses thus a special kind of "reality," which is immanent to the world but which does not exist before or without the world. One can even strengthen the last proposition by saying that time, understood as temporal change in physical bodies, does not exist beyond the world, where the bodies' motions are exhibited. The view that time and the world have foundation in their common otherness led historically, as articulated before, to the replacement of the Hellenistic idea of the *demiurgic creation* of the world in space and in time by the Christian concept of *creatio ex nihilo*. The fundamental change in comprehension of time that accompanied this shift can be commented on as follows.

Since creation out of nothing is not a temporal act in the same sense that we understand temporality in the created world, the creation of the world is not in time; however, it is through the creation that time is held—that is, it is being brought into existence. By following the logic of the created temporal world, we could articulate the "act of creation" in terms that are opposite to time; for example, one could affirm that creation is timeless and that time is brought into existence out of timelessness. But, unfortunately, the term *timelessness* suffers from a deficiency of being produced within the logic of the created world. Indeed, it is introduced into the philosophical lexicon by means of a simple negation of time as temporality and represents a special and rather narrow understanding of eternity, which can be treated in an opposite way as transcendent time—that is, the overall time of all times, which was discussed along with Neoplatonism in chapter 5. But even the transcendent time (eternity as a changeless state of affairs) manifests the mode of the creation, namely, the *invisible* in creation, the world of angelic forms and Platonic ideas. The Greek language denotes eternity as *aeon,* and different aeons measure the spans of existence of different intelligible worlds.

It is because of this that when one asserts that the temporality of the visible creation has its ground in eternity, understood as the opposite to time, one should be very careful, for eternity itself can be an attribute of the created realm and will need further justification in terms of its nonworldly foundation. This reveals the whole scale of the difference between the uncreated realm of the Divine and the created world, leading to the necessity of introducing the third and, according to G. Mantzaridis, the loftiest concept of the *aidion* as the "everlasting," which is "older than all time and eternity in its being."[6] Maximus the Confessor, in some of his texts, elucidates this concept by referring to Scripture, which is saying "that there is something which transcends the age. Scripture has indicated that this thing exists but it has not specified what it is, as the following text shows: 'The Lord rules the age, and above the age, and for ever' (Exod. 15:18. LXX). There is therefore something above the age, namely the inviolate kingdom of God."[7]

It is difficult to articulate further the meaning of the *aidion* in discursive mode except by defining it in purely apophatic terms, which start from negating the time of the visible world. What is interesting, however, is that the Patristic writers, such as Gregory the Theologian (Nazianzus), also anticipated that the understanding of time itself is problematic by definition, for if it is a part of visible creation and falls under the temporal categories itself, how is it possible to define time in categories that assume that they are already temporal? Gregory put this query in the following form: "Is Time *in* Time, or not? If it is, what is the Time it is in? What is the difference between them? How does one contain the other? If Time is not in Time, how acute your wits are to get us non-temporal Time."[8]

The rationale of this quotation is that any attempt to speculate about the foundations of time requires one to abandon language that is inherently temporal, including all simple modes of its expression in terms of timelessness or eternity, in favor of a silent affirmation that God, being the ground of the world and time, is beyond both time and eternity. This observation is important in the methodology of philosophical and theological analysis of scientific concepts of time, and of temporal irreversibility in particular, for any affirmation that time has its foundation in timelessness or eternity is not sufficient in order to be qualified as a theological assertion. This is because, to find the indication of the ultimate ground of time, one should pose both time and eternity in their relation to *aidion* as transcending both of them and being peculiar to the timeless being of the uncreated God. In accordance with the line of reasoning developed in chapters 4 and 5, this implies that the Platonism in arguments for the foundation of time must be reinstated in its Christian version when both empirical time of macroscopic processes and timeless mathematical spaces that mirror these processes through their constitutive difference (*diaphora*) will be referred to the common ground of their unity, that is, to the *logos* of their creation.

The problem of time thus can be seen from a theological perspective as a problem of the relationship of time, either empirical or conceptual, to the everlasting (*aidion*). Still, it is interesting to ask which particular "form" of empirical time (that is, its past, present, or future), the question of its relationship to creation from the everlasting realm of God, it is more appropriate to address, for the human perception of time is always inclined to seek its foundations through the limiting forms of temporal series, which are directed either to the past or to the future. This question cannot be answered on scientific grounds only, for, as will be demonstrated in this section, the appeal to the source of time as existing in the cosmological past (Penrose's model, discussed later in this chapter), as well as the invocation of the source of temporal flow as existing in the underlying level of reality at "present" (Prigogine's theory, also discussed later in this chapter), leads scientific reason inevitably beyond the empirical realm of time, transcending into timeless conceptual realities and making the "historical dimension" of the problem of the origin of temporal flow unimportant.[9]

If, however, one asks the same question in theological terms—that is, from within the perspective of the cosmic history of human beings, the asymmetry between the past and the future (the future that is expressed in eschatological terms as the goal to which human beings as well as the universe are steadily progressing)—then it would be reasonable to argue that the unfolding of the cosmic history goes on toward the future, which comes into the present from the perspective of the ultimate purpose of the world. But the direct analogy between physical time and eschatological time, coming from the kingdom of God, is not simply a working tool in tackling the problem of time from within the scientific context, for the "reality" of the kingdom and the ontology of the coming from the future have a different status in comparison with what is argued in science. This means that the role of the future in the sustenance of time, as its creation from the kingdom, can be articulated only through an appeal to ecclesial and liturgical experience. Can, then, the scientific models of becoming serve as discursive prototypes of the experience of God from his kingdom?[10]

Since the act of creation cannot be conceived as a temporal act, it constitutes an "everlasting" act, which, metaphorically speaking, is *contemporaneous* with all times, for example, with all temporal spans of the evolution of the universe.[11] But the evolution of the visible universe has a beginning, in the time of the created world. The temporality of the visible universe thus represents an aspect of *aidion* that projects the act of creation into its temporal appearance in the visible creation. The creation, however, is initiated from the atemporal and noneternal realm, which means that there is something in it that cannot be projected into the created realm through any form of temporality. It is exactly this remnant that is intuitively sought by science when it attempts to provide the theory of the origin of time. We have seen in chapter 5 that in order to establish the link between the visible universe in its temporal mode of existence and the source of its existence and the source of temporality, scientific means alone have been insufficient. This is because the basic *diastema* in creation can be grasped only through the detection of the presence of the *logoi* of creation in scientific theories. These *logoi* point toward the *logos* of the entire creation, which holds all things together, including irreversible time, with respect to God.

It is clear that such meditations on the nature and origin of time cannot be the task of positive science; that is why scientific experience is destined to accept dispassionately the time of the material world, which manifests itself through the change of sensible things. Despite this acceptance, however, it is amazing to witness how scientific knowledge, being part of the human cognitive faculties, incessantly leads to the production of multiple theories of time. Nevertheless, time, this fascinating feature of all existence in the world around us, inevitably escapes from our scientific understanding into a spiritual world of ideas, becoming again the subject of rather wide contemplative experience, but this time it is the contemplation of meditating scientists, not that of devoted believers.

This shows that there is something about time that will always escape from any attempt of human science to look at it under a microscope. Meditating about the irreversibility of physical time, scientists silently lift their thoughts beyond the physical world, transferring the problem from the sphere of physics to the sphere of ideas.

The proper way to treat the problem here, however, is to apply to it the methods of philosophy and theology.

By saying that physics understands time through material processes, we implicitly accuse physics of a reductionism that might diminish the meaning of the proposed research. We are not afraid of that, however, because this reduction is used only as a starting point for our discussion. We are convinced in advance that any truth about time that we may discover will inevitably urge us to modify our reductionism and that, in consequence, the subject of time will hence be reinstated to its proper place in the sphere of human ideas based on the wholeness of experience. Nevertheless, being respectful to science and its attempts to obtain a glance into the unfathomable depths of a reality that underlies the everyday world of our senses, we consider two particular accounts of irreversibility. We shall see that, irrespective of its search for some ultimate truth about time, this truth turns out to be a metaphysical, and even a theological, truth.

In what follows, we analyze two accounts on the irreversibility of time: the first provided by the theory of Penrose, who argues that the source of this irreversibility lies in special initial conditions of the universe, and the second by the program of Prigogine, who, on the contrary, sought the source of irreversibility from the perspective of new local dynamics, which represents the extension of classical physics.

Irreversibility of Time and Boundary Conditions in the Universe

The issue of design in modern cosmology is closely connected with the fundamental question on the nature of the observed postcollision correlations between "particles" in the universe, which, in our human comprehension, appear as a kind of order or design. The nature of such correlations relates to the present-day value of entropy in the universe, for it is entropy that indicates quantitatively the extent to which the universe is in a state of order/disorder. It is known that this entropy (S) is measured as the number of baryons in the observed universe and that its numerical value is estimated to be $S = s * 10^{80}$, where the specific entropy $s* = 10^8$ is the number of photons per baryon. $s*$ is a fundamental physical parameter that is critical for the existence of stable physical systems: a hypothetical variation of $s*$ by two orders of ten will break the condition for gravitational stability of the stars and galaxies and existence of life in the universe.[12] The thermodynamic understanding of entropy is based on the second law of thermodynamics, which teaches us that the world is in such a state of change that its entropy is constantly growing. This implies that the value of the present-day S is a result of irreversible evolution in the universe from some initial state with the entropy less than S, thus suggesting that there is the universal irreversibility of processes in the universe. The specificity of the universe's present state, which exhibits some order and correlation of its parts, is connected then with special initial conditions, rather than with any possible intrinsic mechanism that drives the flow of time and gives direction to the evolution of the universe to its present designlike state.

Two outstanding attempts to solve the riddle of temporal flow in modern physics exist. The first trend, developed by Prigogine's scientific school, tried to introduce irreversibility at the "local" level, that is, to claim that irreversibility is inherent in some underlying physical laws, which are to be discovered.[13] An alternative approach to the nature of the present state of the universe, as a state with a relatively low entropy and hence a high level of postcollision correlations, dates back to an idea of Penrose's—that the present special state of the universe, which is associated with a kind of design and irreversible flow of time, has its origin in boundary conditions in the remote past of the universe.

The dichotomy that we observe in these two approaches to explaining the entropy and a specific arrow of time in the universe, which is observed by us locally ("here" and "now"), reflects a general difficulty in distinguishing whether this arrow of time is caused by local factors or by the boundary conditions in the distant past or future. Because the universe is unique, it is difficult to distinguish between laws of nature and boundary conditions governing solutions to those laws (any proposal in this regard is untestable scientifically).[14]

In this section, we discuss an attempt to catch the source of the irreversibility of time (leading to the existence of complex systems with a high degree of postcollisional correlations, that is, exhibiting some designlike properties) by appealing to the starting point of its evolution. This approach was developed by Penrose and is based on his firm belief that "if the important local laws are all time-symmetrical, then the place to look for the origin of statistical asymmetry is in the boundary conditions."[15]

Classical dynamics teaches us that boundary conditions can be posed either in the past or in the future. But, as our macroscopic experience shows, imposing boundary conditions in the future presupposes an infinitely precise arranging of the velocity distribution of particles composing the system, so that one would need an infinite amount of information to obtain the present state of the system. Such boundary conditions are separated from what is physically possible by an "entropy barrier."[16]

We accept that lack of information about a system may correspond to a nonzero entropy state and that imposing boundary conditions in the past or future may reduce the entropy to a minimum. The imposition of future low-entropy boundary conditions in this way overcomes the "entropy barrier," which has been shown to be a consequence of the second law of thermodynamics. This means that such a system will evolve in the direction of entropy decrease, which goes against the current view of thermodynamics. To eliminate this apparent contradiction with the second law, we might instead think of the future low-entropy conditions as "time-reversed past conditions."

The relatively small entropy of the present state of our universe, which is evidenced by the existence of stable structures, must stem from the low-entropy conditions at its initial state. The irreversible evolution of the universe toward states with high entropy must hence have its origin in low-entropy conditions at the initial singularity. These are the cause of time's arrow as indicated by the irreversible processes; notice that "time's arrow" is just a shorthand term for the marked tendency of the majority of the observed processes. According to Penrose: "The entropy concept . . . refers to classes of states . . . not individual states."[17]

This shows that the definition of entropy depends on what kind of changes we observe and what methods of description we choose. The very idea of irreversibility, which is associated with the growth of entropy, is relevant not to separate objects following well-known dynamical laws but to aspects of the collective behavior of these objects that is normally observed.

In Prigogine's model of time, the growth of entropy in the universe is driven by the flow of correlations among particles, and the arrow of time, which is related to this mechanism of aging of a system, is associated with a flow of correlation toward complex states involving more and more particles.[18] One must, however, answer a fundamental question: what is the ultimate reason for this flow of correlations to even start? According to Penrose's view, the answer is that the origin of this flow, and of the arrow of time, is hidden in the low-entropy initial conditions for the evolution of the universe.

In itself, the expansion of the universe does not explain time's arrow. Already in 1979, Penrose had pointed out that there is no direct link between the expansion of the universe, the growth of entropy, and the arrow of time. It is easy to understand that, in the approach connecting increase of entropy with a flow of correlations, there is no object in equilibrium in the universe and that the increase of entropy continues forever independently of the universal evolution, whether it be due to expansion or to contraction. This eliminates the idea of a thermal death of the universe, which is inevitable if evolution is considered only in terms of binary correlations.

Classical physics considered entropy to be an attribute of matter attached to such ingredients as radiation and particles. It was assumed ad hoc in classical cosmology that the state of matter near the big bang is approximately in thermodynamic equilibrium with a maximum of entropy (despite the fact that all physical parameters are effectively infinite at the singularity and that any hypothesis on the physical state there is pure speculation). However, it is evident that the state of affairs the universe displays at present is such an ordered state that the entropy of the universe, as a measure of its disorder, is not high enough to prevent the emergence of states showing precise macroscopic after-collision correlations (great disorder in the universe could not support the stable systems, such as clusters of galaxies, galaxies, and star systems). These correlations, observed in a variety of structures, are evidence that a state preceding the present one must show an entropy that is much less if the second law of thermodynamics is true and applicable to the whole universe. This contradicts the hypothesis of maximum entropy at the big bang.

To overcome this paradox, Penrose pointed out that one should take into account the gravitational degrees of freedom of the universe, that is, to consider the state of the universe not only in terms of its matter content (its particles and fields) but also in terms of its geometry linked in general relativity to the gravitational field.[19] He proposed to introduce a new entropy-like property of the gravitational field, later called gravitational entropy (*GE*). Evaluating the possible amount of entropy that can be produced in the universe during the whole period of its evolution from the big bang to the big crunch, he discovered that there is a tremendous lack of entropy in the baryon universe we observe now, namely 10^{88} as compared to the possible value 10^{123}. The reason for this was thought to be found in the low GE condition at the big bang, which suppressed the "disorder" at the very beginning of the evolution of the universe, making this state extremely ordered but leading then to a strong irreversibility in the evolution of the universe, as a change directed toward disorder and a high degree of postcollisional correlations. The second law of thermodynamics, then, can be treated itself as the display of the evolution of the universe from an extraordinary ordered state to a much more probable state with a high degree of disorder.

To express the condition of the order in geometrical terms, it was noticed that the growth of GE corresponds to a clustering of matter that is accompanied by an increase in the degree of anisotropy of the gravitational field, which is itself described by the Weyl curvature (WC). This led Penrose to propose a scenario for the development of the universe in which the evolution begins from a state resembling, in a way, the low GE entropy corresponding to weak gravitational anisotropy and evolves to a high GE state marked by strong gravitational anisotropy, presupposing that WC can be somehow correlated with a quantitative measure of GE. A more precise statement of this idea is his well-known Weyl curvature hypothesis (WCH): "The Weyl curvature tends to zero at all past singularities, as the singularity is approached from future directions."[20]

The physical implications of the WCH for the present state of the universe can be expressed as follows: we regard the character of the actual state of the universe, assuming that it began with a big bang and WC = 0, as being more and more of the "precise correlation" type and less and less of the "low-entropy" type as time progresses. This is consistent with Prigogine's ideas that the complexity of the universe is due to a steady flow of correlations among particles, which can explain a very special state of the present universe. The WCH acquires the features of a special initial condition in the universe, being a local condition, which cannot itself be derived from the retrospective macroscopic dynamics. It is because of this that the WCH is a priori asymmetric with respect to time, for it is not a part of the temporal series of causations that follow the state with WCH. Similarly to Hawking, Penrose believes that this special initial condition is itself subject to some underlying physical law that is asymmetric in terms of time. According to Penrose: "There are in fact . . . laws which only become important near space-time singularities, these being asymmetric in time and such as to force the Weyl curvature to vanish at any initial singular point."[21] This assumes that there must be some laws, "local in time," that are responsible for macroscopic irreversibility; but, in contradistinction to the ideas of Prigogine, these laws are important only at the singularity, that is, in the remote past. As a result, according to Penrose, "the problem of time's arrow can be taken out of the realm of statistical physics and returned to that of determining what are the precise physical laws."[22] In other words, instead of attempting to explain the statistical tendencies in the macroscopic world by using "nondynamic" theory here and now, Penrose proposes to treat all statistical behavior as the remote result of the local and "precise" law, which is only true at the cosmological singularity. Put further in a different way: the observable irreversibility of time, according to Penrose, can be explained not in terms of temporal series themselves, which are displayed because of this irreversibility, but in terms of some yet unknown but theoretically possible local and unique physical law, which is itself not a part of a temporal series.

These laws would have a fundamental importance since they predetermine the entire thermodynamical evolution of the universe and the outcome of this irreversible change, which we contemplate through flow of time and by observing complex structures in nature. From a methodological point of view, such an approach presupposes the search for hidden (unknown) "laws" existing at the singularity, which we can guess at only by observing their macroscopic effects in the present-day universe and which we associate with a kind of design and with the entropy 10^{88}. This means that what is assumed as a hidden physical law at the cosmological singularity in its outcome serves as the explanation of the observable arrow of time and evolving complexity in the present-day universe.

We observe here an interesting shift of the problem of the arrow of time and its particular manifestation through the order and harmony in the present-day universe toward that in the remote past, that is, to the moment of origin of the universe. This means that the issue of thermodynamic irreversibility and its entropic characteristic acquires the colors of the special, original "creation" of the universe. This way of thought is reminiscent of the Kantian treatment of the physico-theological (teleological) argument for God, based in fact on the ideas of design—namely, his demonstration that the design argument, in order to become a theistic argument, assumes its foundation in the cosmological argument, in the idea of totality of the world in space and in time. This is exactly the way of Penrose's logic when the problem of "special entropy at present" is treated as one of a special temporal origination of the universe.

Penrose's Model and Its Theological Interpretation

To illustrate that WCH implies such atypical conditions in the early universe, Penrose appeals to the idea of a "phase space" of different initial conditions for all possible universes.[23] Taking the figure 10^{123} as a maximum potential entropy for a universe of our type, he estimates the phase-space volume corresponding to its possible initial conditions to be $V = 10^{10^{123}}$. But our actual physical universe corresponds to a phase space volume of size $V = 10^{10^{88}}$. This shows that the initial conditions of the universe we live in constitute an infinitesimal part of V, namely: $W/V = 10^{-10^{123}}$; that is, the precision with which the big bang must be set up is nearly infinite.

In different, probabilistic language, the a priori probability for our universe W with a pattern of irreversibility we observe at present approximates to zero. This is because V remains "almost infinite" relative to W. Consequently, the amount of information necessary to select our physical universe, as a particular region in a space V, will likewise be "almost infinite."

Since there is no natural foundation for this kind of event, Penrose introduces the idea of a god powerful enough to "create" all kinds of worlds: only an omniscient creator may possess the knowledge of that infinite amount of information necessary to pinpoint that tiny part of phase space that describes the initial conditions of our own universe.

The function of this creator is only to launch the universe, not to govern it. According to Penrose, it is governed by the time-symmetrical laws of physics. The universe W, where $S = 10^{88}$, which we associate with the presence of a particular kind of irreversibility, appears only because of the very special type of "creation" that is formulated geometrically as the condition WC = 0.

In the rest of this section, we discuss this idea from a philosophical and theological perspective following the lines of methodology we used while discussing Hawking's model of creation out of nothing in chapter 5. The philosophical and theological treatment of Penrose's approach to the source of irreversibility of time will, however, be closer to the genuine philosophy of Penrose himself, for he, in comparison with Hawking's positivistic views, is explicitly Platonist with regard to mathematical physics. According to Penrose, the physical world "emerges out of the ('timeless') world of mathematics."[24] He considers the Platonic world of absolutes as the world of mathematical truth, existing prior to and independently with respect to the physical world. He illustrates his position using a diagram similar to the one shown in figure 6.1, which will be important for our interpretation of his model of special initial conditions.

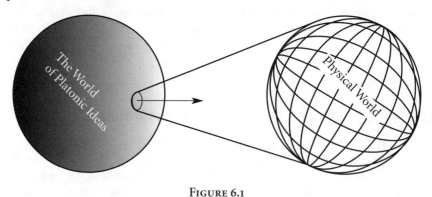

FIGURE 6.1

First let us realize that Penrose introduced the world W as a concept of the visible universe we live in that contains a specific arrow of time and indicates the pattern of design associated with the entropy S. The task of the theory is to explain the origin of the universe W as having special initial conditions. Since what we observe in the universe W is by assumption contained in the initial state of this universe, it is impossible to provide its further explanation in terms of the state of affairs within the universe itself. In other words, we cannot explain the specificity of W in terms of its various elements. It is because of this intrinsic contingency of the universe W and the number $S = 10^{88}$ that the metaphysical understanding jumps from the manifold of the universe in its varied content and unlimited extent to the assumption that the universe is built with some determinate purpose; that is, it is designed. From observing the order that science uncovers in the universe (such as, in modern parlance, large-scale structure, cosmic coincidences, and fine-tuning), one comes next to the conclusion that this order and beauty do belong to the universe contingently, because it is hardly to be believed that the diverse things in the universe could cooperate themselves in order to fulfill the formation of the order to which we attribute purpose and design.[25] At this point, the physical reason appeals to some wise cause, which could be the cause of the world.[26]

Penrose's intention is to remove the contingency of the state of affairs in the universe, as it is now, back to the remote past, where, according to him, there was a "law" that made the contingency, which is observed by us here and now, to be a necessary contingency. In other words, the universe that we observe now as a contingent was not such in the past, because there was an original necessary law that caused the further development of the universe. This law, however, does not belong to the empirical series of causations; that is, it transcends the universe W itself. Indeed, it was necessary for Penrose to introduce two more supernatural ingredients to his explanation, namely, the multitude of the universes with different initial conditions V and the "Creator." The V plays a role of the substratum, which is necessary for the "Creator" to be able to choose our universe W. The "Creator" therefore is not a creator at all: it is an architect of the world (a demiurgic god) who is constructing the world W from the "material" given in V, but who is not the creator of the world out of nothing, for V is not "nothing," but rather the potentiality of all possible states of affairs—that is, in philosophical terms, the maximal symmetrical state of undifferentiated being.

We observe here an analogy with the Kantian criticism of the physico-theological argument for the existence of God. The problem of the physico-theological argument is that one cannot achieve an understanding of the wise cause of the universe W on purely empirical grounds; one needs to appeal to the cosmological argument, that is, to invoke the concept of the world as a totality of the series of alterations. But the concept of the world in this sense does not deviate from the series of appearances, which regresses in accordance with the empirical laws of causality, and therefore it assumes that the world itself is a member of this series. There is no chance, however, to find any first beginning or any highest member (as a primary or ultimate cause) in the series of the world W, for which a concluding term of the series will be in fact the world V.

Science always tries to discover the ultimate source of temporal series in nature by making some regress toward the fundamental but hidden physical law or to the very first beginning of this series somewhere in the remote past. The inevitable consequence of this search for the believed existence of the absolute cause of the irreversibility and order in the universe is a departure from the field of empirical realities and the temporal series in the world W and an appeal to theoretical models, or constructs, such as V: this is the logic of the transition $W \longrightarrow V$ as it is invoked in the thinking of Penrose.

The striking thing, however, is that the constructs of such underlying reality as V, which is supposed to be the first beginning and the highest term in the series of reasoning based on the laws of empirical causation, are far away, by their epistemological nature, from the empirical domain of being; they turn out to be in the world of conceptual realities, or in the world of ideas, which itself does not bear any predicates of temporality. This is why the very cause of temporal flow and irreversibility does not belong to the temporal series. In other words, this ultimate cause of the empirical appearances of irreversibility is not actually the cause of empirical series in a strict sense of empirical causation, because it does not belong to the empirical world. It means that we witness a typical transcendental jump in theoretical thinking from the series of empirical analysis to the series and causation of intelligible nature, that is, to a kind of regress in a conceptual space, where the highest term or the very first "beginning" is revealed not by the methods of empirical advance but by purely logical formulations of the absolute necessity of such a being, which is responsible for the temporal series in the world. One must admit that Penrose's mathematical model (WCH) gives an actual example of such a regress within conceptual realities.

The logic of an inverse transition $V \longrightarrow W$, which describes the actualization of our world W out of V, is then understood from our W perspective as a causation in the conceptual space, whereas for "the Creator," for whom the manifold of the world V, and the world W as a part of V, are given in their *actuality*, the transition $V \longrightarrow W$ means a transition between two ontologically homogeneous objects V and W. This implies that a divine entity that actualizes the world W out of V is seen by us also as a construct from the conceptual space.

We observe here a kind of mental inversion from causation in the temporal series ($W \longrightarrow V$) to causation in the purely intelligible series ($V \longrightarrow W$), the completeness of which is based on the existence of an absolutely necessary cause (the creator). This jump in reflection is based on an inability to build the empirical content of the concept of the unconditioned condition (V + creator) in the series of empirical causes. According to Kant, the special features of the world W, involved in irreversible flux, cannot bring us through the empirical analysis to the existence of such a necessary cause that would not be contingent itself. For Kant, this is why one can state that there is not an absolutely necessary cause or being.

This means, in Kantian parlance, that the idea of the ensemble of possible initial conditions V and the idea of Penrose's creator have no ontological reference in the empirical realm. They both exist in the sphere of thought as logical forms that function instead only for the purpose of the logical justification of W as a contingent and temporal state of affairs with some pattern of design. Some physicists, however, inspired by the idea of many worlds that appears in different parts of physics, believe that V has the same physical ontology as W and that this is why the causation that brings W into existence out of V is sought as a physical law.[27] The same takes place in Penrose's argument when the WCH is formulated metaphysically, that is, as a law imposed by the creator by means of pinning out a "point" in a set of all possible universes.

The clash between the realistic treatment of V and the creator, drawn from Penrose's argument, and the negative result on the same treatment, following from the Kantian analysis, leads us to the only justifiable formula for dealing with the situation, namely, to treat Penrose's statement about the transition $V \longrightarrow W$ as an antinomy, which is similar to the fourth Kantian antinomy on an absolutely necessary being:

Thesis: There belongs to the world the ensemble of all possible universes V with different initial conditions whose existence is absolutely necessary for our universe W with low initial entropy to exist as a part of V; this is a causal condition for the arrow of time in W (there is causal connection between V and W).

Antithesis: There nowhere exists the ensemble of universes V in the world as the cause of our universe W with low initial entropy and the cause for the arrow of time in W; there is no connection between V and W: they belong to different ontological realms (intelligible and empirical correspondingly).[28]

In analogy to what we said in the context of a similar antinomy in Hawking's model, Kant would use this antinomy for a negative conclusion about empirical evidence for the existence of V, playing the role of a cause of the universe W with the arrow of time. He would argue that the V and the *creator* both belong to the intelligible realm and do not have an independent ontological being apart from the thought that brought the ideas of V and the creator into being. From the perspective of Penrose's philosophical position (that is, his Platonism), this will not constitute any trouble, for the world V can be easily treated in Platonic terms as an element of the intelligible realm existing independently from W. The meaning of the transition $V \longrightarrow W$ can then be interpreted in terms of the diagram in figure 6.1 as the transition from the intelligible realm to the sensible realm. This kind of transition we have met before in the context of Hawking's model. To accomplish the theological treatment of this idea, we should add one particular detail to the whole picture, namely, to affirm that the world of Platonic ideas, containing V as well as the visible universe W, constitutes the created world in its differentiation; that is, both are part of the created realm. In this case, the transition between V and W—caused, according to Penrose, by a demiurgic deity—as the "explanation" of the emergence of the visible universe W out of the intelligible ensemble of the universes with different initial conditions means, in a theological context, the differentiation between the intelligible and the sensible in the created domain. In other words, the split between V and W that is presented in Penrose's model as the setting up of the initial conditions in W can be treated through Patristic eyes as the difference (*diaphora*) between the intelligible and the sensible as the constitutive element of creation of both V and W

out of nothing. This treatment can be illustrated with the help of the diagram shown in figure 6.2 (which, in a sense, is a reinterpretation of figure 6.1 through the eyes of Christian Platonism):

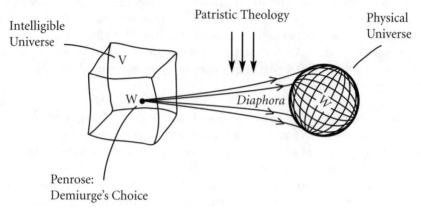

FIGURE 6.2

Finally, this view explains to us what was really indicated in Penrose's model. Definitely it has nothing to do with the *creatio ex nihilo* taken in its pure affirmative form, for the world *V* (out of which the sensible realm *W* emerged) preexisted before the actualization of *W*. The "creator" also belonged to the same realm as *V*, and its work was simply mastering the *W* from the material given in the *V*. Both *V* and the "creator" belong to the intelligible series of causation, as demonstrated earlier.

The Orthodox theological view, which we now employ, is that the *V* is an object from the intelligible domain, whereas the *W*, in its appearance to us, can be considered a part of sensible creation. What, then, does the transition $V \longrightarrow W$ mean? It shows not the creation of *W* out of *V* but, rather, the *differentiation* between the intelligible potentially existing worlds *V* and the sensible world *W*. Indeed, both *V* and *W* exhibit the fundamental *diaphora* in creation. An effort to explain the observable irreversibility of time in *W*, as an attempt to find the foundation of the whole world *W* in the nonbeing of *W*, led us to the scientific model of *diaphora* in the created world. The specificity of the big bang, articulated by Penrose, points in fact to the specificity of the *constitution* of the *creatio ex nihilo*, but not to its ontological mechanism. We contemplate these special constitutive elements of the *creatio ex nihilo* through the model of this difference between *V* and *W*. The difference between the worlds *W* and *V* is the indication of the presence, or absence, of a particular irreversibility of time and the observed order in the universe. This means that the fact of the irreversibility of time in *W* with its specific entropic features can be treated as a constitutive element of the *creatio ex nihilo*, because it provides the characteristic of its difference from other intelligible worlds *V*, where there is no irreversible flow of time, or time's arrow.

The antinomy formulated above in the context of Penrose's model can now be rephrased as an affirmative proposition on the constitution of creation:

God, creating the world out of nothing, sets up the difference between V (plurality of conceptual universes with different initial conditions) as the domain of intelligible creation, and our universe W (with the low initial entropy and hence irreversibility of time and presence of complex structures) as the realm of sensible creation.

From this point of view, the WCH of Penrose can be treated as an attempt to describe this *diaphora* between V and W, as it is seen from within W, that is, in physico-geometrical terms. The presence of the *diaphora* in the created being, detected in the Penrose model, reveals thus the common *logos* of both W and V, that is, that both of them are created (they have nonbeing as the ground for their being).[29] From here, one can conclude that the *logos* of the irreversibility of time (and the complexity and design following from it) is the principle that there is nonbeing of temporal flow, which is the ground for its being. This was exactly demonstrated in the model of Penrose, and it is why we can conclude that Penrose's model, treated through the eyes of Patristic theology, points toward the *logos* of creation.

We see that the problem of the irreversibility of time—that is, an attempt to explain the source of irreversibility of time through the special boundary conditions in the universe—leads inevitably to the result that it can be posed only in the context of the theological concept of *creatio ex nihilo*. This makes it possible to argue that it is in the problem of the irreversibility of time that we witness the presence of fundamental contingency, as the openness of physics to further explanation, coming from philosophy and theology. In this, the phenomenon of time manifests itself as relational upon atemporal reality and the nonintelligible (in human terms) reality of the uncreated God.

Irreversibility of Time through Irreversibility of Processes

In this section, we analyze a different attempt to explain the irreversibility of time, not in terms of geometrical boundary conditions in the universe but as the phenomenon that is driven by some underlying physical law that acts universally everywhere and which is revealed through the behavior of large complex systems. In this approach, which has been developed by Prigogine and his collaborators, empirical time, seen as irreversible temporal flow, is not a primary ontological entity in itself. Instead, it is determined by the processes in physical systems, which are involved in irreversible change because of special deep-level physical laws, so that the deep reason of time is in not the macroscopic world but the underlying (quantum) realm.

Prigogine expresses explicitly his view that the irreversible flow of time is something that can be connected only with a special kind of connection among particles in a complex system: "The arrow of time expresses a relation among the objects—be it among particles or fields. Time is not in the objects, but results from the dynamics; . . . irreversibility is not related to particles but to relations among particles."[30]

The rationale of this statement is straightforward: there is no time as a kind of physical or ontological entity apart and beyond the links and relations among the components of the physical world that are revealed through interactions and collective dynamics. In other words, there is no time and time's arrow as it is in itself. The arrow of time thus is not a mysterious metaphysical entity; rather, it is an *epiphenomenon* of the internal dynamics of physical systems, including the whole universe. This is why, if one wants to explain the nature of irreversibility of time, one should explain, according to Prigogine, why certain processes turn out to be irreversible.

To state this another way, Prigogine seems to assume that the nature of the irreversibility of time in this approach is hidden in some underlying physical factors that may be responsible for physical irreversibility in general. Unfortunately, this approach to the riddle of time in no way brings us closer to solving the riddle of time's irreversibility, because macroscopic flowing time escaped from the scene from the very beginning. Nevertheless, a heroic attempt to solve the mystery of the arrow of time in such an approach exposes further that the problem of the irreversibility of time is a philosophical (or even a theological) problem and can be tackled only by means of a proper discipline.

Let us trace some important stages in Prigogine's program of tackling the problem of time. The major motivation is the existence of the "time paradox" in classical physics, recalled briefly here. According to the commonly accepted view of classical dynamics, represented by either Newton's mechanics or Einstein's relativity, it does not provide in its mathematical expression any adequate means of tracing qualitative transformations in a physical system that could be associated with irreversibility or historical change. Simply speaking, classical mechanics (and actually all physics based on it) is time reversible.

This is because the dynamics of processes in classical mechanics is described by the solutions of ordinary differential equations, which by themselves do not contain any indication of the direction of time or history in the system they describe. In fact, the solutions of these equations are not unique if the set of the boundary conditions is not specified. The relation between the possible solution and the actual dynamics in the physical system can be established only if a particular trajectory is picked up out of many solutions by specifying, for example, its initial point. In fact, the condition that specifies a particular trajectory can be chosen at any point of this trajectory, which makes no difference between "initial" or "final" conditions or any other conditions in the middle. This implies that if one associates the points on this trajectory with a kind of "time" (it can be any parameter that provides a correspondence between the points of trajectory and the set of real numbers; the length measured along this trajectory from its initial point could be a good example), then all "moments" of this time in this dynamics are equivalent in the sense that they are all linked deterministically according to the dynamical law encoded in the differential equations. This means that there is effectively no distinction among "moments" corresponding to different points of trajectory; all of them are uniform and indistinguishable, so that one can affirm that there is no time as irreversible flow of novelty in this system. The complete symmetry between all points of a given trajectory means that "past," "present," and "future" in reversible dynamics simply do not exist. This allows us to guess that time, from the point of view of these simple processes, also does not exist. One concludes, then, that the ideal reversible processes, which are described by classical dynamics, do not contain time and cannot be used in order to study time. One can even speak about the timelessness of these special processes, for there are no temporal distinctions in their nature.

The time paradox appears, then, as an obvious contradiction between the time-reversible laws of classical mechanics and the outcomes of these laws in the macroscopic world, which exhibit irreversible patterns of behavior in complex systems, and the creation of *novelty* in chemical, biological, geological, and other physical phenomena.

Let us formulate the essence of the time paradox in some technical terms. We start with classical dynamics (that is, Newton dynamics and Maxwell-Lorentz theory). From a formal point of view, the dynamics of a free single particle is described by a trajectory in so-called phase space. The phase space corresponding to a single particle constitutes an abstract space of all its possible motions and, for a one-dimensional motion, is presented by a plane with two dimensions: one corresponds to the coordinate of the particle, the other to its momentum. A trajectory that corresponds to some particular motion is represented by a curve (one-dimensional manifold) with two boundary points, which are usually called the initial and final points of the particle's evolution. As pointed out earlier, in the reversible dynamics both of these points are dynamically equivalent as well as equivalent to all other points on this trajectory. The "time," appearing in this description as a parameter marking the points on trajectory from its initial point to the final point, can be easily reversed in the opposite direction so that the dynamics remains, although the logical order becomes reversed. Such reversible dynamics does not feature evolution in a proper sense of this word, because there is no real change in the system and no novelty emerges.

If we generalize this result, we can affirm that if for some physical system the "trajectory" presentation of its dynamics is possible, then the system is time reversible and does indicate the arrow of time.

One might hope that, by considering ensembles of free (noninteracting) particles, we would be able to introduce irreversibility into its dynamics. This is not the case, however, for we can easily replace a single trajectory by a "tube of trajectories" in phase space described by density function ρ. In analogy with our previous result, we can generalize as follows: if for some physical system of many particles the "tube of trajectories" presentation of its dynamics is possible, then the system is time reversible and does not indicate the arrow of time.

If we turn now to a quantum description of dynamics of a single particle—based on the Schrödinger equation for a wave function Ψ, where the location of a particle in space is determined only probabilistically in terms of $|\Psi(x)|^2$—the dynamics of probabilities is deterministic itself, for it follows, in a way, the same deterministic Schrödinger equation. This means that if we consider the motion of a single particle with a constant energy E, the solution of the Schrödinger equation is an oscillating function of time, leading to a trivial result that there is no change at all in the probabilities of locations of the particle, which implies that there is effectively no evolution in the system and, in fact, no time, for there is no distinction between past, present, and future. The same result (in analogy with nonquantum mechanics) holds for an ensemble of noninteracting particles.

We see thus that the reversibility present in dynamical equations of classical and quantum mechanics—or, in different terms, the symmetry of dynamical laws of physics with respect to the inversion of time—leads in fact to the conclusion that physics, based on these laws, does not allow any description of "history" as the emergence of novelty, which is irreversible in the sense that the events of history, being brought into being, cannot be undone or eliminated by "antievents." In this, historicity contrasts with determinism, which is present in the laws of dynamics.[31] Prigogine affirms that a change present in the classical description of trajectories is, in fact, a denial of becoming, for "time" is a mere parameter, which is not affected by the process it describes. This is a manifestation of determinism, which in its ideal denies contingency as well as empirically observed irreversible processes; the growth of complexity in physical, chemical, and biological systems; the emergence of life and the arrow of time. The contrast between the deterministic and time-reversible dynamics, which (according to classical physics) drives the world, and the evidence of irreversible processes and systems—which cannot be precisely described by these laws cannot be understood from within the complete set of given conditions, and requires some extra-factors not described by dynamics—constitutes, according to Prigogine, the "paradox of time." On the one hand, there is no time in the underlying deterministic description of the physical world; on the other hand, there is empirical irreversibility of time observed in complex systems. This paradox, Prigogine argues, must be resolved, for otherwise it leads to dualism in physics.

Irreversibility and Two Views of Nature

Past attempts to resolve the time paradox were based on the common belief that its origin comes from the specificity of the scientific description of the world. In fact, there were two views of nature: one held that the deep, fundamental level of physical reality was described by classical physics and that knowledge about this world is a perfect knowledge; the other was derived from everyday experience and from those parts of experimental physics that demonstrated explicitly the existence of irreversible processes in nature. Scientists tried to explain the irreversibility and irreducibility of its description to deterministic time-symmetric dynamics by referring to the lack of knowledge of microscopic motions of particles involved in macroscopic irreversible processes. If we could know all parameters of microscopic motions with an infinite precision, we might achieve a "perfect knowledge," which would explain away the observable macroscopic irreversibility.

What is striking, however, is that nobody expressed any doubt about the perfectness and exactitude of the underlying reality (or ontology, denoted here as UR), in which the deterministic and time-symmetric physics were supposed to reign and which were supposed to be responsible for the macroscopic (empirical) level of reality (ER), where time irreversibility is undeniable. Nobody could assume that the realm of deterministic and time-reversible physics was a special case of a much more complex state of affairs in the UR, which could be complex and irreversible. Thus the separation of the deterministic and time-symmetric processes in UR and the irreversible processes in ER led to a strange dualism in views about nature.

Historically, however, this was a contradictory dualism, for it was a tendency to explain irreversible phenomena in terms of deterministic dynamics (for example, the attempt by Boltzmann to explain the growth of entropy from dynamical equations). Such attempts manifested the belief that there must be a single level of reality that explains everything. But it was not realized in the past that processes in UR and ER manifested two different types of behavior in physical systems that cannot be ultimately reduced to each other. In other words, an attempt to provide a physically consistent explanation of the transition

$$UR \longrightarrow ER \text{ (fig. 6.1)}$$

by removing thereby the dualism in views of nature did not succeed, because it was an epistemological attempt to reconcile the descriptions of two ontologically different realms, which cannot be described in the same conceptual terms. To succeed with such a unification, one should change the whole physical paradigm so as to be able to justify the transition (fig. 6.1) on the ontological level.

The historical development of classical physics demonstrated that it was unable to solve the mystery of irreversibility and time's arrow, which where observed in the empirical realm (macroscopic world). Classical physics had to recognize that its conceptual basis was not sufficient to tackle the problem of the arrow of time and to accept the arrow as a fundamental ingredient of reality, without further explanation in terms of classical dynamics.

Despite all this, a strong subconscious belief existed that there must be a physical explanation of the origin of the arrow of time. This belief in the ultimate character of the arrow of time and, at the same time, an inability to explain it in a logically consistent way gave rise to an epistemological situation in classical physics that can be described as an antinomy about the origin of the arrow of time:

Thesis: The world is governed by some unknown fundamental physical law, which is the necessary cause for the existence of the arrow of time in the visible universe.

Antithesis: No special but unknown physical law that is a necessary cause for the arrow of time in the visible universe exists in this universe.

Formally, the thesis represents the point of view of a dogmatically optimistic physicist, believing in the existence of the physical cause of the arrow of time, while the antithesis represents the point of view of an empirical physicist who observes the arrow of time but is unable to explain it. Together, the two conflicting views indicate that the arrow of time manifests itself as a brute fact that cannot be explained by positive science and needs for its clarification an intervention from philosophy and theology.

According to our previous experience of dealing with antinomies, we should assert that their presence expresses the fact that classical physics approached closely the borderline between the two distinct realms of being with which it was dealing, with no successful attempt to reconcile them. Namely, there was the world of ideal motions, in which time was not present at all; this was first the world of classical mechanics, by its constitution an intelligible state of affairs, which was described by using abstract mathematical space and nonobservable trajectories in phase space. On the other hand, there was the evident presence of the arrow of time in the empirical realm. The reconciliation of these two realms was problematic by definition, for how could one find the foundation of the arrow of time, which is revealed through the empirical temporal series of causations, by appealing as a cause of it to the laws, which have no indication at all of the presence of temporality, for they represent the "dynamics" in intelligible series, rather than temporal. The trick with using the atemporal physical laws as a limiting term of temporal causations in the empirical realm did not work, for the laws of classical dynamics were considered as acting here and now, rather than from the remote past or future of a temporal series. This makes the problem of time's arrow in classical dynamics different from the problem of time's arrow in the context of the cosmological initial conditions, which was discussed in previous sections.

For Penrose, the time-symmetry of the local physical laws was an indication to look for the source of irreversibility in special boundary conditions, avoiding thereby the time paradox in Prigogine's sense. Whereas, for the latter, the challenge of modern physics is to resolve this paradox without appealing to the remote boundary conditions but, rather, trying to extend the local dynamics enough that it would provide a mechanism of an internal irreversibility here and now. In this case, the transition (fig. 6.1) could be explained on the ontological (physical) level by removing the antinomy of classical physics. It is possible to predict in advance, however, that such an attempt would run into severe difficulties with treating the mechanisms that "take place" in *UR* as physically real. In other words, the hope to change an ontology of *UR*, in order to level it with the ontology of *ER*, is philosophically suspicious, for it leads ultimately to a monistic view of reality. Indeed, if the paradox of time's arrow were to be solved in physical terms, the element of contingency in time, which is present because of the insufficiency of classical mechanics to remove it, as well as expressed epistemologically in the antinomy, would be replaced by an ultimate necessity present in the world, removing the historical change and making it a part of blind and dispassionate universal dynamics.

Prigogine's Treatment of the Time Paradox

According to Prigogine, the key element for resolving the paradox of time must be new dynamics, that is, new laws that could explain the emergence of irreversibility at the fundamental level of reality (in *UR*). This dynamics must be irreversible by definition and must feature two important properties: to contain "interactions" and to be "nonintegrable."

The view that interactions may be responsible for the observed macroscopic irreversibility dates back to the work of L. Boltzmann, who established the general fact that the evolution of a large system with collisions/interactions among its particles leads to disorder because of these interactions. For Boltzmann, the increase of disorder, which can be described formally by the function entropy, can be used to indicate the directed evolution in the system, whereas entropy can be viewed as encoding the growth of time.

One can reassert that macroscopic evolution was associated with the interaction of particles, or the different parts of a large system. We remember, however, that classical physics was always trying to remove an element of irreversibility in its theory, so that its first attempt to keep reversible dynamics in its formalism resulted in an attempt to remove all ingredients in the theory that could lead to irreversibility—the interactions among particles, for example. If this were to be possible—that is, if the interacting particles could be described effectively as noninteracting—then they would follow reversible dynamics, and irreversibility would be excluded. The systems where such a transform is possible are called *integrable*. To establish the dynamics of such a system means to integrate the differential equations that describe it; if it is possible, then it is proved that the system is time reversible. It follows then that the property of a system of particles to be integrable is equivalent to this system being reversible and to its having no internal time.

As is now recognized, the class of integrable systems in nature is quite narrow, so that the reversible processes represent a special case in physics, whereas the majority of realistic systems exhibit such complicated interactions that the integration of the equations and the deterministic description of their motion are impossible. The formal distinction between integrable and nonintegrable dynamical systems was introduced by H. Poincaré.[32] In integrable systems, the potential energy of interaction between parts or particles can be excluded from the expression of the full energy of a system through a suitable transformation of the so-called canonical variables. The system for which this kind of transformation is possible is equivalent to a system of noninteracting particles with reversible dynamics and is called integrable. All systems in which this transformation is impossible are called nonintegrable.

In his famous theorem of 1892, Poincaré proved that, in general, this transformation is impossible. He described a special class of systems, which later were called Large Poincaré Systems (LPS), in which the interactions between the parts of a system could not be excluded due to a special type of behavior (called "resonances") between their degrees of freedom. If there are "enough" resonances, the system is not integrable. As shown later by A. Kolmogorov, V. Arnold, and J. Moser, the evolution of those degrees of freedom that are involved in resonances cannot be described in terms of trajectories.[33] In other words, their trajectories become random and unpredictable, so that the determinism that is usually associated with the trajectory description is lost, and, as a result, the symmetry between past, present, and future is lost in these systems; that is, they manifest irreversible behavior and contain some internal time.

This leads to the important conclusion that classical determinism, which is assumed to be an inevitable consequence of reversible dynamics, is no longer a universal concept and can now be attributed only to very special physical systems.[34]

It is not difficult to realize that the observed irreversible processes are the unavoidable result of the evolution of large complex systems (LPS) in the universe. In fact, the very evolution of the visible universe indicates that the universe itself is an example of LPS.

Coming back to Prigogine's intention to build the new dynamics, we can now formulate more precisely what it means in theoretical terms. We have already mentioned that time-reversible dynamical systems can always be described in terms of trajectories in phase space. It is because of this that the idea of irreversible dynamics on the fundamental level of description is associated with a change such that the trajectory representation in this dynamics will no longer be valid.

What are the philosophical implications of this program? First, when one says that the time-reversible behavior of physical systems in the macroscopic world makes it possible to think of this system as following some trajectory in a phase space, one implies that phase space itself is a more fundamental aspect of physical reality than the variety of observable phenomena, and that the macroscopic properties of the system are somehow predetermined by its development in the underlying phase space. But the phase space is *not* an element of physical reality understood as object in macroscopic space-time. This way of thinking corresponds to the assumption that there is a physical causation from phase space $S \in UR$ to observed irreversibility in space-time in ER that is, that the transition $UR \longrightarrow ER$ is believed to be physical. However, phase space S is an abstract mathematical concept that is believed to have some physical meaning, but its ontological status is unclear.

We are here confronted with an interesting epistemological paradox. We observe time-reversible phenomena on the macroscopic level, describing them in terms of factual appearances. Our understanding then summarizes the multitude of disconnected facts under its own categories to produce some unifying conceptual totality that explains this variety. A striking feature of this description is that it uses mathematical constructs that have no direct correlation with anything in physical reality. To explain the observed physical phenomena, one appeals to elements that belong not to the world of physical reality but to the world of ideas. In this approach, the responsibility for the time-reversible character of some processes is ascribed not to the world of physical phenomena (to ER) but to some kind of conceptual "underlying reality" (to UR), namely, to mathematical phase space S (whose ontological status is quite vague).

From this point of view, Prigogine's program of building irreversible dynamics in phase space that would eliminate trajectories and, as result, lead to macroscopic irreversibility has the following philosophical interpretation: to introduce irreversibility into the description of macroscopic processes, one should attempt to recover irreversible dynamics not from the physical world of phenomena (from *ER*) but from a nonclassical mechanism that operates in the mathematical phase space, which is beyond the empirical realm. If this mechanism, which leads to the destruction of trajectories in phase space, were found, one would be able to claim that it can be used as a base for the new dynamics and is responsible for macroscopic irreversibility. The major philosophical assumption of Prigogine's program, which makes it possible to use such an interpretation, is that there is a physical causal link between the mechanism in phase space and the processes in the empirical realm, that is, that there is some physics behind the transition $S \longrightarrow ER$.

An amazing and nontrivial feature of this program is that, in order to invent a mechanism that can eliminate trajectories from phase space S, one has to make a further appeal to the another underlying reality, so to speak, on the next order, which is in a deeper level than S and which in some sense sustains and explains S. One can name this "reality" provisionally a Hilbert space H. The meaning of H can be illustrated if one presents a trajectory, describing the transition from one state to another in S, as a superposition of all *possible* trajectories, or histories, in H that can cause this particular transition in S. It is important to remember that these "histories" do not belong to the phase space S, because they describe all potential, but not actual, ways by which the system can evolve from one state to another and which are described by a given trajectory in S. This trajectory is presented mathematically as a continuous sum (integral) of all logically possible histories of the system in H in which the integration goes over some parameter k, which corresponds to a given history.

The achievement of Prigogine's group was to demonstrate that for LPS systems, where the so-called resonances between the degrees of freedom take place, the amplitude of the transition between two histories in Hilbert space H becomes a "Fokker-Planck operator" that leads to diffusion in momentum space H and, as a result, to the destruction of trajectories in S. This in turn gives rise to macroscopic irreversibility, which is expressed in terms of the *flow of correlations* among particles. This flow makes it possible to introduce a mechanism of "aging" in many particle systems, that is, to introduce a natural "arrow of time."[35]

Since the interactions among particles may be understood as a flow of correlations from two particles to three particles and from three particles to four particles and so on, the increase of entropy as a measure of irreversibility in LPS will be an unending process due to the tremendous amount of particles in the universe. Since the irreversible processes turn out to be inevitable ingredients of physical reality, it is understood accordingly that they are responsible for all constructive processes in the universe, such as the creation of its large-scale structure of galaxies, stars, planets, human bodies, and so on. These stable structures manifest the effect of long-range coherence, which is possible only because of interactions and instabilities.[36] The top position (in terms of complexity) in the evolving systems belongs to anthropic species. It is because of this that one can affirm along the lines of the so-called anthropic principle that the irreversibility of the universe and the arrow of time constitute the necessary conditions for human beings to come into existence.[37]

From Irreversibility in Physics to Theological Contingency

Let us reflect on the results outlined above. The structure of Prigogine's search for the ultimate source of macroscopic irreversibility can be summarized as a double transition among three types of reality:

Hilbert space $\longrightarrow$ phase space $\longrightarrow$ macroscopic world

This formula demonstrates that in order to explain evolution in the macroscopic empirical world ER, physicists persistently construct the models of its underlying mechanisms using mathematical constructions that are freely created by human reason and that by their constitution do not belong to the physical world ER. Classical physics introduced the idea of phase space S, which for a very long time was identified with the first level of underlying reality. A further synthesis in quantum physics forced a physicist to introduce the idea of the Hilbert space H, which functions as the underlying reality of the second level. The conceptual trajectory description of the dynamics in S received its new interpretation as a sum of all logically possible histories in H. By its logical status, the reality that is associated with H is on a deeper level than that of S, so that the new dynamics of Prigogine in H in a sense justifies the dynamics of trajectories in S. In the same way we say that S underlies ER, we can affirm that H underlies S as well as ER. But both S and H are only two peaks of the evolution of our physical theories, in which we have been steadily forced backward, from abstraction to abstraction, always explaining the coarse and solid of empirical reality by means of the fine and ethereal of the intelligible realm.

If there is the set of histories in H such that it can be integrated and hence can lead to the trajectory in S, then the double transition in the last formula could describe the dynamics of the reversible evolution in a physical system. The presence of irreversibility in the macroscopic world from this perspective can be treated in the framework of classical physics as a puzzle of the transition from the underlying realm UR, with time-symmetric dynamic laws, to the group of irreversible phenomena in ER, which we can denote as ER_{irr}. The problem, then, of classical physics was to explain the irreversibility in ER through the hidden nature of the relationship

$$UR_{rev} \longrightarrow ER_{irr} \in ER \text{ (fig. 6.2)}$$

If we look carefully at the formula (fig. 6.2), we identify immediately some asymmetry between UR_{rev} and ER. The realm UR_{rev} corresponds to time-reversible physical laws, whereas *ER* contains both reversible and irreversible phenomena. As Prigogine showed, one can easily explain the mechanism of the transition $UR_{rev} \longrightarrow ER_{rev} \in ER$, that is, to claim that there are some reversible laws in UR_{rev} that are responsible for the reversible processes in ER_{rev}. It is clear, however, that the class of the underlying structures, such as phase space *S* and Hilbert space *H*, is very special. In other words, the subclass of the reversible phenomena (ER_{rev}) is logically and probably physically connected with a special subset of the underlying realm UR_{rev}.

If we now take into account the results of Prigogine's group, which were explained briefly above, we should admit that it is possible to explain the irreversible phenomena in *ER* only if the structure of the *UR* is radically changed, that is, if the phase space does not contain trajectories (which effectively means that *S* itself no longer exists as a space of trajectories). The most interesting result of Prigogine and Petrosky was to show that the mechanism of the destruction of trajectories, which was initially assumed to be in Hilbert space *H*, destroys the structure of this space, so that neither *S* nor *H* can be used as a conceptual ground for explaining the irreversible phenomena in *ER*; that is, they cannot provide logical or physical causation with ER_{irr}.[38] This implies that the scheme (fig. 6.2) whose explanation was a final dream of classical physics cannot be used for interpretation of irreversible phenomena.

This implies that to explain the existence of ER_{irr} by appealing to some underlying structures, the structures must definitely be different from *S* and *H*; if we denote them as UR_{irr}, then the explanation of phenomena in ER_{irr} would mean providing a physics of the transition

$$UR_{irr} \longrightarrow ER_{irr} \in ER$$

We rearticulate the meaning of this formula because, in order to explain the irreversible phenomena in the empirical realm, one should appeal to mathematical models of the underlying mechanisms of these phenomena, which will be radically different from what is known from classical time-reversible physics (that is, it must be neither phase space *S* nor Hilbert space *H*).

This is a nontrivial consequence of Prigogine's effort to solve the riddle of time, which makes it possible to reformulate the dualism about the nature of reality that was discussed above. One should now recognize how deep is the essential distinction between reversible and irreversible physical processes. They are different not only in their appearance in the empirical realm *ER* but also on the level of the underlying fundamental reality *UR*, which is supposed to be a logical and physical ground of these processes as observable in *ER*. It follows therefore that in order to understand the physics of the irreversible processes, one should change the fundamental description of classical physics.

This change will amount to a substantial shift in our understanding of the physical world in general. We will not ascribe macroscopic irreversibility to a deficiency of our description. On the contrary, we have reason to insist that irreversibility demands consistent and coherent description (by using new mathematical concepts), which, however, leads us beyond the scope of classical physics. Rephrased in philosophical language, one needs an epistemology that can justify a new physics of irreversible processes. We intentionally use the term *epistemology*, not *ontology*, because we are aware that most of the models of underlying reality giving a fragment of a "theory" of irreversible phenomena are, by construction, far beyond the sphere of our immediate cognitive faculties and represent some ideas of physical discursive reason that transcend the world of phenomena, understood as a world of our physical experience *ER*.

In classical physics, we had a dualism between the variety of physical phenomena, including complexity and irreversibility (*ER*) and the underlying reality of perfect physical laws (*UR*). Now, following Prigogine, we have arrived at a more sophisticated dualism, which affirms that there are two complementary kinds of processes in the universe: (1) reversible processes, described in terms of $ER_{rev} \in ER$ and explained in terms of the corresponding $UR_{rev} \in UR$; and (2) irreversible processes as a different subclass of physical phenomena, described in terms of $ER_{irr} \in ER$ and explained, according to Prigogine, in terms of the new dynamics in $UR_{irr} \in UR$.

We feel intuitively that it is a fundamental feature of macroscopic reality to be in motion, to evolve, to pass in time, to produce novelty. We also intuitively feel that the future is open, that it is not fixed or determined in advance. This understanding stimulates our search for an ultimate cause of the passage of time. However, evolution, irreversibility, passage of time always mocks and eludes our rational attempts to grasp everything by subordinating it to our empirical realism of classical physics; it leads us astray from the starting point of its search, from the experience itself. The epistemology that classical physics follows cannot provide a unified description of reversible and irreversible processes. In both cases, it was necessary to appeal to underlying conceptual realities, which by their construction should explain the processes in the *ER*. The new dualism, however, led to the split of the underlying reality into two distinct blocks. We can rearticulate that the new dualism has not removed the duality in views on the interplay between the observable phenomena and the fundamental physics that suppose to describe them from the underlying realm. The logic of Prigogine's approach to the riddle of irreversibility of time brings us to a clear understanding that the irreversibility, if one wants to explain it in physical terms, demands that classical physics change first of all on the conceptual level. This change, however, leads to a split in the ontology of the underlying reality, manifesting thereby the irreducible nature of irreversible physics to one that is reversible in both the empirical and the intelligible realms.

We are inclined to argue that this indicates that the mystery of time's irreversibility cannot be resolved by any theory. Any attempt to appeal to some underlying physical mechanisms that are assumed to be existent ontologically and expressed conceptually through mathematics is doomed not to explain the problem but to shift it onto an underlying level, which will in turn demand its further explanation. The danger of this approach is that the advance toward conceptual realities that can underlie the empirically observable flow of time is probably unending, so that the ultimate term of the chain of intelligible causations that are assumed to describe empirical time cannot belong to the temporal series themselves, leading the search for its source outside physics to the sphere of philosophy and theology.

Let us pause on this last statement. Since UR in both views on nature cannot be observed directly, one might conjecture that there is only some kind of "causality of reason" that, after all, can bridge the difference between UR and ER. The belief that UR as the fundamental reality is responsible for the variety of the phenomena in ER is very close to the philosophical idea of "things-in-themselves" affecting our senses.[39] It is interesting here that the difference in the empirical realm (as to reversible and irreversible processes) as a structure of the ER cascades down toward the underlying reality UR, which is now structured as the difference between UR_{rev} and UR_{irr}. The world of "things-in-themselves" (UR) is structured in the same way as the world of "things-for-us" (ER): we have two types of the empirical realm, which correspond to two types of the underlying reality. Thus we can argue that there two types of causality of reason, which link two pairs of nonintersecting worlds: one that is applicable for justifying the reversible processes $UR_{rev} \longrightarrow ER_{rev}$ and another for irreversible processes $UR_{irr} \longrightarrow ER_{irr}$.

We are now in a position to address whether something has changed in the epistemological status of the idea of time's arrow after the new dualism in views about nature has been brought into physics by Prigogine's ideas. Unfortunately, we have to state that nothing has changed. Despite the fact that his dynamics indicates a source of macroscopic irreversibility inherent in physical reality, the problem of the ontological status of UR_{irr} is unsolved. Since, from a philosophical point of view, we cannot point to any evidence of the objective existence of UR_{irr}—that is, such an existence that could be formulated in terms of physical space and time—we cannot claim that the source of time's arrow belongs to the physical world.[40] What we can do, and have done, is to invent two incompatible hypotheses concerning the nature of UR_{irr}. This leads us naturally to the view that the idea of the arrow of time can be treated only through the antinomian form of thought, setting out the limits of our capacities in tackling this problem of time. The justification for this comes from a simple Kantian formula: that since UR_{irr} is constructed in order to justify the temporal series in ER_{irr}, there must be some connection between them on the physical level so that the temporality of UR_{irr} cascades up toward temporality in ER_{irr}. In this case, UR_{irr}, by logic of the argument, must belong to the same temporal series as does ER_{irr}. On the other hand, since UR_{irr} is a purely intelligible object (that is, it does not belong to the temporal series of causation), the causation in the transition $UR_{irr} \longrightarrow ER_{irr}$ is purely intelligible; that is, the temporal series in ER_{irr} are attempted to be explained by the jump to the ontological origin of this series in an atemporal world of intelligible forms. This situation can be formally described by the following "antinomy of time's arrow":

Thesis: The world is ruled from some unknown physical level UR_{irr}, whose existence is absolutely necessary for the existence of the arrow of time (macroscopic statistical irreversibility) in the visible universe (ER).

Antithesis: There is simply no unknown fundamental-level UR_{irr} as a necessary cause of the arrow of time in the visible universe, either in the world or out of it.

The presence of an antinomy in reasoning about the irreversibility of time indicates, in accordance with the logic established earlier in the context of Hawking's cosmology and Penrose's conjecture, that any attempt to solve the mystery of time's arrow—that is, to find its ultimate foundation in the physical world—leads human reason inevitably to a transcendence beyond the empirical physical world to the realm of intelligible physics, which is considered the foundation of the empirical flow of time. Prigogine's attempt to construct a theory of the mechanism that is pushing time forward revealed with a new force the intuition that the foundation of time is not in the physical world and that theoretical advance in physics is amazingly similar to what is known from philosophy as an endless regressing in causations further from the observable physical world.

Finally, one can argue that Prigogine's theory provides us with more evidence that physics, in its attempt to tackle the ultimate questions, has to deal with a dualistic structure of being (the dichotomy between sensible and intelligible), which, as we have established before, reflects the constitutive differentiation in the created world, its *diaphora*. The significance of this new articulation of the *diaphora* in Prigogine's theory is that it was previously obscured by classical physics, which, by postulating dualism in two views of nature (reversible/irreversible), was attempting to remove it in favor of a monistic description of the world, which was supposed to explain away the contingency of the created realm. It is interesting that Prigogine's attempt to provide a fundamental description of irreversibility through the underlying physical mechanism is similar to the attempt of classical physics to reconcile the visible world with the invisible. What it proves, however, is that the gap between the reversible and irreversible processes is much deeper than was thought in classical physics and that the difference between empirical irreversible phenomena and their explanatory mechanisms in the intelligible realm is much more articulated in terms of the nonclassical and nonvisual nature of the latter.

The lesson of Prigogine's theory strengthens even further the conclusion that the more we deal with the irreversible processes the less we understand their origin. If intrinsic irreversibility drives the life of complex structures, including such systems as the planetary biosphere and individual biological forms, the ultimate origin of these systems cannot be described in temporal terms, for, according to Prigogine, the past of these systems is detached from their present by an infinite entropy barrier, which cannot be overcome. This corresponds to our conclusion that what Prigogine's theory of irreversible processes actually demonstrates is that the riddle of time cannot be explained away by constructing a particular mechanism; it remains the mystery of the whole constitution of the created world, including both the sensible and the intelligible realms—that is, finally it is linked to the problem of fundamental contingency of the world, its creation by God out of nothing.

One should stress, however, that our conclusion about Prigogine's model as rearticulating the contingency of the world upon the ground that is in its nonbeing, or its otherness, is made not as if Prigogine had proved the fundamental irreversibility of everything implying contingency, but from a different perspective: by reducing the problem of time's arrow to the problem of the basic differentiation in the created world between the sensible (with flow of time) and the intelligible (timeless, or with transcendent time).[41] In other words, we treat the arrow of time as the expression of the split in creation between the sensible and the intelligible, which is the manifestation of the contingency of the world in a theological sense. In its essence, this conclusion is similar to what we formulated in the context of Penrose's model. Since the pattern of this split (that is, the basic *diaphora*), is applicable to both reversible and irreversible processes, both types are independently contingent on nonworldly factors. This implies that the link between irreversibility and contingency must not be absolutized; that is, any conjecture about the underlying laws of irreversible natural processes neither explains the contingency away in a monistic sense nor provides any direct evidence for it. This is why one should be cautious when making a distinction between contingency in a theological sense and contingency of processes as the unpredictability of their outcomes, on the one hand, and the lack of determinism in nature in general, on the other. This means that the famous question posed by W. Pannenberg to scientists—"Is the reality of nature to be understood as contingent, and are natural processes to be understood as irreversible?"—must be met with care, for it can give the impression that any display of irreversibility in nature points directly toward contingency in a theological sense.[42] As we have seen in this chapter, the situation is much more complicated, for irreversibility can be caused by special initial conditions (Penrose's case), which implies that it is not irreversibility itself that points toward contingency in this case but, rather, its original cause, which is the initial conditions in the universe. In this case, the whole of physics can be time reversible, but the observable universe will manifest the irreversibility. It is our inability to make a clear distinction between the effects of the remote initial conditions, on the one hand, and the outcomes of the dynamic laws acting here and now, on the other hand, that makes the problem of the link between contingency and irreversibility hardly solvable on purely physical grounds. The confirmation to this was provided in an indirect way by the works of Prigogine and his group.

Prigogine, in his tremendous efforts, wanted to overcome this incompleteness of classical physics in order to restore the unity of the physical realm in such a way that both reversible and irreversible phenomena would be described within one conceptual frame. This means that his new theories of irreversible processes were supposed to explain irreversibility in terms of new dynamics. But what does it mean to explain it? It means to explain the contingency of classical physics away! Yes, his world is irreversible here and now—there is no strict determinism, apart from the statistical one—but there is internal dynamics behind this irreversibility, which means that on the level of ultimate physical reality, according to Prigogine, there is a *law* that drives irreversibility. This implies that, if we want to speak seriously about the contingency that follows from Prigogine's explanation of irreversibility, we must explain the contingency of its underlying (new) physical laws. Irreversibility taken as a brute fact can point toward contingency only in the sense that there is the contingency of the underlying physical laws.

Finally, one can assert that the problem of the irreversibility of processes is linked to the unsolvable mystery of the irreversibility of time, which is not entirely decoded in the physics of these processes.[43] T. Torrance expressed this thought as follows: "Real on-going time which, in metaphorical parlance 'flows', time which 'passes', is intrinsic to all contingent reality and must be interpreted as such, while in the nature of case it retains an open structure like all contingent forms of order. Time thus understood is elusive and cannot, of course, be objectified but requires appropriate modes of apprehension and articulation, and as such needs to be brought into scientific inquiry, not as a linear instrument for measuring velocities, but as an internal dynamic functioning of contingent order."[44]

It is from the perspective of this vision of time as inherent in the contingent order that Torrance gives his view of Prigogine's theory with the operator of time by saying that "while time is brought as an internal operator into physics, real time relations are still not built into the warp and woof of mathematical induction and explanation."[45]

This implies that all modern attempts to give an accomplished physical description of the irreversibility of time are doubtful, for the real effect of the proposed theories, if they are taken without careful philosophical and theological reflection, is not to provide further insights into the contingency of the world but to explain it away. Torrance and Pannenberg argue in a similar direction that a physics must be developed that will incorporate the inevitability of irreversible time not through outwardly allocating a kind of function or operator as substitution for real time but by building time itself into the *logic* of the physics of contingent being.

In analyzing two attempts to tackle the riddles of irreversibility and of time's arrow, we have found similar results. In both cases considered in this chapter, physical reason has brought us to the edge of possible scientific explanation by suggesting models of some ultimate underlying reality that is considered responsible for the observed macroscopic irreversibility of time. These models represent ideas that, while not being abstracted from experience, are at the same time not applicable to the data of sense intuition. These ideas transcend our ordinary experience in the sense that no objects are given, or can possibly be given, within experience that correspond to them. According to Kant, transcendental ideas are produced because of the natural tendency of the human mind to search for unconditioned principles of unity. The transcendental ideas exercise an important regulative function by suggesting scientific explanatory hypotheses; however, all attempts to use the ideas as a foundation of science involve us in logical fallacies and antinomies.

Current ideas about an underlying reality to explain the origin of time all stem from a general tendency of the human mind to look for the wholeness of scientific description beyond the sphere of immediate experience and to invoke the realities of the intelligible realm as the explanatory pattern. Using Kant's method as a methodological tool and placing it in a proper theological frame, we have revealed the meaning of the proposed models of temporal irreversibility as pointing toward its ultimate ground in the otherness of the world, in the transcendent sphere of the Divine.

The problem of the irreversibility of time and processes is thus qualified as a theological problem of the creation of time in the context of the doctrine of *creatio ex nihilo*. Science itself cannot provide a consistent and accomplished theory of irreversibility, in the same way that it cannot explain away the contingency of nature in a theological sense. One can conclude, then, that both models of irreversibility of time—those of Penrose and Prigogine—provide invaluable material for a theological analysis, which uncovers in them the presence of implicit theological ingredients (such as *diaphora* in creation) that outline the similarity between the world at large and the anthropological constitution of humankind as the world in small (microcosm).

7

Humanity as Hypostasis of the Universe

There are in personality natural foundation principles which are linked with the cosmic cycle. But the personal in man is of different extraction and of different quality and it always denotes a break with natural necessity. . . . Man as personality is not part of nature, he has within him the image of God. There is nature in man, but he is not nature. Man is a microcosm and therefore he is not part of the cosmos.

—Nicolas Berdyaev, *Slavery and Freedom*, 94–95

The fact that the universe has expanded in such a way that the emergence of conscious mind in it is an essential property of the universe, must surely mean that we cannot give an adequate account of the universe in its astonishing structure and harmony without taking into account, that is, without including conscious mind as an essential factor in our scientific equations. . . . Without man, nature is dumb, but it is man's part to give it word: to be its mouth through which the whole universe gives voice to the glory and majesty of the living God.

—Thomas F. Torrance, *The Ground and Grammar of Theology*, 4

This chapter develops the idea that the phenomenon of intelligent human life in the universe, which we call the *humankind-event*, is not entirely conditioned (in terms of its existence) by the *natural* structures and laws of the universe. The actual happening of the humankind-event, which is treated as a *hypostatic* event, is contingent on nonnatural factors that point toward the uncreated realm of the Divine. We develop an argument that modern cosmology, if seen in a wide philosophical and theological context, provides indirect evidence for the contingency of the universe on nonphysical factors, as well as its intelligibility, established in the course of the humankind-event, which is rooted in the Logos of God and detected by human beings through the *logoi* of creation. The universe, as experienced through human scientific discursive thinking, thus becomes a part of the humankind-event; that is, the universe itself acquires the features of the hypostatic event in the Logos of God.

Defining the Humankind-Event

Before we discuss the anthropic inference in cosmology, we must look at the phenomenon of human life from a cosmological perspective. We intentionally talk about human life but not about biological life in general, for we are interested here in the meaning of human conscious life, life that has not only natural (physical and biological) dimensions but also hypostatic dimensions, whose essence is to affirm that human beings are not isolated creatures but are relational beings, whose personhood is formed through the relationship of these beings to one another as well as to the source of their existence in the Divine. Thus the phenomenon of human life in the cosmos is to be seen from the point of view of the whole economy of salvation of man, which includes the creation of the world and its redemption and ultimate transfiguration.

This is why we want to separate the issue of biological forms of life in the universe in general from the particular issue of the existence of intelligent human beings, who are able to contemplate the overall order in the universe, its meaning, and to detect the transcendent source of this order, and who can have beliefs and purposes, which can influence their own nature as well as nature of the whole universe.[1] Theology contemplates the meaning of human life as that of *persons* in their relationship to one another and to God. It characterizes humans, who were created in the image of God, through the view that the line that demarcates creature and creator cannot be abolished, yet human beings have the potential of self-transcendence to attain the likeness to God (that is, to be deified). It is through this hypostatic mode of existence that human beings are capable of gratitude to God for creation and can offer the world back to the Creator in thanksgiving, contemplating thus, through their *eucharistic* function, the meaning of the whole world as God's good creation.[2]

What we are affirming here is that the phenomenon of man, if seen from a wide perspective, is not something that is inherent in the story of a large and various universe but, rather, is an *event* in the whole cosmic history (as understood now by modern cosmology). This event is unique not only in a sense of the fine-tuning of some particular aspects of its happening in the universe but literally as the unrepeatable experience of existence in the universe, which cannot be modeled scientifically in different places and different ages of the universe. Our aim, then, is to assert that the whole experience of the world, which is performed by humankind, is a flash of the cosmological memory, incarnate in a particular place in the universe for a fixed aeon, destined to disappear in order to fulfill its eschatological destiny.

Thus the humankind-event can be treated similarly to the Christ-event as a happening of an extraordinary nature, requiring for its explanation the appeal to transnatural principles that will have to elucidate not only the reasons for the humankind-event to happen but also the ultimate purpose of this event for the fate of the entire universe.

When we insist that the phenomenon of humanity is the *event,* we want to make it clear that there is an element of historicity in it, that is, some fundamental, irreversible change in the history of the universe that makes the emergence of human life in the universe not a blind fact of chance but, rather, a hypostasized *existence* that is fundamentally different compared with other forms of matter and different forms of biological life.

In order to convince the reader of this claim, we start with a simple observation: that the phenomenon of man, if seen from a cosmological perspective (that is, from the point of view of the place and age it occupies in the overall history of the universe), and simply in physico-biological terms, represents a tiny island in the vast ocean of physical being. Indeed, according to modern cosmology, the universe is old and large. Its estimated age T varies from between 10 and 15 billion years, and its maximal observable size, corresponding to the distance that light can travel during the time T, is equal to $R_U \approx 10^{28}$ centimeters. If we accept that the humanoid type of life appeared on the earth approximately 1 million years ago, it is not difficult to estimate, in relative units, that the amount of time that human life exists in the universe Δt with respect to the age of the universe T is

$$\Delta t/T \approx 10^{-4}.$$

As to the relative space occupied in the universe by humankind (we mean the earth, with a radius of $R_E \approx 10^9$ centimeters), the ratio will be even more impressive:

$$R_E/R_U \approx 10^{-19}.$$

It is not difficult to realize that the volume occupied by humans on the earth will be $\approx 10^{-57}$ of the volume of the observable universe. The illustration in figure 7.1 makes these calculations even more impressive.

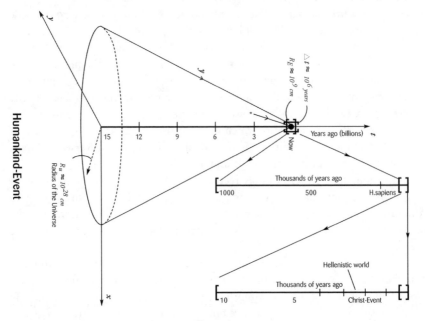

FIGURE 7.1

It is important to realize that the universe, being old and large, was unsuitable for the existence of human life most of the time and is probably unsuitable for life in most of its space (assuming, of course, that when we think about humankind, we mean exclusively our own civilization, refusing any speculations about extraterrestrial intelligent life). This brings us to the conclusion that the universe, understood as overall space-time, is effectively empty and dead in terms of life, with only one exception, the life on the earth.

We can easily illustrate this point by appealing to an anthropic argument that is known as the "fine-tuning" of physical constants and other cosmological parameters in the universe. This argument makes a link between the global physical conditions in the universe and the fact of existence of life on the earth. One of the simplest arguments that life could not exist in the universe's past is that the universe was hot, which prevented the existence of such stable physical states as atoms. The stability of atoms is a fundamental condition for the existence of all possible biological forms of life. This stability is measured in physical terms by binding energy, which for an atom of hydrogen is determined as $E_H = \alpha_e^2 m_e c^2$, where $\alpha_e \approx 1/137$ is the constant of the electromagnetic interaction (the force which makes atoms stable), m_e is the mass of an electron, and c is the speed of light.[3] It is known from atomic physics that in order to destroy atoms, it is enough to expose atoms to external electromagnetic radiation, that is, to highly energetic photons, whose energy is greater than E_H. This implies that since all atomic structures are embedded in the external cosmological background, filled in, for example, with intergalactic gas (IGG) and microwave relict background radiation (MBR), the energy of particles in IGG and MBR must be less than E_H. If we express this condition in terms of the effective temperature of particles and photons, using the connection between energy and temperature $E = kT$ (k is Boltzmann's constant), we can state that

$$T_{MBR}\,[\approx 3K] < T_{IGG}\,[\approx 100K] < T_H\,[\approx 10^4 K].$$

Through experimentation, it is clear that this inequality is satisfied at the current age of the universe. In the universe's past, however, this inequality would not hold, because, for example, the T_{MBR} is the function of the radius of the universe $T \sim 1/a$ and it increases in the past when $a \longrightarrow 0$. At some point, T_{MBR} exceeded T_H and all atoms could not exist, so that no physico-biological form of life would be possible.

Certainly, this simple observation is true if we assume that the constant of electromagnetic interaction α_e does not change in time, that is, that it is a genuine "constant." It is interesting to find, however, that its particular numerical value is critical for the condition of the stability of atoms to hold. Indeed, if we change its value, for instance, if we decrease its value ten times $\alpha_e^* \leqslant \alpha_e/10$, then the corresponding temperature $T_H^* = 10^{-2} T_H \approx 100K$ will be comparable with T_{IGG} and atoms can potentially be destroyed by interactions with the particles from IGG. In a similar way, if we decrease the same constant one hundred times, the corresponding temperature of atoms will be less than the temperature of MBR, so that atoms could not exist in the cosmological background at all. These simple arguments remind us again about the so-called fine-tuning of fundamental physical constants and external cosmological parameters, which provide the sustenance of life in the universe.

What is important for us, however, is that the brute fact of the observable values of the physical constants and cosmological parameters allows us to conclude that the conditions for life, understood in this context only in physical and biological terms, did not exist in the universe forever; that is, the universe was not always "anthropic." On the contrary, one can conclude that it was "anti-anthropic." One can object to this affirmation by saying that the universe is an evolutionary complex and that the emergence of life at a certain point of its evolution and in a given place was conditioned by the previous history of the universe; it is in this sense that one could assert that the universe was anthropic from the very beginning—that is, its initial conditions evolved later on, leading to a cosmic environment such that the *necessary* conditions of the emergence of life were fulfilled. The fact that we stress the word *necessary* (conditions for life) here reflects the weak point of any physical cosmology and even biology as being unable to reflect reasonably on the nature of the *sufficient* conditions for life to emerge in the universe.[4]

The difficulty that cosmology runs into if it attempts to justify the sufficient conditions for the emergence of life can be easily illustrated by referring to what is accepted by modern cosmology as fact that life (again understood in physical and biological terms), existing in the universe here and now, is destined to disappear from its surface because of either terrestrial physical or cosmological reasons. J. D. Barrow and F. J. Tipler provide a possible upper bound for the length of the existence of the earthly biosphere nearly equal to forty thousand years, which could support the evolution of the human species. This is a short future in terms of cosmological scales.[5]

In the astrophysical context, the upper bound on the existence of life on the earth follows from the finite age of existence of the sun (≈ 5 billion years from now), whose termination in an explosion will bring any life in the surrounding cosmos, including the earth, to extinction. Even if we disregard this local cosmic catastrophe and assume that humankind could spread beyond the solar system into outer cosmic space, we still have to face some global cosmological constraints on the duration of its existence, following from the theory: either the eventual collapse of the universe in the big crunch (the so-called closed universe) or the eternal frost of the ever-expanding (open) universe. In the former case, the termination of life is inevitable because the universe will heat up and prevent any possibility for life to survive. In the latter case, some cosmologists have tried to argue that there will be a possibility to extend the "existence" of "life" in the universe by abandoning the human body and adjusting the new form of life to an absolutely different environment. These hypotheses are based on the speculative assumption that life can be defined in terms of mechanisms producing information, so that the question of supporting life in the universe is a question of producing information with no ending. It is enough to remind us the long-standing paper of F. Dyson on life in the cold and dark future of the universe, in which he argued that civilizations can survive there by constantly reducing their rate of energy consumption and information processing.[6] Dyson's argument was that, despite these measures, the total amount of information produced in the universe may still be infinite, which would imply that the posthuman "civilization" could live forever in its subjective time.[7]

Despite the a priori speculative nature of this proposal, which is doubtful first of all on purely anthropological grounds, for it definitely departs far from what is usually understood by humanity as the existence in body and soul, the physics of Dyson's model was revised recently with a very pessimistic conclusion that his scenario of existence forever is physically unachievable.[8]

It is now important to stress that all forecasts for the upper bound of duration of conscious life in the universe assume tacitly that humankind intends to continue to exist and does not participate actively in reducing its chances of survival, avoiding intentionally the situation on the terrestrial scale, which could be called a "doomsday syndrome." The latter is usually associated with the global ecological crisis, nuclear holocaust, some lethal experiments with germ warfare, or experiments with high-energy physics that could lead to the destruction not only of our planet but of the whole universe.[9] It is the possibility of the termination of the humankind-event by conscious beings themselves, when their activity threatens the natural roots of their existence, that points out that the sufficient conditions for the endurance of this event are partially rooted in the sphere of thought of these beings, in the realm of value and ethics, which is not rooted in nature but whose origin is the same as the human hypostasis itself, that is, in the realm of the divine goodness and wisdom.[10]

This brief reference to the future evolution of the universe and the conclusion about the inevitable termination of life in physical and biological terms leads us to the assertion that the universe is essentially (that is, in terms of its nature) "anti-anthropic" in the future, despite that its present state provides the necessary conditions for the existence of life. We can summarize our point in the following formula: The universe is anthropic now. It was anti-anthropic in the past, and it will be anti-anthropic in the future. This leads us naturally to the assumption that the phenomenon of life in the universe, considered at this stage only with respect to its grounds in physics and biology, is *finite* in regard to time and space. This is why we talk about the phenomenon of humanity as the humankind-event, that is, as a physical event whose spatial scale is finite and whose duration, despite being extended in time, is still finite and tiny (if seen from the present) with respect to the age of the universe. This event is not exactly what is usually meant by an event in the physics of relativity, in which an event is assumed to have no temporal extension—that is, it is treated as an instant, the set of which forms space-time. What is important in using the word *event* as applied to the phenomenon of humanity is that this event is not inherent in the cosmological background (there is no ultimate causal link between cosmology and anthropology); it depends on it—that is, the phenomenon of life is conditioned by physics—but only in terms of the necessary conditions. This means that in order for the humankind-event to happen—to become a part of history different from the dynamics of the cosmological background—there must be present some nonnatural factors making the event contingent on these factors. What are the factors? With no ambition of giving a final answer to this question, we will at least discuss this problem in the following sections.

The Humankind-Event and the Anthropic Principle

To elucidate the meaning of the humankind-event as contingent on nonnatural factors, in a cosmological context we should relate it to the series of ideas that are broadly called the anthropic cosmological principle (or AP).[11] The AP has a variety of formulations, which can be found in Barrow and Tipler's work *The Anthropic Cosmological Principle*.[12] This section will discuss only the formulations known as the weak AP (WAP) and the strong AP (SAP).

The WAP concentrates on the privileged spatiotemporal location of intelligent observers in the evolutionary universe: they find themselves at a rather specific site and at a later stage of the history of the universe, for which the physical parameters that are treated as fundamental constants are not arbitrary but, rather, are fine-tuned with the conditions that enable carbon-based life forms to evolve.[13] The WAP emphasizes that there are some *necessary* conditions that make it possible for life to emerge and to continue its existence in the universe. These conditions include, first of all, the size and the age of the universe: the universe must be old and large in order to create the conditions for carbon-based life-forms to emerge. If we translate this into the language of the previous section, the universe must be empty (that is, anti-anthropic) in its past in order to prepare the conditions for its anthropicity at present.

The positive feature of the WAP approach in cosmology is that it does not claim too much; in other words, it does not demand any inherent causality between the cosmological evolution and the emergence of life. It does not say anything about the laws of physics themselves or about the values of the fundamental physical constants, for example, about the actual value of the constant of electromagnetic interaction a_e. It accepts these values as given and then attempts to explain some features of the universe. The WAP simply says that in order for the humankind-event to happen, some cosmological conditions must be fulfilled. The WAP does not link the phenomenon of humanity to the overall evolution of the universe, for example, to the initial conditions in the universe that would inevitably lead to the humankind-event.

In stressing the necessary conditions, the WAP does not, in fact, address the issue of what the actual cause of the humankind-event was. It is also clear that the WAP does not discuss the future of the universe; in other words, it leaves the question of the indefinite continuation of life out of its scope. It is also important to note that the WAP does not attempt to assert causality between the humankind-event and the structure of the whole cosmos, that is, to use the fact of the existence of life to predicate from it to certain special properties of the universe.

The question of whether the anthropic arguments provide some explanation in cosmology is still at the heart of scientific discussions. There have been some attempts to dismiss these arguments as physically explanatory by appealing to so-called string theory, which is not yet confirmed by experiments but which predicts specific values for the fundamental physical constants. If this prediction is correct and unique in its nature, the anthropic reasoning in physics becomes redundant; that is, the fact of the existence of intelligent life in the cosmos cannot be used per se to argue from it to the structure of the universe.[14] But the replacement of the anthropic argumentation by string theory, which consistently justifies the physics of the surrounding cosmos that permits life, does not mean that string theory removes the issue of the origin of conscious life in the universe. Even if this theory provides the explanation of the background that is *necessary* for the existence of life, it cannot address the issue of the sufficient conditions that actually made the potentiality of life become reality, to become the humankind-event.

One can reformulate the last thought by using more philosophico-theological terminology. From a wider system of thought, which is not restricted to the monistic vision of science, it becomes evident that cosmology and physics, although they try to put the conditions of the existence of humanity in a cosmological context, deal only with the *natural* dimension of the humankind-event, that is, with the existence of humans as physico-biological bodies. Physics itself can hardly speculate at present on the nature of human consciousness or the soul, and even less on the human composite hypostasis of body and soul.[15] In other words, physics and cosmology can discuss the human phenomenon only from a perspective of its materiality, in terms of physics and biology, which can be communicated from one being to another and form a large uninatural population. The hypostatic, or personal, dimension of human existence is out of the scope of physics and biology. Certainly, the conscious nature of humans is tacitly present in all cosmological insights, because all are made by intelligent human beings, so that any claim about the universe has sense only in the context of the human intelligence in the cosmos. But cosmology has no key to the explanation of this intelligence itself. The intelligence is not obviously inherent in the cosmological observations and theories; it can be established only by metascientific introspection, not by physics itself.

One establishes, then, a correlation between the terminology used in cosmology and that used in theology. The necessary conditions for life to exist asserted in the WAP correspond in a theological frame of mind to the *natural* conditions for the existence of human persons. The WAP affirms the natural conditions for the humankind-event, but it does not relate to the issue why this event has happened, that is, why the existence of human beings understood as hypostatic creatures, as differentiated persons, became possible, why the humankind-event happened as hypostasized existence, not just as an element in the natural chain of impersonal and dispassionate interplay between chance and necessity. One sees, then, that the problem of the sufficient conditions for life to emerge and to continue to exist in the universe in cosmology correlates with the mystery of the personal, hypostatic existence of human beings in theology. We can anticipate, then, that the issue of the existence of life in the cosmological context cannot be fully addressed without an appeal to theology, for the insufficiency of cosmology to clarify the riddle of intelligent life in the universe points toward the grounds of life, which transcend the cosmological context, making the humankind-event relational (or contingent) upon nonnatural factors.

It follows from what we have just said that the issue of the necessary conditions for intelligent life in the universe must not be separated from the issue of the sufficient conditions. The AP is logically incomplete if it tries to affirm something about the structure of the universe relying only on the natural aspects of human existence. It follows, then, that the genuine anthropic principle must consist of both scientific and theological insights, which would open a route to the demonstration of the contingency of human existence in the universe and to a more intricate involvement of human beings in the communion with the grounds of the intelligibility of the universe.

It becomes clear that even the more speculative strong AP in cosmology does not reach its goal of proclaiming that the whole structure of the universe is to be subordinated to the fact of the existence of intelligent life in the universe: "The universe *must* have those properties which allow life to develop within it at some stage in its history."[16]

An attempt that the SAP makes in subordinating the entire history of the universe to the requirement that life can emerge in this universe has a modest utility in cosmology.[17] However, it raises some problems in a theological discourse. Indeed, if the SAP refers only to the natural aspects of human existence, then it obviously does not address the issue of sufficient conditions for the existence of life in the universe, for even if the universe is physically "designed" to contain biological life, it is still unknown what particular cause led ultimately to the emergence of biological organisms. The problem of consciousness in biological organisms is not even addressed by the SAP inference explicitly. There is some contingent element in the whole story of the appearance of life in the universe that is fundamentally unavoidable if one thinks about it in purely physical terms.

To illustrate this last thought, we employ a simple model of the emergence of complexity (which is often used to describe complicated living systems) in physics to show that it is always accompanied by a fundamental uncertainty, which cannot be resolved on a physical level but requires one to appeal to some transphysical (and nonpredictable) factors. Our example is based on two assumptions. The first is that the phenomenon of life, from a physico-biological point of view (we disregard conscious life in this example), is associated with the "manifestation of the attainment of a particular level of organised complexity in a physical system."[18] It is clear that this definition is an extreme form of reductionism, in which the whole spectrum of biological phenomena is treated from the point of view of physics. It is, however, sufficient for our present purposes to accept this model of living systems. The second assumption is that, for heuristic modeling (not a truly scientific one) of the emergence of the organized complexity, one can use any physical model of complex phenomena that involves an interplay of the necessary and sufficient conditions for the complexity to emerge.

Under these two assumptions, we intend to demonstrate that the emergence of "life," understood simply as a definite level of complexity in a physical system, requires one not only to satisfy the necessary conditions, serving as a background for complex phenomena, but also to realize that a particular outcome of these phenomena (one that could be more precisely associated with the emergence of life) will be a priori unpredictable and contingent on factors that are not conceivable by the physics that operates with the given complex phenomena.

The simplest example of complexity in a physical system is known as the Bernard instability, which provides us with an example of chaotic behavior and emergence of complexity in the physical situation when we consider heat convection in the liquid contained between two planes with different temperatures and embedded in the external gravitational field.[19] The meaning of the Bernard instability can be explained in simple terms as the transition from an initially uniform liquid to the state where this liquid becomes ordered in space, in terms of the Bernard cells, with a typical size of one-tenth of a centimeter, in which 10^{21} molecules experience a special type of correlation. The transition from the uniform liquid to the structured liquid can be compared to the transition from a physical state of the universe with no life to the state when life emerged. In the case of the Bernard phenomenon, the transition from the uniform state to the complex state depends on satisfying some conditions that can be called the necessary conditions. In particular, there must be two factors: (1) the presence of the external gravitational field and (2) the presence of the difference in temperature on the upper and low plains ΔT. When this difference reaches some critical level ΔT_c, one observes the transition from the uniform liquid to the liquid that is formed by cell tubes.

If we make an analogy between the external factors in the Bernard experiment (that is, the external gravitational field and the difference in temperature between the two planes containing the liquid) and the external cosmological conditions that are necessary for the emergence of life (such as the strength of the cosmological gravitational fields and the temperature of the background radiation, which decreases as the universe expands), then the necessary condition for the Bernard phenomenon to occur ($\Delta T > \Delta T_c$) can be paralleled with some cosmological event, when the temperature of the background radiation dropped to such a level that the stability of the constituents of the biological factors on the earth were achieved and life could emerge.

The most intriguing part of the Bernard experiment, however, is that the phenomenon of complexity can be of two different types. The Bernard cell in a given place of the liquid can have either clockwise (right, or R) or counterclockwise (left, or L) chirality, so that the spatial structure of complexity, attained in a fixed point of the liquid, can be depicted as a sequel of cells with different order of chiralities, namely, either A (... RL̲RLRL ...) or B (... LR̲LRLR ...). It is important to realize that the complexity of the Bernard type will necessarily emerge if $\Delta T > \Delta T_c$, that is, the phenomenon is deterministic with respect to the external, necessary conditions. But it is practically impossible to predict what particular outcome—either A or B—

will take place when the necessary conditions are satisfied. This means that if one repeats the experiment, leading to the Bernard instability many times, one can predict only the probability $P_A = 1/2$ that there will be an outcome A and the probability $P_B = 1/2$ that there will be an outcome B.

If we now make a hypothesis in our model, that the state A corresponds to such a level of complexity that leads to "life," whereas the state B is "infertile," then one can affirm that despite the deterministic external conditions (necessary conditions) for complexity to emerge, the actual happening in the system, leading either to "life" or to "no life," is not in causal relation to the necessary conditions (for the actual happening is not conditioned by deterministic "law" but is the outcome of this law corresponding to a broken symmetry between A and B). It is probabilistic in nature and depends on factors that are not described by physical theory. What is the actual cause of a spontaneous choice between "life" and "no life" remains unclear. In other words, the sufficient conditions that led to the emergence of life are not explained. We observe here the display of the fundamental contingency in the physical system that demands for its explanation an appeal to factors that transcend physics.

Some authors, approaching the problem of chaos and organized complexity from a wide philosophical and theological perspective, invoke ideas about *information,* whose input could be a decisive factor in determining whether the complex state will be life-giving or not. J. Polkinghorne defends this idea in the context of chaos theory.[20] Indeed, the information type of consideration is possible in the case of Bernard's instability if we consider the experiment before and after the complex structure emerged. It is clear from what we have said before that the prior probability for the liquid to make a transition either to state A or to state B is the same and equals one-half. This means that the uncertainty in this system can be estimated in terms of the informational entropy I by the formula $I_{before} = P_A \ln P_A + P_B \ln P_B = -\ln 2$. There is, however, no uncertainty after the complexity has been established, for the outcome of the experiment is fixed and a posteriori probability for A and B is distributed either $P_A = 1$, $P_B = 0$ or $P_A = 0$, $P_B = 1$. In both cases, the informational entropy is zero: $I_{after} = 0$. Then, in order for the system to "make a decision" as to what complex state to make a transition (that is, either to A or to B), the system needs to eliminate the informational uncertainty that equals $\Delta I = I_{after} - I_{before} = \ln 2$. This example thus provides some justification for invoking the idea of the active input of information in the chaotic systems in order to deal with an epistemological uncertainty.

What is, however, suspicious in such arguments is that this information is associated sometimes with a sort of divine agency. There are two major objections to this hypothesis. The first is physical and is based on the observation that, in order to overcome the informational uncertainty, one should use some sources of physical energy.[21] The uncertainty in information is connected with the uncertainty in energy according to the second law of thermodynamics: $\Delta I \sim \Delta E/T$ (where T is the temperature of the environment in which the system is embedded). This means that an active input of information needs to be supported by an input of energy from the physical world. In the case of Bernard's instability, this source of energy is hidden in the difference of the temperature ΔT between two flat boundaries of the liquid, which means that an attempt to use the idea of information by contraposing it to physical agency is not justified. The second objection is theological in nature, for it questions whether the information—understood, for example, by Polkinghorne as the divine agency—is part of creation or not.[22]

The Orthodox appropriation of this proposal of Polkinghorne's would be possible only if the notion of information were clearly defined in ontological terms. What is this information? If information is understood in the sense of "theory of information," which is based on the laws of physics, it cannot be treated as an uncreated entity. In this case, it is probably better to refer to the information as some agent from the intelligible realm of the created world. Even in this case, the link between information and divine agency is still unclear, for the Divine is uncreated, whereas the intelligible information is created; since information is part of the creation and any talk about divine intervention (input) into physical process is theologically incorrect. The input of information from the "intelligible heaven" (treated as a noetic entity) can lead, however, to an outcome in a physical system that will have nothing to do with a divine purpose and will. The ontological difference (*diaphora*) in creation between the sensible and the intelligible (which is the constitutive element of the *creatio ex nihilo*) means that any influence (input of information) of the invisible upon the visible is possible only if it has been already encoded in the *creatio ex nihilo* itself; only in this sense can one claim the presence of the divine in their interaction.

It is more consistent, however, to look at the "causal joints" of matter and information from the perspective of the contingency rooted in the created world in both the visible and the invisible realms. This can take different forms, so that the divine action sought by an intellectual mind can be found encoded in the independence and freedom that the created world has received from God through the *creatio ex nihilo*.

When we observe chaos in the natural world and claim that it represents a kind of contingent order that is distinct from predictable aspects of nature, we contemplate, in theological terms, the difference between the *logos* of chaos and the *logos* of predictable and regular processes. The input of active information, to use Polkinghorne's language, could only mean, from an Orthodox point of view, a qualitative change in contingent order that would probably have been caused by a "switching over" of the *logoi* responsible for these two types of processes. We cannot treat this "event" as an input of information because the *logoi* are preexistent in the divine Logos. Thus we are dealing here not with an active input of information (provided by God?) but with a change in the contingent order, which already has its own *logos*.

Finally, one can agree with J. Haught that information as such is a "mystery that science cannot comprehend through its atomising reduction."[23] Similarly to our pointing out that the origin of information lies in the uncreated *logoi*, Haught asserts that informational patterning is a metaphysical necessity for anything to exist, for it must have form, order, or pattern.[24] In other words, the existence of a thing means that there is information about this thing; that is, its existence is the *informed* existence. But what does it mean? The informed existence assumes that there is the *other*, which is informed about the existence of some thing; this manifests the existence of this thing for the other and in the other. This can be rearticulated by saying that there is an inherent intelligible pattern of anything that is revealed through its relation to the other agency, who possesses the ability to enhypostasize this pattern as specific and concrete existence. Here we return to the issue of intelligible agencies in the universe, for only these, by sharing the intelligibility of the universal Logos, can reveal and operate with the information that enters scientific inquiry. It is only in this sense that information can be appropriated as a kind of divine agency, revealing itself through intelligible human beings, capable of grasping forms, orders, and patterns in the universe.

In concluding our discussion of a simple physical model of the emergence of complexity (which can be interpreted in a reductionist way as the emergence of life), we must rearticulate two important achievements: (1) the sufficient conditions for the actual emergence of life in the universe cannot be part of physical theory (this indicates the presence of a fundamental, unavoidable contingency in cosmological theory), and (2) the anthropic arguments deal only with the natural aspects of the humankind-event, whose actual happening is contingent upon some nonnatural grounds. This brings us finally to the understanding that the mystery of the humankind-event and the attempt of cosmology to inquire into it through anthropic arguments is linked with the mystery of the hypostatic existence of human beings; that is, their origin in the divine image and with the whole divine economy followed from the *creatio ex nihilo*. But the mystery of the creation out of nothing, as discussed in chapter 5, is theologically linked with God's plan of the salvation of humankind. This means that the humankind-event, if seen not only from its natural (physico-biological) dimension but also philosophically and theologically, can be understood only through the chain of creation, incarnation, and resurrection.

The strong AP, then, can be reinterpreted, not so much physically but theologically. The status of this interpretation will be, in the parlance of J. Leslie, as a *logical* explanation of the link between the humankind-event and the structure of the universe, rather than a *causal* explanation in physical terms of how the presence of human life in the universe cascades up and down to physics in order to explain its laws and their particular outcomes leading to the existence of life.[25]

This means that the causation that is effectively present in the universe, starting from its creation and up to the point when human life emerges, is subordinated not only to the logic of physics but also to the logic of the divine plan to create such a universe in which human beings, being in God's image, could live and could learn the truth about God and themselves, in particular, that they are not only natural creatures but also hypostatic and ecclesial beings who can enlighten and personify the universe through their presence. It is these human beings who can follow the way of deviation from the necessity of nature in order to transfigure its own cosmological roots according to their ultimate ecclesial aim to achieve the union with God.

It is clear, then, that the theological link between the universe and the humankind-event is not entirely natural. When we talk about the divine plan of salvation of humankind, we assume that this plan is to be incarnate in the realm of contingent creation. This makes it legitimate to assert that since, in the divine reason, the creation of the world out of nothing is linked to the fact of the salvation of humankind, there must be some display of the connection between the world and humanity that is encoded in the theology of creation. In a sophisticated way, this link can be revealed by reasoning we have used several times before in this book, namely, by referring the display of the universe and the presence of human beings in it to their common ground in their otherness, that is, in the transcendent God-Creator. Theologically speaking, the existence of a link between the world and humans is inevitable. The major problem, then, is to articulate this link not only in natural terms, for it cannot be fully expressed from within its worldly manifestations. Otherwise, it would mean expressing in worldly terms the contingency of creation, which cannot be done.[26] The challenge to science is to detect the presence of this contingency in scientific theories with no full explanation of its origin; the latter is exactly what theological methodology can offer.

Cosmology taken in its purely scientific realization can pretend to reveal the fundamental contingency of human existence in its natural dimension on some specific conditions that have been realized in the universe. It will be, however, extremely difficult for cosmology alone (that is, with no support from philosophy and theology) to reveal the ground of the universe and of human beings in it beyond the universe in the realm of the uncreated (we have already seen examples of the theological reasoning on the issue of creation in cosmology and the origin of temporal irreversibility in the universe in chapters 5 and 6 that point toward the transcendent grounds of existence). But this means precisely that cosmology should look for the presence of contingent necessity in its laws and facts about the existence of human beings in the universe (that is, the necessity that by its display in the universe never acquires the features of sufficiency), for the sufficiency, if it were to be possible to reveal it in the display of the universe, by its logical constitution, would be an ultimate ground of contingent necessity in the world, which would correspond to the hidden knowledge of the divine plan of creation and salvation.

If we now look more closely at the affirmation of the SAP—that the universe must have some properties in order to allow human life to develop in the universe—and if we treat this idea theologically, we can see the referral to the creation of the universe with the purpose of the salvation of human beings as creatures with a particular anthropological constitution. For human beings to be made in a particular hypostasis (that is, to be a unity of a body and a soul), there must be conditions for the natural aspects of the human hypostasis to be realized, namely, conditions for the existence of the human body, which is made from the same material available in the universe. The SAP, treated from this perspective, provides in its above form a theological affirmation of the design in the universe in order to fit the human body. But the SAP, as we have established before, deals only with the natural aspects of the humankind-event; that is, it does not address the origin and existence of the human hypostasis as the union between the bodily functions and the abilities to think and contemplate things and ideas as well as to integrate them in a single consciousness. It is exactly at this point that the analysis of the SAP reveals the presence of fundamental contingency, as an inability to provide any inference on the mystery of the hypostatic dimension of human existence.

It must be also noted that the SAP does not address the future of human life in the universe; it does not treat the phenomenon of man as an *event*. An event means not just a happening in the chain of causal physical factors; rather, it is by itself a constitutive element for physical reality, something that makes the undifferentiated matter "the reality." Thus an event itself is a hypostatic notion, which is called to constitute the elements of nature in space and time. Any event by definition is contingent upon some agency that is not entirely rooted in the natural. An event has a beginning and an end. Similarly, the humankind-event has a beginning and an end. This implies that what the SAP asserts is that at some stage of the evolution of the universe, there must be necessary conditions for the humankind-event to happen. This means that the evolution of the universe is *constructive* from the point of view of the history of salvation only up to the humankind-event. This implies in turn that the link the SAP attempts to make between the whole evolution of the universe and the humankind-event is actually subordinated to the latter; yes, the universe must evolve in order to allow the humankind-event to happen, but the future evolution of the universe is not subordinated anymore to the humankind-event, which, according to modern physics and theological eschatology, is finite in time. This implies that the most that the SAP can say about the structure of the universe (in terms of the humankind-event) is to affirm something about its past as contingent on the present, not the future.[27] The final AP of F. Tipler, which attempts to extend the assertion of the SAP to the indefinite future, does not seem to be a plausible version of things in the context of the notion of the humankind-event. The critique of this principle will be touched on briefly later in this chapter.

One can conclude thus that the phenomenon of man in the universe, analyzed in the context of the anthropic arguments in cosmology, is in its essence finite and contingent on nonnatural factors, which can be elucidated only by appeal to the theology of creation. Being an element of creation, the phenomenon of humanity acquires the features of an event. It is in this sense that all assertions of the WAP and SAP can be interpreted as indications of the fundamental contingency present in cosmological theories, open to further explanation and based on nonphysical assumptions.

Hypostatic Dimension of the Humankind-Event

This section articulates in detail what is meant by the hypostatic dimension of the humankind-event. To do this, we start with elucidating the role of human hypostasis in the process of knowing the universe. It can sound tautologous that the very fact that physics can speculate about the universe and the place of humankind in it is based on the ability of humans to contemplate the universe and form a coherent picture of the world. This ability is associated with the intelligence that makes human beings fundamentally different from other forms of biological life. This fact, despite being tacitly present in the very foundation of science, and in cosmology in particular, is disregarded as constitutive for modern knowledge. Human beings as intelligent observers and conscious agencies in the universe are downgraded to the level of passive observers, so that the presupposition of the observations themselves (that is, human consciousness) is excluded from the subject matter of physics. B. Carr stated this situation in physics and cosmology, treated as man's model of the world in which he lives, by saying: "Yet one feature which is noticeably absent from this model is the creator, man himself. That physics has little to say about the place of man in the universe is perhaps not surprising when one considers the fact that most physicists probably regard man, and more generally consciousness, as being entirely irrelevant to the functioning of the universe. He is seen as no more than a passive observer, with the laws of Nature, which he assiduously attempts to unravel, operating everywhere and for all time, independent of whether or not man witness them."[28] The fact that such a vision of humans' place in the universe is fundamentally incomplete can be easily elucidated by a simple example.[29]

Let us analyze a typical diagram from popular scientific books that depicts different objects in the universe, starting from atoms and finishing with galaxies, in terms of their spatial sizes or their masses.[30] The position of human beings in this diagram is seen as mediocre: its typical spatial size is 10^{12} times higher than the atomic one, and the place they occupy in space is 10^{-19} times less than the size of the visible universe. Despite that the existence of human beings depends on atoms and the size (or age) of the universe (this is a typical anthropic line of reasoning), if it is seen from a purely physical point of view, the position of human beings in the universe is insignificant. For every contemplative and psychologically oriented thinker, the internal inconsistency of a purely physical view is hidden in the fact that human reason, which is not present in the diagram explicitly, is encoded in it implicitly, for all objects starting from atoms and finishing with the universe as a whole are integrated in a single logical chain, which is possible only because the human insight is present everywhere. Thus all objects in the chain of physical being are united by human reason in a single consciousness of the whole that is sustained from the "vertical" dimension of human intellect, which is linked to the *natural* conditions of human existence but at the same time transcends this existence, revealing itself as dependent not only on physico-cosmological factors but also on nonnatural or, as we call them, hypostatic factors.[31] This idea is illustrated by the diagram in figure 7.2, which presents the position of humans in being in terms of two dimensions, natural and hypostatic.

One could object to our use of the term *hypostatic* by pointing out that what we mean by it is human intelligence, which assumes the ability to contemplate objects in nature, form their meaning, and communicate this meaning to the whole humankind. Some would say that all these functions of human intellect have naturally emerged, so that they constitute a part of nature, although quite different from

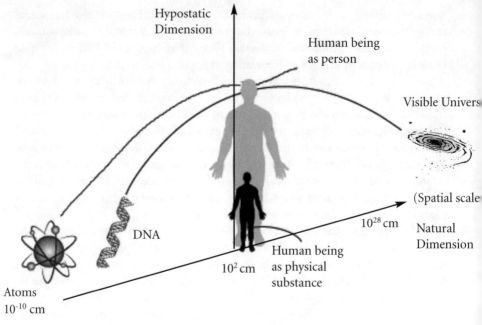

FIGURE 7.2

what one means by physical nature.[32] In this case, one could say that, instead of naming the vertical dimension hypostatic, it would be easy to call it an intellectual (or psychological) dimension and not to make a sharp difference between horizontal and vertical dimensions in figure 7.2. Our response to this objection would be that the presence of intellect and consciousness, even if they are treated in a reductionist way as epiphenomena of physical and biological function, do not explain and justify the aspect of personhood in human existence, that is, genuinely human hypostasis as personified *existence* of human beings in different bodies. The personhood of human beings implies not only that they have self-consciousness (that is, the perception of one's own ego), but also that there is a fundamental distinction from and, at the same time, *relatedness* to other existences, or other hypostases.[33] The personhood as hypostatic existence means that it cannot be communicated to another person (in contrast with the natural, for example, biological factors, which are shared by all human beings and can in principle be communicated from one human being to another, such as the transplantation of organs). Every particular existence is unique and inexpressible in terms of the other. Despite the fact that the hypostatic unity of the human composite of body and soul cannot be communicated in a physical or biological sense, the hypostasis of the human person is formed only through its *relation* to other hypostases (that does not necessarily imply interaction on the level of substance) and to the common source of their origination.[34] In other words, the non-natural aspect of the hypostatic dimension in human beings points toward the fundamentally relational essence of this existential dimension. This literally means that the symbol of human being in figure 7.2 as hypostatic (large and gray) stands for the whole of mankind (in contrast to natural man, small and black) as the community of beings with a common principle (*logos*) of human nature related to God and realized in different hypostases (different persons).[35]

One can say that the integral knowledge of the universe contains in itself an implicit premise that there is a "way" of communication with the universe that would allow human reason to find truth about the universe and to share this truth among the members of the whole community. But the establishment of the "meaning" of what is contemplated by the members of the community presupposes that there is a common ground of sense and intelligibility, which is shared not only naturally (that is, biologically, on the level of the corporeal) but also hypostatically (that is, it is not deduced from nature through a chain of physico-biological and physiological causations), the very possibility of which is rooted in their common relationship to the common source of existence in creation, to the Logos in whom the whole universe and human persons are inherent hypostatically.

Since all things in creation can be treated as effected words of God, knowledge of these things implies the ability to "hear" the words of God, not simply through natural faculties of the body (which provide only the outward impression) but through immediate participation in these words, which takes place on a nonnatural level. The fact that human reason can penetrate space and time and contemplate in different symbols things invisible and nonobservable, microparticles and cosmological structures, points toward man's ability to transcend empirical nature to the realm of intelligible forms. At this point, the importance of the hypostatic dimension for understanding humanity's place in the universe becomes clear. It is because of the hypostatic unity of the body and soul, which forms the *logos* of man and originates from the divine Logos, that it is possible to argue together with Maximus the Confessor and other Patristic writers that man, in a way, imitates in his composition the whole universe, empirical (that is, explicitly visible) and intelligible (invisible); that is, it manifests itself in the basic *diaphora* in creation that points to the *logos*, which holds different parts of creation together.

Maximus developed an allegorical interpretation of the universe as man, and conversely, of man as microcosm and mediator between the parts of the universe and between the universe and God.[36] Maximus articulates the similarity between the composition of human beings and the composition of the universe from the point of view of the hypostatic unity of different parts in them. A passage from Maximus's *The Church's Mystagogy* (chapter 7) elucidates the meaning of this similarity:

> Intelligible things display the meaning of the soul as the soul does that of intelligible things, and . . . sensible things display the place of body as the body does that of sensible things. And . . . intelligible things are the soul of sensible things, and sensible things are the body of intelligible things; . . . as the soul is in the body so is the intelligible in the world of sense, that the sensible is sustained by the intelligible as the body is sustained by the soul; . . . both make up one world as body and soul make up

one man, neither of these elements joined to the other in unity denies or displaces the other according to the law of the one [the Creator] who has bound them together. In conformity with this law there is engendered the principle [*logos*] of the unifying force which does not permit that the [hypostatic] identity unifying these things be ignored because of their difference in nature.[37]

In a scientifico-cosmological context, this text can be interpreted as an insight that can lead a cosmologist beyond the sphere of the visible universe (which is accessible to the senses) to that which is invisible and described in terms of mathematical objects (which human reason, being an analytical part of the soul, operates with because the reason is indwelling in the body), so that through the visible universe the reason reaches the intelligible universe, which also indwells in the visible despite being different from it. It is because of the hypostatic unity of the body and soul in a cosmologist that one can reveal the hypostatic unity of the visible and intelligible universe. A cosmologist relates opposite phenomena: small (atoms) and large (galaxies), visible present cosmos and its invisible past; cosmos as multiplicity of different visible facts (stars, galaxies, distribution of clusters of galaxies) and the mathematical cosmos (as uniform and isotropic space).

The human ability to recapitulate in its knowledge all constituents of the universe, and to recognize that human being is deeply dependent on the structural and nomistic aspects of the microworld as well as of the megacosmos, makes the position of humans in the universe exceptional and unique. The recapitulation of the universe in man takes place not only on the natural level (which is affirmed in the anthropic arguments) but, and this is much more nontrivial, on the hypostatic level; this implies indirectly that human beings are participating in outward hypostasization of their own existence by revealing the meaning of various levels of the universe. The latter is possible because human beings can use their own hypostasis to bring the undifferentiated existents in the universe to their proper, personal existing, that is, as the existence through the apprehension in the persons. Such an existence of the universe through the transferral to it of the personal dimension of humankind can be described in theological terms as the *enhypostasization* of the universe. In different words, human persons, or humankind in general, despite being physically located in one particular point of the universe, share through the fusion of knowledge their existence with all other places and ages of the universe. It is this existence of the universe in the other, that is, in human beings, that means that the universe is enhypostasized by human beings. One can affirm at last that the humankind-event, being made hypostatically inherent in the Logos, is itself the source of further expansion of the hypostatic inherence toward the universe, which has the form of a revelation of the intelligibility of the universe, its purpose and end through the human personhood.[38]

The place of humankind in the universe can be expressed by using the old idea of microcosm, as the world in the small. It is clear, from what we have discussed above, however, that the major feature that puts humans in the "central" position in the universe is the fact that the reality of this universe is articulated by humankind; that is, the universe is revealed to itself in the hypostasis of human being. This adds to the man as microcosm the title of *mediator,* for it is man who establishes the link between the universe and God, not naturally or physically, but hypostatically; that is, the universe as the part of creation is offered to God in the hypostasis of humankind through its thanksgiving wonder of the good creation and its "cosmic liturgy" of knowledge, which, being an open-ended advance of human intelligence, also changes (transfigures) the universe.

The fundamental problem, however, in asserting that the universe is made hypostatically inherent in human apprehension, and that the universe appears to us as intelligible reality, is rooted in the origin of the intelligence of human beings and its relation to the intelligibility of the universe, which is discovered through the scientific quest. It follows from what we have said before that the root of human intelligence lies in the hypostatic dimension of human existence, which can be expressed in such words as the relation to the ultimate source of intelligibility, which is beyond the world. We also stressed that the analogy between human being and the universe, which is expressed in terms of the commonality of their *logoi,* points to the fact that there is contingent intelligibility in the world that is ultimately of the same origin as intelligence in humans. This leads us to the conclusion that the act of making the universe hypostatically inherent in human apprehension means, in fact, recovering the contingent intelligibility of the cosmos (which is not contemplated by the cosmos itself) through the human hypostasis. It is clear, then, that for this to be possible, one should assume that human intelligence is somehow tuned with the intelligibility of the universe. This leads us back to the idea that the intelligence of human beings, rooted in their hypostases, and the intelligibility of the universe, which is not self-evident and which is revealed to human beings when the universe is apprehended and articulated by them, have a common root, one beyond creation and hidden in the Logos of God.

The central position of humankind in the universe can now be described in a different formula by saying that man is positioned between God and the universe in the following sense: human beings are made inherent in the hypostasis of the Logos of God as the accomplished hypostases, whereas the other objects in the universe are made inherent in the Logos without having their own hypostases, so that their existence is not personal and as such is devoid of the realization of purpose and end. It is only through the hypostatic inherence of these objects through human apprehension that they are brought to a realization of their function in the divine plan, when the objects themselves receive their meaning in terms of purposes and ends.

We now have come to the central question in our discussion of the place of man in the universe: Why is the hypostasis of human beings an accomplished one, so that they can mediate between personal God and impersonal nature, or, in other words, Why do human beings exhibit such existences in the universe that resemble the image of the Divine and, at the same time, recapitulate in themselves the whole universe? Repeating the same question in different terms: Why does the humankind-event take place in the universe? We do not expect to reveal the answer in a form like

"God created the universe and human beings in it because of this and this." By posing this question, we simply want to express our main concern and argument that the mystery of the phenomenon of humanity in the universe can only be uncovered partially by the sciences in terms of the natural conditions suitable for the existence of life; the genuine problem of the humankind-event still remains a philosophical and theological issue, in which other (nonscientific) sources of human experience must be invoked. This points precisely to the fact that the human hypostasis is capable of insights and intuitions that are not accessible to discursive thinking.

The question posed above is not scientific in origin. However, it follows logically from what we have discussed in a scientific context. This implies that a response to the question on the position of human beings in the universe will finally be theological in nature, based on the understanding as well as the direct experience of the cosmic meaning of the incarnation of the Logos of God and of the Christ-event. Before we turn to this issue, which is central for this chapter, it is important from a methodological point of view to rearticulate the meaning of the enhypostasization of the universe in the human hypostasis in rather contemporary terms, which are closer to present-day scientific discourse and its dialogue with science.

We leave out for a while the question of the origin of the human hypostasis, assuming that it is somehow in place and that it initiates cognitive faculties in human beings. If describing these faculties empirically, or even philosophically, one can ask what it means that the universe is brought into being (that is, enhypostasized) or selected by observations. In other words, what are the epistemological consequences of our ability to know anything about the universe and how is this reflected in modern discussions about the status of cosmological knowledge as being anthropic by definition? These issues can be illustrated by examples from the concept of the anthropic principle considered in its epistemological dimension.

From Anthropic Transcendentalism to Christian Platonism

Anthropic Inference in Cosmology and Epistemology

The presence of the hypostatic dimension in the humankind-event can be illustrated through analysis of the AP from an epistemological point of view. It sounds nearly tautological that the fact that we observe the universe as it appears to us is deeply embedded in the nature of our cognitive faculties. In other words, we can observe only things in the universe that can enter into the process of our cognition. We cannot observe those "realities" that cannot cause in human being any cognitive or emotional response. This leads us to the simple observation that the visible universe is, in a strange way, selected by acts of human cognition.

This conclusion is not new at all, for in science, especially in the experimental sciences, it was recognized long ago that the instruments and experimental arrangements affect the results of observations and constrain the structure of the sought-for realities. Quantum mechanics, in its Copenhagen interpretation, for example, asserts explicitly that the phenomenon becomes an element of reality only if it is registered, that is, observed and measured.[39] This means that the notion of reality as it is in itself has no sense in such a context. In astronomy, for example, our knowledge of the objects in the universe is predetermined by our ability to see or detect different types of radiation that comes from the cosmos—for example, electromagnetic radiation can be detected by optical telescopes or radio telescopes; gamma rays need a different type of equipment sensitive to them; cosmic rays can be detected by special tracking devices; gravitational waves are expected to be measured by either solid-state antennas or laser-interferometers. The visible universe, as we define it through all different observations, is thus deeply connected with the nature of our cognitive faculties extended by apparata. This reflects the well-known philosophical view that reality can be defined only within a subject-object relation.

It is enough to recall the Kantian treatment of experience as bounded by two forms of sensibility and twelve categories of understanding. It is within this experience that we can know nature and can claim that our knowledge is objective. We can rephrase this by saying that there is an epistemological horizon in the advance of knowledge that is circumscribed by our cognitive faculties. This implies that what we know is, by definition, the world of phenomena, which is self-selected because of our faculties. This line of thought can lead naturally to a claim that the AP is an epistemological tautology, namely, that the visible universe, which is fine-tuned to sustain the life of human beings, is what is called in Kantian terms the phenomenal world, so that it must by its constitution include observers who perceive this world through the "prism" of their cognitive capacities. The question of how particularly the Kantian epistemology can cascade down into the methodology of scientific research was discussed in a paper by W. I. McLaughlin, who tried, for example, to make a link between the number of observed astronomical phenomena and the possible information that can be obtained in principle in this subject area because of the limited number of categories of the understanding.[40] In McLaughlin's approach, the AP is trivial because we can see the world only from within the horizon circumscribed by our faculties, so that what we see is immanent to what we have at our disposal.

Kantian philosophy, however, does not provide any explanation of why we have the cognitive faculties we have and what is the ultimate source of them and, as a consequence, of the structure of the universe we observe. Kant's invocation of the idea of the "noumenal world" (things-in-themselves) was just a way of referring to something that is beyond the world of phenomena but which, being completely inaccessible to us, functions as an empty logical form, playing the role of a delimiter that outlines the boundaries of our knowledge, which separates being from nonbeing. It is important to realize, however, that to affirm that the world of phenomena is self-selected by our cognitive faculties, one should assume, at least in pure thought, that this world is hypostasized in its concreteness with respect to something that transcends it and that is not the world. This assumption, according to Kant, leads to antinomies of the reason that warn that the transcendence of the understanding beyond the world of phenomena is an illegitimate procedure. The paradox here is that, in order to affirm the concreteness of this world, one has to assume that there is nonbeing of this concreteness that cannot be grasped within the human cognitive faculties. According to Kant, transcendence of the world of phenomena was a break beyond the realm that is formed through the relation between subject and object, whereas Kant's follower J. G. Fichte treated this not as a break beyond the subject-object relation but, rather, as the hypostasization of the abstract transcendent realm by the reason within its purely subjective capacity. This means that if, for Kant, the existence of the world of noumena was problematic by its definition, for Fichte, its existence was immanent with the existence of thought itself, which produced this notion.

If we apply this philosophy to the AP, we must admit that the AP functions in modern cosmology as the principle that sets the boundaries to our own knowledge of the visible universe. In other words, any cosmological theory that pretends to describe adequately the visible cosmos should satisfy all the constraints imposed by the strong AP. It does not mean that the AP, as a sheer metascientific statement, explains why the universe is as it is but that the AP acts as the inference that affirms in physico-mathematical terms the concreteness of the visible universe. The novelty of the AP in formulating the specificity of the subject-object relation in cosmology, however, has a profound significance that had not been recognized before this principle was established—namely, it articulates the concreteness of the world, expressed in terms of the fine-tuning of physical and cosmological constants, in terms of its stability. This means that the being of the universe where we live is not an obvious thing, for it is fundamentally unstable with respect to imaginary changes of physical parameters. Stability in this sense is associated with the existence of the visible universe and of human life in it, whereas instability of the universe with respect to small changes of physical constants implies that there is nonexistence of life in all other "imaginary" universes with different sets of fundamental parameters. This fact rearticulates the epistemological dimension of the AP, namely, that in order to assert the concreteness of the visible universe in terms of its adjustment to the cognitive faculties of the observers, one should assume that it is contraposed to its own otherness, that is, to such a state of affairs that excludes life and observers and that can be called the noumenal world in Kantian terms or as a different universe in physical terms. This comparison of the noumenal world with the different universes has a limited validity, for in the Kantian context, the noumenal world is not part of any experience, including the experience of abstract mathematical creativity. It is, however, possible to argue that the concept of different universes, which is invoked in a modified version of the strong AP, functions in cosmology as a "model" of thing-in-itself. These fine distinctions in the pursuit of the idea of transcendence in cosmology are not important in the context of this research, however, for we have already established the vision of the Kantian transcendental method through the eyes of Christian Platonism.

It is evident from what we have said above why the further development of the strong AP led to its reformulation in terms of the ensemble of the universes. Indeed, if the SAP is treated as a principle of self-selection of the visible universe, then to make such a global selection legitimate, there should be that from which to select; otherwise, no justified explanation of the fine-tuning of the universe in ontological terms can be established. Indeed, while the strong AP "explains" why we do not observe universal characteristics incompatible with our existence, it does not explain why the observable characteristics of the universe, evidently compatible with our existence, take place at all. This is why, for a full-value strong anthropic explanation, certain additional assumptions are needed. These are provided by a *world ensemble* hypothesis, the indispensable part of the strong anthropic inference.

The Many-Worlds Hypothesis
and Its Theological Interpretation

The concept of many worlds sounds extremely exotic and nonscientific because it postulates something well beyond the boundaries of what is scientifically "known or knowable" at this time.[41] There is, however, a popular belief among some physicists and philosophers that it can be given some physically realistic meaning based on certain present-day cosmological ideas that depict the universe as a whole as consisting of many physically disjoint domains governed by different laws of their "physics."[42] From this point of view, all possible "physical" arrangements can be realized in small universes comprising the ensemble. At least some universes will, in this case, be suitable for life and intelligence. Further, to explain why we find ourselves in such a well-designed universe—with its specific laws of nature, initial conditions, spatial topology, and so forth—we have to apply the strong AP, which makes our existence impossible in any of the universes that are designed in a different fashion, with no pattern for the fine-tuning necessary for the existence of human beings.

If, then, one assumes in a physically realistic sense that the ontological existence of the ensemble of universes is of the same quality as the visible anthropic universe, then the modified statement of the strong AP (MW-SAP) that "an ensemble of other different universes is necessary for the existence of our Universe" must be critically appraised, for it pretends to be a scientific statement that is subject to verification or falsification on purely scientific grounds.[43] Since this justification is quite problematic, it would be more reasonable to treat this statement not as empirical but as theoretical, that is, mathematical. This implies that it must have, instead, the form of a theorem. The MW-SAP theorem can be formulated in this way: an ensemble of universes *as a part of our world* must exist (its existence is *necessary and sufficient*) for our universe to exist. For our universe to be chosen from something, it is necessary for the ensemble of universes to exist. If the ensemble of universes does exist, it is sufficient for our universe to exist, since the plurality does always contain all kinds of universes, including the one where we live. To attempt a proof of this theorem, there must be established a priori a concept of many universes, which can be done only with a great extent of metaphysical speculation.[44]

The metaphysical concept of the world ensemble refers back to the block of ideas associated with the long-standing concept of plurality of worlds but renewed by ideas either from the many-worlds interpretation (MWI) of quantum mechanics or from chaotic inflationary cosmology (as well as from the old model of the oscillating universe). Probably the best way to give an idea of this model is to quote one of its authors: "The universe is constantly splitting into a stupendous numbers of branches, all resulting from the measurement-like interactions between its myriads of components. Moreover, every quantum transition taking place on every star, in every galaxy, in every remote corner of the universe is splitting our local world on earth into myriads of copies of itself."[45]

Branching in MWI, associated with the measurement-like interaction, is usually said to lead to the creation of copies in interacting subsystems, each representing a separate *world*. Despite the fact that the branching of the universe is supposed to be a physical phenomenon and that it ought to find a precise description within the theory, there is no indication about the *time* and the *way* in which splitting occurs. The claim of the MWI is that all "branches" of the universe "are "actual," none any more "real" than the rest."[46] However, only one outcome of an individual observation is actualized in practice, or, in other words, only one branch of the universe is real in the sense that this is the universe in which we live. This raises the problem of a distinction between *actuality* and *possibility*. Nothing in the theoretical formalism of the MWI accounts for such a distinction.

The fact that the "dynamics" of branching, as well as the branches as separated *worlds*, has no spatiotemporal description leads immediately to the philosophical conclusion that the *plurality* of the worlds must be understood in a logical and philosophical sense.[47] Because of an actual infinity of acts of interactions, the number of worlds with all possible values of the fundamental "physical" constants is actually infinite and contains all potentialities, including the physical constants sustaining our universe. But the possible *worlds* are not part of our visible universe. This requires us to rethink their ontological status, for it appears that they represent conceptual worlds and belong to the nonexperiential realm (what Kant would call the world of pure thought, or the noumena), which we have already encountered many times in the context of theoretical cosmology and call the intelligible world, the world of Platonic ideas.[48]

Such a view of the ensemble of the universes that enters the formulation of the SAP changes radically the whole status of this principle, depriving it of being called scientific. Since the objects that appear in its formula—that is, the visible universe and an ensemble of universes—have absolutely different ontological status (empirical versus intelligible), the SAP needs to be reformulated in order to avoid any contradiction of leveling in its formulation of two ontologically distinct terms. This can be done only if the title "principle" disappears from the anthropic inference in order to give up its place to the *strong anthropic antinomy:*

Thesis: There belongs to the world an ensemble of universes whose existence is absolutely necessary for the visible universe to exist.

Antithesis: There nowhere exists an ensemble of universes as the cause of the visible universe, either in the world or out of it.

We meet here again the epistemological situation in scientific discourse that has been already analyzed in chapter 5 and 6. The idea of many worlds (MW) has been invoked to articulate the specificity of the visible universe (W), its fundamental specificity, and then its instability and contingence on factors that transcend the universe W. In other words, in order to explain W, one should introduce MW as a possible cause of W. On the one hand, it was a way of thought when W was a primary logical cause for introducing MW in the transition $W \longrightarrow MW$; on the other hand, according to the modified version of the AP, it was MW whose existence had been assumed prior to W and that was a "cause" of the existence of W. This can be expressed as the reverse causation $MW \longrightarrow W$.

It is obvious from the nature of this construction that both "causations" have no direct physical meaning on the level of substance (*ousia*). In the direct transition $W \longrightarrow MW$, the invocation of the idea of MW has been methodologically justified as a hypothesis, produced by a simple operation of abstraction from a concrete set of conditions to an indefinite and infinite set of conditions, in which the initial ones have been a part of the whole. In the inverse transition $MW \longrightarrow W$, which is supposed to describe the process of selecting the W out of MW, the actual physical mechanism has not yet been invented, so the causation can be understood only on a hypothetical, explanatory level, with no reference to physics.

The antinomy formulated above reflects the difficulty that inevitably arises if one attempts to level both W and MW ontologically and to predicate about their connection in substantial terms. The way out of this epistemological difficulty, which we have already established in previous chapters, is to treat the antinomy as the indication of a split in the created being between the sensible (W in our case) and the intelligible (MW), which inevitably appears in discursive thinking when it tries to explain away the contingency of the visible universe by subjecting the universe to some necessity that originates from beyond it. In this case, the antinomy instead demonstrates the complex nature of reasoning about the specificity of our universe using the anthropic arguments, which requires one to step out from the visible universe in order to explain its nature from outside. It is at this point that discursive reason is caught by a temptation to ontologize its conceptual schemes of the transcendent universes in the same way it does for the visible universe. It is important, however, to recognize that the ultimate aim of discursive reason is to mediate between conceptual realities and the empirical world. This feature of anthropic reasoning in cosmology underlies again the fundamental fact that human beings are hypostatic creatures who can transcend the realm of the empirical to seek its origin in its otherness. One should point out, however, that in the case of the MW-SAP, this transcendence is not accomplished, for it reaches only the intelligible realm, where all the many universes exist as ideas. Reason that mediates between the sensible and the intelligible reveals itself in hypostatic unity with the human body, thus reflecting that created being is differentiated in itself through basic *diaphora* between the sensible and the intelligible. But this fact has not been revealed by discursive thinking within cosmology itself, for the latter, by trying to explain away the contingency of the visible universe, missed the fact that the many worlds that it treated as a safe ontological ground for the visible universe are themselves contingent because (1) they are created, and (2) because the *MW* is in fact a form of reality that is enhypostasized by human beings; that is, it represents a type of intelligible reality existing in the human hypostasis. This is why the MW-SAP, subjected to antinomial analysis, demonstrates indirectly that human beings occupy a special position in the whole creation, for their hypostasis—that is, the unity of the differentiated body and soul—resembles the basic *diaphora* in creation, whose unity is sustained by God. Thus the MW-SAP does not explain why this is so, that is, why human beings are destined to be a mediator between the sensible and the intelligible in creation, why they resemble the created being at large. What it does provide is an interesting demonstration of how the human hypostasis manifests itself through the process of analytical knowledge by transferring its own principle of existence (*logos*) to the whole universe.

One can probably anticipate the main conclusion to be drawn at this stage, namely, that the MW-SAP, by revealing the basic *diaphora* in creation, leads us again to understanding that the mystery of human hypostatic and natural existence in the universe, as well as the universe itself (their *logoi*), is hidden in God's economy of the creation of the world out of nothing. The universe, as it is enhypostasized through human knowledge, receives, in a way, a second birth through man's participation in the effected words of God about the universe and their articulation in language and scientific discourse. We can state that the universe is created out of nothing by God but that its *logos* is being articulated in the human hypostasis during the whole history of the humankind-event.

It is interesting to note that our analysis of the MW-SAP contributes to the theological assertion that the sustenance of our visible universe is based on a fine split in creation between the visible universe and the intelligible ensemble of universes, which are both held together by the transcendent creator through the *logos* we have revealed. This makes our treatment of the *MW* problem different when compared with what is usually contraposed in the literature as the creator hypothesis versus the *MW* "explanation."[49] Our analysis shows that the creator hypothesis has an advantage if the problem of *MW* explanation is treated a priori from a theological perspective. As pointed out by D. Temple, the creator hypothesis itself does not constitute theology, for the latter is brought into the center of the argument from outside.[50] It is evident, then, that in our analysis the only viable option is to treat the life-permitting conditions of the visible universe, as well as the imagined ensemble of universes where these conditions do not hold, as grounded in the realm of the Divine; that is, the creation hypothesis naturally incorporates the *MW* explanation.

Intelligibility and Meaning of the Universe: The Participatory Anthropic Principle

It is not difficult to realize from what we have just discussed that the question of the intelligibility of the universe is closely connected with the issue of the existence of the universe in human hypostases, that is, in a mode of its articulation that is enhy-postasized by intelligent human beings. The whole question of the existence of the universe in its particular appearance to us is contingent on the existence of human beings, who articulate its existence in data records, theories, language, and so forth. This view is similar to what is known in cosmology as the participatory anthropic principle, which was developed by J. A. Wheeler and formulated in a compact form as follows: "Observers are necessary to bring the universe into being."[51]

The reasoning that underlies this formulation is not at all popular among physi-cists, who find Wheeler's approach "unpalatable in view of its rather mystical over-tones."[52] One should recognize, however, that Wheeler is the only physicist of our time who inquires about the genesis of physical concepts and the meaning of the realities that stand behind them in an ontological sense. He advocates the view that we now enter a "third era of physics," which should operate not with given a priori fundamental concepts, such as space, time, fields, particles, and so forth, but actually explain the genesis of these concepts epistemologically as well as ontologically: "We have to account for all the structure that makes physics what it is."[53] Wheeler believes that the question "What makes meaning?" is the existential question, for it also addresses the issue of our own existence and that of the universe, which has proper-ties that allow us to exist. Can physics itself respond to this question: "Tomorrow, will it not be existence itself that comes under the purview of physics?"[54]

Wheeler argues that his approach to understanding the place and role of human beings in the universe contrasts with the selection mechanism of the MW-SAP in the sense that the participatory AP (PAP) is "founded on construction."[55] In other words, it attempts to explain the genesis of all physical entities in the universe—including human beings and, of crucial importance here, the meaning of objects and the intel-ligibility of the universe in general—as established through conscious communica-tion. He articulates this contrast by comparing the MW-SAP and his PAP as an opposition in views on the place of human beings in the universe as mediocre versus central: "Life, mind, and meaning have only a peripheral and accidental place in the scheme of things in this view [MW-SAP]. In the other view [PAP] they are central. Only by their agency is it even possible to construct the universe or existence, or what we call reality. Those make-believe universes totally devoid of life are (according to this view) totally devoid of physical sense not merely because they cannot be observed, but because there is no way to make them."[56]

Wheeler's argument is similar to our view asserted in the previous section that the many universes assumed to exist prior to the existence of the visible universe, so that the process of selection could be possible, function in the theory of the MW-SAP as intelligible realities that are brought into existence or, phrased in theological terms, enhypostasized by human beings as specific intelligible realities.

The main feature of Wheeler's concept is its ambition to deduce the "meaning" and "reality" of the universe in strictly physical terms. He seeks the meaning of phys-ical objects in acts of observation and in the measurement of certain properties of these objects. The physical happenings that are assumed in a naively realistic view to take place without being observed and measured are contraposed to those *events* that were brought into being through observations irreversibly, so that traces or memories of them cannot be erased.[57] Wheeler believes that the meaning of what is observed does not preexist a measurement itself; rather, it is brought into existence through observation-participation, treated as a complex of the questioning of nature together with the reception of its response, which is correlated with the question.

The important element in Wheeler's scheme of being is the network of observers, who by means of communication establish the intersubjective meaning of what is called physical reality. It is obvious that Wheeler makes a distinction between undifferentiated reality, which brings human beings and their networks into existence, and the reality known and thus defined and structured by human reason. He follows an emergent philosophy here by asserting that consciousness is a product of blind physical forces and myriads of particles in the universe, but that in order to affirm the presence of conscious observers in the universe, this same consciousness must develop the picture of the universe. This, according to Wheeler, has been done at the "late" stage of construction of the universe, when physics, as scientific theory, has been developed, and then the meaning of the universe has been established. It is nearly tautological to claim that the universe is known to us in human rubrics of thought. What is nontrivial in Wheeler's claims, however, is that the universe as the "world of existences" does not exist prior to the phenomenon of humankind in an ontological sense.[58] This is why "observers are necessary to bring the universe into being." The universe thus is a participatory universe, whose existence is relational upon the existence of intelligent observers. Wheeler sincerely believes that a science will be able to provide an explanation of the origins of human intelligence in the future.[59] This corresponds to his desire to treat both intelligence and the intelligible image of the universe as emergent properties.

The humankind-event, then, would be an inevitable result grounded in purely natural factors, and the "tangible reality of the universe" would be simply natural as well, although of a different, animated or self-reflected, order. In one of his famous diagrams, illustrating the transition from the view of the dead mechanical universe to the universe as the world of existences, Wheeler presents the universe as a self-exited circuit, that is, as developing through a cycle (a closed loop) that excludes any reference to a preexistent ultimate foundation of physics and phenomenon of humankind outside this circuit.[60] This means that the self-awareness of the universe through human intelligence, represented by Wheeler as the network of observer-participants, completes the "evolution" of the universe in Wheeler's sense as the movement along the closed circuit. There is no way out from this circuit; there is no further foundation of the circuit itself. From a philosophical point of view, this means that since the circuit is closed, and the universe receives its explanation from within this circuit, no question on the purpose of the universe and its end can be posed; it is just an emergent mode of the world of existences. The world's existence is explained from within itself and results in a monistic view with a closed ontology, which does not require any appeal to transworldly factors. Wheeler argues that his model of a closed circuit escapes the danger of an infinite regress of causations toward the ultimate substance.[61i] Instead, the central notion is the network of human observers who create physics. This removes the search for the ultimate element of the universe from its substantial level (*ousia*) to the existential level, that is, to the community of observer-participants who establish the meaning of what we call the universe. It is in this aspect that it can be affirmed that Wheeler's model is very close to the view that the universe, as we know it through science, is inherent in human hypostasis—that is, that its reality can be thought of only as enhypostasized by human beings.

There is, however, a fundamental difference between Wheeler's model and the Patristic view of the hypostatic feature of the human phenomenon. All human beings are treated theologically as created in the divine image, which is present in the *logoi*, which hold together soul and body in a hypostatic union. This implies that nature, conceived as real and concrete, is objictified through the *logoi* of human beings; that is, in Patristic terms, nature exists as *enhypostasis* of human beings. The latter is similar to some extent to what Wheeler advocates. The difference between Wheeler's thinking and Patristic teaching becomes transparent when one asks about the origin of the human composite. For Wheeler, human consciousness is an epiphenomenon of the network of communications, based on purely physical grounds, and, as a result, is an emergent property of this network. In contrast to this, in theology it is believed that the *logoi* of human beings originate in the Logos of God. The Logos thus is the foundation of both the intelligence of human beings and the intelligibility of the universe.

From a theological point of view there is a gap in Wheeler's reasoning on the universe as the emergent meaning circuit, for it offers no explanation of why the intelligent observers, who reveal the intelligibility of the entire universe, are even possible. Wheeler does not discuss what the ultimate logical premise is that makes the intelligibility of the universe, as realized through the intelligence of observers, a sheer fact.

There is a tacit anthropological assumption present in Wheeler's theory of the universe as a self-exited circuit, namely, the constitution of intelligent observers, as the unities of sensible physical bodies and the analytical soul, which is integrated with a body in order to produce the coherent view of the universe as the unity of impersonal physical agencies (light, pressure, sound) and their hypostatic structuring in the human reason. There is no firm explanation of why this particular structure of the human hypostasis was brought into being. The logic of explanation is different; that is, the universe has a dual structure: as undifferentiated stuff with no meaning (before the observers developed), on the one hand, and as sensible agencies and objects with meaning (or, in different words, as the sensible and the intelligible) after the network of observers developed the intersubjective meaning of what was observed, on the other hand. This is why the observers are necessary to bring the universe into being, to transform it from an undifferentiated state of affairs to something sensible and intelligible. This implies ultimately that the intelligibility of the universe is rooted in the ability of human beings to establish its structures and patterns through communication, starting from some elementary observations/measurements in a quantum sense.

But it is clear to any contemplative mind that the deposit of intelligibility has been tacitly present in the pursuit of Wheeler's scheme of being from the very beginning. Human observers who explain the universe and their own place in it in intelligible terms are already there, as the potentiality of existence itself, which does not logically follow from a simple physicalist view of the universe. This also makes it clear that, despite human beings' "central" position in Wheeler's meaning circuit, the position is not central enough, for the very existence of this circuit, if it is observed from outside as the unity of the universe, is possible because man can transcend from its particular place in this scheme (the top of Wheeler's diagram) and integrate the whole circuit in a single consciousness.[62] This implies that, while being a part of the meaning circuit, human beings transcend it in a sense, that they have an a priori ability to contemplate the universe as a whole and position themselves in it before they appear at some stage of development of the meaning circuit.

This can be clarified by appealing to the analogy with transcendental philosophy. Indeed, if Wheeler claims that the observers bring the universe into being, including its space, time, and so forth, one can reasonably ask: where do human observers dwell at all, if there is no preexistent space and time?[63] This question is reminiscent of the famous Kantian affirmation that human being is *phenomenon* and *noumenon* at the same time. On the one hand, human beings, as natural physical and biological entities, are in space and time. On the other hand, according to Kant, space and time represent transcendental forms of sensibility attributed to the whole humanity; that is, they form absolute and necessary conditions of human experience, including perception of the physical bodies. This means that because human beings initiate space and time from the depths of transcendental unity of their ego, which is prior to any particular form of experience, they "exist" prior to space and time, in the realm of what is called by Kant things-in-themselves. Projected into Wheeler's case, this analogy creates a difficult epistemological situation with respect to Wheeler's affirmations that human beings bring space, time, and the whole universe into being, for the reasonable question arises then: where do they do this from? Wheeler attempts to claim that the meaning of space and time, as well as of all other attributes of the universe, is constructed through observership-participation in quantum acts of immediate cognitions of undifferentiated being; that is, the emergence of space and time in physics is the result of blind interplay between chance and necessity, which leads to the emergence of human beings and their ordering forms of experience, such as space and time. Kant would object by saying that the sense data alone cannot constitute the notions of space and time and that it is the opposite: the ordering of the sense data can be done only in rubrics of space and time, which are a priori forms of human sensibility understood in a transcendental sense. Can physics pretend to solve the mystery of the genesis of space and time as existent in human hypostasis? It is extremely doubtful. If this were possible, it would mean that the emergence of such notions as space, time, fields, and particles (which constitute the structures of the intelligible realm, the *cosmos noeticos*) would be ultimately grounded in the undifferentiated and nonreflective physical world. This would definitely deviate from the Christian Platonic position on the unity of the created being (which is split in itself into the sensible and the intelligible) as having its ground in its nonbeing, in the realm of the Divine.

The Kantian response to Wheeler's conjecture on the nature of space and time, or the universe as a whole, would be to say that they all, as meaningful inductions from experience, are brought into being by transcendental observers out of the world of noumena, which is, by definition, an abstract entity, devoid of any description of the sensible world such as space and time (that is, existing only as an idea of the reason). The philosophical version of the PAP, then, could be rephrased in the following form: the observers (as noumena) are necessary to bring the universe (as a world of phenomena) into being (from the timeless and spaceless realm, that is, from the world of things-in-themselves).

It can be anticipated that any attempt to provide a coherent picture of the "genesis" of the concept of the universe—that is, to speculate about its ultimate grounds on the ontological level (the physical level in Wheeler's case)—will inevitably lead reason to an antinomian difficulty. Indeed, the thesis that "observers are necessary in order to bring the universe into being" makes the notion of the network of observers similar in how it functions in Wheeler's concept to the idea of an absolutely necessary being that appears in the fourth antinomy of Kant. Thus the epistemological situation in the context of Wheeler's proposition can be characterized as a *participatory anthropic antinomy:*

Thesis: The network of intelligent observers understood in a transcendental sense as existing in the realm with no time and no space is absolutely necessary for the visible universe in space and time to be brought into being.

Antithesis: The existence of the visible universe with spatiotemporal attributes is not contingent on the existence of the network of intelligent observers (understood in a transcendental sense) as its cause either in the visible universe or out of it.

According to the methodology of the antinomial monodualism established in chapter 4, we are inclined to treat this antinomy as indicating the dichotomy of what is affirmed and negated, that is, the network of intelligent observers, in the sense that this network is in space and time (that is, in the empirical realm) and, at the same time, transcends space and time, for it establishes the sense of space and time out of certain a priori faculties that define the observers also as intelligible beings. This, according to the method advocated by us, indicates not so much a paradox as a split in the constitution of human beings, between their bodily functions and their analytical soul, which, however, is overcome by positioning it with respect to the common source of both terms of this dichotomy. This means that the phenomenon of humankind, affirmed in a characteristic way by the PAP, if understood with the help of transcendental analysis in the perspective of Christian Platonism, leads us to the affirmation that it has two dimensions: the sensible and the intelligible, which cannot be reduced to each other in any hypothetical theory of the world. The presence of the phenomenal and noumenal in the human constitution (in a Kantian parlance) is treated by us through the eyes of Christian Platonism as the dichotomy between body and soul in human being, which is overcome through the relationship of both of them with respect to the common ground, which is beyond both the sensible and the intelligible in the realm of God, who created human beings in his image.

In the antinomy above, we have articulated again the presence of the basic *diaphora* in the very constitution of human beings. It is because of the similarity of the constitutive principles for both human beings and the universe that the universe can be known and can be presented in the human hypostasis as the unity of the sensible and the intelligible, which is split in itself. Finally, this *diaphora* points toward the hypostatic dimension of human existence, as relational upon God, and, as a result of this, that the universe, as we know it, exists in the human hypostasis; that is, it is enhypostasized by human beings.

Since the human hypostasis cannot be recovered from the impersonal chances and necessities of contingent created being, its presence in the universe can be treated as an event of not entirely natural origin, which we have called the humankind-event. This event is indeed formative for the universe to exist in human hypostasis. The universe itself, as enhypostasized by human beings through contemplation and analytical knowledge, is an event in the whole history of creation and salvation. The mystery of its existence and its knowledge by human beings is thus hidden in the mystery of our abilities to reveal its meaning and intelligence as grounded in the effected words of God. This is why we now turn to the culminating point of this chapter, to the ground of our knowledge of the universe, as well as to the foundation of our destiny, not only to know the universe but also to transfigure it and to bring it back to communion with God. This ground is the incarnation of the Logos of God in nature, in the words of Scripture and in Christ.

The Humankind-Event and the Incarnation

We now address *why* the humankind-event has happened in the universe and what is the ground of possibility for human intelligence to grasp the intelligibility of the universe. The microcosmic position of human beings makes the question of the origin of humanity intimately linked with the issue of the creation of the universe and of humankind in its particular incarnation in nature. However, we have established that the ultimate understanding of why the universe was created—that is, what God's intention was in doing so—cannot be achieved from within scientific or even theological discourse. We recall Maximus the Confessor's assertion that we know from creation that God *is* but that we cannot know God's motivations on creation, for in his essence God is separated from us through the basic *diastema*. Some further clarification to this issue can come from the christological dimension of this problem, that is, when the idea of the humankind-event is linked to the concept of the Christ-event.

The fact that we cannot avoid theological reflection while contemplating the place of humanity in the universe becomes evident in the very definition of humanity. As we have seen, science is able to position all human beings in the universe in terms of their nature, of the physico-biological constants of their existence. This makes it clear that there is no difference whether science speaks about a particular human being or about the whole humankind. Since human nature (that is, physics and biology) is communicable from one being to another, one particular being represents the whole humankind. If follows, then, that what is meant by humankind in the context of physics and cosmology is just an abstract collective of beings functioning at this particular moment of cosmic history. Cosmology and the anthropic arguments do not risk speculating about the links between the universe and humanity, understood in a rather religious sense, as a whole, that is, as those who live now, who lived before, and who will be living in the future. Cosmology does not discuss the *fullness* of humankind as an event that begins from the first born human being and finishes with the last one. It assumes that the phenomenon of man is an inherent, continuous, and indefinite part of cosmic history. In this case, the unity of man in the universe is a result of the ongoing evolution of complexities, so that man is made of whatever material is available in the universe.

For the Patristic writers, such as Gregory of Nyssa, it was clear that a simple articulation of humankind's microcosmic position—that is, its unity with the universe—does not position human beings in the universe in a really central place, not in a cosmographic sense (as in space and time), but in a spiritual sense (as a creature made in the image of God). Gregory writes: "There is nothing remarkable in Man's being the image and likeness of the universe, for earth passes away and the heavens change. . . . In thinking we exalt human nature by this grandiose name (microcosm, synthesis of the universe) we forget that we are thus favouring it with the qualities of gnats and mice."[64]

The central point for Gregory is not to articulate human nature but to stress that all human beings bear the image of God, which makes them united in the fullness of humanity as manifestation of this image. At the same time, this fullness does not dissolve the personhood in human beings, making them one and the other through the hypostatic qualities of existence. This enables human beings to personalize the universe in the sense of establishing its meaning for the whole humankind not only in natural anthropic terms but also from the perspective of the divine image in it. The universe was created by God together with humankind, and it is through humankind that the universe can become aware of its divine origin. It is through knowledge and creative transformation that human beings participate ontologically in affirming and praising things in the universe.

The biblical assertion that human beings are created in the image of God provides us with the understanding of humanity in its fullness, as related (from the first born man to the last one) to its Father, who endowed all human beings with his image.[65] This implies that humanity as an event in the history of salvation recapitulates all human lives in the past, present, and future: "Just as any particular man is limited by his bodily dimensions, and the peculiar size which is cojoined with the superficies of his body is the measure of his separate existence, so I think that the entire plenitude of humanity was included by God of all, by His power of foreknowledge, as it were in one body, and that this is what the text teaches us which says 'God created man, in the image of God created he him.' For the image is not in part of our nature, nor is the grace in any one of the things found in that nature, but this power extends equally to all the race."[66]

This provides a theological weight to our assertion that humankind understood in the Christian sense is worldly only on the part of its particular incarnation in nature in the image of God, whereas in their creaturehood, human beings are hypostatic and ecclesial beings.

Christianity rearticulated the biblical idea of the fullness of humanity by referring it to Christ, the incarnate Logos of God. Irenaeus of Lyons, in developing the idea that it is in the incarnation that the fullness of humanity was recapitulated by Christ, writes that "in times past it was *said* that man was made in the image of God, but not *shown,* because the Word, in whose image man was made, was still invisible."[67] In the incarnation in flesh, "God recapitulated in Himself that ancient handiwork of His which is man,"[68] and "He recapitulated in Himself the long history of mankind."[69] Irenaeus asserts that by taking human flesh, made of the substance of this world, and uniting it to the Divine in Christ, God confirmed that the substance, which God used initially to create human beings, is linked to God's first plan to save humanity, and that the incarnation fulfills this plan. This means that the substance of the world has a fundamental importance for the fulfillment of God's plan. It implies that for the incarnation and recapitulation of all human nature in Christ to take place, the substance of the world was chosen by God in his plan of creation of the world and salvation of humanity, thus making this particular substance to be closely linked to the Divine hypostatically (relationally), that is, existing not as it is in itself but only in the hypostasis of God, who created it. This was demonstrated by the incarnation of the Logos of God with a new force.

One can then speculate that the structure of the natural world has a direct relation to God's providential activity in the world in order to fulfill God's plan. This implies that for the incarnation of God to take place on the earth, in the visible universe, this universe must possess some features such that the making of human beings in God's image, as well as the incarnation of God in human flesh, would be possible. This links the creation of the universe and its structure to the phenomenon of man, and the incarnation articulates this link, making the whole sense of it rather hypostatic (that is, grounded in the will and love of the personal God, who transfers the image of his personality to human beings, who in turn can articulate the universe as being amazingly fashioned in order to sustain life). It is the recapitulation of man in the incarnation that, theologically speaking, links the Christ-event with the humankind-event.

Here we would like to make one critical comment with respect to G. Ellis's attempts to formulate a Christian anthropic principle by linking the presence of life in the universe with the "nature of the creator." Ellis builds his argument on Temple's interpretation of the prologue in John 1:4-5.[70] The words "What came to be in it was Life, and the Life was the light of men, and the light shineth in the darkness, and the darkness did not absorb it" in Temple's interpretation were used by Ellis to state that "we have arrived at the Christian anthropic principle, a profound version of the SAP . . . : the creation *had* to have as its product, life, for that is the nature of the creator."[71] The worrisome aspect of this statement is that it tries to connect the existence of human beings in the universe as it is understood in the SAP—that is, on the substantial (natural) level—with the essence (nature) of God, which, as apophatic theology asserts, is inaccessible to human grasp and hypothesis. This is why it is safer, theologically, to treat life as "the light of men" in the prologue in the sense of God's plan of the salvation of humanity, which preexists the world in the same sense as the Logos of God, who himself, according to the Nicene Creed, was begotten before ages. This means that one can possibly argue that the life is the inherent characteristic of the universe only in a relational sense; that is, that everything in the world, including the lives of human beings, is sustained by the *logoi*, originating from the Word-Logos of God, and that the *logoi* of human beings can be associated with the uncreated light of men. But the meaning of this light was revealed only after the incarnation of the Logos in Christ, in which the Divine and the human were joined by the hypostasis of the Son of God. The physical environment in the universe, as we have established, provides the *necessary* conditions for the existence of human beings. This points toward the contingent necessity displayed in the world and reflecting its dependence on God. But sufficient conditions for human life to exist are deeply rooted in the mystery of humankind's creation, which (being linked to the physical aspects of humanity) is nonnatural and hypostatic. It is only in this hypostatic sense that one can argue that there is a link between the whole creation and life, that is, that the universe and humankind are inherent in the hypostasis of the Logos of God.

The Christ-event has another important meaning, namely, the renewal of the whole humankind to a mode of existence that can be called *ecclesial*. Not only are human beings united to the source of their existence in the Logos of God, but they also participate in the ongoing accomplishment of the body of Christ, God's church, thus making their own existence more hypostatic in an ecclesial sense.[72] The whole universe, then, is seen through the human ecclesial hypostasis in the context of building the body of Christ. This implies that all humans ever living are included in this body, which becomes the definition of humanity. Since the accomplishment of the body of Christ is an eschatological tendency—that is, it must stop together with the formation of man—the humankind-event means that it will have its end; that is, it is indeed an event of cosmological nature and of ecclesial reality. From the Christian perspective, this entails that the whole history of the universe understood as a natural process will transform consequently (as existent in the renewed hypostasis of humanity) toward its ecclesial mode; that is, the universe itself will acquire more hypostatic features.

This observation allows us to conjecture that the development of the universe before the incarnation of the Logos of God in flesh on the earth and after has, theologically speaking, a drastically different meaning. It was necessary for the universe to be in a state of constructive development in order to sustain life on the earth and to allow God to condescend to us and to assume human flesh in order to initiate the new stage of salvation history. This means that nature as it existed before the incarnation (being lost in the sense that it did not know its own divine origin) was transfigured through the knowledge of its meaning and destiny, which it received from humankind, that is, in human hypostasis. This is because the acquisition of the ecclesial hypostasis through the building of the body of Christ leads human beings to the transfigured state, where the balance between their natural and hypostatic qualities should change in favor of the latter; the sustenance of the natural dimensions of human existence, which has been conditioned by the cosmological conditions, probably ceases to function as the precondition of the fulfillment of the divine plan. This confirms our conjecture that the constructive development of the universe as evolving toward the conditions where human beings could exist had to take place only prior to the incarnation.

What will happen afterward, in the remote future, is difficult to say, for, even according to the cosmological predictions, there is a natural limit of the extension of human life in the cosmos. Together with our theological argument, one can reassert that the universe in the future is anti-anthropic in a physical sense, but that it becomes more dependent on humanity in Wheeler's sense when its reality depends on the condition of humankind; the causation between the universe and human life has reversed in relation to what has been proposed by the SAP. The matter of the salvation of the universe becomes, then, an ecclesial activity of the transfiguration of nature and its unification back to God. Humanity is not just a purpose of creation (this would be suggested by the SAP); it can be understood only in the context of the promise of God for its salvation as constituting the locus point of the meeting of God and God's creation, as the mediating agency that is supposed to bring the whole universe through its knowledge to the new creation. This implies that the purpose of the universe is not human beings considered in their natural condition but unique creatures in whom the Logos of God is indwelling and who are chosen to transfigure the universe by bringing it to the ultimate union with God.

The humankind-event, as seen through theological and scientific eyes, thus acquires hypostatic and ecclesial features, which make the position of human beings in the universe similar to the position of the worshiping community in the church: humanity establishes itself as a priest of creation. To develop this thesis as a conclusion to our discussion, we should touch on one particular aspect of the hypostatic dimension of human existence, which can be articulated in terms of space and time.

The nontrivial connection between the problem of the space of the universe and the incarnation of the Logos of God in flesh has been articulated by T. Torrance.[73] This section will develop further his argument that space and time are relational entities whose concepts reflect the contingent rationality of the world, which depends on the transcendent God-Creator. Our intention is to build an argument that the relational nature of space, understood as a physical (natural) place for human beings to live, points toward an ontology of created things and human beings that is relational upon the Logos of God or, in other words, is inherent in the hypostasis of the Logos.

The belief in the incarnation of the Logos of God in flesh plays a central role here; on the one hand, Jesus Christ, being in his nature fully human, lived in the space and time of the empirical world, located in body in a particular place and time of earthly history; on the other hand, Jesus was fully God, who did not leave his "place" in the Holy Trinity and who, being God, not only was present in Palestine two thousand years ago but was always present in all places and times of the universe created by God. We have here a nontrivial, historico-topological relation between the finite track of Jesus in empirical space and time, which in an extraordinary way is linked to the whole history of the visible universe.[74]

Let us provide here a couple of Patristic references. It was Origen who first reflected on the extraordinary position of Christ, being human and God, in the universe in terms of space: "Though the God of the whole universe descends in His own power with Jesus to live the life of men, and the Word which 'was in the beginning with God and was Himself God' comes to us; yet he does not leave His home and desert His state."[75]

Origen stresses here that God, who is the creator and governor of the whole universe, being incarnate in flesh in Jesus Christ, did not cease to be God as a provider of existence and intelligibility of everything at every point in the universe. Being incarnate in flesh—that is, being a human being among humankind, Christ as God was still ruling the whole universe and holding the entire creation together. God, in creating the universe and making sense of it in order to receive his Son-Logos in flesh, prepares a place for himself, but in such a way that, while descending into the created world, in a particular place in Palestine and in a particular time, God still holds the entire creation together, being present in all possible "places" of the universe. One thus says that the incarnation recapitulates the whole creation.

Being incarnate at one point of space and not ceasing from God's "place" as the transcendent creator, holding the wholeness of space through his *logoi*, God demonstrates that his relationship to space is not a spatial relation. Origen asserts this explicitly: "The power and divinity of God comes to dwell among men through the man whom God wills to choose and in whom He finds room without changing from one place to another or leaving His former place empty and filling another. Even supposing that we do say that he leaves one place and fills another, we would not mean this in any spatial sense."[76] God descended to humankind from the kingdom, but God is still there in his kingdom. This means that the message of the kingdom is about human ascension to God (deification), which, being in its movement opposite to God's descension to humankind, has no spatial expression. Rather, it has a temporal expression as an *expectation* of the age to come, as an eschatological future, in which human beings, following the type of the resurrected Christ, will be able to ascend to God and to dwell in God's kingdom forever.

Athanasius of Alexandria expresses the unity of the Divine and the human in Christ in similar terms to Origen, by appealing to the analogy of space. Athanasius explains the incarnation of the Word-Logos of God as follows: "Then the incorporeal and incorruptible and immaterial Word of God entered our world. In one sense, indeed he was not far from it before, for no part of creation had ever been without Him Who, while ever abiding in union with the Father, yet fills all things that are."[77] Athanasius argues in this passage that despite that the Son-Word of God descended to the earth to live with human beings, in a way he did not become closer to us, for he was ever in everything of the universe, which was made by him. Athanasius recognized that there is a paradox that the Son of God is fully present with us in our space and time and yet remains with the Father. This paradox is a serious issue if one employs the receptacle notion of space, which confines God within the receptacle. Athanasius felt intuitively that, in order to resolve this mystery, the receptacle notion of space must be replaced with a relational understanding of space, a form of comprehensibility that is unfolded by the divine agency, who set forth this space in order to reveal himself.[78]

Athanasius develops the thought that by becoming human, the Word of God "became visible through His works and revealed Himself as the Word of the Father, the Ruler and King of the whole creation."[79] Athanasius argues that despite the fact that the Father provided the works of creation as a means by which the maker might be known, this did not prevent men from wallowing in error.[80] Because of this, the Word of God descended to men in order to "renew the same teaching."[81] In *On the Incarnation* (17), Athanasius analyzes the difficulty one can face while dealing with the incarnation of the Word of God.[82] Torrance points out that Athanasius attempted to make an analogy of the human soul and body and its relation in function to what is outside the body, but that this analogy does not hold, for human beings, for example, are unable to control the motion of heavenly bodies by their thought.[83] Space in the case of the Word of God is God's predicate; it is determined by God's agency and is to be understood according to God's nature. This means that the "spatial relationship" between the Father and the Son has no analogies with the spatial relations among creaturely things.

The human nature in Christ was operating within the reality of empirical space and historical time, whereas Christ's divine nature was always beyond the empirical and intelligible aeons, in the uncreated realm of the kingdom of God, which can be expressed symbolically in terms of the boundaries of the created if these boundaries are seen from the vertical (divine) dimension. It is from this "outside" that Christ the Logos of God coordinated the empirical space where he indwelled in the body with the rest of the created universe. This helps us to understand the space-time of the physical universe as the manifestation of the hypostatic mode of the relationship between God and the world.

One can rephrase this idea by using a different analogy. Indeed, space and time are perceived by human beings from within creation. In this sense, one can speculate that this space-time is an internal form of the relation of the universe with the transcendent Divine. This internal form of space and time, being contingent and dependent on the interactions between the parts of the universe and being essential for the existence of human beings and their history, cannot be conceived, however, without its "external" counterpart, its "boundary," which can be articulated only from "outside," from the perspective of the uncreated. This links empirical space and time with its moving "boundary" (which originates from the divine dimension), so that in no way are the space and time of the physical universe accomplished and fixed forever in the shapes that we can comprehend at present.

The question, then, is how the internal space-time of the universe is held in relation to the divine "environment" in which it is embedded, or, in other words, what is the principle of the borderline between the universe and its nonworldly ground associated with the external side of the space of the universe? Here, the analogy with the hypostatic union of two natures in Christ can be employed. Indeed, it is because of the hypostatic union of the divine and the natural in Christ that one can argue by analogy that the interplay between the space and time of the universe and its uncreated ground in God is upheld also hypostatically by God in the course of God's economy of creation. The fulfillment of this economy took place in the incarnation of the Logos of God in flesh, when the link between the humanity of Christ (in space) and Christ's divinity as the Logos (which is beyond space but yet holds all space together) was established. This manifested that space and time are linked to the Divine. It is from this perspective that Torrance's assertions on the relational nature of space, as the form of rationality created by the Logos God to communicate his presence to us, receive further interpretation—namely, that the space and time of the universe manifest in natural (physical) terms the relation between the visible universe and its "external" uncreated and divine "form," which constitutes the ground for the natural one. This implies that a particular appearance of space and time in the physical universe is not complete in itself and is open to the unfolding rationality of God, whose presence in the space and time of the universe has not an essential but a hypostatic character. Indeed, the very relation between the space and time of the universe and its uncreated ground is hypostatic; that is, it exists only in the hypostasis of the Logos God.

When we turn our attention to human beings, we admit that, in their natural mode, they all exist within the internal space-time of the universe. The importance of a particular structure of this space for providing the necessary conditions for existence of human beings can be supported by physical arguments. It is enough to remind the reader that the dimension of space that is equal to three (the number of degrees of freedom of any object in this space) is vitally important for the existence of stable structures in the universe (such as atoms and planetary systems), which contribute toward the natural conditions for the existence of living beings.[84] It is important to assert here that the structure of space is intimately connected with the nature of those interactions experienced by objects in this space. It is difficult to say in abstraction what came first—the dimension of space or the stability of the world—but it remains a fact that both space and the form of physical forces are closely linked to each other. It is also worth remembering that the uniformity of time and space, which is widely exploited in physics, implies the conservation of particle energies and momenta. In fact, empirical physics, which measures the conserved quantities and establishes the laws, is indebted greatly to the relative uniformity of space and time. In general relativity, the links between matter and space-time are even closer.

The SAP and cosmology deal in general with the internal aspect of the "boundary" that separates the created from the uncreated. It is, however, possible to trespass this boundary in pure speculation by appealing again to the idea of many worlds with different geometries. In this case, the positioning of the space-time of the visible universe, with respect to that which is not actualized in physics (but that can be imagined), can be treated as an apophatic affirmation of space-time in its actuality with respect to its possible other being, for example, with respect to the worlds with different dimensions and different topological properties. Here, the relation between actual space-time and conceptual universes can be understood in ontological terms with reference to the idea of the basic *diaphora* in creation that we have already used several times. The conceptually different space-times cannot be treated as an ontological ground for the existence of empirical space and time; they are contingent on their own nonbeing in the uncreated realm. In other words, the MW-SAP–like explanation of the dimension of space $n = 3$ as a selection out of the ensemble of the universes with different dimensions in the visible universe cannot achieve its goal, because it does not explain the nature of the space and time of the visible universe in hypostatic terms, that is, its purpose and end as conceived by the divine hypostasis before all ages. The appeal to the *MW* hypothesis can be treated as an unfortunate attempt to establish the relational nature of space and time with respect to its intelligible nonactuality. As we have argued earlier, the genuine result of this abstraction, from the actuality of space-time to conceptual potentialities, consists in the manifestation of the basic *diaphora* in creation, which points toward their common uncreated ground.

What is important in Torrance's arguments about the links between the incarnation and space-time is that space should be considered in the context of the divine hypostasis, that is, as the expression of the *personal* rationality of God in the world, accessible to us. One should not, however, understand that space and time and their possible theories represent the embodiment of the Logos of God, as was conjectured by W. Pannenberg.[85] Rather, space and time can be treated as a natural counterpart in the hypostatic constitution of the world in its relation to the Divine, which was confirmed through the union between the Divine and the human in the incarnation of the Logos of God, Jesus Christ. It is because of this—that is, that space and time are linked to the ground in the uncreated via the hypostatic (nonontological) union—that any particular perception of space and time and the theory of them is fundamentally open-ended and unfixed in terms of a natural incarnation of the Logos in the flesh in Jesus Christ (which is commonly perceived as the nativity of Jesus). It can mean that the space and time of the universe as we know them were important for the Logos to be incarnate in this particular spatiotemporal form, but, as mentioned before, this fact does not preclude space and time deviating in the future, for the logic of this change follows the logic of the hypostasis of the Logos, who is balancing God's uncreated nature with the world, which has been created by God, rather than by any intrinsic processes in the universe.

It is only through this vision of the universe as held in the hypostasis of the Logos that it is possible to reaffirm that human hypostatic beings occupy a special position in the universe, by being *microcosm* in a very nontrivial sense. In the same way as Christ, being the incarnate Logos of God in a particular place in the space and time of the universe (and, at the same time, not ceasing from his "place" in God, being in all possible places and times of the visible universe as well as in intelligible orders), human beings (whom Christ recapitulated in the incarnation), being present in a particular place of the universe, control it in various locations and times not by power but by their knowledge, recapitulating the universe in a single consciousness. This thought was developed by Maximus the Confessor in his *The Church's Mystagogy,* when he argued that "the word is said to be a man, and in what manner man is a world." Maximus paralleled the basic *diaphora* in creation with the *diaphora* between body and soul, held together hypostatically, in man.[86]

The incarnation of the Logos of God in flesh, which entails the annunciation of the kingdom of God, brings the whole humanity to the realization not only of its *microcosmic* function but also of its *ecclesial* function to build the universal church as the body of Christ and to be a "priest of creation." The whole universe, then, having participated through its creation and the incarnation in the hypostasis of the Logos, is represented for human beings in the holy church, which, according to Maximus, being divided in its outward appearance into sanctuary and nave, is held together hypostatically ("through their relationship to the unity").[87] It is from this analogy that one sees again the meaning of the incarnation: for the whole church represents the world, and it is Christ who is the head and the foundation of the church; the universe, being mirrored in the church, is held hypostatically by the Logos of God, who is the head of the universe understood as a church.

The incarnation thus reveals for Christians and affirms for modern science the ecclesial nature of the universe as well as of human beings. This is why knowledge and exploration of the universe in the context of the science–religion dialogue can be treated as an activity of uncovering the hypostatic features of the universe, which can mean at the same time the praising of the personal creator of the universe. This activity reinstates the existing split between the church and the universe, returning them to their unity in the communion with God, revealing thus the work of scientists as a para-eucharistic work.[88]

To make a final refinement in our vision of the humankind-event in the universe as a hypostatic happening, we refer here to Torrance's analysis of the arguments of Athanasius of Alexandria about the difference in relationships between Christ and his Father, on the one hand, and between humanity and God, on the other hand. These can be illustrated as the difference in spatial constitution of Christ as being in space and, at the same time, being with the Father beyond all space versus human beings as enclosed in the place as contingent things. Athanasius's argument assumes the presence of a parallel relation between human nature and God, which points beyond the natural aspects of existence. Torrance quotes a passage from Athanasius in this context that is important here: "We shall not be *as* the Son, nor equal to Him for we and He are different. The word *as* is applied to us inasmuch as things differing from others in nature become as they, in view of certain reference beyond them. Wherefore the Son is simply and without any reservation in the Father, for that belongs essentially to Him by nature, but so far as we who are not like that by nature are concerned, an image and a *pointer* are needed."[89]

Torrance stresses that the presence of the word *pointer*, as translation of the Greek *paradeigma*, is crucial in order to articulate the image of God deposited in human nature without transgressing the difference between them. In other words, the pointer does not touch on the ontological relationship between human nature and God; rather, it points toward the hypostatic dimension of human existence as originating in the Logos of God. The Christ-event, being thus the manifestation of the spatiotemporal relationship between God and the physical universe, and being expressed as an open-ended interaction between God and human beings, "eternal and contingent happening,"[90] recapitulates the humankind-event in the universe, making the latter the expression of an interaction between humankind and God and of contingent happening in the eternity of God.

In a similar manner, by referring to the resurrectional aspect of the Christ-event, it is plausible to argue that while Christ after resurrection and ascension left us with a message about God in space and time, which we know, on the one hand, through the history of succession in the church and, on the other hand, eschatologically through the presence of God's kingdom in the liturgy of the church, the present historical reality of the humankind-event in the universe experiences an eschatological pause, which is granted to cosmic humanity to transfigure and deify the universe. In the same way that church and its liturgy manifests explicitly the historical and eschatological presence of Christ among us, the ecclesial essence of human beings in the universe manifests that the universe and its knowledge are revealed to us in the hypostasis of the divine Logos.

The Universe as Hypostatic Event

Humankind-Event and the Destiny of the Universe

Now we come to the discussion of the finality of the humankind-event. We have recognized earlier that the humankind-event is understood as constructive for forming the inward existence of the universe and its self-conscious expression in the apprehension of human beings and their creative activity in the cosmos. It has also been recognized that hypostatic human beings are dependent on those conditions in the universe that allow them to sustain the unity of their soul with a material body; it is in this sense that the process of giving the universe its existence in the hypostasis of human beings is deeply rooted in the universe as itself hypostatically inherent ("prior" to human beings) in the Logos of God. In other words, the physical conditions of the universe and the environment on the earth form the necessary conditions for human beings to exist. It is important to understand, however, that the position of human beings in nature, despite their ability to transcend it, was very passive up to some point in history, that is, human beings were not able to change the natural conditions of their existence using the power of their intellectual and technological activity, so that the environment was stable and immutable, experiencing no serious influence from human activity. The balance between the intellectual exploration of the intelligible and sensible worlds and the stability of the natural environment was considered as an obvious fact; human apprehension of the universe and its technological implications had never before threatened the natural physico-biological conditions of human existence.

This balance between hypostatic and natural in human beings—the balance between the human longing for the spiritual and human beings' rootedness in nature—assumed that any particular development of human thought, being directed toward nature, should not cross a line such that the apprehension of nature and its implications in technology could be detached from the morality and wisdom inherent in human hypostasis and responsible for preserving the gift of life and for supporting the balance between natural and spiritual. What we observe nowadays is a shift in this balance, when human reason, freed from its living fullness of spiritual apprehension of the universe and the Divine, attempts to explore peculiar aspects of creation and to develop artificial conditions of living and technologies, which can, because of either an accident or just human naïveté and ignorance, threaten the natural conditions of living for humans.[91] This creates a serious philosophical and theological problem as to how to balance the human ability to think and to discover novelties in nature and technology with the fact that the progress of this development must preserve the very possibility of these hypostatic human beings to function on the natural level. One can question to what extent the development of the human intellect and its apprehension of the universe and its technological transformation can advance while preserving the unity of the sensible and intelligible in humanity, that is, in its hypostatic constitution, with which human beings were endowed by God.

It is interesting to note that the problem of human survival in the course of technological progress came into existence only in the twentieth century, when the expansion of technology brought human beings for the first time in the history of the humankind-event to the point where they can influence global conditions of their own existence and even terminate existence as such by destroying its natural dimensions. In the words of the Russian philosopher N. Berdyaev, man has become a cosmic force, or *"cosmiurger,"* who not only passively observes nature but also participates in its formation and transformation. The impact of the technological revolution that has been taking place since the eighteenth century has changed the relation of human beings to nature, resulting in the replacement of the belief in the immutable and objective order in nature, in which human life was embedded and to which it was subordinated. This has happened because the power of technology destabilizes the human world and the cosmos connected with that world. Berdyaev wrote as far back as 1933 that "it will be soon that peaceful scientists will be able to make shocks not only of historical but of cosmic character," since "man has in his hands the power, by means of which he can operate the World and he can annihilate the most part of mankind and culture."[92]

When we studied the humankind-event from a cosmological perspective above, we realized that the natural conditions of the existence of human beings in the cosmos cannot be sustained forever. This is why we have introduced the terminology of the humankind-event: to underline the finitude of the human phenomenon in the universe. The questions important for our discussion here, however, are as follows: If the humankind-event is a constructive event for the whole universe in both the physical and the hypostatic senses, how then can the cessation of the natural dimension of the humankind-event affect the existence and destiny of the universe? What would be the consequences for the universe itself if the humankind-event were to be untimely terminated by an accident or by intentional suicide? Would there be a big difference, in terms of the finality of humankind, between a global disaster on earth (for example, being a hit by an asteroid), which would terminate the existence of human beings prematurely, and the passive expectation of humankind's extinction in the course of the predicted cosmological evolution? One anticipates that religion and theology should play the pivotal role in answering this question, for it is for human beings to decide what particular future for which to expect and to hope. The future can be defined by the power of human intellect in different ways, using either ideas from scientific fantasies and utopias or religious beliefs and prophetic visions. It is crucial here to recognize that the very existence of the future of human beings in the universe is entirely open to their own hypostatic definition and judgment. It can also clearly be seen here that the issue of morality and ultimate values in the definitions of the future arises: "All becomes dependent on the spiritual and moral state of man, on what will be the goal to use his power and on what kind of spirit he has."[93]

To make this point stronger, we can appeal to the observation made in previous sections that, theologically speaking, the constructive evolution in the universe, which is aimed to create conditions that allow the human body to function, was decisive prior to the incarnation of the Logos of God in flesh. This implies that the future of the universe as such does not have any particular goal if it is not seen from the perspective of the destiny of human beings, the vision of which can be established only theologically, not scientifically. What this means is that the role of human beings, in the future development of the universe, is crucial, for it is human beings who can impose goals on the development of the universe according to their own vision. The role of religion and theology becomes indispensable indeed for making any feasible predictions about the future of humankind and the universe, if these predictions are supposed to be rooted in ethics and wisdom. The Christian vision of the destiny of human beings and their function in the universe as microcosm as well as mediator with God is deeply rooted in the ability of human beings to transcend actuality, being hypostatically inherent in God, and to perceive their place and the place of the universe in the context of the deification and transfiguration of the universe, that is, through unification with God in God's kingdom.

Indefinite Humankind-Event in Final Anthropic Cosmology

Despite the fact that human life, seen in a theological perspective, transcends its natural appearance (being inherent in the hypostasis of the Logos of God), science tends to treat the phenomenon of human life monistically, reducing it to physico-biological factors and making the intellectual dimension of human existence purely epiphenomenal. In some "scientific" futuristic accounts, one can see scenarios of the future based on the idea of indefinite human life in purely naturalistic terms, in which it is assumed that the human phenomenon had a beginning in time (and, in this sense, is finite in the past), but in which it is also hoped that this phenomenon will endure indefinitely in the future. What is important in these models is that human beings are assumed to be capable of directing the development of the universe to a very special end.

Let us analyze briefly, as a case study, some ideas of F. Tipler that he calls the "Omega Point theory," the "theory of evolving God," or the "physics of immortality," which offer an eschatological scenario for life to exist forever in the universe.[94] These ideas have their origin in the final anthropic principle (FAP), which attempts to extend the validity of the weak and strong anthropic inferences beyond the present-day state of affairs in the universe toward the remote evolutionary future.[95] In general, cosmology predicts that the future of the universe may be extremely anti-anthropic, leading ultimately to the fireball of the final collapse (the big crunch) in a closed universe or to the "eternal cold" (the open universe). The FAP postulates the eternity of life (understood in a reductionist way as the running of software on a computer): "Intelligent information-processing must come into existence in the Universe, and, once it comes into existence, it will never die out."[96]

The fundamental inconsistency of this proposition is rooted in the fact that the life the FAP is talking about is the "life" of machines, some kind of intelligent automata, but not of hypostatic human beings. Tipler make this clear by saying that intelligent life is associated with a computer: "A living human being is a representation of a definite program, rather than the program itself,"[97] and "a living being" is any entity that codes "information." Thus life is a form of information processing, and "the human mind—as well as the human soul—is a very complex computer program."[98] This is why it is believed that life (understood in such a strange way) could be possible not only in a human body but also in other material structures where the processing of information is possible.

The very existence of the phenomenon of intelligent life, then, is dependent on natural conditions: "If the laws of physics do not permit information processing in a region of space-time, then life simply cannot exist there. Conversely, if the laws of physics permit information processing in a region, then it is possible for some form of life to exist there."[99] This is true in any case even if life is treated in ordinary biological terms: it needs an appropriate physical environment in order to function. But the natural conditions constitute only the conditions necessary for the existence of life; life's actual coming into existence remains a mystery and cannot be understood in terms of nature alone. The same is true with respect to the endurance of life. From what we have discussed above, it is clear that the actual continuation of intelligent life on the earth now depends on the will and aspirations of humankind, its desire to survive in worsening ecological conditions as well as to avoid a social and political situation that could lead to global nuclear conflict, which could wipe out life from the surface of the planet. This explains why Tipler's assertion that *if* life comes into existence "it will never die out" is very optimistic.

If life did depend entirely on physical and biological conditions, then, indeed, the survival of this life would require a suitable universe; according to Tipler, it would be enough to have a universe that allows for intelligent information processing to continue all the way to the future, final temporal boundary of the universe. This kind of a universe must be closed and must contain a single final point (the Omega Point, in Tipler's terms) in which the world lines of all events in the universe will coincide and in which there will be no horizons. The quantity of information processed in all these curves coming to the Omega Point must be infinite, since "only if there is an infinite number of thoughts in the future it is reasonable to say that intelligent life has existed 'forever.'"[100] The Omega Point itself acquires some "divine features" replacing space and time and containing all information about the universe.

We have no intention of discussing here the flaws and problems associated with the pseudo-theological terminology employed in this context, for it has been done elsewhere.[101] The epistemological naïveté of some claims of the theory of the evolving God have also been analyzed before.[102] Here, we are mostly concerned with the implications of the FAP (certainly in a purely hypothetical form) with respect to the universe as nature, as well as to the fate of human beings as hypostatic unities of bodies and souls. Elementary physics contained in the assumptions of the FAP tells us that, in order to produce an infinite amount of information in the universe, all structural elements of the material universe must be effectively destroyed. Theologically speaking, if one believes in the natural order in creation provided by God, this order is supposed to be not only distorted but also removed. One can make a rough analogy by saying that the sensible creation is supposed to be entirely replaced by the realm of intelligible forms, to which the Omega belongs.[103] The FAP, it can then be said, tends to remove, or at least to modify, the basic ontological difference in creation (the *diaphora*) between the sensible and the intelligible. It is not surprising, then, that this intention, which is tacitly present in Tipler's theories, led him to the affirmation of the divine properties of the Omega Point, for, indeed, it is only in the power of God to set a particular structure of the world as a constitutive element of the *creatio ex nihilo*. Theology affirms that the basic *diaphora*, as the ontological difference between sensible and intelligible creation, is not subject to any change, even in the process of deification, which, leading to union with God, does not touch on the basic ontological difference.

One can then speculate that if the setting up of the basic *diaphora* is associated with the providential activity of the Logos of God, in the course of creation of the universe, its replacement, implied in the FAP, corresponds to something that is opposite to the *creatio ex nihilo*. Indeed, the attempt to claim that the Omega Point is immanent and transcendent to the universe is a tacit assertion that the difference between the created and the uncreated is removed in such a way that the ultimate union with the "evolving god" assumes de facto the annihilation of the world. Amazingly, the initial anthropic motivation of the FAP turns out to be absolutely anti-anthropic, for the destruction of physical nature implies the destruction of the physico-biological component of human existence.

Taking a strong stance, one can argue that the Omega Point theory of Tipler proposes a mathematical prescription as to how to organize intentionally the "cosmological crisis" (that is, the "ecological crisis" on cosmic scales).[104] This immediately leads to two theological observations. First, by destroying nature, the "posthuman" kind of intelligent processing machines desanctifies the good creation of a good God, which is tantamount to the view that the sensible creation is evil and is worth replacing in favor of an intelligible world, which is full of disembodied "softwarelike" souls. The second unsatisfactory feature of this scenario is that the human hypostatic constitution is supposed to be destroyed together with the divine image with which human beings are endowed.

One fears that such a scenario probably indicates a deep spiritual crisis of human scientific thought, in which the vision of nature as sacrament, as well as the understanding of human life as deeply rooted in the reality of the Divine, is lost.[105] Why does this happen? Why does the exaggeration of the naturalistic dimension in anthropic cosmology lead in theory to the eclipse of the human-divine image and to the lack of balance and responsibility for nature, which God handed to human beings?

To answer these questions, it should be reemphasized that cosmology in general has been a powerful tool in sketching the picture of the world and influencing the beliefs of society; it has always entered the social institutions under the cover of some ideology. The social function of cosmology was active in practically all human cultures that existed before Christianity and that coexist with it nowadays. Cosmology orientates a community in its world, in the sense that it defines, for that community, the place of humankind in the cosmic scheme of things. Such cosmic orientation tells the members of the community in broad terms who they are and where they stand in relation to the rest of creation; it is also active in the prescription of a system of norms contributing to the normative ethics of the community. This system of norms circumscribes the aspirations of the community, which are proportional to its expectations. Expectations, in turn, depend on the information summarized in the concept of the environment. This conception, built on local, empirically accessible data about the environment, shapes the expectation in simple ways, but since the nature and stability of the local environment depend on remote cosmological factors, the shaping of expectations, and, hence, moral norms, social order and ecological strategy themselves are dependent on cosmologies.[106] Cosmology not only plays an eschatological function for societies but also had a direct impact on the practical life of ancient societies, which projected the cosmic order onto their institutions, for example, through the spatial arrangement of ancient settlements and cities on the basis of their correspondence to the images of the cosmic environment such that the information about the universe was encoded in the track a particular society left in its earthly history.[107]

This social function of cosmology was implemented sometimes as a cosmic religion, in which the gods were positioned in the cosmic space in planets and stars and the whole cosmos was endowed with a "cosmic soul." Cosmological views were often used either to defend or to refute a particular form of religiosity. Cosmology can be used in opposite ways too, either to affirm the importance of the human phenomenon in the universe, an exceptional role that human beings are destined to play in the universe, or to condemn humanity to its purely natural state of existence, which implies its insignificant and indifferent position in the cosmos. The adoption of different views on the role of man can have different social implications if the relationship between man and the universe is projected into the relationship between a person and society.[108]

Cosmology can also penetrate the minds of people in the form of so-called *cosmism*, which is a philosophical and spiritual longing for fusion with cosmic entities. Cosmism in this sense means not only the affirmation of our commonalities with nature and our contingence upon its laws and accidents but also a much more sophisticated kind of spirituality, which longs for fusion with "cosmic life" and its mystery and which is ecstatic in its essence. Berdyaev called this spiritual tendency "the lure of the cosmos" and described it as man's slavery to cosmos (and nature in general), as opposed to the freedom of hypostatic existence in the divine image.[109] The danger of this kind of cosmism is evident nowadays, when the cosmic fantasy of science fiction and endless television serials makes the dream of cosmic travel and indwelling to be the psychological enervation of the masses, appealing to cosmic nostalgia as the last resort in their attempt to overcome the discomfort and stress of modern life here on the earth.[110] This is why the science-fiction cosmologies, such as Tipler's cosmological physics of immortality, are capable of competing with all sorts of paganistic religions, whose tendency is to turn the minds and souls of human beings from the contemplation of the God-Creator of the universe in order to enslave them spiritually to the impersonal and unarticulated forces of the cosmos, visible or invisible. The Omega Point of Tipler's theory or his "evolving god," which represent the final destination for "human" disembodied programs to exist, thus strongly resemble those impersonal cosmic deities of the Hellenistic philosophy that were so strongly rejected by the Fathers of the early church. The coming of paganism through the back door of scientific terminology indicates, from a Christian perspective, the loss of the perception of the human-divine image in modern scientific discourse by those who invent such cosmic fantasies.

The apology for slavery to the forces of nature and the lure of existing forever through physical machinery, which is present in finalistic cosmologies, indicate the lessening of the soteriological and ecclesial perception of human existence, its sacred qualities and function in creation as microcosm and mediator, transfigurer, and redeemer. It is interesting to observe that a single theological fallacy—namely, the distortion of the human image in the perspective of its link to God—leads, if it is implemented in cosmology, to the cascade of philosophical, methodological, and physical obscurities. This shows that no genuine and adequate cosmology is possible if the anthropological dimension of the universe is not properly taken into account. It is at this point that Tipler's cosmology deviates considerably from the Christian view of the universe as the hypostatic inherence in the Logos of God, an existence articulated by hypostatic human beings. The latter view implies that the inward existence of the universe is possible only in conjunction with hypostatic human beings, so that any deviation from Christian anthropology in theory should lead to a change in the inward existence of the universe. If this anthropology is replaced at all in favor of disembodied computer programs, the inward existence of the universe should change too, so that its "physics" would be non-anthropic and unarticulated in human terms.

This argument demonstrates once more the fallacy hidden in the final anthropic cosmology, which treats people as finite state machines and in which the fullness of human life is substituted by "intelligibility" treated as computability of thoughts. It is clear, however, that there is something in human beings that is completely noncomputable and irreducible to any objective expression. Faith (and revelation in response to it), mystical experience, and various individual feelings and emotions can hardly be reduced to any kind of objective computation and reproduced through their encoding in a computer program. This is why a "life" in the final anthropic cosmology has some remote similarity to what is meant by human life as the experience of personhood.

The scale of the distortion of the idea of human life through reduction to computer software becomes manifest when compared with Christian anthropology. Christianity offers an alternative idea of divine humanity that establishes the norm for man. Christ, our idea about Christ, is the perfect model by reference to which we can answer the question about who are we are. He is *the* man, "the first-born of every creature" (Col. 1:15), the archetype of which every human being is, in terms of his or her potentialities, the image. The difference between Christ and us is that Christ is eternally God's son, while we are God's sons because we are created in the image of Christ's divine humanity. To be a son of God is to have the Divine as the determining element of our being, that is, to be inherent in the divine hypostasis. It is precisely this that makes us human and that constitutes our humanity. To the degree to which we fail to attain a full realization of this, we fail to be human.

If it is true that without the divine dimension the genuine human dimension would be deprived of reality, it is equally true that without the human dimension the divine would be deprived of self-manifestation. If one allows the divorce with God (let us say, only in thought), one, in fact, risks denying the existence of God and hence the existence of human beings. It is not surprising, then, to hear from Tipler that the "traditional God is superfluous," for he denies not only the existence of the

Christian God but also the existence of all human persons as hypostatic unities of body and soul inherent in the Logos of God.[111] In a way, we observe here an explicit logical and ethical contradiction to the initial aim of the final anthropic cosmology to promote human life in the universe. The future of the universe predicted by a theory that contains this contradiction is sorrowful, as we have argued before. In the words of P. Sherrard: "Having rejected the understanding that his life and activity are significant only in so far as they incarnate, reflect and radiate that transcendent spiritual reality which is the ground and center of his own being, man is condemned to believe that he is the autocratic and omnipotent ruler of his own affairs and of the world about him, which it is his right and duty to subdue, organize, investigate and exploit to serve his profane mental curiosity or his acquisitive material appetites."[112]

For although the body of human beings comes into existence from the underlying matter of the world and is independent of the soul in some ways, there is an indissoluble hypostatic relationship between soul and body that has an affinity with the Divine. This gives human beings a key position and role in the universe. They stand as mediators between God and the material world, between heaven and earth. Nothing is external to them, for everything is articulated, enhypostasized by human beings. This is in sharp contrast to the scientific view of things that presupposes that the universe is an object external to humanity and that it is possible to manipulate the universe without limit without the risk of losing one's own roots in it. In this picture, there is a loss of the consciousness in which nature is considered a part of the subjectivity of human beings; consequently, there is a loss of the sense of humanity's decisive role in relationship to the rest of creation.

Christian theology teaches that the destiny of the universe is in the hands of human beings, who are made in the image of God, because it is only through humanity's fulfilling its role as mediator between God and the world that the world itself can fulfill its destiny and be transfigured in the light and presence of God. This is a possible Christian theological alternative to all scientific utopias of the indefinite cosmological future.

Humankind-Event and the Transfiguration of the Universe
The discussion of the destiny of the universe in the Orthodox context requires one to emphasize one particular point of its eschatology, namely, a close link of Orthodox eschatology to the theology of creation of the universe and its further articulation (enhypostasization) by human beings, whose existence forms the humankind-event. This is why the future of the universe can be understood only in the perspective of the final destiny of human beings. The existence of the universe for us (that is, its articulated existence) is inseparable from the continuity of human consciousness, beginning from the very "first" event, when consciousness contracts its existing in the hypostasis of the Logos, and finishing with the "last" event, which accomplishes human history, so that the articulation of the universe as the display in space and time and as a set of different happenings and physical events ceases to be inherent in the human apprehension.

St. Gregory of Nyssa describes this final stage of the humankind-event in terms of the ceasing of human generation, which, because of the divine plan of salvation, will have fulfilled it purpose, so that flowing time will stop:

> God, Who governs all things in a certain order and sequence . . . foreknew the time coextensive with the creation of men, so that the extent of time should be adapted for the entrances of the predetermined souls, and the flux and motion of time should halt at the moment when humanity is no longer produced by means of it; and that when the generation of men is completed, time should cease together with its completion, and then should take place the restitution of all things, . . . and also humanity should be changed from corruptible and earthly to the impassible and eternal.[113]

According to Gregory, the possibility of the end of the world in the sense described above is connected with the fact of its beginning (understood either as the *creatio ex nihilo* in an absolute sense or as the creation as articulation of the world through human apprehension).[114] However, if one asks about how and when the end of the world is supposed to happen, Gregory insists that this question must be abandoned, for the end of the world as well as its creation is a mystery, which is inconceivable to our grasp.[115]

What is important here is that Gregory describes the end of the world in terms of the end of humanity, for with no humanity there is no universe as articulated existence. This implies immediately that the universe itself, being articulated through human apprehension, acquires the features of a hypostatic event, in the same sense that the humankind-event is inherent in the hypostasis of the Logos. This thought provides another argument to assert that the change of human hypostatic constitution, its progress toward the dominance of the ecclesial mode in human existence, its deification and return to the kingdom of God, will result in a complete change of the articulation of the universe. This change can be called its renewal or transfiguration.

For Maximus the Confessor, for example, the transfiguration of the universe was directly linked to the mediating function of human beings, who remove all divisions in creation on the level of morality and will, so that the change of human hypostatic constitution itself results in the changes in the universe (the removal of the divisions in it). These changes can be understood as changes of the image of the world and its articulation, as being inherent in the hypostasis of the Logos of God, by human beings who are supposed to restore the integrity of their personhood in Christ. As the perception of flowing time in the ordinary life of a human being is transfigured into an atemporal "instant" of eternity through the liturgical invocation of the kingdom of God in church, suspending the temporal order[116] and bringing the praying community in the eschatological realm, the physical time of this age is supposed to be transfigured by the whole community of human beings through their mediating function between creation and God, so that the cessation of the humankind-event in the universe will mean, in fact, the cessation of a temporal image of the universe, which, in physical terms, will mean its end. In no way, however, does the change of the image of the universe as a result of the cessation of the humankind-event assume the destruction of the universe and its natural order. On the contrary, the universe itself will probably be seen through the light of the Logos, manifesting itself as the ultimate sacrament, united back to God.

It is important to realize, finally, that it is the Christ-event that can be paralleled with the humankind-event and which can be said to have recapitulated the humankind-event, its beginning and its end, setting thus a vision of the destiny of humankind and the universe in the perspective of the resurrection.

Christ himself was treated as "the New Man" and the last Adam. The divine plan of salvation was consummated, the kingdom of God inaugurated through Christ, but the ultimate things were yet to come in fullness and glory. The king had come, but the kingdom was still to come. The promise of the kingdom was granted to the church by the Holy Spirit. The church has lived since then in two dimensions: in sight of ongoing secular history and world events in the time of decay and oblivion, but also in the time of the heavenly kingdom inaugurated by the risen savior (in which the church has lived *epicletically* in the expectation of the kingdom).[117]

The coming of Christ and the resurrection changed completely the human situation, for in fallen existence, the time form of the world is characterized by law (*nomos*); this implies that humans were involved in an irreversible chain of decay and corruption, which led them to mortality with no hope of undoing the things they had done. Everything that had been done became ontologically necessary, so that there was no way to overcome this necessity, which is indicated by the word *law*. The coming of Christ and the resurrection relieved us from this law; we are still living in the world of "fallen" temporal order, but we are relieved from the necessity of the law; that is, we have a chance of renewal and of entering the kingdom, cleansing ourselves through constant participation in the resurrection of the Lord.

Christian thought acquired a fundamental change in the understanding of history through the expectation of the kingdom. Since history has not been accomplished through the historical resurrection of Christ, the whole historical development is treated now as from the perspective of the completion of the work of Christ, that is, from the completion of his body, the church, in its ultimate, final understanding as an "event" of the eschatological future. Even the mystery of the incarnation now receives eschatological meaning: in order to accept death, and to be resurrected, Christ must have a body.[118] One can speak of the historical Jesus from birth to resurrection as "sheer miracle or downright *resurrection* from the beginning to end."[119]

That is why Gregory the Theologian in his *Orations* (45) preaches on the celebration of Pascha, the mystery of the Passover, as celebration of "both the Birthday and the Burial of Him Who was born for thee and suffered for thee."[120] We do the same in the service of Palm Sunday when we celebrate during the Paschal service the economy of the incarnation, exalting, "Blessed is he that cometh in the Name of the Lord."[121] It has some correlation with the baptismal overtones of the same service when, to enter the new life of resurrection, the baptized must be symbolically buried together with Christ in order to be resurrected through baptism to the new life.[122] In this ceremony, Christ's coming inaugurates the eschatological age when the fulfillment of his promise is seen from the perspective of the age to come, from the age of the kingdom.

We have thus seen that the eschatological vision of history links two elements of Christian history—the incarnation and the resurrection—both of which we comprehend as the divine design for the salvation of man. The eschatology of the age to come, of the kingdom of God, does not mean, however, that there will be no "end" in the historical progression that moves us along and sets us in the kingdom to come. Rather, it means that nothing is static in our eucharistic experience of communion with the kingdom.[123] This implies not only that the whole creation is in movement but that this movement is irreversible and progressive toward its eschatological end.

As discussed earlier, the Christian eschatology is conceivable only in connection with the concept of the true creation, the *creatio ex nihilo*. This is because, if we have the beginning of the world through the creation, we can grasp the meaning of the expectation for the age to come, when the whole creation will be transfigured and space and time will be redeemed through the resurrection.[124] Gregory the Theologian makes this link with the creation in Paschal celebration explicit when he starts his preaching from the exposition of the Cappadocian understanding of God and his ecstatic love, resulting in the free creation of the world and of humankind.[125] Gregory insists that the history of the creation is an inevitable part of the celebration of the Passover.[126] This is why we read the first chapter of Genesis at the beginning of the Easter vespers: the creation of the world is a Passover or Easter event and, in fact, the first of all Passover events.[127]

There is a correspondence between Old Testament creation and the "new creation," the "Paschal creation" of the Christians (2 Cor. 5:17; Gal. 5.17). We observe here the development of the motif present in the Old Testament that results in the correspondence between creation and redemption, between creation to the new life through the resurrection and the fulfillment of the Lord's promise for the kingdom to come. The creation of the world, the redemption, and the eschatological salvation are all interrelated as three paschal events at the beginning, middle, and end of time: "The one God who acts paschally through his 'word' is at once creator of the world (*Gen 1:1*), 'creator of Israel' (*Is 43:1, 15*), and creator of 'new heavens and new earth' (*Is 65:17; Rev 21.1*)."[128]

We know about the kingdom of God and the ultimate destiny of this world because we know the Christ-event. Christ through the cross, resurrection, and ascension left us with historical memory of the event and liturgical memory of the kingdom. The condescension of the Logos of God into the world through the incarnation in Christ, and Christ's coming back to the kingdom through the resurrection and ascension, provide Christians with the typology of the events that will happen to human beings, in particular with the image of the end of the world and the human being, as both transfigured and united back to God, leaving behind the images of the world in its present state of flowing time.

One can imagine that when human beings reintegrate their personhood in God, so that their hypostatic constitution will no longer resemble the divisions in creation, human apprehension will change fundamentally. The vision of the universe, its articulation in space and in time, will cease to function at all, resembling more and more the hypostatic "apprehension" of the universe by the Logos himself, for whom the whole universe in its spatial and temporal span exists as an instant of truth, as the "eighth" boundless day, the aeon with no duration.

Abbreviations

ANF   Library of the Ante-Nicene Fathers. Translated into English with prolegomena and explanatory notes. Second series. Ann Arbor, Mich.: Eerdmans, 1955.

Contra   Athanasius of Alexandria *Contra Gentes.* English translation: Library of the Nicene and Post-Nicene Fathers. Translated into English with prolegomena and explanatory notes. Second series. Edinburgh: T & T Clark; Grand Rapids, Mich.: Eerdmans, 1996.

ET   English translation

NPNF   Library of the Nicene and Post-Nicene Fathers. Translated into English with prolegomena and explanatory notes. Second series. Edinburgh: T & T Clark; Grand Rapids, Mich.: Eerdmans, 1996.

PG   Migne, J. P., ed., *Patrologiae cursus completes.* Series Graeca. 161 vols. Paris: Migne, 1857–66.

Strom.   Clement of Alexandria *The Stromata, or Miscellanies.* English translation: Library of the Ante-Nicene Fathers. Translated into English with prolegomena and explanatory notes. Second series. Ann Arbor, Mich.: Eerdmans, 1955.

Notes

Chapter 1

1. Peacocke, *Theology for a Scientific Age,* 3.
2. Harakas, "Orthodox Christianity Facing Science," 7–15.
3. See, e.g., Lindberg, *The Beginnings of Western Science;* and Lindberg, "Science and the Early Church."
4. Pelikan, *Christianity and Classical Culture,* 5.
5. Schmemann, *The Historical Roads of Eastern Orthodoxy.*
6. As an example, one can point to an outstanding book of the Russian philosopher and theologian V. Nesmelov, *Faith and Knowledge from the Point of View of Gnoseology,* in which he argued that scientific rationality and religious belief have a common source so that in no way can they constitute an opposition or be in a state of conflict.
7. Gregorios, *The Human Presence,* 83. Some references to other writings on the concept of nature and creation are provided in this book, including Florovsky, "Creation and Creaturehood"; Evdokimov, "Nature"; and Schmemann, *The World as Sacrament.* There are also some references to the papers of the French Orthodox theologian Olivier Clément in French. The recent English translation of one of his books, under the title *On Human Being,* develops ideas on the position of human beings in the universe.
8. The full list of sources on science and religion in the Orthodox context, including some titles in Russian, can be found in section B of the bibliography.
9. The Sherrard books are *The Rape of Man and Nature* and *Human Image: World Image.* On Orthodox bioethics, see Breck, *The Sacred Gift of Life;* and Engelhardt, *The Foundations of Christian Bioethics.* On science and religion in general, see Vucanovich, *Science and Faith;* Puhalo, *The Evidence of Things Not Seen;* and Woloscahk, *Beauty and Unity in Creation.*
10. Staniloae, *Theology and the Church,* 224, 226.
11. Zizioulas, *Being as Communion,* 119–20.
12. Sherrard, *The Rape of Man and Nature,* 84.
13. Yannaras, *Elements of Faith,* 37–38.
14. Staniloae, *Theology and the Church,* 214.
15. Staniloae, *Theology and the Church,* 216.
16. Gregorios, *The Human Presence,* 91.
17. K. Ware, *The Orthodox Way,* 46.
18. Sherrard, *The Rape of Man and Nature,* 101–2.

19. This implies in turn that any hope of getting closer to the so-called final theory (or theory of everything) is fundamentally flawed by the fact that this hope is set within an ideal of the all-embracing power of the human intellect, which is able to grasp the totality and the meaning of the world. Theology, by asserting the contingency of the world, always cautions the ambitious reason from any attempt to explain the contingency away through "final explanation."

20. V. Lossky, *The Mystical Theology of the Eastern Church*, 106.

21. Compare with T. Torrance, who argued in his books that the problem of theology and science requires one to develop a *new* theological language. See, e.g., his *Theological Science*.

22. Bishop Basil (Osborne) of Sergievo, "Beauty in the Divine and in Nature," 28–37.

23. Torrance, *Space, Time and Resurrection*, 179–80.

Chapter 2

1. Drapper, *History of the Conflict between Religion and Science*, 51–52.

2. See, e.g., Hooykaas, *Religion and the Rise of Modern Science*; and Jaki, *The Savior of Science*. These sources do not deal seriously with the impact of Christianity and Hellenistic science. There is, however, an underlying desire to shape the relationship between Christianity and science in an idealized way in which historical contingencies are disregarded. This makes the nature of these claims rather apologetic, which promotes a simplified view of Christianity as a stimulating force for scientific development.

3. Lindberg, "Science and the Early Church," 19–48.

4. See, e.g., Daniélou, *Gospel Message and Hellenistic Culture*; and Chadwick, *Early Christian Thought and the Classical Tradition*.

5. It was in this period, generally known as the Patristic period, that the fundamental Christian doctrines were fixed by the Fathers of the church in a series of church councils. The Patristic period as understood within Orthodox Christianity is often extended far beyond these "official" historical limits until at least the fourteenth century, the century of St. Gregory Palamas. In a sense, however, the Patristic era never ended: "In the eyes of Orthodoxy the 'Age of the Fathers' did not come to an end in the fifth century, for many later writers are also 'Fathers.' . . . It is dangerous to look on 'the Fathers' as a closed circle of writings belonging wholly to the past, for might not our own age produce a new Basil or Athanasius?" T. Ware, *The Orthodox Church*, 212.

6. St. Gregory the Theologian (Nazianzus) *Orations* 28 [ET: NPNF, 300–301]. It is interesting to note that the recent translation of the same oration instead of the word *science* uses the word *knowledge*, which probably reflects more accurately the usage of the terms related to the particular sciences in the time of St. Gregory. See F. W. Norris, *Faith Gives Fullness to Reasoning*, 242.

7. It is known that religion or theology is considered by some modern scientists as being irrelevant in any scientific context. Some of the educated public treat religion as giving important insights when it deals with some scientific beliefs in the field of biological evolution and cosmology. This feature of knowledge, its integrity and all-encompassing domain, is quite unpopular and even hostile to the modern understanding of sciences as strongly differentiated branches of research with quite narrow and strictly professional applications. Knowledge as a universal intellectual and cultural attitude to the world is not pursued now as part of the educational agenda in the average university.

8. See, e.g., M. L. W. Laistner, *Christianity and Pagan Culture in the Later Roman Empire*, ch. 3.

9. Gregory the Theologian (Nazianzus) *Orations* 43.11 [ET: NPNF, 398–99].

10. This long-standing problem is still at the center of present-day dialogue between science and religion. It is unfortunate, however, that the analysis of this problem in Patristic writers (that is, the Patristic synthesis of faith and knowledge) is nearly forgotten now.

11. Justin Martyr *I Apology* 59.1–5 [ET: 182–83].

12. R. A. Norris, *God and World in Early Christian Theology*, 53.

13. St. Irenaeus of Lyons *Against the Heresies* 2.10.4 [ET: ANF, 370].

14. In modern parlance, this position can be named *panentheism*.

15. This is why Clement is considered the first thinker to use the term *theology* in the Christian context.

16. It is important to remember that the general attitude of the Christians to classical philosophy was suspicious and even antagonistic. For example, Hippolytus of Rome in his *Refutation of All Heresies* associated philosophies with heresies; Tertullian denounced philosophy as unworthy of use or study by Christians.

17. Clement of Alexandria *The Stromata, or Miscellanies* 1.5 (hereafter abbr. *Strom.*) [ET: 305–7].

18. It is because of this that the Fathers could not just condemn pagan philosophy and education in general; instead, they warned those Christians who were in preparation or training against using some philosophical or scientific ideas literally in order to argue for or against Christian faith. They understood all advantages of education in its formal side, that is, as a method of training and demonstration. It is interesting that all philosophical systems, as seen from this perspective, are similar as far as Christian theology is concerned. Vladimir Lossky expressed this thought very clearly when he wrote that "the question of the relations between theology and philosophy has never arisen in the East" and that is why "there is no philosophy more or less Christian." See V. Lossky, *The Mystical Theology of the Eastern Church*, 42.

19. "Christian theology is able to accommodate itself very easily to any scientific theory of the universe, provided that this does not attempt to go beyond its own boundaries and begin impertinently to deny things that are outside its own field of vision." V. Lossky, *The Mystical Theology of the Eastern Church*, 106.

20. Unfortunately, however, neither cosmology nor biology is considered in some modern scientific circles as cooperating factors in our search for truth. Some contemporary scientists not only dismiss Christian theology as irrelevant for scientific discourse but also claim that science itself can provide an access and criteria for truth. This tendency in intellectual thought would be unimaginable for Clement.

21. The Fathers do not call creation "nature" in general. They make a distinction between *ousia* (being) and *physis* (nature), despite the fact that some of them spoke of both terms as parallel entities. Gregory of Nyssa treats "nature" or *physis* as such in which the existence of beings was comprehended (*De anima ressurectione* [ET: 52]). This view obviously leaves out everything in creation that has not yet been comprehended or that cannot be comprehended at all (for example, some intelligible worlds or different aeons). An interesting discussion of the Fathers' understanding of nature can be found in Gregorios, *The Human Presence*, 20–22. The only comprehensive study on nature in Greek Patristics that is currently available is Wallace-Hadrill, *The Greek Patristic View of Nature*.

22. The notion of the *logoi*, which was extensively developed in the theology of St. Maximus the Confessor in the sixth century, can be also found in the church writers before him. For example, in Gregory the Theologian *Orations* 18.16; 30.20. [ET: NPNF, 259–60; 316–17]; in Gregory of Nyssa *On the Making of Man* 24 [ET: 414]; in Basil the Great *The Hexaemeron* 1.7–8 [ET: 55–57]; in Dionysius the Areopagite *The Divine Names* 5.7–8 [ET: Rolt, 138–41]; and in Evagrius Ponticus *The Praktikos* 92 [ET: 39]. The concept of the seminal reasons, similar to the *logoi* and discussed later in this chapter, was also developed by Augustine of Hippo. The parallelism in the usage of the terms *logoi* and *energeia* of God, which were employed by Vladimir Lossky in *The Mystical Theology of the Eastern Church*, should also be mentioned here. The problems of this parallelism have been discussed by Lars Thunberg in *Man and the Cosmos*, 137–43.

23. Gregory the Theologian (Nazianzus) *Orations* 28.29 [ET: NPNF, 299].

24. This attempt to show that the theological categories of thought are adequate to the interpretation of nature and the natural sciences can be qualified in modern terms as "theology of nature" in contradistinction to natural theology understood as an argument from nature to God.

25. Lindberg, *The Beginnings of Western Science*, ch. 10; see also his "Science as Handmaiden," 518–36.

26. See, e.g., Whitakker, *Space and Spirit*. The historical shift from the Platonic vision of realities to the method of Aristotle, which took place after the twelfth century, consisted of a treatment of natural phenomena in which, instead of explaining them in terms of the higher order and perfect structural forms, phenomena could be exposed to further empirical analysis. This approach to nature later formed the method of research that is usually called modern science. See, e.g., McMullin, *The Inference That Makes Science*. An interesting Orthodox interpretation of the transition to the modern views on reality can be found in Sherrard, *The Rape of Man and Nature*. Science thereby acquired the features independent of metaphysics and theology.

27. Basil the Great *Hexaemeron*, 5.1 [ET: 76].

28. The view that the physical regularities exhibited in the universe are taken as a brute fact needing no further explanation (that is, need no creator) is known as atheism (in contemporary settings, it appears under the title of evolutionary naturalism).

29. Eusebius *Praeparatio evangelica* 6.6 [ET: Wallace-Hadrill, 106].

30. Many contemporary theologizing scientists are eager to reveal the so-called divine actions—in particular, natural phenomena—which, according to them, point to "special divine actions" that are "local" in

space and time. This search assumes tacitly a panentheistic ontology (that is, the finite world is ontologically present in the infinite God), where no difference is drawn between the ontological grounds of the natural law, on the one hand, and God's direct intervention into the world through special action, on the other hand. See, e.g., Clayton, *God and Contemporary Science*, ch. 4. On the Orthodox treatment of panentheism, see, e.g., K. Ware, *Through the Creation to the Creator*, 9–10. The evidence for these special actions is usually sought in such scientific fields as theory of complexity and chaos as well as from quantum mechanics. See, e.g., (on chaos) Polkinghorne, *Belief in God in an Age of Science*, ch. 3; and Russell et al., eds., *Quantum Cosmology and the Laws of Nature*.

31. Gregory the Theologian (Nazianzus) Letter 81 [ET: NPNF, 461].

32. Basil the Great *Hexaemeron* 1.1 [ET: 52].

33. Nemesius of Emesa *De natura hominis* 43.63 [ET: 431–32].

34. The large-scale account of how this mediation was supposed to work through humans was developed by Maximus the Confessor. See, e.g., Thunberg, *Microcosm and Mediator*, ch. 6; and Louth, *Maximus the Confessor*.

35. Irenaeus of Lyons *Against the Heresies* 5.33.4 [ET: ANF, 563].

36. Origen *De principis* 1.6.4 [ET: 57–58].

37. See Thunberg, *Microcosm and Mediator*, 382.

38. Athanasius *De incarnatione verbi Dei* 12 [ET: 39].

39. Athanasius *Contra gentes* 35.4 (abbr. *Contra*) [ET: 22].

40. Kant argued later that the inference from the order of the universe can only prove an *architect* of the world "who is always very much hampered by the adaptability of the material in which he works, not a creator to whose idea everything is subject." Kant, *Critique of Pure Reason*, 522.

41. Athanasius *De incarnatione verbi Dei* 14 [ET: 42].

42. Athanasius *De incarnatione verbi Dei* 14 [ET: 42].

43. Athanasius *De incarnatione verbi Dei* 14 [ET: 45].

44. The interplay between the concept of the incarnation and space is discussed by T. F. Torrance in *Space, Time and Incarnation*.

45. This view rejects the Hellenistic idea that there is a partial order in the world.

46. See, e.g., Jaki, "Christology and the Birth of Modern Science," 69.

47. Torrance, "Creation, Contingent World-Order, and Time," 207–10.

48. On Maximus's theory of the *logoi*, see, e.g., Thunberg, *Microcosm and Mediator*, 64–79; and Thunberg, *Man and the Cosmos*, 134–43.

49. See, e.g., Thunberg, *Microcosm and Mediator*, 105.

50. Clément, *On Human Being*, 29

51. Thunberg, *Microcosm and Mediator*, 105.

52. One should mention, however, that the natural contemplation that St. Maximus used to describe knowledge of the *logoi* in their unity, which provides an access to the Logos of God, being organically a sort of communion with God, assumes that the Holy Spirit is present in this communion. This means that God opens his mystery not to those who only speculate abstractly about the high being and origin of the world but rather to those for whom the communion through the works of the Logos is accompanied by the communion through Scripture as well as by the sacramental communion with Christ. See, e.g., Zizioulas, *Being As Communion*, 191.

53. Maximus the Confessor *The Ambigua* 22. (P.G. 91, 1257 AB) [ET: Thunberg, 140]. These ideas of Maximus on the *logoi* of creation and their accessibility to a scientific research understood spiritually will be developed further later in the book to provide a sophisticated theological methodology of mediation with science.

54. Thunberg, *Man and the Cosmos*, 127.

55. See Thunberg, *Microcosm and Mediator*, 397.

56. See, e.g., Cochrane, *Christianity and Classical Culture*, 377.

57. As we have seen earlier, this position was shared by some of the Greek Fathers, in particular by Clement of Alexandria and Gregory the Theologian.

58. See the more detailed account in Lindberg, *The Beginnings of Western Science*, 133–51.

59. Lindberg, *The Beginnings of Western Science*, 163–82, 203–6.

60. Augustine *Letter to Consentius* [ET: 27–28].

61. Augustine *Confessions* 10.35 [ET: Library, 233–34].

62. Augustine *Confessions* 4.16 [ET: NPNF, 77].

63. Augustine *On Christian Doctrine* 1.31 [ET: NPNF, 531].

64. Augustine *Epistolae* 120 [ET: 708].

65. On the role of faith and the rational understanding to which Augustine believes it should lead, see Kretzmann, "Faith Seeks, Understanding Finds," 1–36.

66. Augustine *On Christian Doctrine* 1.40 [ET: 534].

67. Augustine *On Christian Doctrine* 1.40 [ET: 534].

68. Augustine *On Christian Doctrine* 1.40 [ET: 534].

69. Augustine *The Literal Meaning of Genesis* 2.9 [ET: 59].

70. Augustine *The Literal Meaning of Genesis* 2.9 [ET: 59].

71. Augustine *On Christian Doctrine* 1.39 [ET: 534].

72. Augustine *On Christian Doctrine* 1.39 [ET: 534].

73. Augustine *The Literal Meaning of Genesis* 1.19 [ET: 42–43].

74. Augustine *Enchiridion* 3.9 [ET: 342].

75. Compare the appreciation of nature by the Greek Fathers.

76. Augustine *On Christian Doctrine* 1.4 [ET: 523].

77. A couple of illustrations where Augustine uses natural sciences to interpret Genesis can be found in Lindberg, "Science and the Early Church," 36.

78. On the implications of this idea of science as handmaiden of theology in later medieval history, see Lindberg, "Science as Handmaiden," 518–36; and Lindberg, "Medieval Science and Its Religious Context," 60–79.

79. Wolfson, *The Philosophy of the Church Fathers*, 282.

80. Gilson, *The Christian Philosophy of St. Augustine*, 206.

81. Augustine *On the Trinity* 3.8.13 [ET: Bourke, 103].

82. Augustine *The Literal Meaning of Genesis* 4.33.51 [ET: 143].

83. Ernan McMullin cautions against the use of Augustine's theory of seminal principles to justify the doctrine of evolution, which has been done by some Catholic writers. He notes that "Augustine did not hold that one species could arise out of another, his theory of forms as ideas in the mind of God would have rendered such an hypothesis quite implausible." McMullin, "Introduction: Evolution and Creation," 15.

84. Compare Gilson, *The Christian Philosophy of St. Augustine*, 207. In modern physical parlance, this can be illustrated by saying that it is in the act of *creatio ex nihilo* that God brought into existence all space and all times, so that any particular "development," as movement in space and time, is only the appearance of the underlying seed corresponding to this development, which in a physical language contains all future "development" from the moment of its creation. This implies that there is no development at all in this case, for everything is predestined at the initial seed. No history as creative novelty is possible.

85. David Lindberg, in "Science and the Early Church," 37, supports the observation made by R. A. Markus that Augustine's doctrine of seminal reasons leads to the concept of natural law, which was discussed earlier in the context of the Greek Fathers. See Markus, "Augustine: God and Nature," 398–99.

86. Augustine *On the Trinity* 3.9.16 [ET: NPNF, 62].

87. The investigation of the whole scale of these differences would require extensive historical research of the Greek and Latin Fathers, which is not the aim of this book.

88. Roger Bacon played a key role in an ambitious attempt to reform the system of learning in the Christian world to involve natural philosophy and the sciences, which became available after major Greek Classical writings were translated into Latin. He faced the same problem that had been addressed by Augustine eight hundred years earlier. It was the same challenge of the Classical tradition, which became more prominent in thirteenth-century Europe in terms of writings as well as more powerful in terms of its appeal to the public. On the role of Roger Bacon in the historical development of science, see Lindberg, *The Beginnings of Western Science*, ch. 10; and Lindberg, "Science as Handmaiden."

89. Wolfson, *The Philosophy of the Church Fathers*, 283.

90. The communication of grace to humans was possible, according to Augustine, within the boundaries of the earthly church.

91. Sherrard, The *Rape of Man and Nature*, 90–112.

92. See detailed discussion in Sherrard, *The Greek East and the Latin West*, chs. 6, 7.

Chapter 3

1. Daniélou, *Gospel Message and Hellenistic Culture,* 308.

2. Evagrius Ponticus *On Prayer,* 61 [ET: 62].

3. Gregory the Theologian (Nazianzus) *Orations* 27.3, 28.1 [ET: Norris, 218–19, 224]. Compare with St. John the Klimakos's affirmation that "the climax of purity is the beginning of theology." Scalara Paradisi 30 [ET: 108].

4. Evagrius *On Prayer* 61 [ET: 57].

5. On the notion of cosmic liturgy in Maximus, see Thunberg, *Microcosm and Mediator,* 397–98.

6. Maximus the Confessor *Four Hundred Texts on Love* 2.26 [ET: 69].

7. Maximus the Confessor *Two Hundred Texts on Theology* 1.83, 2.15 [ET: 132, 141].

8. Gregory Palamas *The Declaration of the Holy Mountain in Defence of Those Who Devoutly Practise a Life of Stillness* [ET: 421].

9. Vasileos, *Hymn of Entry,* 22–23.

10. See "Theology," in the glossary of Palmer et al., eds., *The Philokalia.*

11. One should mention the difference between the words *participation* and *communion* that was developed by the Greek Fathers. *Participation* was used only in the context of creatures in their relation to God and never was applied to God's relation to the created. *Communion* represents a more general notion. It was used to express the truth of God's being as communion of love. *Communion* has deep ontological connotations, for to participate means to take part in something that is separate and prior with respect to the agency participating, whereas to commune means to be involved in one's own otherness, which constitutes one's very existence. In other words, communion is an existential and ontological category, whereas participation represents knowledge, or only an epistemological dependence. See, e.g., Zizioulas, *Being As Communion,* 94.

12. See Allchin, "The Appeal to Experience in the Triads of St. Gregory Palamas," 323–28.

13. Irenaeus of Lyons *Against the Heresies* 2.19.1 [ET: ANF, 385]; see also 4.38.4 [ET: ANF, 522].

14. Irenaeus of Lyons *Against the Heresies* 4.18.5 [ET: ANF, 486].

15. Peter of Damaskos, *Twenty Four Discourses* [ET: 277]. The question of truth in theology—that is, what makes us sure that the theological experience is true—can thus be considered as an ontological question. Truth of theology is guaranteed by the fact that theology through its function in the church's tradition creates reality in the same way that God reveals himself to us. Theology that is not ontological, that is, whose mode of existence is nonhypostatic, is just an illusion and a fallacy.

16. Irenaeus of Lyons *Against the Heresies* 3.24.1 [ET: ANF, 458].

17. Reference to this feature of the eucharist can be found in the first canonical documents of the church, such as *Didache* and *Apostolic Tradition.* For a full discussion of this issue, see Zizioulas, *Being As Communion,* 81–2, 118, ch. 4, 5.

18. V. Lossky, *The Mystical Theology of the Eastern Church,* 8–9.

19. T. Ware, *The Orthodox Church,* 215.

20. Yannaras, *Elements of Faith,* 15.

21. Yannaras, "Theology in Present-Day Greece," 207.

22. Torrance, *Theological Science,* 39 (emphasis added).

23. Diadochos of Photiki *On Spiritual Knowledge* 7 [ET: 254].

24. As we have seen before, this experience includes prayer, *katarsis,* communion (eucharist), and *charisma.*

25. "Discussion of theology is not for everyone. . . . Nor, I would add, is it for every occasion, or every audience; neither are all its aspects open to inquiry." Gregory the Theologian (Nazianzus) *Orations* 27.3 [ET: Norris, 218].

26. Gregory the Theologian argued that theology can be pursued by those persons who combine the Christian faith and Greek *paideia;* theology "is not for all men, but only for those who have been tested and have found a sound footing in study, and, more importantly, have undergone, or at the very least are undergoing, purification of body and soul." Gregory the Theologian (Nazianzus) *Orations* 27.3 [ET: Norris, 218].

27. V. Lossky, *Orthodox Theology,* 16.

28. See Clement of Alexandria *Strom.* 2.4 [ET: 349–51].

29. Augustine *Epistolae* 120.

30. Torrance, *Theological Science*, 36.

31. We discuss the difference between the spiritual intellect (*nous*) and the reason (*dianoia*) later. See the glossary of Palmer et al., eds., *The Philokalia*.

32. Sherrard, *The Greek East and the Latin West*, 152. Compare with Clement of Alexandria (knowledge requires an ultimate presupposition, which is faith) or with Augustine (one should believe in order to understand).

33. Isaac the Syrian *Homilies* 51 [ET: 243].

34. Isaac the Syrian *Homilies* 51 [ET: 243, 246].

35. Isaac the Syrian *Homilies* 51 [ET: 246].

36. Isaac the Syrian *Homilies* 51 [ET: 250].

37. Athanasius of Alexandria *De decretis* 2 (P.G. 25.411c) [ET: 367].

38. See, e.g., Yannaras, *Elements of Faith*, 16, 150.

39. Florovsky, "The Lost Scriptural Mind," 14.

40. Florovsky, "St. Gregory Palamas and the Tradition of the Fathers," 109.

41. Zizioulas, *Being As Communion*, 117.

42. Zizioulas, *Being As Communion*, 118.

43. V. Lossky, *Orthodox Theology*, 15. Florovsky conveys the same message: "Apart from life in Christ theology carries no conviction and, if separated from the life of faith, theology may degenerate into empty dialectics, a vain *polylogia*, without any spiritual consequence. Florovsky, "St. Gregory Palamas and the Tradition of the Fathers," 108. The academic theology can be characterized as disincarnate faith, which constitutes the matter of opinion and subject of vain discussions.

44. Torrance, *Theological Science*, 9.

45. Florovsky, "St. Gregory Palamas and the Tradition of the Fathers," 108.

46. Basil the Great *Letters* 7 [ET: 115].

47. For a more precise explanation of the difference between *dianoia* and *nous*, see the entries for the terms *reason* and *intellect* in the glossary of Palmer et al., eds., *The Philokalia*.

48. See, e.g., McMullin, *The Inference That Makes Science*.

49. Maximus the Confessor *Two Hundred Texts on Theology* 1.8 [ET: 115].

50. Glossary of Palmer et al., eds., *The Philokalia*.

51. In chapter 4, we will mark the limit of the reason by investigating the boundaries of rational reasoning exercised in its attempt to catch the divine from within the world. We will see that the rationality based on the execution of syllogism in theology must be replaced by antinomial-like structures of comprehension, which lead the reason ultimately to silence, that is, to a humble acceptance of its own limits.

52. Glossary of Palmer et al., eds., *The Philokalia*.

53. Maximus the Confessor *Various Texts on Theology* 3.31 [ET: 215].

54. Maximus the Confessor *Various Texts on Theology* 3.31 [ET: 276].

55. Maximus the Confessor *Two Hundred Texts on Theology* 1.9 [ET: 116]. Compare this affirmation with a similar thought of Clement of Alexandria in chapter 2, p. 26.

56. See Thunberg, *Microcosm and Mediator*, 105.

57. Maximus the Confessor *Four Hundred Texts on Love* 4.50 [ET: 106].

58. Maximus the Confessor *Four Hundred Texts on Love* 4.50 [ET: 106].

59. V. Lossky, *Orthodox Theology*, 18.

60. The word *economy* (*economia*) stands for the Greek οικονομια, literally, "housekeeping" or "household management," that is, the activity of God in the created world.

61. Florovsky, "St. Athanasius' Concept of Creation," 52.

62. We discuss later the concept of the uncreated energies and their link to the concept of the *logoi* employed in the theology of St. Maximus the Confessor. It is through immanent aspect of the *logoi* that one receives the manifestation of God in the created world, and it is the transcendent aspects of the *logoi* that link all the *logoi* in the Divine Logos and that constitute the principle of being for the immanent *logoi*.

63. See V. Lossky, *In the Image and Likeness of God*, 15.

64. See Polkinghorne, *Belief in God in an Age of Science*, ch. 2.

65. This correlates with a Kantian vision: that the truth of the appearances of things subsists in their spatial and temporal forms, which, according to Kant, form a frame of the integrated transcendental experience and the last resort, and guarantor, of truth. See Kant, *Critique of Pure Reason*, 194.

66. See, e.g., Torrance, *Space, Time and Resurrection,* chs. 7, 8.

67. This constitutes the essence of the so-called eucharistic ecclesiology, which has been developed by J. Zizioulas.

68. On the elaborate exposition of the concept of the tradition in Orthodoxy, see, e.g., Florovsky "The Function of Tradition in the Ancient Church." On the importance of the presence of the Patristic mind in the church, see Florovsky, "St. Gregory Palamas and the Tradition of the Fathers." See also V. Lossky, "Tradition and Traditions"; and Meyendorf, *Living Tradition.*

69. See Zizioulas, *Being As Communion;* see also McPartlan, *The Eucharist Makes the Church.*

70. The relationship between science and theology is often described in modern sources by using such words as *consonance, compatibility, consistency, conflict,* and *confrontation.* See, e.g., Russell et al., eds., *John Paul II on Science and Religion.* One finds different classifications of the relationship between science and religion, which are made under different headings. See, e.g., Barbour, "Ways of Relating Science and Theology." See also Barbour, *Religion in an Age of Science;* and Drees, "A 3 X 3 Classification of Science-and-Religion."

71. Hilary of Poitiers *The Trinity* 1.15 [ET: 15–16].

72. The term *contemplation* (Gk. θεορια) is defined in the glossary of Palmer et al., eds., *The Philokalia.*

73. See Thunberg, *Microcosm and Mediator,* 78.

74. Maximus the Confessor *Various Texts on Theology* 1.94, 3.33 [ET: 186, 217].

75. Torrance, *Space, Time and Incarnation,* 21.

76. Latin, *docta ignorantia.*

77. Despite the historical dimension of theology as teaching and thinking in terms of space and time, theology understood Patristically, as silent gnosis or communion with God, transcends history and space-time. Thomas Torrance uses the term *divine dimension,* which makes sense of any creaturely expressions of the theological teaching, and opens us to a special form of rationality where we can conceive the foundation to our divine affinity. See Torrance, *Space, Time and Incarnation.*

78. V. Lossky, *Mystical Theology,* 42.

79. V. Lossky, *Mystical Theology,* 42.

80. V. Lossky, *Mystical Theology,* 106 (emphasis added).

81. V. Lossky, *Mystical Theology,* 106.

82. Compare Torrance, *Space, Time and Resurrection,* 179–80.

83. It is worth noting that theological treatment of science does not necessarily mean a *theistic* interpretation of scientific facts and theories; the latter would take place if we were to develop a natural theology. The treatment proposed deals rather with a methodological evaluation of science in general from a theological perspective. This differs crucially from what is called "the philosophy of science," not only because of the difference in epistemological schemes of philosophy and theology but also because of different purposes of the evaluation of science.

84. The simplest illustration of this principle is the very possibility of science. To exercise science, one should believe at least in the existence of the reality of what is investigated. This is, rather, a metaphysical belief. If one wishes to maintain the line that scientific research has a purpose, this purpose can be derived ultimately only from the reality of what is investigated. This implies that nature itself has a purpose. The last inference is definitely theological in origin.

85. On the role of philosophical principles in forming scientific theories, see, e.g., McMullin, *The Inference That Makes Science;* Margenau, *The Nature of Physical Reality;* Chalmers, *Science and Its Fabrication;* Gillies, *Philosophy of Science in the Twentieth Century;* and Newton-Smith, *Rationality of Science.* On the social determination of scientific knowledge, see, e.g., McMullin, ed., *The Social Dimensions of Science.* An interesting paper written by famous quantum physicist W. Heisenberg, "Scientific and Religious Truth," offers some valuable insights on how the ideologies of particular societies influence the choice of scientific paradigm of the time.

86. J. Polkinghorne, in his *Belief in God in an Age of Science,* argues that the dialogue between science and theology demands more involvement of theologians. This is quite coherent with our view of science as a mode of religious experience. It is not enough to reflect on scientific theories in order to claim whether this experience can enhance theology or vice versa. One should attempt the theology of science, which would be methodologically similar to philosophy of science in its function, but fundamentally different in its particular conceptual realization.

Chapter 4

1. "God . . . remains transcendent, radically transcendent by His nature, in the very immanence of His manifestation." V. Lossky, *Orthodox Theology*, 23.

2. Dionysius the Areopagite *The Divine Names* [ET: Rolt, 51].

3. "Very existence itself (*per se*), as an existence which is real and not just an object of thought (whoever might be the thinker), is subsistent; it is hypostatic, the absolute hypostatic existence." Staniloae, *The Experience of God*, 131.

4. Maximus the Confessor *Two Hundred Texts on Theology* 1.1 [ET: 114].

5. Compare to the with famous Kantian skepticism on the existence of the absolutely necessary being if the latter is inferred from the intelligible chain of causations.

6. Maximus the Confessor *Two Hundred Texts on Theology* 1.7 [ET: 115] (emphasis added).

7. Maximus the Confessor *Two Hundred Texts on Theology* 1.68 [ET: 127–28] (emphasis added).

8. Maximus the Confessor *The Ambigua* 10.37 (PG 91: 1180 D) [ET: Staniloae, 133–34; see also Louth, 139].

9. Yannaras, *Elements of Faith*, 19.

10. V. Lossky, *The Mystical Theology of the Eastern Church*, 39.

11. According to V. Lossky: "The cataphatic way leads us to some knowledge of God, but in an imperfect way. The perfect way, the only way which is fitting in regard to God, who is of His very nature unknowable, is the apophatic theology, which leads us finally to total *ignorance*." V. Lossky, *The Mystical Theology of the Eastern Church*, 25. This expresses "that fundamental attitude which transforms the whole of theology into contemplation of the mysteries of revelation. Christian Apophatic theology forbids our thought to follow its natural ways and to form concepts which would occupy the place of spiritual realities because it is not a philosophical system of abstract concepts, but is essentially a communion with the living God." V. Lossky, *The Mystical Theology of the Eastern Church*, 42.

12. Some contemporary Orthodox theological writers make a clear distinction between the Eastern apophaticism as the experience of God and the Western negative theology. Yannaras places the Western negative theology under the name of "Western rational theology," stressing its academic and nonexperiential nature. From his point of view, there is no value in the "affirmative" theology. See Yannaras, *De l'absence et de l'inconnaissance de Dieu*. Yannaras and V. Lossky insist that the apophatic approach to theology is based on the knowledge of the personal character of God. This makes it clear why they both do not allow any value to the cataphatic, impersonal approach to God. As we will see later, this position, if accepted in its extreme, could bring our attempt to mediate between science and theology to a standstill, for the modern theologizing science is cataphatic by construction. It is because of this that the author shares the position of Romanian theologian D. Staniloae, who argues that both apophatic and cataphatic ways of knowledge of God are valuable, if they are considered in their mutual dynamics and grounded in the living experience of God. See Staniloae, *The Experience of God*, ch. 6.

13. This dynamics of the cataphatic and apophatic can be observed in St. Gregory the Theologian's *Orations*: "God always was, and always is, and always will be. Or rather, God always Is. For Was and Will be are fragments of our time, and of changeable nature, but He is Eternal Being. And this is the Name that He gives to Himself when giving the Oracle to Moses in the Mount. For in Himself He sums up and contains all Being, having neither beginning in the past nor end in the future; like some great Sea of Being, limitless and unbounded, transcending all conception of time and nature, only adumbrated by the mind, and that very dimly and scantily . . . not by His Essentials, but by His Environment; one image being got from one source and another from another, and combined into some sort of presentation of the truth, which escapes us before we have caught it, and takes to flight before we have conceived it." *Orations* 38.7 [ET: NPNF, 346–47].

14. See Danto, "Naturalism," 448.

15. See Hawking and Penrose, *The Nature of Space and Time*, 121. See also Hawking, *A Brief History of Time*, 9, 139.

16. Hawking, *A Brief History of Time*, 141. A detailed analysis of Hawking's cosmological views will be provided in chapter 5.

17. See, e.g., Craig and Smith, *Theism, Atheism and Big Bang Cosmology*, ch. 10.

18. Kant, *Critique of Pure Reason*, 522.

19. See Davies, *The Mind of God.* On the latter, see, e.g., Leslie, *Universes,* 198 : "...The fine tuning is evidence, genuine evidence, of the following fact: that God is real, and/or there are many and varied universes."

20. Polkinghorne, *Belief in God in an Age of Science,* 19, 20.

21. Polkinghorne, *Belief in God in an Age of Science,* 20.

22. See the discussion in chapter 3.

23. Maximus the Confessor *The Ambigua* 41 (PG. 91, 1305A) [ET: Louth, 156].

24. The world is *contingent* upon its maker, God the creator. That is why it is usually said that science is adjusted in its operations to the contingent (created) order. It is because of the *contingency* of the world that the empirical sciences are possible. See, e.g., Torrance, *Divine and Contingent Order.*

25. Dionysius the Areopagite introduced the term *Divine Darkness* with respect to God as he is in himself to describe that it is impossible to speak of or know God in terms of senses and thoughts, because God is beyond all of this. See *The Mystical Theology* 1 [ET: Rolt, 191].

26. Thunberg, *Microcosm and Mediator,* 408–10.

27. V. Lossky, *The Mystical Theology of the Eastern Church,* 28.

28. Thunberg notices that both types of apophatic theology (that of extreme purification and that of extreme negation) lead to immanentism, which eliminates the proper concern of negative theology: the difference between empirical man in the world and God as he is in himself. Thunberg, *Microcosm and Mediator,* 410.

29. Thunberg, *Microcosm and Mediator,* 411.

30. Maximus the Confessor *Two Hundred Texts on Theology* 2.39 [ET: 147]. See also Maximus the Confessor *The Church's Mystagogy,* prologue [ET: 185–86].

31. Thunberg, *Microcosm and Mediator,* 413.

32. ET: 114–15.

33. ET: 116.

34. For example, we attempt to predicate about God, using the notions applicable to the created things. This quotation is from V. Lossky, *The Mystical Theology of the Eastern Church,* 29. See also another English translation by Rolt, 201.

35. Dionysius the Areopagite *Mystical Theology* 1.2 [ET: Rolt, 192–93] (emphasis added).

36. See, e.g., Fichte, "Second Introduction to the Science of Knowledge."

37. On the difference between the *nous* and the *dianoia,* see chapter 3.

38. See Thunberg, *Microcosm and Mediator,* 413.

39. Florensky, *The Pillar and Ground of Truth,* 163.

40. Latin, *docta ignorantia,* the concept developed by Nicholas of Cusa.

41. The Russian religious philosopher Semen Frank offered the term *antinomial monodualism,* affirming that any knowledge, if it is aimed toward the ultimate aspects of things, should follow this pattern. See Frank, *The Unknowable,* 97.

42. Maximus the Confessor *The Ambigua* 10.19 (PG. 1133C) [ET: Louth, 113].

43. See, e.g., Polkinghorne, *Belief in God in an Age of Science.* In a systematic book on physics and theology, M. W. Worthing discusses the argument from design, reincarnated by modern cosmology, and its implications for theology. Worthing's conclusions are quite reserved: he is cautious about making any straightforward theological inferences from physical arguments. See Worthing, *God, Creation, and Contemporary Physics.*

44. Kant, *Critique of Pure Reason,* 520.

45. Chapter 2 quotes the passages from Athanasius of Alexandria where he argued that it is possible to infer from the order of things to the Word of God, who is the cause of this order.

46. Kant, *Critique of Pure Reason,* 522.

47. Kant, *Critique of Pure Reason,* 415.

48. Kant, *Critique of Pure Reason,* 490.

49. Kant, *Critique of Pure Reason,* 492.

50. Kant, *Critique of Pure Reason,* 500.

51. See, e.g., the applications of this epistemology in McLaughlin, "Kantian Epistemology as an Alternative to Heroic Astronomy," 611–39.

52. On the concise account of Greek monism in early Christian times, see Florovsky, "The Patristic Age and Eschatology," 235–50.

53. It is assumed in cosmology, for example, that the big bang has the same ontology as the observable universe; in all theories involving the idea of the plurality of worlds, the ontological status of all worlds is assumed to be the same as it is for our universe, despite the fact that all other universes are not observable in principle. The list of these examples can be continued indefinitely.

54. The term *hypostasis* marks a concrete being, that is, every particular realization of this being, its concrete independence and intrinsic constitution. In the *hypostasis* of being, we find the incarnation of all its essence or common features, but in an individual, distinct, and unrepeatable way. See Prestige, *God in Patristic Thought.*

55. Zizioulas, *Being as Communion*, 83.

56. Florovsky, "St. Athanasius' Concept of Creation," 39–62.

57. Zen'kovski, *The Foundations of the Christian Philosophy.*

58. The expression of an absolute ontological distinction between creator and creation, according to C. Gunton, "is to be preferred to the well-known and misleading expression, 'infinite qualitative difference,'" which implies something rather different." See Gunton, *The Triune Creator,* 67.

59. Florovsky, "St. Athanasius' Concept of Creation."

60. Zizioulas, *Being as Communion,* 86 (emphasis added).

61. See Torrance, *Divine and Contingent Order,* 1997.

62. Clément, *On Human Being,* 29.

63. The latter dualism is named by some Patristic and Byzantine writers as basic dichotomy in creation.

64. Torrance, "Creation, Contingent World-Order, and Time," 206.

65. It is worth mentioning that R. Penrose is nowadays an enthusiastic proponent of Platonism in modern mathematical physics. In one of his books, he explicitly states that the physical laws we observe on the level of their empirical appearance have an underlying ontology that is rooted in the world of Platonic ideas. Despite the interplay between the ideas and the facts, their ontologies are different. See, e.g., Penrose et al., *The Large, the Small and the Human Mind.*

66. This argument is based on the christological anthropology that man's body and soul have the same hypostasis that is rooted in the divine Logos—according to Maximus the Confessor, for example, the human nature is itself enhypostasized. The mediation between sensible and intelligible in man's creaturely condition is justified through an analogy with Christ, who can mediate between the sensible and the intelligible (see the account of theology of mediation in theology of Maximus in Thunberg, *Microcosm and Mediator,* 398–404). The analogy works under the observation that both the unity of the human and divine in Christ and the unity of body and soul in man are hypostatic. The difference, however, is that the unity in Christ is hypostatic only (that is, nonnatural), whereas the unity of body and soul in man is also ontological (natural). See Thunberg, *Microcosm and Mediator,* 105–6.

67. See the account by St. Athanasius on the inference from design to the Word of God in chapter 2.

68. Kant, *Critique of Pure Reason,* 416.

69. V. Lossky, *The Mystical Theology of the Eastern Church,* 76.

70. V. Lossky, *The Mystical Theology of the Eastern Church,* 69.

71. See Thunberg, *Man and the Cosmos,* 132–43.

72. See, e.g., Maximus the Confessor *Four Hundred Texts on Love* 2.26 [ET: 69]. Maximus applies contemplation in this passage with respect not only to sensible things but also to intelligible beings. More often, he applies the term *contemplation* only in the context of sensible realities. See *Four Hundred Texts on Love* 1.94,97 [ET: 64].

73. Maximus the Confessor *The Ambigua* 10.18 (PG 1129B) [ET: Louth, 110].

74. Thunberg, *Man and the Cosmos,* 138.

75. Thunberg, *Man and the Cosmos,* 139.

76. Gregorios, *The Human Presence,* 61.

77. See the discussion of the notion of participation in Gregory of Nyssa in Balas, "*Metousia Theou.*"

78. Thunberg, *Man and the Cosmos,* 127.

79. According to Maximus the Confessor, the mediation between sensible (visible) and intelligible (invisible) was effected by Christ as he ascended through the "divine and intelligible ranks of heaven" with *soul and body,* that is, with the whole human nature. In this ascension, Christ "showed the convergence of the whole of creation with the One according to its most original and universal *logos.*" *The Ambigua* 41 (1309C) [ET: Louth, 160]. This mediation between two parts of the created being is possible with the

whole human nature because of the incarnation of Christ the Logos. There is only one way to God the Father, the way through Christ and the way like that of Christ. It means for us that the mediation between sensible and intelligible with our whole human nature is the way to find the "most original and universal *logos*" which is common for things visible and invisible. As soon as we achieve the contemplation of unity of things empirical (visible) and those that are theoretical (invisible), we approach the ultimate limit of our natural ability to synthesize the manifold of our creaturely experience. This limit in a mode of meditation will bring us to the *logos* of creation (this will be a response to our inquiry into why God created at all). See details in Thunberg, *Microcosm and Mediator*, 398–404.

80. Maximus the Confessor *The Ambigua* 41 (1312B) [ET: Louth, 160].

81. Maximus the Confessor *Various Texts on Theology* 5.71 [ET: 277]. A similar formula can be found in Maximus's *Ambigua:* "The human being, consisting of both soul and sensible body, by means of its natural relationship of belonging to each division of creation, is both circumscribed and circumscribes: through being, it is circumscribed and through potency, it circumscribes. So in its two parts it is divided between these things, and it draws these things through their own parts into itself in unity." *The Ambigua* 10 (1153AB) [ET: Louth, 124].

82. It is worth pointing out here the similarity between the antinomial formula on humankind's position in the universe, which was formulated by Maximus, and that intuition of the Kantian philosophy that human beings, being a *phenomenon* in empirical appearance and function, are at the same time a *noumenon,* and the latter forms a ground for the former. Man, as a part of the world, is circumscribed and defined, and through his spiritual power he holds the parts of the world together in its unity, because the world is a subject of his perception. Kant did not believe, however, that any speculation about unity of human nature can have an ontological foundation. His monism stopped him from going beyond antinomies toward the common principle of human nature, that is, to the principle that man is a *microcosm* as well as to the one principle of being in large, to the idea of *macrocosm* and that both microcosm and macrocosm have a similar *logos*, responsible for their constitution.

83. Maximus the Confessor *The Ambigua* 41 (1312B) [ET: Louth, 160].

84. Thunberg, *Microcosm and Mediator,* 401.

85. Maximus the Confessor provides an allegorical interpretation of a particular place in the divine liturgy as the gathering of people in one single unity, which signifies the human limit in ascension to God; the next step is possible only with the help of God's grace alone. See *The Church's Mystagogy* 23 [ET: 196–97].

86. Basil the Great, Letter 236, [ET: 278].

87. Torrance, *The Ground and Grammar of Theology,* 100.

88. See e.g. Florovsky, "St. Athanasius' Concept of Creation."

89. One can apply the distinction of nature and hypostasis to human beings. All human beings have common nature (similar biology) so that blood and flesh can be shared. However, human beings are different *persons* with distinct existences, which cannot be communicated. In the Patristic model of a human being the body and soul are both created and have different natures, but the same hypostasis: they are *co-hypostasized* by the Logos of God (Maximus the Confessor). See, for example, Thunberg, *Microcosm and Mediator,* 106.

90. See, for example, Florovsky, *The Byzantine Fathers of the Sixth to Eighth Centuries,* 191–203. Florovsky refers to the terms used by Leontius by saying that *enhypostasis* points towards something which is not self-contingent, but has its being in the other and is not contemplated as it is in itself. *Enhypostasis* is the reality in the other hypostasis.

91. Maximus the Confessor *Various Texts* 1.7 [ET: 165].

92. Maximus the Confessor *Various Texts* 1.6 [ET: 165].

93. Maximus the Confessor *Various Texts* 1.3 [ET: 164].

94. Maximus the Confessor *Various Texts* 1.8 [ET: 166].

95. Gregorios, *The Human Presence,* 83.

96. Compare with Maximus the Confessor *Two Hundred Texts on Theology on Theology* 2.3 [ET: 138].

97. Prestige in order to illustrate how the apprehending knowledge becomes hypostatic existence refers to Clement of Alexandria (*Strom.* 4:22, 136:4). Prtestige writes: ". . . apprehension extends by means of study into permanent apprehension; and permanent apprehension, by becoming, through continuous fusion, the substance of the knower and perpetual contemplation, remains a living hypostasis. This

appears to mean that knowledge becomes so bound up with the being of the knowing subject, as to constitute a permanent entity" (*God in Patristic Thought,* 176).

98. Maximus the Confessor *Two Hundred Texts on Theology* 2.5 [ET: 138].

99. Maximus the Confessor *Two Hundred Texts on Theology* 2.5 [ET: 138].

100. See Levinas, *Time and the Other,* 42–43.

101. Levinas, *Time and the Other,* 43.

102. On co-inherence see Prestige, *God in Patristic Thought,* ch. 9.

Chapter 5

1. May, *Creatio ex nihilo.*

2. See, e.g., Athanasius of Alexandria *Contra gentes* 8, 34, 38, 40 [ET: 7, 22, 24, 25].

3. Irenaeus of Lyons *Against the Heresies* 3.5.3, 3.24.2, 4.5.1, 5.29 [ET: ANF 418, 458–59, 460, 558].

4. Irenaeus of Lyons *Against the Heresies* 2.3.1–2 [ET: *Scandal,* 28].

5. See, e.g., Florovsky, "St. Athanasius' Concept of Creation."

6. Athanasius of Alexandria *De incarnatione verbi Dei* 43 [ET: 68].

7. Torrance, *Divine and Contingent Order,* ch. 1.

8. See chapter 4.

9. We will deal more with this issue in chapter 7.

10. Irenaeus of Lyons *Against the Heresies* 5.16.2 [ET: *Scandal,* 56].

11. Irenaeus of Lyons *Against the Heresies* 3.18.6 ET: *Scandal,* 58].

12. Irenaeus of Lyons *Against the Heresies* 3.13.1 [ET: *Scandal,* 59].

13. Irenaeus of Lyons *Against the Heresies* 5.1.1 [ET: *Scandal,* 56].

14. Irenaeus of Lyons *Against the Heresies* 5.1.2 [ET: *Scandal,* 58].

15. Irenaeus of Lyons *Against the Heresies* 4.6.6 [ET: *Scandal,* 50].

16. Athanasius of Alexandria *De incarnatione verbi Dei* 14 [ET: 42].

17. Athanasius of Alexandria *De incarnatione verbi Dei* 14 [ET: 42]. It is similar to the thought of Irenaeus on recapitulation of the whole creation in the incarnation.

18. It is exactly this *necessity* that is revealed in the science of the contingent world order. The difficulty of science, however, is to recognize that the necessity of the laws and processes it investigates is not *absolute* in itself, that is, to recognize that the necessary laws are yet contingent.

19. Athanasius uses various means to demonstrate that from the order in the world one can conclude to the existence of the maker of this order, the Word of God. See chapter 2.

20. Torrance, *Divine and Contingent Order.*

21. Hawking, "Is the End of Theoretical Physics in Sight?" 15–16.

22. Hawking, *A Brief History of Time,* 160.

23. Chalmers, *What Is This Thing Called Science?* 156.

24. This issue was a matter of interesting discussions in the papers of J. A. Wheeler in 1960s through the 1980s. The full bibliography can be found in his *At Home in the Universe,* 351–54.

25. One should remember that dust stands here for the uniform distribution of clusters of galaxies, which are treated as noninteracting particles (similar to the concept of the ideal gas).

26. The list of references on inflationary cosmology is astronomical. A simple model of what has been said in the text can be found, for example, in Gunzig et al., "Inflation and Thermodynamics"; and Gunzig et al., "Inflationary Cosmology."

27. See Tryon, "Is the Universe a Vacuum Fluctuation?"; and Isham, "Creation of the Universe as a Quantum Process."

28. E. McMullin points out that the position of Newton was a departure from the medieval Aristotelians, who were not inclined to separate creation of matter and time. McMullin, "Is Philosophy Relevant to Cosmology?" 44.

29. Kant, *Critique of Pure Reason,* 396.

30. McMullin, "Is Philosophy Relevant to Cosmology?" 46.

31. Basil the Great *The Hexaemeron* 1.5 [ET: 54].

32. Basil the Great *The Hexaemeron* 1.5 [ET: 55]. In a different passage, Basil argues that the creation

of the world was not a spontaneous origination (that is, conception by chance) but, on the contrary, the world was created with a purpose and a reason. See Basil the Great *The Hexaemeron* 1.6 [ET: 55].

33. Basil the Great *The Hexaemeron* 1.6 [ET: 55].

34. Augustine *Confessions* 11.5 [ET: Chadwick, 225].

35. Augustine *City of God* 11.6 [ET: 435–36].

36. J. Barrow argues that the global initial conditions do not provide much use for conclusions about the visible universe. See his "Unprincipled Cosmology," 116–34; and *Between Inner Space and Outer Space*, 26–27. He mentions the "no boundary" condition proposed by S. Hawking and J. Hartle (we discuss this theory in detail later in this chapter); the "outgoing quantum wave condition" by A. Vilenkin, "Quantum Cosmology and the Initial State of the Universe" (see the discussion of this proposal in C. J. Isham "Quantum Theories of the Creation of the Universe"); and a minimum "gravitational entropy" condition of R. Penrose (which we will discuss in chapter 6).

37. See, e.g., Wheeler, "From Relativity to Mutability."

38. Hawking, *A Brief History of Time*, 123. See also 133.

39. See, e.g., Isham, "Creation of the Universe as a Quantum Process" and "Quantum Theories of the Creation of the Universe."

40. From the address delivered at the 80th Assembly of German Natural Scientists and Physicians, Cologne, Germany, September, 21 1908. See Minkowski, "Space and Time," 65.

41. Hawking and Penrose, *The Nature of Space and Time*, 66.

42. Hawking, *A Brief History of Time*, 134.

43. Hawking, *A Brief History of Time*, 134.

44. Hartle and Hawking, "Wave Function of the Universe," 2960–65.

45. See, e.g., Wheeler, "From Relativity to Mutability."

46. One should remember, however, that, according to Hawking himself, the no-boundary proposal is merely a proposal; it is not a principle that is deduced from a more fundamental theory. In a way, it is (using the language of Clement of Alexandria) the ultimate premise, which cannot be demonstrated syllogistically. As Hawking affirms: "Like any other scientific theory, it may initially be put forward for aesthetic or metaphysical reasons" (*A Brief History of Time*, 136). One can only add that this is exactly true, that is, the no-boundary proposal is a metaphysical (nonphysical) proposal that is dictated by some undemonstrable belief in reality as "self-contained and not affected by anything outside itself" (*A Brief History of Time*). How similar this intention is to the long-standing pretensions to monism professed by numerous defenders of the sovereignty of the universe against God.

47. Hawking and Penrose, *The Nature of Space and Time*, 84–86.

48. Hawking, *A Brief History of Time*, 139.

49. Hawking, *A Brief History of Time*, 139. It is appropriate to ask, however, for the description of what entity Hawking is talking about—in other words, what is his ontological position? As we will see below, the answer to this question will contain a mixture of positivism, deism, and, as we will argue, Platonism.

50. See, e.g., a good review paper of D. Coule, "Quantum Creation and Inflationary Universes." In this paper, the healthy criticism of the creationist pretensions of quantum cosmology is developed. The author rightly affirms that the issue of "creation" is overstated in quantum cosmology and that its aim is to provide "quantum determination of the cosmological state" rather than to claim the "creation."

51. Hawking, *A Brief History of Time*, 140.

52. Hawking, *A Brief History of Time*, 140.

53. Hawking, *A Brief History of Time*, 141, emphasis mine.

54. Hawking, *A Brief History of Time*, 141.

55. See, e.g., Drees, *Beyond the Big Bang*; Craig, "'What Place, Then, for a Creator?'"; and Le Poidevin, "Creation in a Closed Universe or, Have Physicists Disproved the Existence of God?" See also Worthing, *God, Creation, and Contemporary Physics*, ch. 3.

56. Hawking, *A Brief History of Time*, 9 (emphasis added). See also a similar affirmation at 139.

57. Hawking and Penrose, *The Nature of Space and Time*, 121.

58. Hawking and Penrose, *The Nature of Space and Time*, 121.

59. Hawking, *A Brief History of Time*, 175.

60. In his book *The End of Science* (ch. 4), J. Horgan discusses the implication of Hawking's cosmological model in the context of his claims about the end of physics as soon as the ultimate theory of every-

thing will be built. Horgan accepts a view that cosmology in the form as it is developed by theoretical physicists such as Hawking departs from any experimental base (in comparison with astronomy, for example). He calls this cosmology *ironic* rather than scientific, concluding that the trend it takes in its extreme speculation provides not an end of science as ultimate knowledge of everything but, rather, the "epitaph" for cosmology itself as a scientific discipline.

61. Craig, "'What Place, Then, for a Creator?'"

62. Craig, "'What Place, Then, for a Creator?'" 300

63. Craig, "'What Place, Then, for a Creator?'" 293, 291–92.

64. Craig, "'What Place, Then, for a Creator?'" 293.

65. See, e.g., Craig, "'What Place, Then, for a Creator?'"; and Worthing, *God, Creation, and Contemporary Physics*.

66. See Wheeler, *At Home in the Universe*.

67. For details, see Plass, "Timeless Time in Neoplatonism."

68. Hawking, *A Brief History of Time*, 139.

69. See again Craig, "'What Place, Then, for a Creator?'"

70. Damascius offered an interesting geometrical analogy in explaining the nature of empirical time as the radiance that circles the intelligible center, the unity of all time, which preserves the order of time in the empirical world. See Sambursky and Pines, *The Concept of Time in Late Neo-Platonism*, 64–93. Intelligible time in this picture is the cause of the coherent continuity of the temporal flow. This makes the empirical time united with the intelligible one as the radii are united in the center of a circle. Damascius argues, then, that the whole time exists at once as all radii exist at once at the center of a circle. He then concludes that the whole time exists simultaneously in the same way as the whole space of the cosmos (it is interesting that this intuition is very similar to the spatialization of time that is often done in the context of relativity theory). The Hawking model of imaginary time offers something similar, for its finite universe covers the whole span of all possible real times in a single spacelike structure, whose existence, according to Hawking, is not in the flux of time but, rather, represents a hidden form of time, its encapsulated form.

71. Craig, "'What Place, Then, for a Creator?'"

72. The physico-mathematical problems that arise in this matching are discussed in Hawking and Penrose, *The Nature of Space and Time*, in particular ch. 7.

73. Regarding the term *noetic*, see K. Ware, *The Orthodox Way*, 49. Regarding *kosmos noetos*, see Armstrong and Markus, *Christian Faith and Greek Philosophy*, 28, and the references therein.

74. Armstrong and Markus, *Christian Faith and Greek Philosophy*, ch. 3.

75. We have already discussed the role of man as mediator between intelligible and sensible creation, in chapter 4.

76. Thunberg, *Microcosm and Mediator*, 51–56. It was stated in the context of christological debate on the Chalcedonian Creed that there is the remaining *diaphora* (that is, the *difference* of the two natures in Christ after their hypostatic union) but not the *diairesis* (the *division*).

77. Dionysius the Areopagite *The Divine Names* 5.8 [ET: 138–39]; and *The Celestial Hierarchies* 4.1 [ET: 32].

78. See, e.g., Wheeler, "Genesis and Observership"; "The Quantum and the Universe"; "Physics as Meaning Circuit"; and "World as a System Self-Synthesized by Quantum Networking."

79. This is the meaning of Hawking's claim that the quantum universe with imaginary time can be a more fundamental and genuine level of reality, whereas the visible distinction between space and time in the classical universe is merely a figment of our imagination.

80. Kant, *Critique of Pure Reason*, 415.

81. We have already mentioned this formula of Maximus the Confessor many times before.

Chapter 6

1. See, e.g., Isham and Polkinghorne, "The Debate over the Block Universe."

2. N. O. Lossky, *Sensible, Intellectual and Mystical Intuition*.

3. For a general review, see Prigogine, *From Being to Becoming*; and Prigogine and Stengers, *Order out of Chaos*.

4. See also Nesteruk, "Temporal Irreversibility."

5. See Philo of Alexandria *On the Account of the Creation of the Worlds as Given by Moses* 7, [ET: 6].

6. Mantzaridis, *Time and Man*, 7. See the distinctions between *aeon* and *aidion* in the glossary of Palmer et al., eds., *The Philokalia*, under the rubric "Age."

7. Maximus the Confessor *Two Hundred Texts on Theology* 86 [ET: 159].

8. Gregory the Theologian (Nazianzus) *Orations* 29.9 [ET: Norris, 250].

9. One can agree in this case with W. Pannenberg that "scientific knowledge participates in a certain sense, despite its position in time, in the perspective of eternity.... Such participation in eternity ... seems to be confirmed also in the function of knowledge which causes unity." See Pannenberg, *Toward a Theology of Nature*, 102.

10. Compare with W. Pannenberg, who pointed out that "of the modes of time, the one closest to the eternal act of creation would not be the past but the future. From the future is the world, even with its already past periods of world process, created." See Pannenberg, *Toward a Theology of Nature*, 102.

11. This can be illustrated by figure 5.4.

12. Barrow and Tipler, *The Anthropic Cosmological Principle*.

13. Prigogine, *From Being to Becoming*; Prigogine and Stengers, *Order out of Chaos*. We will analyze Prigogine's program later in this chapter. See also Nesteruk, "Temporal Irreversibility."

14. See, e.g., Ellis, "Modern Cosmology and the Limits of Science," 11.

15. Penrose, "Singularities and Time-Asymmetry," 586.

16. Prigogine, *From Being to Becoming*.

17. Penrose, "Singularities and Time-Asymmetry," 588.

18. Prigogine and Stengers, *Order out of Chaos*.

19. Penrose, "Singularities and Time-Asymmetry."

20. This hypothesis was originally formulated by R. Penrose in "Singularities and Time-Asymmetry" and reproduced later in a series of papers and books. See, e.g., *The Emperor's New Mind*.

21. Penrose, "Singularities and Time-Asymmetry," 632.

22. Penrose, "Singularities and Time-Asymmetry," 633.

23. Penrose, *The Emperor's New Mind*, 344.

24. Penrose et al., *The Large, the Small and the Human Mind*, 2.

25. Compare with the reasoning of St. Athanasius that we considered in chapter 2.

26. The notion of contingency is applied only to the form of the world, not to its *substance*. See Kant, *Critique of Pure Reason*, 522. The *idea* of the wise cause of the world cannot have its *object* (518). Kant denies any causation between an *idea* and its hypothetical *object* because he denies logical predetermination, or the existence of a forming principle of object.

27. For example, the many-worlds interpretation of quantum mechanics or chaotic inflation in the context of the strong anthropic principle.

28. Kant, *Critique of Pure Reason*, 415.

29. It is similar to what was affirmed by Maximus the Confessor on the mediation between sensible and intelligible realms. See the discussion in chapter 4.

30. Prigogine, "What Is Time?"

31. Prigogine, "La redécouverte du temps," 6.

32. Poincaré, *Methods nouvelles de la mécanique céleste*.

33. See Arnold and Avez, *Ergodic Problems of Classical Mechanics*.

34. Prigogine, "La redécouverte du temps."

35. For more technical details, see, e.g., Prigogine, "Why Irreversibility?"

36. Prigogine, *From Being to Becoming*; Prigogine and Stengers, *Order out of Chaos*.

37. See, e.g., Barrow and Tipler, *The Anthropic Cosmological Principle*.

38. Petrosky and Prigogine, "Thermodynamic Limit."

39. This is just a vague analogy, for the things-in-themselves in the Kantian sense are beyond any experience, including the mathematical one that attempts to model *UR*.

40. It should be stressed, however, that an accomplished model of UR_{irr}, which, according to Prigogine's results, should be a radical modification of phase space and Hilbert space, does not yet exist.

41. See the discussion in chapter 5 on the Neoplatonic theory of time.

42. Pannenberg, *Toward a Theology of Nature*, 21.

43. Pannenberg, *Toward a Theology of Nature*, 21.

44. Torrance, "Creation, Contingent World-Order, and Time," 220.

45. Torrance, "Creation, Contingent World-Order, and Time," 220.

Chapter 7

1. R. Swinburne defines human life as the embodiment of conscious creatures. He makes a clear distinction between animal life and the life of the human conscious being, who possesses free will, which is not rooted in the laws of nature. See his "Argument from the Fine-Tuning of the Universe."

2. For more on theological vision of the distinct position of humans in the universe, see K. Ware, *Through the Creation to the Creator*, 15–23.

3. See Barrow and Tipler, *The Anthropic Cosmological Principle*, 305, where it is mentioned that the value of a_e together with the ratio $m_p/m_e = 1837$ (m_p is the mass of a proton) provides a strict condition for the possibility for the replication of DNA.

4. This point will be discussed intensively later.

5. Barrow and Tipler, *The Anthropic Cosmological Principle*, 565–66. This estimate has been made on the basis of Carter's formula, derived from the assumption that life is improbable in the universe. The accuracy of this estimate is dependent on our accurate knowledge of many factors that sustain the stability of the biosphere, in particular, the physics of the atmosphere's stability.

6. Dyson, "Time without End," 447.

7. A similar way of thinking was developed later by F. Tipler. See, e.g., Barrow and Tipler, *The Anthropic Cosmological Principle*, ch. 10.

8. Krauss and Starkman, "Life, the Universe, and Nothing."

9. See Leslie, *The End of the World*, and the references therein. On the latter issue, see pp. 108–22.

10. Compare with Leslie, *Value and Existence*, in which the author argues that the ultimate reason and values of all existing things belong to the realm of Platonic ides, which cause the things to exist.

11. The list of references on this topic is vast. The main systematic source before 1988 is Barrow and Tipler, *The Anthropic Cosmological Principle*; a list of different published papers before 1991 can be found in Balashov, "Resource Letter AP-1." See also Leslie, *Universes*, and the references therein.

12. See pp. 16–23.

13. Barrow and Tipler, *The Anthropic Cosmological Principle*, 16.

14. See, e.g., Kane et al., "The Beginning and the End of the Anthropic Principle."

15. R. Swinburne asserts that there cannot be a scientific explanation for the occurrence of consciousness. See Swinburne, "Argument from the Fine-Tuning of the Universe," 163. See also Swinburne, *The Evolution of the Soul*, 10.

16. Barrow and Tipler, *The Anthropic Cosmological Principle*, 21 (emphasis added).

17. See, e.g., Carr, "On the Origin, Evolution and Purpose of the Physical Universe"; and Leslie, "The Anthropic Principle Today." Leslie makes a point that in spite of the AP sounding like a tautology its explanatory and predictive power is very limited, but he affirmed that the AP can *enter* the explanation and prediction (295, 301).

18. Barrow, *Between Inner Space and Outer Space*, 19.

19. For details, see, e.g., Nicolis and Prigogine, *Exploring Complexity*.

20. See, e.g., Polkinghorne, *Belief in God in an Age of Science*, ch. 3.

21. The well-known example is the refutation of Maxwell's demon in thermodynamics. See, e.g., Brilluoin, *Science and Information Theory*.

22. Polkinghorne, *Belief in God in an Age of Science*, 63.

23. Haught, *God after Darwin*, 76.

24. Haught, *God after Darwin*, 76.

25. Leslie, "The Anthropic Principle Today," 296.

26. See Torrance, *Divine and Contingent Order*.

27. E. McMullin, in his critical appraisal of the SAP, points out that the problem with it is in the phrase "must be," which appears in its formulation. He argues that if "must be" is understood in the sense "that, antecedently, the universe had to be of the sort that would make the appearance within it of observers unavoidable, then it is not just strong, it is entirely groundless." See McMullin, "Fine-Tuning the

Universe?" 112.

28. Carr, "On the Origin, Evolution and Purpose of the Physical Universe," 152.

29. This makes all claims of physics and cosmology about the position of humankind in the universe limited and insufficient in principle. This follows from a separation, typical for natural sciences, of what is supposed to be described as objective reality from the *subject*, who affirms this reality, who hypostasizes this reality as existing in the knowledge of this subject.

30. The reader can find these diagrams in many books. See, in particular, Barrow,' *The Artful Universe*, 49, 53; and Barrow, *Between Inner Space and Outer Space*, 20. See also Penrose et al., *The Large, the Small and the Human Mind*, 5.

31. The difference between natural and hypostatic in human constitution can be illustrated in terms of space and time. Indeed, is it possible for a human individual to exist at different places at the same time? If human beings are considered only as physical bodies animated by soul, it seems inconceivable. If, however, by its hypostatic constitution, human beings are related to God, and through him to the whole world, its physical presence here and now does not exhaust its potential from being present everywhere in the universe by the power of *relation* to it, which is not so much epistemological as ontological (not based on the substance of nature).

32. See a bright exposition of this view in Dennet, *Consciousness Explained*.

33. In Greek Patristic literature, it was a prevailing view that the state of human being as it exists in the natural environment includes the body, soul (including the *dianoia* as an analytical part of the soul), and spirit, which had never been dissociated from the Holy Spirit. Human spirit stands here for the *nous* (spiritual intellect, the organ of faith), linking the human person to its dynamic relationship to God and to the world. It is natural congeniality with God, which is articulated by the presence of the Holy Spirit in human being. But the Holy Spirit is the creator of both body and soul, whose unity forms a particular human person. The presence of the Holy Spirit in human constitution thus makes the human person open upward through its calling to the Divine as its destiny. Without the Spirit, the Greek Fathers assert, the human being is incomplete and imprisoned through the conditions of the created nature. V. Lossky reaffirms this point by saying that "the distinction between person and nature reproduces in humanity the order of divine life, expressed by the dogma of the Trinity." See V. Lossky, *Orthodox Theology*, 128.

34. The acquisition of personhood can be achieved only in community. This is the meaning of what J. Zizioulas calls the ecclesial existence. See Zizioulas, *Being as Communion*.

35. For a better understanding that the hypostasis of human beings relates not purely to their cognitive faculties or to consciousness but represents an ontological, existential notion, it may be useful to comment on its meaning by using the language of E. Levinas. Levinas, in his approach to hypostasis, starts with the ontological notion of one's existing. He writes: "It is thus the being in me, the fact that I exist, my existing, that constitutes the absolutely intransitive element, something without intentionality or relationship. One can exchange everything between beings except existing. In this sense to be is to be isolated by existence. Inasmuch as I am, I am a monad. It is by existing that I am without windows and doors, and not by some content in me that would be incommunicable." In order to overcome the isolation of the existent in its existing—that is, for the existent to come into existence—there must be, according to Levinas, an ontological event when "the existence contracts its existing." Levinas calls this event hypostasis. See Levinas, *Time and the Other*, 42–43.

In the language used in this chapter, this thought could be rephrased as that the existent, who was brought into being as the composite of the body and soul, contracts its existing in the hypostatic event, when the unity of the body and soul of a particular individual is related to a similar unity of another individual not naturally, but hypostatically (that is, when the existing of the one becomes the existence for the other).

36. One should note that the idea of man as microcosm in Maximus is a Christian transformation of the old pagan idea of man as microcosmos, which recapitulates in itself all natural elements of the universe.

37. ET: 196. The words in brackets are imported from the Russian translation of the same text, which better clarify the sense of Maximus's assertion. See Maximus the Confessor, *Collected Works*, vol. 1 (in Russian) (Moscow: Martis, 1993), 167–68.

38. It should be mentioned here that, despite the nonscientific origin of the idea that the reality of the universe is brought into existence through the process of its contemplation and knowledge, the articula-

tion of this idea has at least been attempted in modern physics by J. A. Wheeler, who proposed the so-called participatory anthropic principle. Discussion of the PAP can be found later in this chapter.

39. This expresses the essence of the Bohr's principle: "No elementary phenomenon is a phenomenon until it is a registered ('observed') phenomenon." See, e.g., Bohr, *Atomic Physics and Human Knowledge.*

40. See McLaughlin, "Kantian Epistemology as an Alternative to Heroic Astronomy." See also Balashov, "Transcendental Background to the Anthropic Reasoning in Cosmology."

41. Temple, "The New Design Argument," 137.

42. For the variety of different theories of multiple universes, see Leslie, *Universes,* ch. 4.

43. Barrow and Tipler, *The Anthropic Cosmological Principle,* 22.

44. E. McMullin mentions in this context that the *MW* hypothesis represents simply a shift in a much wider metaphysical indifference principle, in which our mediocre location in space is replaced by our mediocre membership in the ensemble of universes. See McMullin, "Fine-Tuning the Universe?" 109.

45. De Witt, "Quantum Mechanics and Reality," 33.

46. Everett, "Relative State Formulation of Quantum Mechanics," 459.

47. A certain philosophical approach known as modal realism can be used to clarify the above-mentioned distinction between the actual and the possible in the context of MWI. See, e.g., Lewis, *On the Plurality of Worlds.*

48. Compare with Penrose's phase space of all possible initial conditions of the universe, which was discussed in chapter 6.

49. See, e.g., Leslie, "Modern Cosmology and the Creation of Life."

50. Temple, "The New Design Argument," 134–35.

51. Barrow and Tipler, *The Anthropic Cosmological Principle,* 22.

52. Carr, "On the Origin, Evolution and Purpose of the Physical Universe," 158.

53. Wheeler, "On Recognising Law without Law," 404.

54. Wheeler, "On Recognising Law without Law," 404.

55. Wheeler, "How Come the Quantum?" 310.

56. Wheeler, "How Come the Quantum?" 310.

57. Wheeler, "How Come the Quantum?" 311.

58. See Wheeler, "World as a System Self-Synthesized by Quantum Networking."

59. See, e.g., Wheeler, *At Home in the Universe,* 307.

60. See, e.g., Wheeler, *At Home in the Universe,* 293.

61. Wheeler, *At Home in the Universe,* 300; Wheeler, "How Come the Quantum?" 313.

62. See Wheeler, "How Come the Quantum?" 305.

63. See Wheeler, "World as a System Self-Synthesized by Quantum Networking."

64. Gregory of Nyssa *On the Making of Man* 16.1. ET: quoted in O. Clément, *On Human Being,* 34.

65. The affirmation of this *community* aspect of human existence in relation to the Father is manifested in the "Lord's Prayer," whose entry words "Our Father . . ." signify the positioning of all human beings with respect to their common source of origin, thus making all beings to be the same, that is, to be the community, which is formed through the communion with God.

66. Gregory of Nyssa *On the Making of Man* 16.17 [ET: 406].

67. Irenaeus of Lyons *Against the Heresies* 5.16.2 [ET: *Scandal,* 56].

68. Irenaeus of Lyons *Against the Heresies* 3.18.7 [ET: *Scandal,* 58].

69. Irenaeus of Lyons *Against the Heresies* 3.13.1 [ET: *Scandal,* 59].

70. Temple, *Readings in St. John's Gospels.*

71. Ellis, "The Theology of the Anthropic Principle," 396–97.

72. Zizioulas, *Being as Communion.*

73. Torrance, *Space, Time and Incarnation.*

74. A similar relation is established in the humankind-event, which being finite in space and time, is related through human apprehension to the whole universe.

75. Origen *Contra celsum* 4 [ET: Bettenson, 213].

76. Origen, *Contra celsum* 1 [ET: Chadwick, 187].

77. Athanasius of Alexandria *De incarnatione verbi Dei* 8 [ET: 33].

78. On the receptacle and relational notions of space in theology, see Torrance, "The Relation of the Incarnation to Space in Nicene Theology." See also Torrance, *Space, Time and Incarnation.*

79. Athanasius of Alexandria *De incarnatione verbi Dei* 16 [ET: 45].

80. Athanasius of Alexandria *De incarnatione verbi Dei* 12, 14 [ET: 39, 42]. In modern terms, it means that any natural theology is insufficient in order to know truth about God.

81. Athanasius of Alexandria *De incarnatione verbi Dei* 14 [ET: 42].

82. See the quote in chapter 2, 24–25.

83. Torrance, "The Relation of the Incarnation to Space in Nicene Theology," 365.

84. See., e.g., Barrow and Tipler, *The Anthropic Cosmological Principle*, 260.

85. Pannenberg, *Jesus—God and Man*, 166.

86. Maximus the Confessor *The Church's Mystagogy* 7 [ET: 196–97].

87. Maximus the Confessor *The Church's Mystagogy* 7 [ET: 188].

88. Compare with Zizioulas, *Being as Communion*, 119–120.

89. Athanasius of Alexandria *Contra arianos* 3.23 [ET: 369–70] (emphasis added).

90. Torrance, "The Relation of the Incarnation to Space in Nicene Theology," 371.

91. See, e.g., Leslie, *The End of the World*.

92. Berdyaev, "Man and Machine," 157.

93. Berdyaev, "Man and Machine."

94. Tipler, "The Omega Point Theory"; Tipler, "The Omega Point as *Eschaton*"; and Tipler, *The Physics of Immortality*.

95. Barrow and Tipler, *The Anthropic Cosmological Principle*, ch. 10.

96. Barrow and Tipler, *The Anthropic Cosmological Principle*, 23.

97. Barrow and Tipler, *The Anthropic Cosmological Principle*, 659.

98. Tipler, "The Omega Point Theory," 317.

99. Tipler, "The Omega Point as *Eschaton*," 223.

100. Barrow and Tipler, *The Anthropic Cosmological Principle*, 660.

101. See, e.g., Stoeger and Ellis, "A Response to Tipler's Omega-Point Theory."

102. Nesteruk, "The Final Anthropic Cosmology as Seen by Transcendental Philosophy."

103. See the argument on this in Nesteruk, "The Final Anthropic Cosmology as Seen by Transcendental Philosophy."

104. See Nesteruk, "The Metaethical Alternative to the Idea of Eternal Life in Modern Cosmology"; Nesteruk, "Ecological Insights on the Anthropic Reasoning in Cosmology"; and Nesteruk, "The Idea of Eternal Life in Modern Cosmology."

105. Philip Sherrard argued strongly along similar lines that the desanctification of nature takes place as the result of the dehumanization of humankind, so that the ecological crisis is in its essence anthropological and manifests the spiritual disorientation of human beings. See Sherrard, *The Rape of Man and Nature*; and Sherrard, *Human Image: World Image*.

106. See, e.g., Mathews, *The Ecological Self*.

107. See, e.g., some examples from ethnology in Lévi-Strauss, *Structural Anthropology*.

108. It is worth pointing out W. Heisenberg's modern treatment (probably a little anachronistic) of the famous conflict of Galileo with the Roman Catholic Church, in which he made an interesting connection between a change in the world outlook induced by scientific and technological progress and the problem of stability of the society whose integrity is based upon a particular view of reality based on tradition (for example, religious tradition). Heisenberg linked new cosmological perspectives on humankind's place in the universe following from Copernicus's and Galileo's (arguably just or not) with the risk of obscuring the vision of the whole in the consciousness of the individual, so that the living community could suffer and be threatened with decay. See Heisenberg, "Science and Religious Truth," 225.

109. On "The Lure of the Cosmos," see Berdyaev, *Slavery and Freedom*, 93–102.

110. See, e.g., Wilkinson, *Alone in the Universe*, 144.

111. Tipler, "The Omega Point Theory," 314.

112. Sherrard, *The Rape of Man and Nature*, 43.

113. Gregory of Nyssa *On the Making of Man* 22 [ET: 412].

114. See Gregory of Nyssa *On the Making of Man* 23 [ET: 413]. There is a deep contrast between the Christian eschatological vision of being and that of Hellenistic philosophy, in which the whole world was in a steady, cyclic motion, that is, in a mode of endless repetition of its states. The eschatology is not possible in the Hellenistic world, for it cannot be the end of the world if it did not have the beginning. On a

detailed account of the Christian eschatology versus Hellenistic cosmology, see Florovsky, "The Patristic Age and Eschatology."

115. Gregory of Nyssa *On the Making of Man* 23 [ET: 413].

116. See Mantzaridis, *Time and Man,* 100–105.

117. See Torrance, *Space, Time and Resurrection,* 99.

118. This was one of Athanasius's main arguments in his *De incarnatione verbi Dei* 21 [ET: 51].

119. Torrance, *Space, Time and Resurrection,* 94.

120. Gregory the Theologian (Nazianzus) *Orations* 45.21 [ET: NPNF, 430–31].

121. Hapgood, ed., *Service Book,* 204.

122. Hapgood, ed., *Service Book,* 204.

123. See Zizioulas, "The Eucharist and the Kingdom," pt. 1, 6.

124. See Zizioulas, "The Eucharist and the Kingdom," pt. 3, 12.

125. Gregory the Theologian (Nazianzus) *Orations* 45.5–9 [ET: 424–26].

126. Gregory the Theologian (Nazianzus) *Orations* 10 [ET: 203–4].

127. Füglister, "The Biblical Roots of the Easter Celebration," 24–26.

128. Füglister, "The Biblical Roots of the Easter Celebration," 26.

Bibliography

A. Classical and Patristic Writers (with the source for the English translation)

Athanasius of Alexandria

Contra Gentes	NPNF, series 2, vol. 4.
De Incarnatione Verbi Dei	*On the Incarnation.* Crestwood, N.Y.: St. Vladimir's Seminary Press, 1998.
De decretis (P.G. 25.411c)	Quoted in Torrance, "The Relation of the Incarnation to Space in Nicene Theology."
Contra Arianos	Quoted in Torrance, "The Relation of the Incarnation to Space in Nicene Theology."

Augustine of Hippo

Confessions	NPNF, series 1, vol. 1; or The Library of Christian Classics. Vol. 7. London: SCM Press, 1955; or *Saint Augustine Confessions.* Trans. H. Chadwick. New York: Oxford University Press, 1991.
City of God	Augustine. *Concerning the City of God against Pagaus.* Trans. H. Bettenson New York: Penguin Books, 1980.
Letter to Consentius	A fragment in Lindberg, "Science and the Early Church."
On Christian Doctrine	NPNF, series 1, vol. 2.
Enchiridion	The Library of Christian Classics. Vol. 7. London: SCM Press, 1955.
Epistolae	Goldbacher, A., ed., *Corpus Scriptorum Ecclesiasticorum Latinorum,* vol. 34. Vienna: Tempsky, 1895.
On the Trinity	NPNF, series 1, vol. 3; or Bourke, V. J., ed. *The Essential Augustine.* Indianapolis: Hackett, 1975.
The Literal Meaning of Genesis	Taylor, J. H. *St. Augustine: The Literal Meaning of Genesis.* New York: Newman, 1982.

Basil the Great (of Caesarea)

The Hexaemeron	NPNF, series 2, vol. 8.
Letters	NPNF, series 2, vol. 8.

Clement of Alexandria

The Stromata, or Miscellanies	ANF, vol. 2.

Diadochos of Photiki

On Spiritual Knowledge	Palmer et al., eds. *The Philokalia,* vol. 1.

Dionysius the Areopagite

The Divine Names	C. E. Rolt. "Dionysius the Areopagite, The Divine Names and The Mystical Theology." Trans. C. E. Rolt. London: SPCK, 1979. Some quotations are from V. Lossky, *The Mystical Theology of the Eastern Church.*
The Celestial Hierarchies	*The Mystical Theology and the Celestial Hierarchies of Dionysius the Areopagite.* Godalming: The Shrine of Wisdom, 1965.
Mystical Theology	C. E. Rolt. "Dionysius the Areopagite, The Divine Names and The Mystical Theology." Trans. C. E. Rolt. London: SPCK, 1979.

Eusebius of Caesarea
Praeparatio evangelica   E. H. Gifford, *Preparation for the Gospel.* Eugene: Wipf & Stock
                              Publishers, 2002; or Wallace-Madrill, *The Greek Patristic View
                              of Nature.*

Evagrius Ponticus
The Prakticos   Bamberger, J. E. "The Praktikos, Chapters on Prayer." Trans. J. E.
                              Bamberger. Kalamazoo, Mich.: Cistercian, 1981.
On Prayer   Palmer et al., eds., *The Philokalia*, vol. 1.

Gregory of Nyssa
De anima ressurectione   Roth, C. P., *The Soul and the Resurrection.* New York: St.
                              Vladimir's Seminary Press, 1993.
On the Making of Man   NPNF, series 2, vol. 5.

Gregory Palamas
The Declaration of the   Palmer et al., eds., *The Philokalia*, vol. 4.
Holy Mountain in Defence
of Those Who Devoutly
Practise a Life of Stillness

Gregory the Theologian (Nazianzus)
Orations   NPNF, series 2, vol. 7; or F. W. Norris, *Faith Gives Fullness to
                              Reasoning.*
Letters   NPNF, series 2, vol. 7.

Hilary of Poitiers
The Trinity   McKenna, S. *The Trinity.* Washington, D.C.: Catholic University
                              of America Press, 1954.

Irenaeus of Lyons
Against the Heresies   ANF, vol. 1; or *The Scandal of the Incarnation: Irenaeus "Against
                              the Heresies."* Ed. H. U. von Balthasar. Trans. J. Saward. San
                              Francisco: Ignatius, 1990.

Isaac the Syrian
Homilies   Wensinck, A. J. *Mystical Treatises by Isaac of Nineveh.*
                              Amsterdam: Koninklijke Akademie van Wetenschappen, 1923.

John the Klimakos
Scalara Paradisi   Quoted in Florovsky, *Bible, Church, Tradition,* 108.

Justin Martyr
I Apology   ANF, vol. 1.

Maximus the Confessor
The Ambigua   Thunberg, *Man and the Cosmos;* or Louth, *Maximus the
                              Confessor;* or Staniloae, *The Experience of God.*

Four Hundred Texts on Love	Palmer et al., eds., *The Philokalia,* vol. 2.
Two Hundred Texts on Theology	Palmer et al., eds., *The Philokalia,* vol. 2.
and the Incarnate Dispensation	
of the Son of God	
Various Texts on Theology,	Palmer et al., eds., *The Philokalia,* vol. 2.
the Divine Economy,	
and Virtue and Vice	
The Church's Mystagogy	*Maximus Confessor. Selected writings.* Trans. G. C. Berthold, 181–225.

Nemesius of Emesa

De natura hominis	*Of the Nature of Man.* The Library of Christian Classics. Vol. 4. London: SCM Press, 1955.

Origen

De principis	*On First Principles.* Trans. G. W. Butterworth. Gloucester, Mass.: Peter Smith, 1973.
Contra celsum	Bettenson, H. *The Early Christian Fathers.* New York: Oxford University Press, 1969; or *Origen: Contra Celsum.* Trans. H. Chadwick. Cambridge: Cambridge University Press, 1965.

Peter of Damaskos

Twenty Four Discourses	Palmer et al., eds., *The Philokalia,* vol. 3.

Philo of Alexandria

On the Account of the Creation	Philo Judaeus. The Essential Philo. Ed. N. N. Glatzer.
of the World as Given by Moses	New York: Schocken Books, 1971, 1–41.

B. Titles Related Directly to the Eastern Orthodox Perspective in Science

Allchin, A. M. "The Theology of Nature in the Eastern Fathers and among Anglican Theologians." In *Man and Nature,* ed. H. Montefiore, 143–54. London: Collins, 1975.

Berdyaev, N. "Man and Machine." ET from the Russian, "Chelovek i mashina," *Voprosy Filosofii* 8 (1991): 147–62.

———. *Slavery and Freedom.* London: Centenary, 1944.

Bishop Basil (Osborne) of Sergievo. "Beauty in the Divine and in Nature." *Sourozh: A Journal of Orthodox Life and Thought* 70 (1997): 28–37.

Breck, J. *The Sacred Gift of Life: Orthodox Christianity and Bioethics.* Crestwood, N.Y.: St. Vladimir's Seminary Press, 1998.

Cavarnos, C. *Biological Evolutionism.* Etna, Calif.: Center for Traditionalist Orthodox Studies, 1994.

Clément, O. *On Human Being: A Spiritual Anthropology.* London: New City, 2000.

Demopulos, D. "Genetic Engineering and Ethics." In *Ethical Dilemmas: Crises in Faith and Modern Medicine,* ed. John Chirban, 91–99. Lanham, Md.: University Press of America, 1994.

Dobzhansky, T. *The Biology of Ultimate Concern.* New York: New American Library, 1967.

Engelhardt, H. T. *The Foundations of Christian Bioethics.* Exton, Pa.: Swets & Zeitlinger, 2000.

Evdokimov, P. "Nature." *Scottish Journal of Theology* 18:1 (1965): 1–22.

Flegg, C. G. "Review of *Science and Belief* by J. Polkinghorne." *Sobornost incorporating Eastern Churches Review* 17:2 (1995): 60–67.

Florovsky, G. V. "Creation and Creaturehood." In *Creation and Redemption*, 43–78. Belmont, Mass.: Nordland, 1977.

———. "St. Athanasius' Concept of Creation." In *Aspects of Church History*, 39–62. Belmont, Mass.: Nordland, 1975.

Gregorios, P. M. *The Human Presence: Ecological Spirituality and the Age of the Spirit*. New York: Amity House, 1987.

———. *Science for Sane Societies*. Rev. ed. New York: Paragon House, 1987.

Harakas, S. S. "Christian Faith Concerning Creation and Biology." In *La Théologie dans l'Église et dans Le Monde*, 226–47. Geneva: Chambesy, 1984.

———. "The Eastern Orthodox Tradition." In *Caring and Curing: Health and Medicine in the Western Religious Traditions*, ed. R. L. Numbers and D. W. Amudsen, 146–72. New York: Macmillan, 1986.

———. "Orthodox Christianity Facing Science." *Greek Theological Review*, 37:1–2 (1992): 7–15.

Nesmelov, V. I. *Faith and Knowledge from the Point of View of Gnoseology*. Kazan: Central Printing Office, 1915.

Nesteruk, A. V. "Design in the Universe and the *Logos* of Creation (Patristic Synthesis and Modern Cosmology)." In *Design and Disorder: Perspectives from Science and Theology*, ed. N. H. Gregersen and U. Görman, 171–202. New York: T & T Clark, 2002.

———. "The Final Anthropic Cosmology as Seen by Transcendental Philosophy: Its Underlying Theology and Ethical Contradiction." *Studies in Science and Theology* 5:1 (1997): 43–54.

———. "Patristic Theology and the Natural Sciences." Parts 1 and 2. *Sourozh: A Journal of Orthodox Life and Thought* 84 (2001): 14–35; 85 (2001): 22–38.

———. "Polkinghorne on Science and God: A Review Essay." *Sourozh: A Journal of Orthodox Life and Thought* 77 (1999): 34–41.

———. "Theology of Human Co-Creation and Modern Physics." In *Mémoire du XXIᵉ Siecle*, no. 3–4, Cahiers transdisciplinaires, *Création et transcréation*, 163–75. Paris: Éditions du Rocher, 2001.

Patriarch Ignatius IV of Antioch. "Three Sermons," *Sourozh: A Journal of Orthodox Life and Thought* 38 (1989): 1–14.

Puhalo, L. *The Evidence of Things Not Seen: Orthodoxy and Modern Physics*. Dewdrey, British Columbia: Synaxis, 1996.

Schmemann, A. *For the Life of the World: Sacraments and Orthodoxy*. Crestwood, N.Y.: St. Vladimir's Seminary Press, 1995.

Sherrard, P. "Christianity and the Desecration of the Cosmos." In *Christianity: Lineaments of a Sacred Tradition*. Edinburgh: T & T Clark, 1998.

———. *The Greek East and the Latin West*. Limini, Evia, Greece: Denise Harvey, 1995.

———. *Human Image: World Image, the Death and Resurrection of Sacred Cosmology*. Ipswich, England: Golgonooza, 1992.

———. *The Rape of Man and Nature: An Enquiry into the Origins and Consequences of Modern Science*. Suffolk, England: Golgonooza, 1991.

Staniloae, D. *Theology and the Church*. Crestwood, N.Y.: St. Vladimir's Seminary Press, 1980.

———. "The World as Gift and Sacrament of God's Love." *Sobornost* 5:9 (1969): 662–73.

Vucanovich, V. *Science and Faith: Order in the Universe and Cosmic Evolution Motivate Belief in God*. Minneapolis: Light and Life, 1995.

Wallace-Hadrill, D. S. *The Greek Patristic View of Nature*. Manchester, England: Manchester University Press, 1968.

Ware, K. (Bishop of Diokleia). *Through the Creation to the Creator*. London: Friends of the Centre, 1997.

Woloscahk, G. E. *Beauty and Unity in Creation*. Minneapolis: Light and Life, 1996.

Zizioulas, J. *Being as Communion: Studies in Personhood and the Church*. Crestwood, N.Y.: St. Vladimir's Seminary Press, 1997.

———. "Preserving God's Creation: Three Lectures on Theology and Ecology." Parts 1–3. *King's Theological Review* 12 (spring 1989): 1–5, 12; 12 (autumn 1989): 41–45; 13 (spring 1990): 1–5.

C. General Bibliography

Allchin, A. M. "The Appeal to Experience in the Triads of St. Gregory Palamas." In *Studia Patristica*, vol. 8, 323–28. Berlin: Akademie Verlag, 1966.

Armstrong, A. H., and R. A. Markus. *Christian Faith and Greek Philosophy*. London: Darton, Longman & Todd, 1964.

Arnold, V. I., and A. Avez. *Ergodic Problems of Classical Mechanics*. New York: Benjamin, 1968.

Balaguer, M. *Platonism and Anti-Platonism in Mathematics*. New York: Oxford University Press, 1998.

Balas, D. "*Metousia Theou:* Man's Participation in God's Perfection according to St. Gregory of Nyssa." In *Studia Anselmiana*, vol. 55, 1–185. Rome: Herder, 1966.

Balashov, Y. V. "Resource Letter AP-1: The Anthropic Principle." *American Journal of Physics* 59:12 (1991): 1069–76.

———. "Transcendental Background to the Anthropic Reasoning in Cosmology." *Man and World* 25 (1992): 115–32.

Barbour, I. G. *Religion in an Age of Science*. San Francisco: Harper & Row, 1990.

———. "Ways of Relating Science and Theology." In *Physics, Philosophy and Theology: A Common Quest for Understanding*, ed. R. J. Russell et al., 21–48. Vatican City State: Vatican Observatory, 1988.

Barrow, J. D. *The Artful Universe*. Oxford: Clarendon, 1995.

———. *Between Inner Space and Outer Space: Essays on Science, Art and Philosophy*. New York: Oxford University Press, 1999.

———. "Unprincipled Cosmology." *Quarterly Journal of the Royal Astrological Society* 34 (1993): 117–34.

Barrow, J. D., and F. J. Tipler. *The Anthropic Cosmological Principle*. New York: Oxford University Press, 1986.

Berthold, G. C., trans. *Maximus Confessor: Selected Writings*. New York: Paulist Press, 1985.

Bohr, N. *Atomic Physics and Human Knowledge*. New York: Wiley, 1959.

Bolgar, R. R. *The Classical Heritage and Its Beneficiaries from the Carolingian Age to the End of the Renaissance*. Cambridge: Cambridge University Press, 1954.

Brilluoin, L. *Science and Information Theory*. New York: Academic Press, 1956.

Brooke, J. H. *Science and Religion: Some Historical Perspectives*. Cambridge: Cambridge University Press, 1991.

Carr, B. J. "On the Origin, Evolution and Purpose of the Physical Universe." In *Modern Cosmology and Philosophy*, ed. J. Leslie, 152–57. New York: Prometheus, 1998.

Chadwick, H. *Early Christian Thought and the Classical Tradition: Studies in Justin, Clement and Origen*. Oxford: Clarendon, 1966.

Chalmers, A. F. *Science and Its Fabrication*. Minneapolis: University of Minnesota Press, 1990.

———. *What Is This Thing Called Science? An Assessment of the Nature and Status of Science and Its Methods*. 2d ed. Indianapolis: Hackett, 1994.

Clayton, P. D. *God and Contemporary Science*. Grand Rapids, Mich.: Eerdmans, 1997.

Cochrane, C. N. *Christianity and Classical Culture*. New York: Oxford University Press, 1972.

Coule, D. "Quantum Creation and Inflationary Universes: A Critical Appraisal." *Physical Review D* 62 (2000): 124010–17.

Craig, W. L. "'What Place, Then, for a Creator?' Hawking on God and Creation." In W. L. Craig and Q. Smith, *Theism, Atheism and Big Bang Cosmology*, 279–300. Oxford: Clarendon, 1993.

Craig, W. L., and Q. Smith. *Theism, Atheism and Big Bang Cosmology*. Oxford: Clarendon, 1993.

Daniélou, J. *Gospel Message and Hellenistic Culture*. London: Darton, Longman & Todd, 1973.

Danto, A. C. "Naturalism." In Edwards, ed., *The Encyclopedia of Philosophy*, vol. 5. New York: Macmillan, 1967.

Davies, P. C. W. *The Mind of God: The Scientific Basis for a Rational World*. New York: Simon and Schuster, 1992.

Dennet, D. *Consciousness Explained*. New York: Penguin, 1993.

De Witt, B. S., "Quantum Mechanics and Reality." *Physics Today* 23 (1970): 30–35.

Drapper, J. W. *History of the Conflict between Religion and Science*. London: Henry S. King, 1876.

Drees, W. B. "A 3 X 3 Classification of Science-and-Religion." *Studies in Science and Theology* 4 (1996): 18–32.

———. *Beyond the Big Bang: Quantum Cosmologies and God*. La Salle, Ill.: Open Court, 1991.

Dyson, F. J. "Time without End: Physics and Biology in an Open Universe." *Review of Modern Physics* 51:3 (1979): 447–60.

Ellis, G. F. R. "Modern Cosmology and the Limits of Science." *Transactions of the Royal Society of South Africa* 50 (1995): 1–26.

———. "The Theology of the Anthropic Principle." In *Quantum Cosmology and the Laws of Nature*, ed. R. J. Russell, N. Murphy, and C. J. Isham, 367–406. Vatican City State: Vatican Observatory; Berkeley, Calif.: Center for Theology and the Natural Sciences, 1993.

Everett, H. "Relative State Formulation of Quantum Mechanics." *Reviews of Modern Physics* 29 (1957): 454–62.

Farrington, B. *Greek Science*. London: Penguin Books, 1966.

Fichte, J. G. "Second Introduction to the Science of Knowledge." In *The Science of Knowledge*, ed. and trans. P. Heath and J. Lachs, 29–85. New York: Cambridge University Press, 1982.

Florensky, P. *The Pillar and Ground of Truth* (in Russian). Moscow: Pravda, 1990.

Florovsky, G. *Bible, Church, Tradition: An Eastern Orthodox View*. Belmont, Mass: Nordland, 1975.

———. "The Byzantine Fathers of the Sixth to Eighth Centuries" In *Collected Works*, vol. 9. Valduz: Büchevertriebsanstalt, 1987.

———. "The Function of Tradition in the Ancient Church." In *Bible, Church, Tradition: An Eastern Orthodox View*. Belmont, Mass.: Nordland, 1972.

———. "The Lost Scriptural Mind." In *Bible, Church, Tradition: An Eastern Orthodox View*. Belmont, Mass: Nordland, 1975.

———. "The Patristic Age and Eschatology: An Introduction." In *Studia Patristica*, vol. 2, ed. K. Aland and F. L. Cross, 235–50. Berlin: Akademie Verlag, 1956.

———. "St. Athanasius' Concept of Creation." In *Aspects of Church History*, 39–62. Belmont, Mass.: Nordland, 1975.

———. "St. Gregory Palamas and the Tradition of the Fathers." In *Bible, Church, Tradition: An Eastern Orthodox View*. Belmont, Mass: Nordland, 1975.

Frank, S. *The Unknowable: An Ontological Introduction to the Philosophy of Religion*. Athens: Ohio University Press, 1983.

Füglister, N. "The Biblical Roots of the Easter Celebration." In *Celebrating the Easter Vigil*, ed. R. Berger and H. Hollerweger, 3–35. New York: Pueblo, 1983.

Gillies, D. A. *Philosophy of Science in the Twentieth Century*. Oxford: Blackwell, 1993.

Gilson, E. *The Christian Philosophy of Saint Augustine*. London: Victor Gollancz, 1961.

Gunton, C. E. *The Triune Creator: A Historical and Systematic Study*. Grand Rapids, Mich.: Eerdmans, 1998.

Gunzig, E., R. Maartens, and A. Nesteruk. "Inflation and Thermodynamics." *Classical and Quantum Gravity* 15 (1998): 923–32.

Gunzig, E., A. Nesteruk, and M. Stokley. "Inflationary Cosmology with Two-Component Fluid and Thermodynamics." *General Relativity and Gravitation* 32 (2000): 329–46.

Hanson, N. R. *Patterns of Discovery: An Inquiry into the Conceptual Foundations of Science*. Cambridge: Cambridge University Press, 1958.

Hapgood, I. F., ed. *Service Book*. Englewood, N. J.: Antiochian Orthodox Christian Archdiocese, 1996.

Hartle, J. B., and S. W. Hawking. "Wave Function of the Universe." *Physical Review D* 28 (1983): 2960–75.

Haught, J. *God after Darwin: A Theology of Evolution*. Boulder, Colo.: Westview, 2000.

Hawking, S. *A Brief History of Time: From the Big Bang to Black Holes*. London: Bantam, 1988.

———. "Is the End of Theoretical Physics in Sight?" *Physics Bulletin* (January 1981): 15–17.

Hawking, S., and R. Penrose. *The Nature of Space and Time*. Princeton, N.J.: Princeton University Press, 1996.

Heisenberg, H. "Scientific and Religious Truth." In *Across the Frontiers,* trans. Peter Heath, 213–29. New York: Harper & Row, 1974.

Hooykaas, R. *Religion and the Rise of Modern Science*. Grand Rapids, Mich.: Eerdmans, 1972.

Horgan, J. *The End of Science*. London: Little, Brown, 1996.

Isham, C. J. "Creation of the Universe as a Quantum Process." In *Physics, Philosophy and Theology: A Common Quest for Understanding*, ed. R. J. Russell et al., 375–408. Vatican City State: Vatican Observatory, 1988.

———. "Quantum Theories of the Creation of the Universe." In *Quantum Cosmology and the Laws of Nature*, ed. R. J. Russell, N. Murphy, and C. J. Isham, 51–89. Berkeley: Center for Theology and the Natural Sciences, 1996.

Isham, C. J., and J. C. Polkinghorne. "The Debate over the Block Universe." In *Quantum Cosmology and the Laws of Nature*, ed. R. J. Russell, N. Murphy, and C. J. Isham, 139–47. Berkeley: Center for Theology and the Natural Sciences, 1996.

Jaki, S. L. "Christology and the Birth of Modern Science." *Ausbury Theological Journal* 45:2 (1990): 61–72.

———. *The Savior of Science*. Washington, D.C.: Regnery-Gateway, 1988.

Kane, G. L., M. J. Perry, and A. N. Zytkow. "The Beginning and the End of the Anthropic Principle." Astro-ph/0001197, Los Alamos Archives, 28 January 2000.

Kant, I. *Critique of Pure Reason*. 2d ed. Trans. N. K. Smith. London: Macmillan, 1933.

Krauss, L. M., and G. D. Starkman. "Life, the Universe, and Nothing: Life and Death in an Ever-Expanding Universe." *Astrophysical Journal* 531 (2000): 22–30.

Kretzmann, N. "Faith Seeks, Understanding Finds: Augustine's Charter for Christian Philosophy." In *Christian Philosophy,* ed. T. P. Flint, 1–36. University of Notre Dame Studies in the Philosophy of Religion 6. Notre Dame, Ind.: University of Notre Dame Press, 1990.

Laistner, M. L. W. *Christianity and Pagan Culture in the Later Roman Empire*. Ithaca, N.Y.: Cornell University Press, 1967.

Le Poidevin, R. "Creation in a Closed Universe or, Have Physicists Disproved the Existence of God?" *Religious Studies* 27 (1991): 39–48.

Leslie, J. "The Anthropic Principle Today." In *Modern Cosmology and Philosophy*, ed. J. Leslie, 295–305. New York: Prometheus, 1998.

———. *The End of the World: The Science and Ethics of Human Extinction.* New York: Routledge, 1996.

———. "Modern Cosmology and the Creation of Life." In *Evolution and Creation*, ed. E. McMullin, 91–120. Notre Dame, Ind.: University of Notre Dame Press, 1985.

———. *Universes.* London: Routledge, 1989.

———. *Value and Existence.* Oxford: Blackwell, 1979.

———, ed. *Modern Cosmology and Philosophy.* New York: Prometheus, 1998.

Levinas, E. *Time and the Other.* Pittsburgh: Duquesne University Press, 1987.

Lévi-Strauss, C. *Structural Anthropology.* London: Allen Lane and Penguin Press, 1968.

Lewis, D. *On the Plurality of Worlds.* Oxford: Blackwell, 1986.

Lindberg, D. *The Beginnings of Western Science: The European Scientific Tradition in Philosophical, Religious, and Institutional Context, 600 B.C. to A.D. 1450.* Chicago: University of Chicago Press, 1992.

———. "Medieval Science and Its Religious Context." *Osiris* 10 (1995): 60–79.

———. "Science and the Early Church." In *God and Nature: Historical Essays on the Encounter between Christianity and Science*, ed. D. C. Lindberg and R. L. Numbers, 19–48. Berkeley: University of California Press, 1986.

———. "Science as Handmaiden: Roger Bacon and the Patristic Tradition." *Isis* 78 (1987): 518–36.

Lossky, N. O. *Sensual, Intellectual and Mystical Intuition* (in Russian). Moscow: Respublika, 1995.

Lossky, V. *In the Image and Likeness of God.* Crestwood, N.Y.: St. Vladimir's Seminary Press, 1997.

———. *The Mystical Theology of the Eastern Church.* London: James Clarke, 1957.

———. *Orthodox Theology: An Introduction.* Crestwood, N.Y.: St. Vladimir's Seminary Press, 1997.

———. "Tradition and Traditions." In *In the Image and Likeness of God.* Crestwood, N.Y.: St. Vladimir's Seminary Press, 1997.

———. *The Vision of God.* Crestwood, N.Y.: St. Vladimir's Seminary Press, 1983.

Louth, A. *Maximus the Confessor.* London: Routledge, 1996.

Mantzaridis, G. I. *Time and Man.* Trans. Julian Vulliamy. South Canaan, Pa.: St. Tikhon's Seminary Press, 1996.

Margenau, H. *The Nature of Physical Reality: A Philosophy of Modern Physics.* Woodbridge, Conn.: Ox Bow Press, 1977.

Markus, R. A. "Augustine: God and Nature." In *The Cambridge History of Later Greek and Early Medieval Philosophy*, ed. A. H. Armstrong, 398–99. London: Cambridge University Press, 1967.

Mathews, F. *The Ecological Self.* London: Routledge, 1991.

May, G. *Creatio ex nihilo: The Doctrine of 'Creation out of Nothing' in Early Christian Thought.* Edinburgh: T & T Clark, 1994.

McLaughlin, W. I. "Kantian Epistemology as an Alternative to Heroic Astronomy." *Vistas in Astronomy* 28 (1985): 611–39.

McPartlan, P. *The Eucharist Makes the Church: Henri de Lubac and John Zizioulas in Dialogue.* Edinburgh: T & T Clark, 1993.

Meyendorf, J. *Byzantine Theology.* New York: Fordham University Press, 1998.

———. *Living Tradition.* Crestwood, N.Y.: St. Vladimir's Seminary Press, 1978.

———. *A Study of Gregory Palamas.* Crestwood, N.Y.: St. Vladimir's Seminary Press, 1998.

McMullin, E. "Fine-Tuning the Universe?" In *Science, Technology, and Religious Ideas*, ed. M. H. Shale and G. W. Shields, 97–125. Lanham, Md.: University Press of America, 1994.

———. "How Should Cosmology Relate to Theology?" In *The Sciences and Theology in the Twentieth Century*, ed. A. R. Peacocke, 17–57. Notre Dame, Ind.: University of Notre Dame Press, 1981.

———. *The Inference That Makes Science*. Milwaukee, Wis.: Marquette University Press, 1998.

———. "Introduction: Evolution and Creation." In *Evolution and Creation*, ed. E. McMullin, 1–56. Notre Dame, Ind.: University of Notre Dame Press, 1985.

———. "Is Philosophy Relevant to Cosmology?" In *Modern Cosmology and Philosophy*, ed. J. Leslie, 35–56. New York: Prometheus, 1998.

———. "Models of Scientific Inference." *CTNS Bulletin* 8:2 (1988): 1–13.

———, ed. *The Social Dimensions of Science*. Notre Dame, Ind.: University of Notre Dame Press, 1993.

Minkowski, H. "Space and Time." In H. A. Lorentz, A. Einstein, H. Minkowski, and H. Weyl. *The Principle of Relativity: A Collection of Original Memoirs on the Special and General Theory of Relativity*, trans. W. Perrett and G. B. Jeffery, 73–91. New York: Dover, 1952.

Murphy, N., and G. F. R. Ellis. *The Moral Nature of the Universe: Cosmology, Theology, and Ethics*. Minneapolis: Fortress Press, 1996.

Nesteruk, A. V. "Ecological Insights on the Anthropic Reasoning in Cosmology: Ecological Imperative versus Cosmological Eschatology." In *Proceedings of the First International Conference "Ecology and Democracy: The Challenge of the 21st Century,"* Ceske Budejovice, Czech Republic, September 1994, 110–13.

———. "The Idea of Eternal Life in Modern Cosmology: Its Ultimate Reality and Metaethical Meaning." *Journal of Ultimate Reality and Meaning* 17:3 (1994): 222–31.

———. "The Metaethical Alternative to the Idea of Eternal Life in Modern Cosmology." *DIOTIMA* (Espace cosmique et philosophie) 21 (1993): 70–74.

———. "Temporal Irreversibility: Three Modern Views." In *Time, Creation and World-Order*, ed. M. Wegener, 62–86. Acta Jutlandica, vol. 74, no. 1; Humanities Series, vol. 72. Aarhus, Denmark: Aarhus University Press, 1999.

———. "The Weyl Curvature Hypothesis and a Choice of Initial Vacuum for Quantum Fields at the Cosmological Singularity." *Classical and Quantum Gravity* 11 (1994): L15–L21.

Newton-Smith, W. H. *Rationality of Science*. Boston: Routledge, 1996.

Nicolis, G., and I. Prigogine. *Exploring Complexity: An Introduction*. New York: Freeman, 1989.

Norris, F. W. *Faith Gives Fullness to Reasoning: The Five Theological Orations of Gregory Nazianzen*. Supp. to Vigilae Christianae, vol. 13. New York: Brill, 1991.

Norris, R. A. *God and World in Early Christian Theology: A Study in Justin Martyr, Irenaeus, Tertulian and Origen*. London: Adam & Charles Black, 1965.

O'Hear, A. *An Introduction to the Philosophy of Science*. Oxford: Clarendon, 1990.

Osborne, E. F. *The Philosophy of Clement of Alexandria*. Cambridge: Cambridge University Press, 1957.

Palmer, G. E. H., P. Sherrard, and K. Ware, eds. *St. Nikodimos of the Holy Mountain and St. Makarios of Corinth, The Philokalia: The Complete Text*. 4 vols. London: Faber, 1979–95.

Pannenberg, W. *Jesus—God and Man*. London: SCM Press, 1968.

———. *Toward a Theology of Nature: Essays on Science and Faith*. Louisville, Ky.: Westminster John Knox Press, 1993.

Peacocke, A. *Theology for a Scientific Age: Being and Becoming—Natural and Divine*. Minneapolis: Fortress Press, 1993.

Pelikan, J. *Christianity and Classical Culture: The Metamorphosis of Natural Theology in the Christian Encounter with Hellenism*. New Haven: Yale University Press, 1993.

Penrose, R. *The Emperor's New Mind*. New York: Oxford University Press, 1989.

———. "Singularities and Time-Asymmetry." In *General Relativity: An Einstein Centenary Survey*, ed. S. W. Hawking and W. Israel, 581–638. Cambridge: Cambridge University Press, 1979.

Penrose, R., with A. Shimony, N. Cartwright, and S. Hawking. *The Large, the Small and the Human Mind*. Cambridge: Cambridge University Press, 1997.

Petrosky, T., and I. Prigogine. "Thermodynamic Limit, Hilbert Space and Breaking of Time Symmetry." *Chaos, Solitons and Fractals* 11 (2000): 373–82.

Plass, P. C. "Timeless Time in Neoplatonism." *Modern Schoolman* 55 (November 1977): 1–19.

Poincaré, H. *Méthhodes nouvelles de la mécanique céleste*. 1892. Reprint, New York: Dover, 1957.

Polkinghorne, J. *Belief in God in an Age of Science*. New Haven: Yale University Press, 1998.

Prestige, G. L. *God in Patristic Thought*. London: SPCK, 1955.

Prigogine, I. *From Being to Becoming*. New York: Freeman, 1980.

———. "La redécouverte du temps." *L'Homme* 28:4 (1988): 5–26.

———. "What Is Time?" In *Metaphysics as Foundation: Essays in Honor of Ivor Leclerc*, ed. P. A. Bogaard and G. Treash, 285–94. Albany: State University of New York Press, 1993.

———. "Why Irreversibility? The Formulation of Classical and Quantum Mechanics for Nonintegrable Systems." *International Journal of Quantum Chemistry* 53 (1995): 105–18.

Prigogine, I., and I. Stengers. *Order out of Chaos*. London: Heinemann, 1984.

Russell, R. J., N. Murphy, and C. J. Isham, eds. *Quantum Cosmology and the Laws of Nature*. Berkeley: Center for Theology and the Natural Sciences, 1996.

Russell, R. J., W. R. Stoeger, and G. V. Coyne, eds. *John Paul II on Science and Religion: Reflections on the New View from Rome*. Vatican City State: Vatican Observatory, 1990.

Sambursky, S., and S. Pines. *The Concept of Time in Late Neo-Platonism*. Jerusalem: Israel Academy of Sciences and Humanities, 1971.

Sandys, J. E. *A History of Classical Scholarship*. 2 vols. Cambridge: Cambridge University Press, 1903–8.

Schmemann, A. *The Historical Roads of Eastern Orthodoxy*. Crestwood, N.Y.: St. Vladimir's Seminary Press, 1997.

———. *The World as Sacrament*. London: Darton, Longmann & Todd, 1966.

Staniloae, D. *The Experience of God*. Brookline, Mass.: Holy Cross Orthodox Press, 1998.

Stoeger, W. R., and G. F. R. Ellis. "A Response to Tipler's Omega-Point Theory." *Science and Christian Belief* 7 (1995): 163–72.

Swinburne, R. "Argument from the Fine-Tuning of the Universe." In *Modern Cosmology and Philosophy*, ed. J. Leslie, 161–63. New York: Prometheus, 1998.

———. *The Evolution of the Soul*. Oxford: Clarendon, 1986.

Temple, D. "The New Design Argument: What Does It Prove?" In *Science, Technology, and Religious Ideas*, ed. M. H. Shale and G. W. Shields, 127–39. Lanham, Md.: University Press of America, 1994.

Temple, W. *Readings in St. John's Gospels*. London: Macmillan, 1961.

Templeton, J. M., Sir, ed. *Evidence of Purpose: Scientists Discover the Creator*. New York: Continuum, 1994.

Thunberg, L. *Man and the Cosmos: The Vision of St. Maximus the Confessor*. Crestwood, N.Y.: St. Vladimir's Seminary Press, 1985.

———. *Microcosm and Mediator: The Theological Anthropology of Maximus the Confessor*. Chicago: Open Court, 1995.

Tipler, F. J. "The Omega Point as *Eschaton*: Answers to Pannenberg's Questions for Scientists." *Zygon* 24:2 (1988): 217–53.

———. "The Omega Point Theory: A Model of an Evolving God." In *Physics, Philosophy and Theology: A Common Quest for Understanding*, ed. R. J. Russell et al., 313–31. Vatican City State: Vatican Observatory, 1988.

———. *The Physics of Immortality: Modern Cosmology, God and the Resurrection of the Dead.* London: Macmillan, 1995.

Torrance, T. F. "Creation, Contingent World-Order, and Time (A Theologico-Scientific Approach)." In *Time, Creation and World-Order*, ed. M. Wegener, 207–10. Acta Jutlandica, vol. 74, no. 1; Humanities Series, vol. 72. Aarhus, Denmark: Aarhus University Press, 1999.

———. *Divine and Contingent Order.* Edinburgh: T & T Clark, 1998.

———. *The Divine Meaning: Studies in Patristic Hermeneutics.* Edinburgh: T & T Clark, 1998.

———. *The Ground and Grammar of Theology: Consonance between Theology and Science.* Edinburgh: T & T Clark, 2001.

———. "The Relation of the Incarnation to Space in Nicene Theology." In *The Ecumenical World of Orthodox Civilization, Russia and Orthodoxy*, vol. 3, *Essays in Honor of Georges Florovsky*, ed. A. Blane and T. E. Bird, 43–70. The Hague: Mouton, 1974.

———. *Space, Time and Incarnation.* Edinburgh: T & T Clark, 1997.

———. *Space, Time and Resurrection.* Edinburgh: T & T Clark, 1998.

———. *Theological Science.* Edinburgh: T & T Clark, 1996.

Tryon, E. P. "Is the Universe a Vacuum Fluctuation?" In *Modern Cosmology and Philosophy*, ed. J. Leslie, 222–25. New York: Prometheus, 1998.

Vasileos, A. *Hymn of Entry.* Crestwood, N.Y.: St. Vladimir's Seminary Press, 1984.

Vilenkin, A. "Quantum Cosmology and the Initial State of the Universe." *Physical Review D* 37:4 (1988): 888–97.

Ward, K. *Religion and Creation.* New York: Oxford University Press, 1995.

Ware, K. *The Orthodox Way.* Crestwood, N.Y.: St. Vladimir's Seminary Press, 1996.

———. (Bishop of Diokleia). "Theological Education in Scripture and the Fathers." Unpublished paper presented at the 5th Consultation of Orthodox Theological Schools, Halki, Turkey, 13–20 August 1994.

Ware, T. *The Orthodox Church.* New York: Penguin, 1997.

Wheeler, J. A. *At Home in the Universe.* New York: American Institute of Physics, 1994.

———. "From Relativity to Mutability." In *Symposium on the Development of the Physicist's Conception of Nature in the Twentieth Century, Miramare, Italy (Trieste), 1972*, ed. J. Mehra, 202–47. Dordrecht: Reidel, 1973.

———. "Genesis and Observership." In *Foundational Problems in the Special Sciences*, ed. R. Butts and J. Hintikka, 1–33. Dordrecht: Reidel, 1977.

———. "How Come the Quantum?" In *New Techniques and Ideas in Quantum Measurement Theory*, ed. D. M. Greenberger, 304–16. New York: New York Academy of Sciences, 1987.

———. "On Recognizing Law without Law." *American Journal of Physics* 51 (1983): 394–404.

———. "Physics as Meaning Circuit." In *Frontiers of Non-Equilibrium Statistical Physics*, ed. G. T. Moore and M. O. Scully, 25–32. New York: Plenum, 1986.

———. "The Quantum and the Universe." In *Relativity, Quanta, and Cosmology in the Development of the Scientific Thought of Albert Einstein*, ed. M. Pantaleo and F. de Finis, 807–25. New York: Johnson Reprint, 1979.

———. "The Universe as Home for Man." In *The Nature of Scientific Discovery*, ed. O. Gingerich, 261–96. Washington, D.C.: Smithsonian Institution Press, 1975.

———. "World as a System Self-Synthesized by Quantum Networking." *IBM Journal of Research and Development* 32 (1988): 4–15.

Whitakker, E. *Space and Spirit.* London: Thomas Nelson, 1946.

Wilkinson, D. *Alone in the Universe: Aliens, the X-Files and God.* Crowborough, England: Monarch, 1997.

Wolfson, H. A. *The Philosophy of the Church Fathers.* Cambridge: Harvard University Press, 1976.

Worthing, M. W. *God, Creation, and Contemporary Physics.* Minneapolis: Fortress Press, 1995.

Yannaras, C. *De l'absence et de l'inconnaissance de Dieu.* Paris: Éditions du Cerf, 1971.

———. *Elements of Faith: An Introduction to Orthodox Theology.* Edinburgh: T & T Clark, 1998.

———. "Theology in Present-Day Greece." *St. Vladimir's Seminary Theological Quarterly* 16:4 (1972): 195–214.

Zen'kovski, V. *The Foundations of the Christian Philosophy* (in Russian). Paris: YMKA-Press, 1964.

Zizioulas, J. "The Eucharist and the Kingdom." Parts 1–3. *Sourozh: A Journal of Orthodox Life and Thought* 58 (1994): 1–12; 59 (1995): 22–38; 60 (1995): 32–46.

Index

Christian Church, 30, 57, 61, 151, 246: canonical documents of, 254; as historical reality, 58–59; as eschatological reality, 59; as the Body of Christ, 1, 43, 59, 229, 230, 235, 246; Eastern Orthodox, 1–2, 5, 36, 58–59; early, 13, 44, 63, 65, 242; Latin, 28; liturgical experience of, 58, 61–62 (*see also* liturgy); mysteries of, 57–58, 60; the Fathers of, 6–7, 12, 14–15, 20–22, 27–31, 36–39, 41–43, 49, 52–54, 56, 60, 63, 65–67, 69, 76, 78–79, 99, 104–6, 119, 120–23, 125, 153, 195, 242, 250–51; dogmas (definitions) of, 19, 44–45, 49–51, 65; Roman Catholic, 268; tradition of, 44, 58–59, 254; the presence of the Holy Spirit in, 44, 143 (*see also* Holy Spirit); Western, 29, 33, 38

Clement of Alexandria, 16–19, 30–31, 41, 78, 251–52, 255, 260, 262

contingency: contingent order, 99, 119, 133, 192; contingent intelligibility, 111, 213; contingent laws, 118; contingent necessity, 123, 207; contingent rationality, 123, 230; notion of, 119; of the world upon God, 10, 12, 21, 25, 70–71, 90, 93, 95, 98, 109; 111, 118, 120–25, 143, 151–52, 154, 158, 161, 173, 177, 191–92, 194, 220, 226, 234, 258, 261; of time, 182; of the act of creation, 35, 120

cosmology: as *cosmism*, 242; anthropic, (see anthropic principle); Classical (non-quantum), 126–27, 140, 169; Greek, 36, 118, 151; Hawking's, (see Hawking); inflationary, 140, 218, 261; quantum, 134, 137, 140, 142, 145, 148, 150–52, 155–56, 158–59, 262

Craig, W., 143–44, 149

creation: as *creatio ex nihilo*, 34–35, 118–21, 124–25, 134, 143, 145, 153–55, 158–59, 164, 176–77, 205–6, 220, 240–41, 245, 247, 253; as good, 24, 36, 241; as "everlasting" act, 166; as timeless, 164; demiurgic, 164

Damascius, 263

deification, 42, 63, 117, 124–25, 231, 240, 245

deism, 21, 140, 262

Diadochos of Photiki, 41

design: argument from, 92–93, 95–96, 98, 125, 258–59; divine, 247; in the universe, 170–74, 177, 202, 207, 217

diairesis (division), 154

dianoia (discursive reason), 52–54, 63, 65, 71, 77, 90, 255, 258, 266

diaphora (difference in being), 108, 129, 146, 152, 154–55, 158–59, 161, 165, 175–77, 191, 205, 211, 219–20, 226, 234–35, 240–41, 263: as a principle of variety and unity in creation, 154; scientific model of, 176

diastema (distance), 103–5, 108, 109, 116, 120, 166

Dionysius the Areopagite, 11, 56, 76, 83–84, 88, 102, 154, 258

dualism: between sensible and intelligible creation, 100, 145, 153, 259 (*see also diaphora*); Cartesian, 33; in human constitution, 52, 98; in views of nature, 180–81, 187–90; ontological, between the world and God, 66–68, 73–75, 78–79, 98–99, 101, 105, 128

Dyson, F., 198–99

energeia, 97, 101, 105, 120–21, 251: divine and uncreated energies, 39, 56, 101–2, 104–5, 113, 120, 143, 255

enhypostasis, 113, 116–17, 223, 260

entropy, 168–72, 175, 177: gravitational, 169, 262; growth of, 181, 183, 185

epistemology, (open-ended) 65–66, 68, 74

eschatology: Christian theological, 151, 161, 244, 247, 208, 269; cosmological, (see final anthropic principle); Hellenistic, 268–69

Evagrius Ponticus, 41–42, 83–84

Fichte, I., 87, 216

Florensky, P., 69, 89

Florovsky, G., 56, 249, 255, 260
Frank, S., 258

God: apophatic definitions of, 42, 76–77,
84–86, 258 (*see also* apophaticism); as
creator, 10, 20, 22, 33, 38, 79, 98,
100–101, 130, 142, 153, 226–27, 242
(*see also* creation as good); as he in
himself, 56, 62; as the Father, 24, 110,
122, 152, 260, 267; as trinity, (see
Holy Trinity); as transcendent, 75, 80,
82, 94, 112, 143, 207, 331; communion with (participation in), 2, 7, 27,
39, 41–47, 59, 60, 75, 84, 98–99, 102,
105–6, 113, 143, 235, 252; charismatic
manifestations of, 44; economy of,
56–57, 112, 115, 162, 220; effected
words of, 211, 220, 226; *energeia* of,
(see *energeia*); essence of, 56, 97–98,
100, 119–20, 226; evolving (in Tipler),
239–42; experience of, 1, 7, 36, 42–43,
52, 54–56, 60, 62, 65–69, 79, 82, 90,
141; grace of, 38, 42, 53; incarnation
of, (see Christ); intelligibility of, 65;
kingdom of, 59, 60, 124, 151, 164,
231–32, 235–36, 239, 245–47; knowledge of, 4, 17, 23, 28, 30, 35, 42,
43–44, 48, 51, 55, 63, 71, 75–76,
79–80, 83–84, 89–90, 98, 103, 107,
113, 158, 257; life in, 8, 11, 30, 69;
logoi of, (see *logoi*); love for, 55; name
of, 59; person (hypostasis) of, 111,
113, 228; plan of salvation of, 60, 110,
119–21, 206, 228; praise and glorifica-
tion of, 12, 30–31; relationship
between the world and, 17, 20–21, 57,
61, 67–68, 73, 84, 103–4, 108, 115–17,
236; revelation of, 16, 55, 79, 122;
traces in creation of, 35; Son of, (see
Christ, Logos of God); Spirit of, (see
Holy Spirit); union with, 6, 22, 25, 42,
63, 69, 117, 206, 230 (*see also* deification); vision of, 45–46, 50, 67, 82, 89;
will of (as different with essence of),
17, 21, 56, 91, 95, 97, 112, 119,
120–21; wisdom of, 18, 24

Gregorios, P., 6, 104
Gregory the Theologian (Nazianzus),
14–15, 21, 41, 165, 246–47
Gregory of Nyssa, 102–5, 120, 227, 245,
251, 259
Gregory Palamas, 42–43, 46, 110, 250

Harakas, S., 4
Haught, J., 205
Hawking, S., 80, 125, 132–34, 137–46,
148–52, 157–59, 170, 172, 175, 190,
262–63
Heidegger, M., 2
Heisenberg, W., 256, 268
Hilary of Poitiers, 62
Hippolytus of Rome, 250
Holy Spirit, 1, 32, 39, 42–44, 50, 55, 63–64,
120, 143, 246, 252, 266
Holy Trinity, 31, 42, 56–57, 77, 84, 97, 110,
116, 120, 123, 231, 266
Horgan, J., 262–63
horos (limit, horizon, boundary of faith),
49
humanity: as inherent in the Logos, 111,
113, 238–39, 259; as microcosm, 68,
108, 211–13, 226–27, 235, 238, 243; as
mediator, 12, 22, 68, 107–9, 153, 158,
211, 213, 220, 238, 243–45, 252, 259,
263; as hypostasis of the universe,
115, 266 (*see also* universe, as enhypostasized by humanity); phenomenon of, 222–23, 225, 238; as divine
image, 21, 23, 26, 105–6, 111, 113,
121, 194–95, 206, 223, 226, 228–36,
238, 241, 244–45, 252, 259–61; hypostatic unity of body and soul in, 212,
219, 223, 240, 245, 259, 266 (*see also*
hypostasis, human); natural conditions of existence of, 237–38; as cosmic force ("cosmiurger"), 237; as
priest of creation, 235; transfiguration
of nature of, 63; fullness of (as recapitulated by Christ), 12, 225, 227–28,
235, 243
humankind-event, 220, 222, 238: as contingent, 200, 206; as hypostatic event,

260; detachment from, 28; interpretation of, 20; laws of, 21–22, 25, 35, 194, 209, 265; meaning of (in Christ), 27, 36, 38, 106; suffering in, 22; transfiguration of, 22, 117, 230, 239, 244–45

Nesmelov, V., 249

Newton, I., 128, 178–79, 261

Nicene Creed, 152–53

no-boundary proposal, 138: *See also* Hawking, S.

nous (spiritual intellect), 25, 52–55, 60, 63–64, 66–67, 70–71, 75, 77, 82, 90, 105, 255, 258, 266: as inner self and person, 55

Origen, 41, 123, 231–32

Osborne, B., 11

ousia (substance, essence), 97, 104–5, 112, 147, 157, 219, 223, 251

panentheism, 104, 116, 250

pantheism, 20, 27

Pannenberg, W., 191–92, 234

participation: as co-creation (through articulation of the universe), 99, 111, 117, 212–13, 220–21, 224, 227, 244–45; in God, (see God, effected words of and communion with); in ecclesial reality (liturgy and tradition), 44–45, 48, 106, 110; in Christ-event, 60; in relationship between the world and God, 117

Patristic synthesis, 2, 5, 7, 17, 36: *See also* theology, Patristic

Peacocke, A., 4

Penrose, R., 132, 142, 165, 167–77, 182, 190, 259, 262, 267

perichoresis (co-inherence), 116–17

Petrosky, T., 187

Philo of Alexandria, 163

philokalia, 53

Philoponus, J., 25

philosophy, 1, 17, 19–20, 28, 31, 37, 65, 67, 71, 73–75, 78, 80, 155, 161, 167, 177, 189: as mediator between science and; theology, 73; Hellenistic (pagan), 13-16, 18, 30–31, 36, 39–41, 118–19,

163–64, 251; emergent, 222; natural, 31, 253; of science, 256; phenomenological, (see Levinas); transcendental, 65, 91, 95–96, 128, 224, 260: *See also* Kant

physics, 8, 13, 26, 33, 41, 58, 71, 110–11, 125–27, 129–30, 132–36, 138, 142, 152, 156, 159–61, 163, 163, 166–70, 172, 174, 177–78, 180–83, 185–92, 197, 199, 200–204, 206, 208–9, 219, 221–24, 227, 234, 240, 242, 251, 258–59, 262, 266–67

.physis (nature), 112, 251

Plato, 14, 16, 20, 29

Platonism, 22, 31, 34–37, 66, 95, 100–101, 129, 144–45, 153, 160–61, 165, 251, 262: Christian, 39–40, 100–101, 140, 145, 150, 155, 176, 214, 216, 225–26; Neoplatonism, 103, 147–49, 151, 164; of Penrose, 143, 172, 175, 259

personhood (human), 26, 45–47, 52, 54–55, 67, 74, 99, 101, 114, 152, 157, 194, 201, 210, 213, 227, 243–45, 248, 260, 266

Polkinghorne, J., 81–82, 204–5, 256

Prestige, G., 260

Prigogine, I., 160, 162–63, 165, 167–70, 177–78, 182–92, 262

Proclus, 147

prosopon (persona), 97, 112

Pythagoras, 14

relativity (theory): general, 126, 131–34; special, 136, 160–61, 178

salvation, (see God, plan of)

second law of thermodynamics, 168–69, 204

seminal reasons, 33–35, 251, 253

Schrödinger, E., 134–35, 138

science: and religion, 2, 4–6, 29, 36, 92, 97, 141, 235; and theology, 4–6, 10–13, 19, 29–30, 33, 40, 48, 61–62, 66–74, 79, 91, 117, 145; as theological inquiry, 70; infinite advance of, 34, 125; liturgical vision of, 2, 7, 235

Sherrard, P., 6, 12, 39, 48, 244, 251, 268

Staniloae, D., 6, 9, 257
Swinburne, R., 265

time: arrow of, 168; as an image of eternity, 161; as overall time of all times, 164; as flow of events, 146, 148, 160; deconstruction of, 146, 147; empirical, 139, 147–48, 161; frozen, 147, 160; geometrization of, 137; imaginary, 136–38, 140, 145–46, 148–50, 158; irreversibility of, 160–63, 166–72, 176–80, 183, 188, 190–93; living, 147; pre-existent, 139; real, 139–40, 149; timeless, 145, 147, 150; transcendent, 147–48, 150, 164; problem of, 161; participated and unparticipated, 147–48; paradox of, 178
Tertullian, 250
theology: apophatic, 56, 66, 69, 79, 80–84, 91, 107, 109, 142, 257–58 (*see also* Apophaticism); as communion, 45; as direct experience of God, 45, 62; as fruit of interior purity, 45; as mysticism, 45; as *theologia*, 41, 52, 54–57, 61–64, 82–83, 91, 109; as worship and liturgy, 57; Byzantine, 29; cataphatic, 56, 79, 80–82, 257; economic, 56–57, 62–63, 82; natural, 1, 48, 91, 110–11, 251, 268; of creation, (see creation); Orthodox, 1–2, 4–8, 10, 12, 30, 38, 42–43, 45, 48, 51, 54, 60, 65, 67–69, 74, 106, 110, 140, 257; Patristic, 6, 13, 40, 42, 53, 62, 96, 99, 102, 111, 112, 114, 145, 176–77; revelational, 48; Trinitarian, 57, 97, 102, 116, 120
Thomas Aquinas, 29, 38
Thunberg, L., 83, 258
Tipler, F., 198, 200, 208, 239–43, 265
Torrance, T., 2, 12, 45–46, 65, 99, 110–11, 124, 192, 194, 230, 232, 234–36, 250, 252, 256

tradition: Anglican, 4; Eastern Orthodox, 1, 6–7, 12, 45, 51, 256; Hebraic, 110; Hellenistic (classical), 13, 17, 28–29, 33, 36, 60, 253; Latin, 4, 36; Patristic, 4; scriptural, 78; Western, 6
Tryon, E., 127, 129
universe: anthropic 198–99, 217; anti-anthropic, 198–99, 230; as church, 235; as enhypostasized by humanity, 212, 214, 221, 223, 226, 236–37; as hypostatic event, 194, 208, 236, 245; as inherent in the Logos of God, 112–13, 116–17, 237, 243; as "world of existences", 222; block-universe, 160–61; closed 198; destiny of, 236; expansion of, 126, 169; Hellenistic, 147, 151; historical 148–50, 155, 158; open, 198; quantum (primordial, Euclidean; intelligible) 148–50, 152, 156–58; transfiguration of, 239, 244–45; visible (classical, empirical), 128–34, 139, 141, 148–52, 155–57, 159, 166, 172, 175, 181, 184, 189–90, 210, 212, 214–16, 218–21, 225, 231, 234, 262; wave function of, 138

Vilenkin, A., 262

Wallace-Hadrill, D., 251
Ware, K., 10, 45
Weyl curvature hypothesis (WCH), 170: *See also* Penrose, R.
Wheeler, J., 221–25, 230, 261

Yannaras, C., 8, 45–46, 257, 267

Zizioulas, J., 7, 50, 98, 256, 266